D0847953

Secret City

Secret City

The Hidden Jews of Warsaw,
1940–1945

Gunnar S. Paulsson

Yale University Press
New Haven and London

For information about this and other Yale University Press publications, please contact:
U.S. Office: sales.press@yale.edu   yalebooks.com
Europe Office: sales@yaleup.co.uk   www.yaleup.co.uk

Set in Columbus MT by Fakenham Photosetting Limited, Fakenham, Norfolk
Printed in Great Britain by St Edmundsbury Press, Suffolk

Library of Congress Cataloging-in-Publication Data

Paulsson, Gunnar S.
Secret city: the hidden Jews of Warsaw, 1940–1945/Gunnar S. Paulsson.
p.   cm.
Includes bibliographical references and index.
ISBN 0-300-09546-5 (cloth)
1. Jews—Poland—Warsaw—History—20th century.   2 Holocaust, Jewish (1939–1945)—
Poland—Warsaw.   3. World War, 1939–1945—Jews—Rescue—Poland—Warsaw.
4. Warsaw (Poland)—Ethnic relations.   I. Title.
DS135.P62 W3265 2002   940.53´18´094384—dc21   2002002005

A catalogue record for this book is available from the British Library.

10 9 8 7 6 5 4 3 2 1

Contents

3 The Secret City   97

Introduction 97 • *Life in Aryan Warsaw* 98

4 The City Under Siege   138

Threats from the German Side 138 • *Threats from the Polish Side* 141
Conclusions 162

5 The Warsaw Uprising and its Aftermath   165

Introduction 165 • *The Course of the Uprising* 166
The Jewish Experience of the Warsaw Uprising 168
Jewish Perceptions of the Uprising 170 • *Atrocities: The Prosta Street Massacre* 173
Other Atrocities 177 • *Jewish Participation in the Uprising* 183
The Treatment of Jewish Civilians by the Insurgent Authorities and Population 187
The Aftermath of the Warsaw Uprising 189 • *Summary and Conclusions* 196

6 Numbers   199

Introduction 199
Study 1. How many Warsaw Jews Were Hiding on the Eve of the Warsaw Uprising? 201
Development and Finances of ŻKN 206
Study 2. How Many Warsaw Jews Survived the War? 210
Summary and Conclusions 229

Summary and Conclusions   231

Notes   249

Bibliography   273

Index   288

Illustrations

Plates

Tables

Maps

Figures

Foreword

Terminology: 'Aryan' and 'Non-Aryan'

It is impossible to describe life in a Nazi-occupied country, or to write about the Holocaust, without using Nazi terms such as 'Final Solution', 'deportation', 'resettlement', 'pacification', 'special handling' – all frequently euphemisms for mass murder – or the various Nazi 'racial' definitions. Such expressions described fundamental categories in the universe that the Nazis created, and fundamentally affected the situation and treatment of the people to whom they applied. Thus, for example, the distinction between 'Aryans' and 'non-Aryans' was universally accepted as part of the vocabulary of the time, used in Poland by Poles and the Jews themselves as well as the Germans. Simply, the concept and the distinction were created by the Nazis and no non-Nazi term quite captures the flavour.

Forced to use such words, we might place them in inverted commas; but they crop up so often that this would quickly grow tiresome in an extended work such as this one. I have therefore elected to follow Fowler's advice on inverted commas: if a word is right for the job, use it without apologies. Therefore I shall speak of Aryan Warsaw, Aryan documents, an Aryan appearance and so on, without holding these terms at arm's length. The inverted commas are implied, so to speak, and anyone wishing to quote from this book is welcome to add them as required.

Who is a Jew?

The question 'who is a Jew?' has of course been much debated. According to *Halakhah* (Jewish religious law), a Jew is anyone who has been properly converted to Judaism, or who has a Jewish mother. The State of Israel, following the so-called 'Rufheisen precedent', regards as a Jew anyone who is Jewish under *Halakhah* and has not accepted another religion: thus, it is possible to be, say, a

Catholic Jew under *Halakhah*, but not under Israeli law. For the purpose of award-ing the title 'Righteous among the Nations', given in principle to people who risked their lives to rescue Jews, the Rufheisen definition is relaxed somewhat, to allow for conversion as a survival strategy. Arbitrarily, Yad Vashem accepts as Jews people who converted from Judaism to another religion from the beginning of 1941 until the end of the war.

Nazi law was much more inclusive. Under the First Regulation to the Reich Citizenship Act – the third of the Nuremberg Laws – a Jew was anyone who was descended from three or more grandparents who were 'full Jews by race' (the defi-nition was therefore circular). Someone who was descended from two such grand-parents was a *'Mischling* of the first degree' (*Mischling ersten Grades*), and from one grandparent, a *'Mischling* of the second degree' (*Mischling zweiten Grades*). Under some circumstances, *Mischlinge* of the first degree were considered to be Jews as well. Except for the purpose of determining the classification of a *Mischling*, a person's current religious affiliation was irrelevant to this 'racial' definition.

The Nuremberg Laws as interpreted in Poland were still more inclusive. According to Nazi racial logic, a German *Mischling*'s one-half or three-quarters of good German blood was sufficient to overcome the taint of Jewishness, if the *Mischling* did not associate with the Jewish community or betray other signs of Jewishness; but the blood of Slavic *Untermenschen* could not so easily compensate. Under a decree of 24 July 1940 pertaining to the General Government (German-occupied Poland), any full Jew or *Mischling ersten Grades* was considered Jewish by race, as also was anyone who was a member of the Jewish *gmina* (organized com-munity) on 1 September 1939, or had a Jewish spouse, or was born after 31 May 1941 as a child of Jewish parents.[1] Thus, in a Catholic family consisting of a father whose grandparents were converted Jews, a mother with an impeccably Aryan pedigree, one child born before 31 May 1941 and another born after that date, in Poland all would have been considered Jews except the elder child. In Germany, all would have been considered Aryans.

This definition naturally included many people who did not regard themselves as Jews, and were not regarded as Jews by either their Jewish or their Polish neigh-bours (bar some political extremists). It included many people who are not regarded as Jews by Yad Vashem, who are routinely excluded from scholarly studies of the subject and who do not appear in any census or population statis-tics as Jews. Nevertheless, for present purposes it is the only workable definition. I will consider as Jews all those who were at risk at the hands of the Nazis; who had to conceal their identity or ancestry; who were forced to live in the ghetto or lived illegally if they chose not to enter it. I will except only non-Jewish spouses.

It may be objected that someone who was accepted as non-Jewish by Polish society was not at risk on the Aryan side of the ghetto wall to nearly the same extent as a self-identified Jew, and did not face nearly the same problems and difficulties. This is true enough. The difference is one of degree rather than of kind, however. There was a gradation of risk: a *Hassid* who spoke only Yiddish and lived in complete isolation from Polish society was obviously at greater risk than an assimilated, Polish-speaking Jew, and the latter was in turn at greater risk than a convert who not only spoke Polish fluently but was well versed in the Catholic religion and in Polish customs as well. All were nevertheless in some danger. All could easily find themselves preyed upon by *szmalcowniks* (extortionists and blackmailers), who could somehow detect the merest hint of Jewishness even in the most assimilated Jew. All had to be provided with forged documents, and all were eligible for aid from the underground organizations that sprang up to care for Jews in hiding. Apart from anything else, purely as a practical matter it is no longer possible to distinguish between one class of Nuremberg-Law Jew and another on the basis of the surviving records.

This inclusive definition of 'who is a Jew' makes a slight contribution to the estimates here of the number of Jews in hiding, of Jewish survivors and so on, which are higher than one is accustomed to seeing elsewhere in the literature. But there were only some 1,700 converts in the Warsaw ghetto, and perhaps an equal number who chose to remain outside it. Converts were thus a rather marginal element in this large Jewish community, less than 1 per cent of the whole. Their prospects of survival were no doubt somewhat better than the others'; but even so they can have contributed at best a few hundred souls to the final tally of survivors. The converts played an important role by establishing a bridgehead on the Aryan side, an essential link that made mass escape from the ghetto possible; but in purely numerical terms, they are hardly significant, and no adjustments will be necessary to take them into account. The high estimates presented here are not the result of a difference of definition – they reflect a real phenomenon and are supported by evidence that will be put forward in due course.

'A German', 'the Germans', 'the Nazis'

A German, as the term is used here, is anyone who identified himself or herself as a member of the German nation, and was so accepted under the Nazi laws. This includes *Reichsdeutsche* (RD), German citizens of the Reich, and also, where appropriate, *Volksdeutsche* (VD), persons of German descent who had signed the Volksliste (VL), declaring themselves to be German. *Deutschstämmige* (persons of German descent who had not signed the VL) are not regarded as Germans in principle, but German statistics sometimes do not allow them to be disentangled from the VD. German Jews of course cannot be considered Germans for the present purpose.

This definition is simple but sometimes problematical. *Deutschstämmige* came under coercive pressure to sign the VL, so that this declaration was not always voluntary; and even when it was, the motive was often opportunistic – to take advantage of higher rations and lower prices and the many other privileges available to Germans, to try to have relatives released from PoW camps, and so on. But in the simplified moral categories of wartime, VD were regarded as traitors and collaborators by most Poles, and so willy-nilly were forced into the German milieu. Their children had to join the *Hitlerjugend* and undergo Nazi indoctrination, and in the best totalitarian tradition were expected to inform on their parents. In Warsaw, most VD – and also many *Deutschstämmige* – lived in the loosely defined German district. At the end of the war, knowing the probable fate that awaited them in post-war Poland, most of them retreated with the Wehrmacht and lived in Germany after the war. According to official German statistics, there were some 16,000 RD, 16,000 VD and 10,000 *Deutschstämmige* in Warsaw in 1944, not counting more than 50,000 occupation troops and non-German auxiliaries stationed in barracks.[2]

The term 'the Germans', used to signify a historical agent, is simply a historian's *façon de parler*. It is not at any time to be taken to refer to all Germans or to the German nation as a whole. I can think of no proposition about 'the Germans' in this sense that is entirely true (not even, say, 'the Germans speak German', since many VD did not). Here, depending on context, it means the German occupation authorities, or the German residents of Warsaw, or some specific group of Germans currently under discussion. In each case, the meaning should be clear from the context.

A Nazi is taken to be anyone who embraced the principles and ideology of the Nazi party. By this definition, not all party members were Nazis, and not all Nazis were party members (or Germans). Oskar Schindler is the best-known example of a 'non-Nazi Nazi', but others will figure in this book. Many Germans would prefer the authorities of the Third Reich to be referred to as Nazis rather than Germans; unfortunately, most of the police, military and bureaucratic apparatus of the Nazi state was not made up of party members or politicized fanatics but of Christopher Browning's 'ordinary men'.

It was the universal practice in occupied Europe to refer to all non-uniformed German police (and to policemen wearing SS uniforms) as the Gestapo, ignoring all fine distinctions between the actual Gestapo, the SD, the Security Police (Sipo), the Criminal Police (*Kripo*) and so on. In most cases, these distinctions are not very important for the present purpose, and it is often impossible to tell, for example in survivor accounts, which police force is meant. Therefore I have often followed contemporary practice and used 'Gestapo' as a catch-all term, which has the virtue of preserving something of the victims' point of view. Similarly, distinctions between the various kinds of uniformed police were not rigorously observed at the time, such police often being called the gendarmerie (a term that properly applies only to the *Feldgendarmerie* of the Wehrmacht and a few other specific units). They are not rigorously observed here, either.

Other Issues

I sometimes speak of 'the ghetto' as a corporate person: for example, 'the ghetto did not understand German plans'. It is proper to speak of a group in this way, I believe, when it displays coherent behaviour from which a common intention can be deduced. The case is similar to R.G. Collingwood's example of a run on the bank: just as we can easily work out the thought-processes of depositors in a panic to withdraw their funds, so can we also work out those of the inhabitants of the ghetto, all faced with the same overwhelming problems. We can indeed imagine 'the ghetto' thinking, trying to guess, deciding among the limited possibilities that presented themselves.

Warsaw, here, is the City of Warsaw within its 1939 boundaries. The 'Warsaw area' in principle means the area of operations of the Warsaw group of activists connected with the Polish and Jewish aid organizations; it therefore extends to such nearby locations as the Kampinos forest and Wyszków woods, towns like Pruszków, Milanówek, Otwock, Józefów and so on. The 'Warsaw District', on the other hand, is the German administrative division of that name, which was still larger. When I speak of Jews hiding in Warsaw, I generally mean the Warsaw area.

For the sake of consistency, Polish spellings will be used for the names of persons, places, and so on, except where there is an accepted anglicization (Warsaw, Cracow, the Vistula). I intended at first to use English translations of Warsaw street names, whose colourful medieval and Catholic character is otherwise not apparent to the English-language reader. Thus:

Ulica Świętojerska = St George Street;
Ul. Świętokrzyska = Holy Cross Street;
Aleje Jerozolimskie = Jerusalem Avenue;
Plac Zbawiciela = Square of the Redeemer;
Plac Trzech Krzyży = Three Crosses Square;
Ul. Złota, Żelazna, Kamienna = Gold, Iron, Stone Streets;
Ul. Dzielna, Dzika = Brave Street, Wild Street;
Ul. Krzywa, Prosta, Śliska = Crooked, Straight, Slippery Streets.

By doing so, I also meant to try to reduce the exaggerated sense of exoticism with which we tend to view foreign countries, increasing our psychological distance and lending credibility to extreme conclusions. There are in addition certain ironies that are lost on the reader who does not speak Polish: that the main command centre of the Warsaw Ghetto Uprising was located in Pleasant (Miła) Street, for example; or that the two most notorious Gestapo prisons were in colourfully named Peacock (Pawia) and Goose (Gęsia) Streets. One of the entrances to the ghetto was, appropriately, at Iron Gate Square (Plac Żelaznej Bramy), from which Border (Graniczna) Street ran along the ghetto wall. The well-guarded street that separated the ghetto from the Jewish cemetery was Trench (Okopowa) Street.

This procedure, however, would cause difficulty for readers who are familiar with the Polish names from other sources, but not with their meanings, and it would pose problems in incorporating quotations, which mainly use the Polish names. I have therefore somewhat reluctantly opted for the Polish names, except in certain cases where the English translation seemed natural or usual (e.g. Three Crosses Square). Occasionally, the Polish is followed by an English translation in parentheses where the context seemed to allow it without undue awkwardness, or where it seemed to have some immediate point.

Reference has already been made to *szmalcowniks*, extortionists and blackmailers. In Polish, the wartime slang term *szmalcownik* (plural: *szmalcownicy*) in principle meant people who accosted their victims in the street, demanding relatively small sums, whereas the more serious criminals who followed Jews to their hideouts and stripped them of all they had were called *szantażysci* (blackmailers, from the French *chantage*). I have rendered these as 'extortionist' and 'blackmailer', respectively. These distinctions were not strictly observed, however, and *szmalcownik* often served in practice as a catch-all term. For present purposes it has proved convenient to use *szmalcownik* in this way, following the normal practice in the Jewish and English-language historiography, with the terms 'extortionist' or 'blackmailer' reserved for cases where the distinction seemed important. In English, the forms *shmaltsovnik* (plural: *shmaltsovniks* or *shmaltsovnikes*) are often encountered; these are transliterations from the Yiddish. In keeping with my general policy of using Polish spellings, I have not adopted these forms, but I have compromised by using the plural *szmalcowniks*, feeling that English-speakers will not easily 'hear' *szmalcownicy* as plural.

The Polish police force serving under German orders was known before the war as the State Police (*Policja Państwowa*). During the war it was pressed into service by the authorities, with the top posts being filled by Germans. It kept its navy-blue uniforms, but all insignia alluding to the Polish state were removed, except for the designation 'PP'. This was reinterpreted by the Germans as *Polnische Polizei*, one of the few occasions when the adjective *polnisch* was retained: normally, *nichtdeutsch* was preferred. The Poles generally rejected both the designation and its implication, regarding these men as corrupt and *vendu*:

> The police, which let no one dare to call Polish, has especially earned punishment and decided contempt. These navy-blue louts, squeezing bribes out of whomever they can, resorting to threats and blackmail, snapping to attention in front of every Hun, have demonstrated such a collapse of human and national dignity that they deserve no excuse.[3]

In everyday speech, Poles referred to this force as the *policja granatowa* or navy-blue police; the Jewish Order Service, because of its yellow hat-bands, was similarly called the *policja żółta*, or yellow police. In the English-language literature, the terms 'Blue police' and 'ghetto police', respectively, are the most frequently used, and I have adhered to these.

There has recently been some discussion of the spelling of 'antisemitic', 'anti-semitism' etc. The accepted spelling is 'anti-Semitism' *et simile*, but the objection is raised that this implies that there is something called 'Semitism' to which one might, possibly legitimately, be opposed. I am of the opinion that such molehills turn into mountains as a result of debates of this kind; but given that the mountain has been conjured up, and having to choose between raising eyebrows in some circles and giving offence in others, I would rather see the eyebrows go up. Therefore antisemitism it is.

Glossary

AAN	*Archiwum Akt Nowych*: Modern Records Archive (Warsaw)
AK	*Armia Krajowa*: Home Army, the mainstream Polish military underground
AL	*Armia Ludowa*: People's Army, the Polish Communist military underground
AWIH	*Archiwum Wojskowego Instytutu Historycznego*: Archives of the Army Historical Institute (Warsaw)
AŻIH	*Archiwum Żydowskiego Instytutu Historycznego*: Archives of the Jewish Historical Institute (Warsaw)
BBWR	*Bezpartyjny Blok Współpracy z Rządem*: Non-Party Bloc for Co-operation with the Government. Political party of the *Sanacja* under Piłsudski
Bleter far Geshichte	Yiddish-language journal of ŻIH
BLHG	*Beit Lohamei HaGetaot*: Ghetto Fighters' House (Nahraiyya, Israel). Archive and museum
Bund	The General Jewish Workers' Bund: Jewish socialist and anti-Zionist party
BŻIH	*Biuletyn Żydowskiego Instytutu Historycznego*: Polish-language journal of ŻIH
Centos	*Centrala Opieki nad Sierotami*: Central Organization for Orphan Care. In the Warsaw ghetto an agency of the Jewish Council, headed by Dr Adolf Berman
Chadecja	Christian Democracy, a pre-war right-wing Catholic party
Chadek	Supporter of Christian Democracy
CKŻH	*Centralny Komitet Żydowski Historyczny*: Central Jewish Historical Committee, historical research branch of CKŻP, predecessor of ŻIH
CKŻP	*Centralny Komitet Żydów w Polsce*: Central Committee of Jews in Poland, post-war umbrella Jewish organization
Delegatura	Representation of the Polish Government-in-Exile in Poland. Consisted of the Delegate (Jan Jankowski) and representatives of underground military and civilian organizations
Endecja	Roman Dmowski's National Democratic party and its successors. A right-wing, antisemitic political movement, mainly represented during the war by the SN and its offshoots, ONR, Falanga, OWP and others
Endek	Supporter of the Endecja
Falanga	One of the factions of ONR
FOP	*Front Odrodzenia Polski*: Front for the Rebirth of Poland. An association of right-wing and centrist Catholic intellectuals. Participated in RPŻ

Front Morges	Pre-war opposition bloc formed at the home of Ignacy Paderewski in Morges, Switzerland; leading figures included General Władysław Sikorski. This group was the nucleus of the Polish Government-in-Exile, which formed in Angers, France, in 1940, and moved to London after the fall of France
General Committee	See GK
GG	*Generalgouvernement*: General Government; the central part of Nazi-occupied Poland, headed by Governor-General Hans Frank, which included Warsaw
GK	The General Commission for the Investigation of German Crimes in Poland. A committee of the Polish Interior Ministry, Prosecutions Branch, established in 1945 to co-ordinate the activities of regional commissions investigating Nazi war crimes in Poland. In 1953 its name was changed for political reasons to the General Commission for the Investigation of Hitlerite War Crimes in Poland. After 1989 its mandate was broadened to include Soviet war crimes and it was renamed the General Commission for the Investigation of Crimes against the Polish Nation; subsequently it was absorbed by the Institute of National Memory (IPN)
GL	*Gwardia Ludowa*: People's Guard. (1) PPS newspaper (2) Predecessor of AL
JDC	Joint Distribution Committee. American Jewish organization that carried out relief work in Poland. It had an office in Warsaw until the German declaration of war against the US (21 December 1941), and continued underground after that
The Joint	The JDC. The English word was used in Polish
KPP	*Komunistyczna Partia Polski*: the pre-war Communist Party of Poland, dissolved in 1938 by the Comintern
NSZ	*Narodowe Siły Zbrojne*: National Armed Forces; extreme right-wing military underground organization, independent of AK, formed mainly by members of ONR and OWP
melina	Hiding place. From the Hebrew *melunah*, kennel
ONR	*Obóz Narodowo-Radykalny*: Extremist party modelled on the Italian Fascists, which broke away from the SN in 1934. Co-founded NSZ
Oneg Shabbat	Sabbath joy. So called because it met on the Sabbath, this circle of intellectuals was formed by the historian Emmanuel Ringelblum and included, among others, the diarist Abraham Lewin. *Oneg Shabbat* worked to document and record the life of the Warsaw ghetto. Its archive was concealed in milk cans and tin cases and buried; most of it was recovered after the war. The surviving portion of the *Oneg Shabbat* archive forms the most important source of historical information about the Warsaw ghetto.
OWP	*Obóz Wielkiej Polski*: Great Poland Camp; Right-wing faction of SN. Co-founded NSZ
OZN or OZON	*Obóz Zjednoczenia Narodowego*: National Unity Front. Government party, successor to the BBWR, formed in 1936
PAL	*Polska Armia Ludowa*: Polish People's Army. Military arm of RPPS
PPR	*Polska Partia Robotnicza*, Polish Workers' Party. Communist party formed in 1942
PPS	*Polska Partia Socjalistyczna*, Polish Socialist Party
PPS-WRN	*Polska Partia Socjalistyczna – Wolność, Równość, Niepodległość*: Freedom-Equality-Independence; right-wing wartime faction of the PPS
PS	*Polscy Socjaliści*: left-wing wartime faction of the PPS; later, RPPS
RGO	*Rada Główna Opiekuńcza*: Main Welfare Council. Polish welfare organization, sponsored by the occupation authorities

RPPS	*Robotnicza Partia Polskich Socjalistów*: Workers' Party of Polish Socialists. Successor of PS
RPŻ	*Rada Pomocy Żydom*: Council to Aid Jews. See *Żegota*
Sanacja	The Pilsudskiite movement. Its party was the BBWR (1926–36), thereafter OZN
SD	(1) *Stronnictwo Demokratyczne*: Democratic Party. Centrist party formed in 1938 by former supporters of Piłsudski opposed to the governing OZN
	(2) *Sicherheitsdienst*: Security Service. The internal police force of the SS
SL	*Stronnictwo Ludowe*: People's Party. Mainly rural party formed by union of the centrist SL-Piast and the left-wing SL-*Wyzwolenie* ('Liberation')
SN	*Stronnictwo Narodowe*: National Party. The main political party of the Endecja
SOS	*Społeczna Organizacja Samopomocy*: Social Self-Help Agency. Underground welfare agency created by the Democratic Party (SD). Its Jewish section, headed by Zofia Kossak-Szczucka, served mainly as a liaison between Żegota and religious institutions hiding Jewish children
SPP	*Studium Polski Podziemnej* = UPST
SSPF	*SS- und Polizeiführer*: SS and Police Leader. The SSPF for the Warsaw District, subordinate to the HSSPF for the General Government, was Ferdinand von Sammern-Frankenegg. He was replaced in April 1943 by Jürgen Stroop, who headed the military operation against the Warsaw Ghetto Uprising
szmalcownik	Blackmailer or extortionist. See discussion on p. xiv
TKPŻ	*Tymczasowy Komitet Pomocy Żydom*: Temporary Committee to Aid Jews = TRPŻ
TRPŻ	*Tymczasowa Rada Pomocy Żydom*: Temporary Council to Aid Jews; predecessor of *Żegota*, founded in September 1942
Umschlagplatz	'Marketplace': the yard to the north of the Warsaw ghetto where Jews were held prior to being loaded onto deportation trains
UPST	Underground Poland Study Trust (London)
WRN	See PPS-WRN
WSM	*Warszawska Spółdzielnia Mieszkaniowa*, Warsaw Housing Co-operative. Large housing co-operative in Żoliborz, operated by PPS, in which many Jews were hidden
YV	Yad Vashem, the Holocaust Heroes and Martyrs' Remembrance Authority. In citations, its archives
YVS	*Yad Vashem Studies*: leading Holocaust studies journal, published by Yad Vashem
Żegota	Codename of RPŻ; also *Komitet im. Konrada Żegoty*, Konrad Żegota Committee. Organization formed by TRPŻ in December 1942, including representatives of ŻKN and Bund, to carry out relief work among Jews in hiding. An official organization of the Delegatura
ŻIH	*Żydowski Instytut Historyczny*: Jewish Historical Institute
ŻKK	*Żydowski Komitet Koordynacyjny*: Jewish Co-ordinating Committee; often rendered in English as Joint Co-ordinating Committee. Committee to co-ordinate activities of ŻKN and Bund; political arm of ŻOB
ŻKN	*Żydowski Komitet Narodowy*: Jewish National Committee. Umbrella organization of Zionist parties, excluding Revisionists
ŻOB	*Żydowska Organizacja Bojowa*: Jewish Combat Organization; military wing of ŻKK
ŻTOS	*Żydowskie Towarzystwo Opieki Społecznej*: Jewish Social Welfare Society; welfare agency of the Jewish Council
ŻZW	*Żydowski Związek Wojskowy*: Jewish Military Union; military wing of Revisionist Zionists

Guide to Polish Pronunciation

Polish is an extremely phonetic language, easy to pronounce once you know the rules but with some unfamiliar combinations. The spelling is usually more daunting than the pronunciation. For example, if you can pronounce 'Khrushchev', you can pronounce the szcz combination: pszczoła (bee) is pronounced psh-choh-wah.

Vowels
Vowels are usually pronounced just as written, according to the rules below. There are no diphthongs, long or short forms, or rising or falling inflections, and with one exception they are never silent. Thus 'nauka' (science) is pronounced 'nah-oo-kah'; 'mile' (kindly) is pronounced 'mee-leh'.

a   as in *father*
e   as in *bet*
i   as in *litre*
o   as in *hot*
ó   like oo but slightly shorter
u   identical to ó
y   as in *lynx*

i 'softens' the preceding consonant and is run together with it; e.g. biedny (poor) = byed-nyh, ciemny (dark) = chem-nyh, siny (blue) = shee-nyh

Nasal vowels
ą   like French *on*
ę   like French *in*

Consonants
Consonants are pronounced as in English, with the following exceptions:
c   ts
ć   ch (soft)

ch   as in Scottish *loch*
cz   ch (hard)
g   always hard, as in *get*
j   like y in *yet*
ł   w
ń   like n in *onion*
r   rolled, but short
rz   zh (hard)
ś   sh (soft)
sz   sh (hard)
w   v
ż   zh (hard, identical to rz)
ź   zh (soft)

The combinations ci, ni, si and zi are pronounced like ć, ń, ś and ź. When they are followed by a vowel the 'i' sound disappears (this is the one case of a silent vowel in Polish). So ci = chee, cie = che (as in *check*).

Poles distinguish between the 'hard' sounds cz, rz, sz and the corresponding 'soft' sounds, ć, ś and ź, but the English ear cannot usually tell the difference. Those who can 'do' accents might try the Irish or American pronunciation for the 'soft' sounds and 'received' English (or the French or German equivalents) for the 'hard' ones.

Double consonants are pronounced separately; e.g. Anna = An-na.
Consecutive vowels are also pronounced separately, e.g. zoologia = zoh-oh-log-ya.

Usually the penultimate syllable is stressed.

Examples:

ciuchy	*choo*-hyih	second-hand clothes (sold for food)
Gęsiówka	Gen-*shoof*-ka	prison in Gęsia (*Gen*-sha) Street
Pawiak	*Pah*-vyak	prison in Pawia (*Pah*-vya) Street
placówka	plats-*oof*-ka	work gang working outside the ghetto
szaber	*shah*-ber	loot
szabrować	shah-*broh*-vach	to loot
szmalcownik	shmahl-*tsov*-nik	extortionist or blackmailer
Z otchłani	zot-*hwah*-nee	*From the Abyss* (title of a volume of poetry)
Góral	*Goo*-rahl	Carpathian mountaineer; 500-zł note
swój	svooy	'one of us'

Acknowledgments

I owe a debt, first of all, to my doctoral thesis co-supervisors, Peter Pulzer in Oxford and Jerzy Tomaszewski in Warsaw, who waded through my many drafts and preliminary papers and in so many ways kept me from losing my way. I am indebted also to the late Teresa Prekerowa, who gave generously of her time and knowledge and also read much more of my material than her busy schedule ought to have allowed. To Jeremy Gurofsky, Berel Lang, Larry Powell and Thomas Sandkühler, who read the typescript and offered many constructive suggestions. To David Cesarani, Tony Kushner, Rainer Liedtke, Antony Polonsky, David Rechter, Jonathan Webber, Stephan Wendehorst and Joshua Zimmerman, for providing the opportunity for my work-in-progress to mature through public exposure.

At Yad Vashem in Jerusalem, I received valuable comments and advice from Israel Gutman and Shmuel Krakowski and much practical assistance from Mordechai Paldiel, Director of the Department of the Righteous, and his secretary, Viola Wein; also from archivist Hadassah Modlinger; Iris Berlatzky, Head of the Oral History Department, and many others. I am indebted to Igra Moos for translating key materials from the Hebrew for me. At Beit Lohamei Hagetaot, I was helped by archivist Ewa Feldenkreis, and by Dorka Sternberg, who made all the physical arrangements for my stay there. I am grateful also for having met Zvi Eisenman, possibly the last of the Yiddish-language poets of Warsaw, who became a sincere friend.

In Warsaw, I received much help from Marek Józ´wik, archivist at the Jewish Historical Institute. Dariusz Stola and Małgorzata Melchior also shared time and material, including copies of their books,[1] which I found most useful. I owe especial thanks to Barbara Engelking-Boni, who shared research material with me, introduced me to Helena Merenholc, an authentic heroine of those days, and became and has remained a friend. Her trilogy on the experience of the Holocaust and her 'Baedecker' of the Warsaw ghetto have an honoured place on my bookshelf.[2]

I am unable to thank in detail all those friends in cyberspace who have contributed in one way or another. I owe gratitude to the moderators and all the subscribers of the H-HOLOCAUST e-mail list, who have provided a sounding-board and much feedback. In particular, I owe thanks to Kenneth Waltzer, who sent me a pre-publication copy of the memoirs of Jacob Celemeński in English translation, and to Chaim Ellenbogen, who made this important source available.

In Toronto, I owe thanks to Michael Marrus for teaching me most of what I know about the Holocaust in History, and for supervising my Masters' thesis, a pilot study for the present work. Thanks also to all those connected with the Polish–Jewish Heritage Society in Toronto, particularly to Rabbi Dow Marmur and Frank Białystok, for providing a forum where I listened and learned a great deal.

In Oxford, Jonathan Glover, who describes himself as an 'applied moral philosopher' with a special interest in the Holocaust, gave me many hours of his time for discussion of the knotty problems in ethics which the Holocaust presents: I hope my contribution to his work was one-tenth as helpful as his to mine.[3] Thanks also to Johannes Brozi, who taught me most of the Yiddish I know, and to the several teachers at the Oxford Centre for Hebrew and Jewish Studies who tried with limited success to teach me Hebrew. Others in Oxford and London who provided advice, a sounding board, or other forms of help include Chimen Abramsky, Norman Davies, R.A.E. Ellis, Oliver Freeman, Timothy Garton Ash, Piotr Grabowski, Ewa Huggins, Wanda Kemp-Welch and Jolanta Kisler-Goldstein. Special thanks to Leszek Kołakowski for providing a meeting-place and much interesting discussion.

Space does not permit me to name all the individuals who contributed to this project in one way or another; apologies therefore to all those whom I have failed to mention. It need hardly be added that any merit this book may have is due in part to all those who helped me, while its faults are entirely mine.

Money is alas the root of all, and those without whose financial contributions this project would have been impossible include the Council of Vice Chancellors and Principals of British Universities, the Commonwealth Scholarship Foundation and the Social Sciences and Humanities Research Council of Canada.

I have left until last those who contributed far more than money and advice: the many Holocaust survivors and Catholic Poles with whom I conversed, formally or informally, in the course of shaping my understanding. For reliving their painful memories, sometimes for many hours at a time, and for their patience with my ignorance and their forgiveness of my lapses in tact, I must extend thanks with the greatest sincerity to Nina Assorodobraj-Kula, Janina Brandwajn-Ziemian, Renia Brus, Daniel Falkner, Louis Lenkinsky, Helena Merenholc, Diana Sternick, the late Przemysław Wodzinowski, Halina Zrubek, and others who did not wish to be named.

Finally, and above all, I owe gratitude to my late mother, *née* Alicja Pelcer – A.P. in the following account – who shared her memories with me over the course of many years. To her I owe my interest in the subject, my knowledge of Polish, whatever 'feel' I have for the period, and of course my life. To her memory I dedicate this work.

inappropriate that the day in the Jewish calendar that has been chosen to commemorate the Holocaust, *Yom ha-Shoah*, is linked to Warsaw and the Warsaw Ghetto Uprising.[4]

Most histories of Jewish Warsaw end with this event. Yet after the defeat of the uprising, after the complete destruction of the ghetto, after nine-tenths of its Jews had been murdered, there still remained in Warsaw the largest clandestine community of Jews anywhere in Europe, in fact probably the largest community of people that has lived in hiding in any city, ever. Estimates of its size vary widely. Raul Hilberg, on the basis of German reports, maintains that there were only 5,000–6,000 Jews in hiding in Warsaw,[5] but all others have put forward much higher figures: 10,000–15,000 (Emmanuel Ringelblum), 15,000 (Shmuel Krakowski), 15,000–20,000 (Joseph Kermish, Israel Gutman and others), 25,000 (Krakowski, elsewhere), to as many as 42,000 (Tatiana Berenstein and Adam Rutkowski) or even 50,000 (Marek Arczyński). The great disparity between these estimates reflects the lack of solid knowledge until now. The Chairman of the Jewish National Committee, Adolf Berman, was closest to the situation, since his organization did relief work among the fugitives and kept records. Berman estimated that there were still 15,000–20,000 Jews in hiding in 1944, the survivors among a presumably much larger number of escapees a year or two earlier. This book will find support for Berman's claim, on the basis of a close analysis of his records and a broad variety of other sources. It will show that about 28,000 Jews lived 'on the Aryan side' in Warsaw at one time or another, having either stayed out of the Warsaw ghetto when it was formed, or escaped from it, or come to Warsaw to hide.

The general subject of escape and hiding as a Jewish response to the Holocaust has been virtually ignored by historians, so that accurate comparisons are hard to come by. Many Jews in Paris and Budapest went into hiding for brief periods, but in neither city was the situation comparable to that in Warsaw. Paris had no ghetto, hence no 'Aryan side', and 30,000 Jews lived in the city openly until liberation.[6] The Budapest ghetto existed for only three months, and while only a third of Budapest's Jews entered it, most of those who stayed outside lived not in hiding but more or less openly under the protection of Raoul Wallenberg and other foreign diplomats. It is estimated that 20,000–25,000 Jews went into hiding in the Netherlands and a similar number in Belgium. The Dutch Jews were concentrated in Amsterdam, where the number in hiding may have reached 20,000. There, too, the situation was not entirely comparable, since Amsterdam had an 'open' ghetto in which 14,000 Jews were still living legally at the time of liberation; but it probably offers the best comparison available. The Belgian Jews were divided between Antwerp, Brussels, Liège and Charleroi; Antwerp was the largest Jewish centre, but it is unlikely that as many as 10,000 were hidden there. There are thought to have been about 5,000 Jews hiding in Berlin, probably rather fewer in Vienna. The 5,000 Jews hidden by the 5,000 citizens of Le Chambon-sur-Lignon in France represent undoubtedly the densest concentration of Jewish fugitives anywhere; but in absolute terms, and among large centres, Warsaw accounted for the largest number of Jews in hiding by far.

I have characterized these 28,000 Jews – together with the many non-Jews who helped to hide them, and the criminal element that ceaselessly hunted them – as not merely a collection of isolated individuals, but a 'secret city'. Secret it certainly was, of course: not only did it have to be concealed from the Polish population at large as well as the Germans and their minions, but its inhabitants themselves were barely aware of its existence. Each Jew in hiding knew of a few others – family, friends, people with whom they were sharing hiding places – and also of a few Polish friends who could be counted on to help. Each Jew had to deal with various strangers, perhaps friendly and perhaps not, who provided services usually for money. Each Jew was also confronted with an army of blackmailers, denouncers, policemen and so forth, and faced a huge, impassive city of strangers who had to be presumed hostile until proven otherwise. Jews in hiding therefore felt themselves to be isolated and alone, with few friends and many enemies, and this is the impression that prevails in the many memoirs of the period.

Unbeknownst to the Jews, however, these various groups of friends, paid helpers and other Jews in hiding intertwined to form a large network, connecting every Jew in hiding to every other. No one was fully aware of this network, which came into being spontaneously through personal contacts rather than any organized effort, but there are many strands of evidence that testify to its existence. For one thing, nearly all the Jews in hiding were victimized by *szmalcowniks* (extortionists and blackmailers), showing immediately that their isolation was not so great as it seemed. For another, a common language developed: a hiding place was called a *melina*; if it was discovered, it was said to be 'burnt'; Jews in hiding were called 'cats'. The word *szmalcownik* was itself a coinage of the time. Again, 3,500 Jews fell into the Hotel Polski trap (described in Chapter 4): about one in seven of the Jews in hiding at the time. Nearly all the Jews heard about this scheme, which was advertised strictly through word of mouth. The speed and thoroughness with which the news spread is testimony to the extensive communications networks that linked the secret city, just as the number of victims helps to demonstrate its scale.

The secret city also had its institutions, consisting mainly of a group of charitable organizations devoted to bringing aid to the Jews: the joint Polish and Jewish Council to Aid Jews (codenamed 'Żegota'), its member Jewish organizations, the Jewish National Committee (*Żydowski Komitet Narodowy* – ŻKN), representing the Zionist parties, and the Bund. These organizations between them eventually reached about 8,900 of the Jews in hiding, and formed the single most important link in the network. There were also a number of other institutions: the Socialist (PPS), Communist (PPR) and Democratic (SD) parties, which helped their Jewish members directly; the Social Self-Help Organization (*Społeczna*

Organizacja Samopomocy – SOS), founded by the Democratic Party, which acted as a liaison between Żegota and Catholic welfare institutions; the Warsaw Housing Co-operative (*Warszawska Spółdzielnia Mieszkaniowa* – WSM), run by the PPS, which harboured a large number of Jews and gave employment to a few; the Co-ordinating Committee of Democratic and Socialist Physicians (PPR, PPS and SD), which provided medical assistance to Jews in hiding; and even the tiny Association of Tartar-Muslims, which provided a few Jews with false documents ('Aryan papers') and an explanation for being circumcised. The provision of false documents was not of course limited to the Muslims: Żegota and the mainstream Polish underground operated a vastly larger 'legalization' enterprise, which produced documents for people in hiding in general, including Jews.

Besides institutions, the secret city had a cultural life of sorts, and literary achievements. These include four important books: Ludwik Landau's chronicles, *Kronika lat wojny i okupacji*, a fundamental source for the period; Emmanuel Ringelblum's *Polish–Jewish Relations during the Second World War*, a volume of poetry, *Z otchłani* (From the Abyss); and Jakub Wiernik's memoirs, *Rok w Treblince* (A Year in Treblinka). The latter two were published during the war, and were even smuggled out of the country and published in London and New York in 1944. Ringelblum also wrote other manuscripts: a series of biographical sketches of prominent Warsaw Jews, which was published after the war, and a history of the Trawniki labour camp, which has unfortunately been lost. In addition, he carried on a correspondence with Adolf Berman, which has been preserved. In July 1944 ŻKN published an underground bulletin, *Głos z otchłani* (Voice from the Abyss), in which an anonymous author wrote:

> Our publications are without precedent in history. They are put out by people over whom there constantly hangs the sentence of death, who work in the nightmarish conditions of a double underground. They are published by the same factors in Jewish society that raised the flag of battle for the human and national dignity of the Jews, those circles whose slogan was and is 'to live with dignity and to die with dignity'. The idea of dedicated self-help and armed resistance, which lighted our path through all the phases of the martyrdom of the Jews of Poland, even now remains the engine of our work. Under the sign of self-help and battle we fulfil our social duty, despite persecutions, on the boundary between life and death.

Besides these 'official' efforts, many diaries were kept in hiding, some of which survived, and some of which formed the basis of subsequent memoirs. There were also Polish literary works on the plight of the Jews, such as Maria Kann's *Przed oczyma świata* (Before the Eyes of the World), also published during the war, and Czesław Miłosz's poems *Campo di Fiori* and *Biedny polak patrzy na ghetto* (A Poor Pole Looks at the Ghetto) which appeared in the *Z otchłani* volume. There was a social life of a kind, too: there were restaurants and cafés whose clientele included Jews in hiding, and the activists' circles provided a social milieu as well as a working group.

The secret city's criminal element consisted not only of *szmalcowniks* and police agents, but of people who were prepared to cheat and rob Jews in other ways. These elements were also intertwined with the network that formed the city: that is how they found their victims. Some of the more sophisticated *szmalcowniks* infiltrated the city by playing a double game, helping Jews and providing hiding places, and then blackmailing them. Dishonest landlords and people who stole property that Jews had entrusted to them were also an integral part of it. Conversely, the secret city had a rudimentary justice system, arising late in the day and necessarily small and limited in power, which passed and carried out death sentences on collaborators, including a few of the *szmalcowniks*.

The secret city also carried out military operations. The Jewish Combat Organization (ŻOB) continued in hiding after the Ghetto Uprising, with satellite partisan operations in the Wyszków and Łomianki woods. There was a ŻOB cell in the tractor factory in Ursus, to the west, and another in the southern suburb of Okęcie. The fighters of the Revisionist ŻZW, who had made their way out of the ghetto during the uprising, took their weapons into hiding with them. One group died in a gun battle with German police on 16 June 1943, when their hiding place was discovered; another joined Polish Communist partisans in Michalin and were also killed in battle. When the Warsaw Uprising broke out in August 1944, both ŻOB and ŻZW fighters took part, as well as hundreds of Jews who had been in hiding or were liberated from German prisons.

The secret city of the Jews in hiding in Warsaw was thus a unique and extraordinary phenomenon. Consisting of 28,000 Jews, perhaps 70,000–90,000 people who were helping them, and 3,000–4,000 *szmalcowniks* and other harmful individuals, its population numbered more than 100,000, probably exceeding the size of the Polish underground in Warsaw, which fielded 70,000 fighters in 1944. The study of other cities in occupied Europe may ultimately provide other, comparable examples, but it is unlikely that these will prove to be as large, as varied or as complex as this one. There has never been anything quite like it.

Prior Literature

While there is a very considerable memoir literature, and an extensive historiography on various related topics, serious historical writing on this important group of fugitives has been limited to a few articles and a few paragraphs, sometimes chapters, in books devoted to other things. On the whole, Jewish Warsaw during the Holocaust is taken to be synonymous with the ghetto. Characteristically, Israel Gutman's classic study *The Jews of Warsaw* bears the dates 1939–43, ends with the destruction of the ghetto and spends only a few paragraphs on the fate and experience of the survivors.[7] One particularly enigmatic episode, the Hotel Polski affair, has received some attention,[8] and there is a substantial literature on the related topics of Polish–Jewish relations and Polish assistance to Jews. All of these neighbouring bodies of work naturally have something to say about the Jews in hiding, but more often than not this takes the form of polemical assertions inadequately grounded in research, supported (if at all) by selected anecdotes or the opinions of contemporary witnesses. Such assertions have usually been meant to prop up one or another author's theses about Polish behaviour and attitudes, rather than to propose realistic conclusions about the Jews themselves.

There have been a few books on Jews in hiding, though none specifically on Warsaw. The most notable is Michael Borwicz's three-volume *Arishe papirn* (Aryan Papers), and the abbreviated French version, *Les vies interdites*.[9] The larger work has a few chapters on Warsaw; in the shorter, these have been removed to make way for material on France. *Arishe papirn* is a serious and important treatment of the subject, and remains even today the only continent-wide survey of hiding, but it has shortcomings. Writing in 1955, Borwicz could not benefit from the many sources, especially memoirs, that have become available since then, not to mention the vast corpus of modern literature on the Holocaust as a whole. His work therefore remains indispensable, but is not the last word.

One cannot go on without mentioning Emmanuel Ringelblum's *Polish–Jewish Relations during the Second World War*, written while the author was himself hiding in a 'bunker' on the Aryan side in Warsaw. Two chapters of this extraordinary book are devoted to the Aryan side, and the English-language edition is provided with an introduction and copious footnotes by its editors, Joseph Kermish and Shmuel Krakowski, which are themselves a significant contribution to the field. Artur Eisenbach has performed a similar service for the 1988 Polish edition, the first to appear unbowdlerized in the original language. I have presented an analysis of Ringelblum's book elsewhere,[10] and more will be said below; for now, it should be noted that Ringelblum himself regarded his work as only a preliminary sketch, a 'contribution for a future historian', and that although it is a remarkable achievement given the conditions under which it was written, it has obvious limitations. I have treated it mainly as a primary source.

A work that follows in Ringelblum's footsteps is Israel Gutman and Shmuel Krakowski's *Unequal Victims*, mainly about Polish–Jewish relations, but again with substantial material on the Aryan side, of which a small amount is on Warsaw. Gutman and Krakowski describe Jewish experiences and Polish responses, supported by a range of anecdotal evidence, but (unlike Ringelblum) they generally do not venture numbers. Without numbers, we have no sense of scale, and we are left with the authors' opinions as to the relative significance of the phenomena that they note. In addition, more needs to be said about the situation of the Poles than simply to report, *in vacuo*, the range of their behaviour towards the Jews. The conditions of the German occupation on both sides of the ghetto wall need to be considered, not to prove that the Jews suffered more, which has never been in doubt, nor to provide excuses for the Poles, but to understand how these conditions defined and limited the possibilities of action by Poles and Jews alike. In any event, *Unequal Victims* does not pretend to be more than incidentally about the present subject. Like the Polish polemical works to which it is intended as a response, it is more about the bystanders than the victims, who are treated as either passive objects of persecution or passive recipients of aid. This book, I must emphasize, is not about bystanders. It is not about the Poles, or Polish–Jewish relations, or altruism, or rescue, or efforts to help Jews, though something will be said about all these things. It is about the Jews, and their active efforts to help themselves and each other.

At the same time I must also emphasize that this is not a book about 'Jewish resistance to the Holocaust', a phrase that, as I shall shortly argue, has become so diluted as to be nearly meaningless. In any case, escape and hiding have rarely been included in even broad discussions of resistance; in fact, they have hardly been included in historical studies at all. *Rethinking the Holocaust,* Yehuda Bauer's recent overview of Holocaust historiography, confirms this point: though there is a chapter entitled 'Unarmed Resistance and Other Responses' where these questions might have been raised, escape and hiding are not discussed.[11] This is not negligence on Bauer's part: systematic historical study of Jewish attempts to save themselves – of Jews during the Holocaust who, without taking up arms, were at least to some extent masters of their own fate – virtually does not exist.

Evasion, the Unexplored Continent of Holocaust Studies[12]

That so little has been written on escape and hiding so far, given the enormous literature on the Holocaust published over the past sixty years, is something of a puzzle. It is instructive to try to work out why historians have taken such a distorted view of Jewish responses, and to consider how this book can usefully redress the balance.

Raul Hilberg proposed five categories of responses made by victims of the Holocaust (indeed, by victims in general): *resistance, alleviation, evasion, paralysis* and *compliance.* Hilberg himself emphasized the passive responses – paralysis and especially compliance – as the most characteristic, ingrained, according to him, as the result of thousands of years of life in exile. In particular, he asserted controversially that '[t]he reaction pattern of the Jews is characterized by an almost complete lack of resistance'.[13] Hannah Arendt went further, declaring that 'without Jewish help in administrative and police work ... there would have been either complete chaos or an impossibly severe drain on German manpower',[14] from which she concluded that 'if the Jewish people had really been unorganized and leaderless, ... the total number of victims would hardly have been between four and a half and six million people'.[15]

In Holocaust studies, the scholarly agenda has very often been driven by accusations and defensive reactions, and this proved no exception. The Hilberg–Arendt thesis of Jewish passivity and compliance – virtually alleging that the Jews had collaborated in their own destruction – aroused a storm of protest, especially in Israel, where Jewish armed resistance, the Warsaw Ghetto Uprising in particular, has had the status of a founding myth. In one of the first in what has become a torrent of books and articles, Reuben Ainsztain responded to Hilberg with an enormous polemic, which over nearly a thousand pages surveyed the military history of the Jewish Diaspora, from the Jewish soldiers of Cyrus the Great to Captain Dreyfus, before giving a panoramic view of Jewish armed resistance during the Holocaust.[16] The very first Yad Vashem Conference, in 1968, was devoted to 'Manifestations of Resistance in the Holocaust': its participants tried to meet the Hilberg–Arendt challenge not only by documenting Jewish partisan activity and various uprisings in ghettos and camps, but by broadening the definition of resistance to include anything that served to frustrate the Nazis' aims, even simply staying alive. Yehuda Bauer offered the following definition: resistance was 'any group action consciously taken in opposition to known or surmised laws, actions or intentions directed against the Jews by the Germans and their collaborators'.[17] More recently he has proposed including some individual actions as well.

Another response came in the form of Isaiah Trunk's great study of Jewish leadership, *Judenrat*, and the 1976 Yad Vashem Conference on 'Patterns of Jewish Leadership'. Trunk and the other conference participants stressed the dilemmas faced by Jewish leaders, portraying them by and large as honest men doing their best to ease the lot of the Jews in their charge under impossible conditions.

Returning to Hilberg's taxonomy, it can thus be seen that Hilberg and Arendt stress compliance and paralysis as Jewish responses to the Holocaust, against which Trunk stressed the attempts of the Jewish councils at alleviation, while Ainsztein (and many others) documented resistance in painstaking detail. Lost in all these polemics was, and still is, the third of Hilberg's five categories, evasion. Even at the first Yad Vashem conference, with its all-inclusive definition of resistance, no study of evasion was presented. Properly so, in fact. While all such classifications are of course arbitrary, there are good reasons for wanting to preserve the distinction between resistance and evasion. First of all, 'fight' and 'flight' are basic and universal psychological categories, and if we erase the difference between them we are left unable to understand the dilemmas which the Jews faced. In Warsaw, in particular, we have to understand that resistance and evasion were to some extent antagonistic: those Jews who went into hiding within the ghetto were not, as the ghetto fighters claimed, engaging in 'passive resistance' in support of the fighters, but were trying to evade the roundups; and the uprising, with the subsequent total destruction of the ghetto, was a calamity for them. This subject will be taken up further in Chapter 2. Second, it has become deeply unfashionable to speak of compliance or paralysis, since these terms are rightly seen as inappropriately judgemental, so that the whole spectrum of Jewish responses to the Holocaust has tended to become telescoped into the single subject of resistance (compliance and paralysis being cast as 'failure to resist'). This has led to the situation I encountered at a recent conference, in which the topic of 'Jewish resistance' – in reality, Jewish responses *in toto* – was allocated a single session in which seventeen papers on the most varied subjects had to be squeezed into one and a half hours, making sensible discussion impossible. Finally, the marginalization of evasion as a topic, the result of its being treated as a mere footnote to the story of resistance, has led to many distortions. Hilberg, who did preserve the distinction, nevertheless, having minimized resistance, minimized evasion still more. 'We know', he claimed, 'that only a few thousand Jews escaped from the ghettos of Poland and Russia, that only a few hundred Jews hid out in the large cities of Berlin, Vienna, and Warsaw, that only a handful of Jews escaped from camps.' He attributes this alleged refusal of the victims to save themselves to their own attitudes: 'In the main, the Jews looked upon flight with a sense of futility; the great majority of those who did not escape early did not escape at all.'[18]

Even at the time Hilberg wrote, many of his assertions were known to be wrong: he even contradicts himself, reporting (as I have noted) that 5,000–6,000 Jews had managed to flee during the liquidation of the Warsaw ghetto.[19] Hilberg himself was among the 350,000 Jews who left the Greater Reich before war broke out: he characterizes this movement as forced emigration rather than flight, but that was by no means always the case. (The Swiss became so concerned about the number of Jews entering their country illegally that they asked the German authorities to stamp Jewish passports with a 'J', and I know of at least one German survivor whose family made its way illegally to Belgium through an organized 'underground railroad'.) During the course of the war, across Europe, perhaps 400,000 Jews went into hiding, and perhaps an equal number fled across international borders: from Norway and Denmark to Sweden, from the Low Countries to France, from France to Spain, Switzerland and Italy, from Romania to Palestine, from Poland to Lithuania, Slovakia and Hungary. A few Jews even made it to Shanghai and the Americas. Hilberg discounts the largest mass flight of all – that of 300,000 Polish Jews to the Soviet occupation zone in 1939–40, and subsequently of 700,000 Jews to the Soviet interior in 1941–2 – because non-Jews also fled, and because a few were activists afraid of political rather than racial persecution.[20] In short, Hilberg treats the reactions of the two million or so people who fled or went into hiding – surely the most reasonable and human of all responses to an overwhelming hostile force – briefly and dismissively.

It is odd, therefore, that this particular failure of analysis on Hilberg's part – and Hilberg, it scarcely need be said, is the seminal figure in modern Holocaust historiography – has provoked only the most meagre response. Arendt took up the topic briefly, as part of her attack on the Jewish Councils. She describes a scene during the Eichmann trial, when the testimony of Pinchas Freudiger, a prominent member of the Budapest Jewish Council, was interrupted by shouted accusations from the audience. Freudiger, she writes,

> was shaken: 'There are people here who say that they were not told to escape. But fifty percent of those who escaped were captured and killed' – as compared with ninety-nine percent, for those who did not escape. 'Where could they have gone to? Where could they have fled?' – but he himself fled, to Rumania [....] 'What could we have done? What could we have done?'[21]

Arendt then cites the case of the Netherlands, where, she says, 10,000 Jews survived out of 20,000–25,000 who 'escaped the Nazis – and that means also the Jewish Council'.[22] But she does not take the argument further.

Leonard Gross's book on the Jewish fugitives in Berlin, which is rather popular in tone, is a good beginning but hardly exhausts the subject. As to Vienna, I have been able to discover nothing at all. The figure on Amsterdam cited above had to be inferred from general books and articles on the Holocaust in the Netherlands: no detailed study of Jewish fugitives either in the city or in the country as a whole is available, so far as I know, and the reliability of extant figures is in doubt.[23] Nor is there much systematic treatment of flight across borders. Even the mass movement of Jews to and within the Soviet Union has received very little attention from historians, beyond approximate estimates of numbers and some rudimentary discussion of motives.[24] Who were these fugitives? Why did some escape, and not others? How far were they aware of the Holocaust as it unfolded, and did they know what was happening to relatives left behind? What did the Soviet government know? Could the fugitives exert any influence on it? All these questions, and many others, await an industrious author, who had best undertake the work while there are witnesses still alive.

The sparsity of the literature on evasion as a response to the Holocaust can be explained, I think, by psychological and political factors. There is a stigma attached to flight, which was often seen as an act of betrayal by the ghetto communities, and even by the fugitives themselves: 'survivors' guilt' has been particularly acute among those who escaped, often leaving family members behind in the ghetto. There has therefore not been much pressure from survivors to set things straight. This kind of guilt, though understandable, is misplaced: life in hiding was not at all easy or safe, and those who fled often took up the battle later, as partisans, in the 1944 Warsaw Uprising, or by joining the army once Poland was liberated. Flight did not preclude fight. In any case, people do not need an excuse for trying to save themselves. Politically, the existence of a practical third way between compliance and resistance – which, of the three, turned out to offer by far the best prospects of survival – is an awkward fact. It was all very well to use this fact as a springboard to attack the Jewish Councils, as Hannah Arendt did; but armed resistance, particularly the Warsaw Ghetto Uprising, is a different matter. Hilberg maintained that resistance was rarely attempted; a serious consideration of evasion as an alternative suggests that when attempted it may not always have been wise.

In Warsaw especially, the assumption that flight to the Aryan side was well-nigh impossible, and offered little prospect of survival, was an essential part of the calculations of the Jewish resistance movement: otherwise a suicidal uprising made no sense. If it turns out that this assumption was mistaken, then a number of uncomfortable questions would suggest themselves. Even if we grant (as I would) that a show of armed resistance was a political, emotional and moral necessity, might not the welfare of the civilian population have been taken into account? Might preparations for the uprising not have included plans for evacuating at least part of the remaining ghetto population? The ŻZW adopted the strategy of defending strongholds, having previously prepared their retreat by digging tunnels to the Aryan side. Why did they not arrange to evacuate civilians through these tunnels, while they still held their strongholds? Why did they not make the locations of their tunnels generally known as they withdrew, so that more people could use them, not just the few who discovered them by accident? Why did the mainstream ŻOB not build tunnels or give any prior thought to evacuation? Was it really wise to fight to the death, instead of withdrawing early, as the Revisionists did – living to fight another day, perhaps undertaking partisan raids on the deportation trains which might have allowed more people to escape? Might not an early withdrawal have prevented the physical destruction of the ghetto, making more living space available in post-ghetto Warsaw and so easing the problem of finding *melinas*? Could not what remained of the ghetto's wealth have been smuggled out in good time, to help sustain the fugitives? Were the magnitude of the flight from the ghetto and the seriousness of the problems faced by the fugitives properly communicated to or understood by the Polish authorities, Western governments and Jewish communities abroad, and could they in turn not have done more to provide practical and material support? There are many more awkward questions of this kind.

For sixty years, the standard answer to such questions has been that anyone who raised them did not understand the situation: the scarcity of hiding places, the appalling conditions faced by the fugitives, the indifference or hostility of the surrounding population, the prevalence of denunciation and blackmail. Flight from the ghetto was for the favoured few who had money, contacts and a 'good' (non-Semitic) appearance, and who spoke flawless Polish; and even then

[t]he Jews on the Aryan side could expect no help except from a handful of individuals. They were a hunted pack, living twenty-four hours of the day and

every second of the hour in torment and terror. Their chances of survival were negligible, and the prospect of death ominous and all-pervading.[25]

Such has been the general view. Yet all these assertions are based on no solid research, and this book will show many of them to be mistaken. Indeed, careful contemporary observers also realized that the widespread fear of the Aryan side, though it had an objective basis, was greatly exaggerated. Ringelblum spoke of a 'psychosis of fear' among the fugitives, and added that

> there are far fewer dangers than the Jew [in hiding] imagines. It is [the] imaginary perils, [the] supposed observation by the neighbour, porter, manager or passer-by in the street that constitute the main danger, because the Jew [...] gives himself away by looking around in every direction to see if anyone is watching him, by the nervous expression on his face, by the frightened look of a hunted animal, smelling danger of some kind everywhere.[26]

(A Gypsy proverb puts it succinctly: 'fear has big eyes'.) This psychosis of fear also found its way into the ghetto, inhibiting escape. A survivor writes:

> Stories circulated about those who had fled to the Aryan side and, once outside the wall, were surrounded by Polish blackmailers who took everything they possessed and then handed them over to the Gestapo. The fugitives were shot on the spot. This was true, but little was said about those who were lucky enough to escape.[27]

The psychological mechanisms behind such filtering of information will be discussed in Chapter 2. People living under such extreme circumstances clearly cannot be expected to exercise purely rational judgments or to act with historical hindsight. There is no excuse, however, for historians supposedly writing *sine ira et studio* to filter information in the same way. In Chapter 6 it will be shown that about 11,500 of these fugitives lived to see the end of the war, a little more than 40 per cent. Their chances of survival were therefore not good, but they were considerably better than 'negligible'. Hannah Arendt put the main point well enough: half or more of those who fled may have perished, but so did 99 per cent of those who did not flee.

It would be very wrong to raise it as an accusation that the majority had somehow 'failed' to flee when they could have, or to offer the posthumous advice that they 'should' have fled. Hilberg, for one, does seem to make this accusation, which might be phrased as follows: 'they didn't resist, they didn't even try to run away; they were passive and helpless'. But there are perfectly comprehensible reasons why most Jews did not try to flee, even when opportunities presented themselves: chiefly, that they lacked accurate, timely information about the Nazis' plans and intentions, and thus believed that reasonable alternatives existed when there were none. They were trapped, in other words, by the unprecedented and unbelievable nature of the Nazi programme, by the secrecy and improvisational style with which it was carried out, and by the Nazis' divide-and-conquer tactics, which deliberately fostered illusions even to the door of the gas chamber. In just the same way, German Jews did not try to flee in large numbers until the *Kristallnacht* pogrom in 1938 – not because they were paralysed, as Hilberg would have it, but because they had as yet little reason to believe that the Nazi regime would last, or that the Nazis really meant what they said. To say that more opportunities to flee existed than were taken advantage of, in Germany as in Poland, is more an acknowledgment of the deadly effectiveness of Nazi methods than a criticism of the victims, whom we are in any case hardly in a position to judge.

With all necessary caveats, however, we can still draw conclusions about flight in the objective realm. Of all the options that seemed to be available to the Jews, including armed resistance, flight unquestionably offered *in practice* the best chance of survival, and, contrary to the prevailing belief, it did take place on a massive scale. It is certainly wrong to dismiss flight – evasion, in general – as a marginal phenomenon, and the dilemmas involved in the decision to flee raise many important issues. The neglect of this topic by the historical community is unjustified.

A proper consideration of the 'missing topic' of evasion will have an important effect on all aspects of Holocaust studies, not only the assessment of Jewish responses. Most obviously, the question of Jewish–Gentile relations will have to be assessed in the light of new research in this area, since their nature clearly affected both the chances of evasion available to the Jews and their prospects of survival. It was the Jews who escaped whose fate depended most directly on the attitudes of their Gentile neighbours, who were otherwise mainly passive and mainly impotent onlookers to the drama that was unfolding before them. Only a few heroes will actively intervene to save others, especially at the risk of their own lives, but most people will respond to a direct plea for help if they can. Their attitudes will of course influence their actions, but without sound research we cannot know in what manner and to what extent. Thus, for example, assertions made hitherto about the role of traditional antisemitism in sealing the fate of the Jews may be open to question.

The topic of rescue, related both to evasion and to Jewish–Gentile relations, must also be reassessed. Rescue, viewed in the light of widespread attempts at evasion from the Jewish side, becomes the story, not of rare, altruistic 'righteous gentiles' reaching out to help hapless victims, but of initiative, courage and endurance on the part of those who escaped, helped by bystanders who had to be approached, often at great risk, and who were usually paid. This form of narrative does not by any means diminish the heroism of those who risked their lives to help, especially those thousands of great hearts who immersed themselves in this enterprise with no thought of compensation. But it complements this inspiring story with the equally inspiring story of self-help (including institutional self-help), instead of misrepresenting the victims as passive.

To consider another aspect of rescue, the Allies have been taken to task for lack of generosity towards Jewish refugees, but only rarely for not providing sufficient aid to encourage and support escape. The Allies can indeed be criticized, much more than they have been, for their indifference to and even sabotage of the efforts of Jewish organizations to save Jews. One such effort, for instance, tried to exploit prisoner exchange programmes, using often forged or questionable consular documents. Had officials been more prepared to turn a blind eye to these irregularities, for the sake of saving lives, thousands of Jews might have survived. Conversely, the work of the Jewish organisations to support and promote Jewish self-help in occupied Europe deserves to be better known.

Even the perpetrators have to be considered differently, since they were often the best-placed to help as well as hinder evasion. One can rarely speak of uniformed Germans as rescuers, but in certain circumstances they played a significant role in making evasion possible. In short: once we take seriously the fact that millions of Jews made an effort to get away from the Nazis and that possibly two million succeeded, we must also change our outlook on everything else as well.

Escape and Hiding in Warsaw

This book makes a start at the systematic study of evasion as a response to the Holocaust by looking in detail at one particularly significant instance of mass escape. Were the title not spoken for, we might aptly call it 'the Great Escape' since it dwarfs that celebrated event in scale, and was arguably the largest prison-break in history. Perhaps we should call it 'the Greatest Escape'. At the same time, the majority of the Jews of Warsaw did not escape, so that much of the discussion here is not only a celebration of success but also an accounting of failure. Chapter 2 will show that escape did not become a rational option for most ghetto-dwellers until the liquidation of the ghetto got under way in the summer of 1942, and that escape was physically difficult while the liquidation action continued. The Nazis concealed their plans, and when they did move, it was so rapidly and on such a massive scale that the Jews, under the conditions of isolation that the Nazis had imposed, had no time to react. Therefore – for tragic but perfectly rational reasons – the bulk of escapes did not, could not, take place until after the great majority of Warsaw Jews had been killed. For very similar reasons, serious preparations for armed resistance did not begin until that point either. Thus, at the very time the ghetto fighters were laying their plans in the sincere belief that escape was impossible, a very substantial proportion of the remaining inhabitants of the ghetto – perhaps as many as a quarter – were in fact making their way to the 'other side'. The rest, as we shall see, generally chose not resistance but another form of evasion, the construction of bunkers within the ghetto, on the theory that the Germans would not liquidate their workforce until the last possible moment. The ghetto-dwellers could then disappear into the bunkers, wait a few weeks and the war would be over. One way or another, evasion and not resistance was the dominant Jewish response to the liquidation of the Warsaw ghetto.

This is, then, the first detailed historical study not only of the 'Greatest Escape' and of the extraordinary secret city to which it gave rise, but of evasion in general as a Jewish response to the Holocaust. What factors made it possible? What factors limited it? What happened to the Jews who did escape? What were their chances of survival? What do their experiences tell us about the surrounding society, its responses, good and bad, and their effect on the Jews? On a more universal level, what is the psychology behind the decision to stay or flee? Were those who did not flee the victims of 'paralysis', as Hilberg would have it, or did they make a rational calculation, and if they did calculate, was their calculation right or wrong in hindsight? Those who fled had to endure a state of continual fear, under difficult physical and emotional circumstances; how did they manage? How did the competing impulses of altruism and prejudice resolve themselves among bystanders, who were themselves not entirely free agents but also faced difficult and frightening circumstances? What sort of judgments, if any, can we validly make about people in such circumstances, whether victims or bystanders?

These questions are not meant to be either exhaustive or to provide a check-list of subjects covered in this book. They are meant only to suggest that the terrain opened up here is enormously rich and productive. I hope that many more explorers will follow, and that in time a detailed historical picture will emerge of this phenomenon across Europe.

Sources

The most important information about the period comes from autobiographical accounts of various kinds, which I have taken for the most part from two archival collections – those of the Jewish Historical Institute (*Żydowski Instytut Historyczny*, ŻIH) in Warsaw, which are designated as AŻIH in citations, and of Yad Vashem in Jerusalem, designated as YV – and from published memoirs. These have been supplemented by a smaller number of accounts drawn from other sources: manuscripts that I have received from survivors or colleagues (designated in citations as 'in author's possession'); a few accounts from the archives of the Hebrew University (designated as HU); a few from YIVO in New York, of which copies were on file at Yad Vashem and which are designated by their Yad Vashem file numbers (collection YV-O17); short accounts and other materials from the archives of the Underground Poland Study Trust in London (designated UPST); and, most important, a number of interviews with Jewish survivors and Catholic Poles.[28]

Of these autobiographical sources, the most extensive collections are AŻ IH 301 ('Relations'), AŻIH 302 ('Memoirs'), YV-O3 ('Testimonies') and YV-O33 ('Memoirs'). ŻIH distinguishes between lengthy 'memoirs' and shorter 'relations'; Yad Vashem between 'testimonies' collected by its Oral History Department and 'memoirs' of any length that it has acquired in various ways. For present purposes, these distinctions are not very important. By 'the memoirs', I mean all of these kinds of accounts, collectively. When distinctions need to be made, I sometimes refer to 'relations', 'depositions' or 'shorter accounts', as against 'longer accounts', and to 'oral', as against 'written', testimonies, depositions, etc. Another distinction is more important: 'memoirs' are in principle accounts written after the fact, regardless of length or provenance, whereas 'diaries' or 'contemporary accounts' are those written at the time, or at any event during the war or immediately after-wards – *na gora, co*, 'on the hot', as the Poles say.

AŻIH 301 contains more than 7,000 relations (the number continues to grow), more or less evenly divided between accounts by Poles and by Jews. It proved impracticable to examine all of them; instead, a sample of 2,600 was surveyed, of which 308 or nearly 12 per cent turned out to pertain to the Aryan side in Warsaw. AŻIH 302 contains 293 manuscripts, most of which are of substantial length. Fully 104 of them pertain to Warsaw, of which 101 are first-hand Jewish accounts. YV-O33 contains 'some 2,500' memoirs, of which 1,580 are described in the published index.[29] Indexed material on the Aryan side in Warsaw amounts to twenty-eight manuscripts, totalling 5,139 pages – only 1.8 per cent of the total, but one should keep in mind that the Yad Vashem archives pertain to the whole of occupied Europe, whereas the ŻIH files cover Poland alone. Collection YV-O62 (interviews conducted by Michal Borwicz for *Arishe papirn*) yielded another six accounts.

Another important source at Yad Vashem is the files of the Department of the Righteous. These contain one folder for each of the more than 19,000 individuals and families who have been awarded the title 'Righteous among Nations'. Dr Mordecai Paldiel, Director of the Department of the Righteous, estimates that 500 of these folders pertain to Warsaw, each containing depositions from Jews who were rescued. Although this is potentially a rich source, it is unfortunately not indexed by city, and time did not permit an exhaustive search. Instead, Dr Paldiel was kind enough to provide me with an alphabetical list of all the 'Righteous' from Poland, and when I encountered someone in the memoirs who seemed to deserve the title, I consulted this list. In the process, I discovered that a disappointingly small number of the people who appear to merit this distinction have received it; nevertheless, in this way I was able to find my way to fifteen of these files, which helped particularly in tracing the networks described in Chapter 1.

In addition to memoirs and other autobiographical sources, both published and archival, I have made use of the surviving records of three of the organizations that provided material assistance to the Jews in hiding: the Council to Aid Jews

(Żegota), the Bund and the Jewish National Committee (*Żydowski Komitet Narodowy – ŻKN*), a Zionist umbrella group.

What appear to be complete lists of people under the care of the Bund, held at the Modern Records Archive in Warsaw, were brought to my attention by the late Teresa Prekerowa, who had also previously published a list of more than 600 people who were receiving money from Żegota.[30] By far the largest collection of activist records, however, is the Berman Archive at the Ghetto Fighters' House in Israel. This archive contains the records of the ŻKN, and includes not only lists of recipients but much other fascinating material as well. To my knowledge, neither the Berman archive nor the Bund lists have previously been used for historical research.

The lists kept by the activists allow, for the first time, direct, if partial, confirmation of activists' claims about the number of people under their care, as well as furnishing a variety of details about the recipients. Taken together, these sources were used to construct a database of more than 9,300 records, on the basis of which a number of studies were conducted (see Chapter 6).

Still other lists were consulted, notably a list of more than 58,000 Jewish survivors in Poland, compiled in June 1945 by the Central Committee of Jews in Poland (CKŻP); a list of Holocaust survivors in Sweden, about 175 of them from Warsaw, also published in 1945; a list of about 6,000 Warsaw Jews in the US occupation zone of post-war Germany; and a list of some 32,000 Holocaust survivors living in the US and Canada, published by the National Gathering of Holocaust Survivors.[31] These are also analysed in Chapter 6.

Methods

These various sources are used in two ways: in an objective, 'positivist' way as a source of factual information, on the basis of which statistical analyses are developed; and in a more subjective way, as a source of insights into the psychology and state of mind of the witnesses. In the first case, the most important consideration is reliability: the question is simply whether to accept or reject statements made by witnesses according to some assessment of their factual accuracy. In the second, every statement made by a witness is grist for the mill, whether factually correct or not: the question is not 'did it happen?', but 'what does it mean?'

There are various possible standards of evidence, for example the standard of 'beyond reasonable doubt', applicable to a criminal trial, or that of 'balance of probabilities', used in civil cases. The news reporter's standard is to reject witness statements unless they can be corroborated. Jan T. Gross, on the other hand, has recently proposed what he calls a 'New Approach to Sources':

> When considering survivors' testimonies, we would be well advised to change
> the starting premise in appraisal of their evidentiary contribution from a priori

critical to in principle affirmative. By accepting what we read in a particular account as fact *until we find persuasive arguments to the contrary*, we would avoid more mistakes than we are likely to commit by adopting the opposite approach, which calls for cautious skepticism toward any testimony *until an independent confirmation of its content has been found*. The greater the catastrophe the fewer the survivors. We must be capable of listening to lonely voices reaching us from the abyss.[32]

Gross has been much criticized for this statement, but in truth this procedure is standard in writing about the Holocaust from the perspective of the victims. As Gross observes, because this is a story of almost complete destruction, there has also been an almost complete destruction of evidence, and we therefore have to make do with whatever traces the past has been kind enough to leave us. Raul Hilberg, as a purist, apparently believes that we should prefer to write about the perpetrators, who left behind a good, traditional trail of documentary evidence. But that is hardly a satisfactory answer. Unlike the jury in a criminal trial, historians do not have to worry that their decisions will send someone to prison; unlike news reporters, they do not ordinarily have to worry about libel suits. History can therefore afford to be more flexible in its approach to evidence, and can take the 'balance of probabilities' approach. That is what I have done in this book: in general, I have chosen to believe witness testimony, including third-person, hearsay accounts, if, on balance of probabilities, it seems likely to be true. This is perhaps slightly more restrictive than Gross's 'until we find persuasive arguments to the contrary'.

Literature usually relies not on an accumulation of facts but on the sensitive observer to establish truth. Rafael Scharf has put this view: 'One can argue the accuracy of statistics and round off a percentage here and there (I do not decry the value of work done in this field, I value it highly), but the Jews have no need of statistics, they know how it was.'[33] I have great respect for Dr Scharf, whom I count as a friend, but in this instance I have to disagree with him: people are rather notoriously poor at 'knowing how it was', especially when strong emotions are involved – as in the case of the Holocaust they naturally nearly always are. Nor can we establish the truth by democratic means, as Scharf does when he invokes the collective 'the Jews'. Leaving aside the fact that there are many things about which Jewish witnesses disagree, any number of witnesses may easily suffer from the same illusions. Scharf of course knows this; he qualified his remarks soon after in the same talk: 'the truth is complicated and has many dimensions; we are sensitive to some of its aspects, blind to others; only some segments are accessible to each of us.' He adds: 'The sheer awareness that this is so seems to be a step in the right direction.'[34]

Statistics is thus not a matter simply of 'rounding off a percentage or two', the more so since much of the data presented here has never been quantified before. In quantification, I believe, lies the key to solving many of the dilemmas facing historians in this area. If we establish, for example, that about 5 per cent of the population of the Warsaw ghetto managed to escape, then we may still not agree on whether this number was large or small, or even the right one, but at least we shall know what we are arguing about. Scharf is right in saying that what matters most is not whether it was really 5 per cent or perhaps 4 or 6 per cent: any reasonable approximation is an improvement over 'some' or 'many' or 'few', which mean different things to different people. Quantitative analysis is the backbone of this study, or rather the skeleton, which though cold and hard and lifeless nonetheless serves to set the proportions. Most of the quantitative work is consigned to the final chapter, so as not to impede the flow of the argument; statistically minded readers may want to read it first.

Putting flesh on the skeleton requires evidence of the more traditional, subjective kind, and this raises questions of selection, interpretation, balance and voice. Because I have counted on quantitative analysis to provide the proper proportions, I have felt fairly free to raise topics that seemed worth discussing, and to select appropriate illustrations for them, without worrying too much about whether they are representative. Thus selection and balance are only background concerns.

I have quoted witness testimony in three different ways. When I believe something to be true (on the weight of the evidence), I prefer, when possible, to let a witness make the point in his or her own words. When I believe (again on the weight of the evidence) that something a witness says is not true, then I try to reconcile perception and reality by analysing (or to use the fashionable term, deconstructing) the reasons for the discrepancy. When the evidence is ambiguous, I often cite contradictory or doubtful testimony to introduce discussion. My manner of handling evidence therefore depends crucially on whether I believe it or not.

This may strike some readers as wilful: it looks on the face of it a good deal like what Jacques Barzun calls 'source mining', starting with a preconceived notion and then finding the evidence that fits – the very sin against scholarship. There is a crucial distinction here, however: it is not a prior agenda, but the 'weight of the evidence', and above all the quantitative work, that has led me to believe some things and not others. I hasten to add that I have rarely disbelieved witnesses on points of fact. What I have taken with a pinch of salt is rather perceptions and statements of opinion. In other words, I have evaluated impressions and beliefs on the basis of whether they agree with the facts, rather than facts on the basis of whether they agree with impressions and beliefs.

To take an example, many witnesses agree with a statement that I quote in Chapter 4: 'if they had known who I was, they surely would have betrayed me.' This is speculation, that is to say, opinion, which is not borne out by the statistics on the actual frequency of betrayal. What needs to be explained here is not why betrayal was so frequent, but why so many witnesses believed it to be more frequent than it was. That is, this statement needs to be 'deconstructed' (or, according to one of my early readers, 'blatantly deconstructed') as a psychological rather than a physical fact. On the other hand, I have observed that nearly all the longer memoirs mention encounters with *szmalcowniks*; on this basis, I have accepted that nearly all the Jews in hiding had such encounters. But here it is not a matter of speculation or opinion, but of direct eyewitness evidence: 'I was black-mailed' is different from 'I surely would have been blackmailed'.

In other words, I have adopted different standards of proof for different kinds of evidence: I accept statements about what actually happened as true unless there is good reason not to (Gross's standard, in its weaker version). But I accept statements of opinion only when there is good corroborating evidence (the reportorial standard), other than further statements of opinion; otherwise these statements are treated as psychological facts, to be analysed and explained. All this is really fairly standard historical practice: the only real departure is that I treat hearsay in the same way as direct evidence. Statements about rather than by Jews in hiding are 'the voice from the abyss' about which Gross speaks, in most cases the only evidence we have about people who did not survive. Indeed, because non-survival rather than survival was the typical experience, I have often privi-leged hearsay over direct evidence: I have based many statistics on 'third-person studies', using statements about rather than by Jews in hiding, so as not to bias the sample in favour of survivors.

The basis of the quantitative estimates will be explained in detail at the begin-ning of Chapter 6. In general, however, the following method is used. First, where there is sufficiently solid evidence, some absolute numbers are developed. For example, Nathan Eck's study of the Hotel Polski episode established forty years ago that some 3,500 Jews fell into this trap, and there is no good reason to doubt his numbers. Again, I have established from the records of the various Polish and Jewish underground aid agencies, the single most important source for this study, that these organizations had between them some 8,900 people under their care during the period of their most intense activity, that is to say, between October 1943 and the outbreak of the Warsaw Uprising in August 1944.

Given these two bedrock figures, other estimates are developed by studying samples of cases drawn from the memoirs. Thus I have concluded, by comparing the names of people known to be in hiding during this period with the lists of aid recipients, that the 8,900 cases of which we have more or less direct evidence represent only about half of the people in hiding at the time. After some further deliberations, I conclude that some 17,000 people were still in hiding at the outbreak of the Warsaw Uprising (1 August 1944). Given that 3,500 people sur-rendered at the Hotel Polski in the summer of 1943, we then have fairly reliable evidence of at least 20,500 people in hiding immediately after the defeat of the Ghetto Uprising. Of course, we must take attrition into account as well.

To estimate attrition, the fates of people mentioned in memoirs (not counting the memoirists themselves, to avoid a bias in favour of survivors) are categorized and tabulated. On this basis we arrive, among other things, at the proportion of people who are said to have surrendered at the Hotel Polski, and from this we can work out the numbers in the other categories. An estimate of 28,000 Jews in hiding follows from this. If this total is correct, it also follows (on the evidence of the memoirs) that the total number of people who died 'on the Aryan side' must have been about 16,500, and that the number of final survivors must therefore have been about 11,500. This latter figure is then checked against several independent sets of post-war survivor records and other lines of evidence, and is found to be consistent with all of them. This very satisfying outcome lends confidence not only to the estimate of final survivors, but to the whole enterprise, which seems to fit together like a jigsaw puzzle.

But there is still one more 'sanity check' for these figures. On these estimates, the attrition among these Jews, prior to the outbreak of the Warsaw Uprising in 1944, amounted to about 6,800 people or 24 per cent, a modest enough figure under the circumstances. Were we to suppose that fewer people were in hiding, then the rate of attrition would have to be lower – in fact, we might feel, implausibly low. If, on the other hand, we were to set the number in hiding any higher, we would confront other problems. As we shall see in Chapter 2, the bulk of the escapees were drawn from the relatively small number of Jews who survived the Great Deportation of 1942. On the stated estimates, it will turn out that nearly a quarter of the Jews remaining in the ghetto at that time managed to escape. This is already a surprisingly high figure, and if the overall number of people in hiding were any greater, it would have to be higher still – in fact, implausibly high. The estimate of 28,000 Jews in hiding is thus very securely grounded: not so much because it can be verified by tests of statistical significance, but because it is consistent with a number of independent lines of evidence, and because it passes two contrasting tests of historical credibility more satisfactorily than any other estimate would. Again, this lends additional confidence to the whole procedure and to the other estimates based on it.

There will of course be mistakes. When it is a matter of counting cases, the possible errors in any one memoir do not matter very much, since idiosyncratic cases will be lost in the statistical shuffle, while random errors (for example, in reporting the time and manner of leaving the ghetto) will cancel each other out so long as their direction is not consistent. In these cases we can count on the 'law of large numbers' to come to the rescue, provided the numbers are large enough. The question of the reliability of autobiographical evidence is more important, however, when we reach to the memoirs for descriptive material, examples, assessments and other evidence of a qualitative and subjective nature.

There are of course many problems associated with the use of autobiographical materials as sources, particularly in the case of memoirs written sometimes many years after the event. There is first of all the question of authenticity. For example, the authenticity of one of the published memoirs, *Dziewczynka z ulicy Miłej*,[35] seems highly doubtful to me: the editor tells us nothing about the author or the provenance of the manuscript, and its content is in places antisemitic. Every Jew mentioned seems to be portrayed in a negative light, every Pole positively. While it is possible that a Jewish author had such experiences – and of course it would not be the first time that a Jew, especially an apostate, had expressed antisemitic opinions – this memoir is so much at odds with all the others that I should want sure evidence of its authenticity before accepting it. The purported author, Sara Kraus-Kolkowicz, does not appear in the post-war survivor lists, and the manuscript is not on file at either ŻIH or Yad Vashem. At the moment I should judge it to be an antisemitic fabrication; it was not used for this study. Doubts have also been expressed in Poland about the authenticity of a second published memoir, *Hana, pamiętnik Żydówki*,[36] largely on the grounds that nowhere is the author's full name mentioned, and again that nothing is said about the provenance of the manuscript. The publishers have, however, corrected these faults by publishing an 'annex' to it; in addition, by good fortune, one of the writer's relatives lived near me, and was able to confirm that she (Hana Gorodecka) is indeed a real person and the author of the memoir.

After authenticity, the next problem is credibility. Occasionally, one encounters a memoirist who seems unbalanced, such as one unfortunate who writes that 'I clearly feel that I am electronically surveyed by various Polish German Nazi groups'.[37] We can readily accept this memoir as evidence of the long-term effects of such traumatic experiences, but need to be very careful about the author's description of the experiences themselves. Most autobiographies are of course to some extent self-serving, sometimes subtly, sometimes less so. The occasional tall tale does not necessarily affect the credibility of all parts of a memoir. One can, for example, be skeptical about Samuel Willenberg's accounts of his amorous exploits on the road back to Warsaw after his escape from Treblinka without doubting his descriptions of the camp or of his life in hiding. Jack Eisner's memoir is regarded as doubtful in Poland, and indeed some of the author's purported experiences in the concentration camps seem far-fetched; but his stories of his experiences as a child smuggler ring true, and agree with other sources. In general, I have discounted the numerous testimonies in the ŻIH archives from Poles who claim to have helped Jews, unless these are corroborated by statements from the Jews themselves, or unless the individual concerned has been recognized as a 'Righteous Gentile' and has therefore passed extensive scrutiny by Yad Vashem. Such statements are often accompanied by requests for financial assistance, which of course renders their authors' motives suspect.

Even the most respected memoirists sometimes fall prey to the frailties of human perception and memory. For example, Marek Edelman, writing in 1945, maintains that news of the Chełmno death camp reached Warsaw in the spring of 1941, which would have been something of a feat since the camp did not open until December of that year.[38] In fact, news about Chełmno reached Warsaw in February 1942.[39] Edelman's mistake is not merely a typographical error, since the event fits into the flow of his narrative as if it had happened early in 1941. Errors of this kind are of two sorts. First, there are random errors (similar to 'signal noise' in communications theory), in which facts are forgotten, distorted, conflated or invented without any particular pattern; in such cases we can rely on external evidence to identify the error, as above, or, in quantitative work, we can assume that such errors will cancel each other out. In qualitative work, erroneous reports, once identified, can be ignored, or treated where relevant as psychological facts. Second, and more problematically, there are systematic errors, the results of distortions that are characteristic of the human perceptual apparatus, especially under the influence of strong emotion or prior 'sets'. In particular, there is the problem of 'the dog that didn't bark in the night': that people are apt to notice what is noticeable and remember what is memorable, and to ignore what is mundane and everyday – that is to say, what is actually typical. If most memoirists mention something, it cannot be concluded that it was therefore a common phenomenon, or vice versa: indeed, the fact that something is frequently mentioned often means that it is particularly striking and hence uncommon, whereas things that are mentioned rarely are often so common that they are taken for granted. An example in Chapter 4 concerns Jews who gave their possessions to Poles for safekeeping and then returned to claim them. Some people in this situation were cheated, but contrary examples are rarely mentioned. Here one must take into account that such Poles were chosen because Jews believed them to be trustworthy, and betrayal was therefore unexpected and especially wounding. Conversely, in the rare cases when memorists explicitly say that they were not cheated (that is to say, that the dog did not bark in the night), it usually turns out that the Poles in question were known to be antisemites, and therefore were again acting contrary to expectation. On the other hand, those who were trusted and did not betray their trust behaved as they were expected to, so that their behaviour is rarely considered worth mentioning. Since memoirists invariably allude to encounters with *szmalcowniks*, they would surely be even more likely to mention cases when they were robbed by people they had trusted. To conclude from the mere numbers of cases mentioned that in this situation most Poles cheated Jews would show insufficient psychological insight. A similar procedure is conversely used to evaluate Nechama Tec's conclusion that the great majority of landlords did not regard money as a condition of rescue. Most memoirs are silent on the subject, so it is again probably the exceptional cases (landlords who cheated their tenants and altruistic landlords) that tend to be mentioned, while the expected case of the honest paid landlord tends to be ignored. The principle in both these examples is that 'silence implies assent' – to the unspoken yet common-sense assumption that people usually behave as one expects them to.

The Gestalt psychologists have identified various mechanisms that lead to systematic distortions of perception; among other things, figure–ground effects (an example can be seen in the paired quotations that open Chapter 3) and the need for closure (facts will be added, omitted or changed to make sense out of a story, to make it more dramatic, to make it fit storytelling conventions or the author's or reader's expectations). In Chapter 5, we shall see that a massacre was perpetrated whose witnesses and investigators interpreted it in different ways according to their respective ethnic and political perspectives, with both sides demonstrably inventing facts. For example, a speech is attributed to an individual who was not there, the details of which are clearly embroidered as the story passes from mouth to mouth. In some cases we can do no better than marshal all the various accounts and then use our judgement.

I might mention in concluding that I have learnt something about methodology from the 'Polish memoir school' of sociologists, founded by Florian Znaniecki with his landmark study *The Polish Peasant in Europe and America*.[40] Znaniecki's method was to use subjective evidence – in this case, letters written by Polish peasants in America to their families in Poland – as a source of social rather than individual facts. Znaniecki combed these letters for stereotyped formulas through which, he believed, the culture rather than the individual was speaking. Certain formulaic elements occur in the memoirs examined here as well: for example, many memoirs end with an account of the post-war fates of the various *dramatis personae*. The fate of those persons who died during the war, when it is known, is usually mentioned at the appropriate point in the narrative, so that the purpose of this final accounting is mainly to enumerate those who survived. Anyone whose fate is not mentioned at all, therefore, will usually have died in unknown circumstances. It can be added, for those readers who are still dubious about all this 'blatant deconstruction', that in each case the conclusions drawn are consistent with the quantitative evidence, whereas the *prima facie* conclusions would not have been.

Representativeness of the Memoirs

Problems associated with the use of memoirs as sources are not limited to issues of factual reliability, which I have addressed above; there is also the question of how far they are representative. There is first of all the issue of survivor bias, which I have already partly dealt with. The great majority of accounts were written by survivors: *ipso facto*, therefore, they represent relatively favourable experiences. A partial solution is the method discussed above, the use, whenever possible, of third-person studies to redress the balance by privileging hearsay over direct testimony. Another is to use several different methods of calculation for the most important statistics, so that the results obtained from the memoirs can be checked against other lines of evidence. Generally these cross-checks give reassuringly similar results, lending credibility to the general approach and showing that survivor bias is perhaps not such a strong effect after all.

Another objection might be that memoirists are more literate than the average, and are therefore drawn mainly from the educated classes. But this objection is unjustified. Most of the 'memoirs' on which I have relied are in fact oral testimonies rather than written ones; the Central Jewish Historical Commission, which gathered this evidence immediately after the war, actively sought people out and tried to induce them to record their memories, rather than relying on those who came forward on their own. The Jewish community in Poland at that time had still not segregated itself into its three post-war streams (broadly: Zionists, who went to Palestine; diasporists, who went west; and assimilationists, who stayed in Poland), so that testimonies collected at that time probably represent a reliable cross-section of survivors. In any case, the Jews who experienced life on the Aryan side were actually selected in favour of the educated classes, since it was mainly such people who managed to escape.

Limitations

I have, for reasons of time and space, been forced to accept certain limitations. Relatively little is said here about issues such as Polish assistance to Jews, or about the Polish and Jewish activists who were involved in this effort. In part, that is because this area has already been explored in the extensive Polish literature on Żegota (and the much less extensive Jewish literature on the ŻKN). In addition, the impetus for this book was the observation that, while much has been written in general on the subject of rescue, of which the Jews are depicted as passive beneficiaries, very little has been said about ordinary Jews themselves as active agents of their own survival. That is therefore where the emphasis in this book lies. Polish helpers and Jewish activists have in turn been consigned to the background, which is perhaps unfair to them. But to do justice to these subjects would require another work of the length of this one, and there is enough food for thought here as it stands. All this and much else will have to await another day.

1 Networks

Introduction

The secret city of the Jews in Aryan Warsaw could not have come into existence without a substantial network of contacts between the city's Polish and Jewish communities, despite the religious, cultural and linguistic barriers that had separated these communities for centuries. This chapter will examine the nature, origin and extent of this network, and will probe, by means of a case study, its development during the war. In the process, various propositions will be put in summary form that will be developed more fully in later chapters.

The secret city crystallized around three separate nuclei. The first, which already existed before the war, consisted of Jewish assimilants and converts. Such people generally had longstanding personal, professional and often family contacts with the Polish milieu, and were well-enough integrated into Polish society not to attract attention outside the ghetto. The second consisted of Jews and Poles who formed their contacts during the ghetto period, mainly through illegal trade. The third comprised Jewish and Polish activists, whose connections were mainly institutional, through fraternal political parties or social organizations. Many of these connections had existed for years, but others were formed as a result of wartime conditions. For example, some Jewish activists acted as couriers on the Aryan side while the ghetto still existed, and some Polish activists became involved in forging documents and providing other kinds of aid for the small number of Jews in hiding at that time. Besides these underground connections, there were overt links between the Polish city administration and the Jewish Council, and between charitable organizations within and outside the ghetto. Of particular importance was the connection between CENTOS, which cared for orphans within the ghetto, and the main aboveground Polish relief agency, the RGO, as well as the Polish Red Cross. The initial group of Polish activists drawn into helping Jews came from this milieu; many of them also had Jewish spouses or other connections with the Jewish community.

Those Jews who never entered the ghetto, or left it at an early stage, were almost all converts and assimilationists. They were anathematized by most Jews, who regarded them as traitors and probably antisemites; but in truth they often brought assistance to relatives and friends within the ghetto, and later found hiding places for them and helped to smuggle them out. Their numbers were small, but they formed the kernel of the secret city, which could not have arisen without them.

As the number of Jews in hiding grew, so did the possibilities for this kind of Jewish self-help. To these early helpers belonged also the small group of Poles who, on their own initiative, maintained contacts with their Jewish friends in the ghetto, and again later helped to smuggle them out or to hide them after their escape. This Polish milieu also expanded with time, as those Poles already involved in helping Jews drew in others, and as Jews needing help drew in their Polish friends.

The contacts formed during the ghetto period, primarily through underground trade, consisted mainly of people, both Poles and Jews, whose interest was mercenary rather than humanitarian. From these circles arose the *machers* (fixers), who for a price seemed to be able to arrange anything, including escape from the ghetto, Aryan documents and hiding places. On the Jewish side, the ghetto police were heavily involved in the underground trade. They dealt every day with the Polish and German policemen, who guarded the ghetto gates, and who could often be bribed to turn a blind eye to the smuggling of goods, guns and people. Underground trade also gave rise to the criminal elements: *szmalcowniks*, who started by extorting money from food smugglers, particularly children, and later preyed on Jews in hiding; and corrupt policemen who, when the liquidation of the ghetto deprived them of the chance to earn money from bribes, turned to blackmailing instead. There is evidence that such people co-operated and passed information to each other, and this underworld was also rather easy for the Gestapo to infiltrate with agents and informers. The enemies of the Jews had their networks, too.

An organized joint effort to help the fugitives did not appear until relatively late in the day, emerging at the end of 1942 almost as an afterthought to the development of Jewish armed resistance. The bulk of escapes took place at about this time (see Chapter 2), but almost entirely independently of the political and social activists, both Poles and Jews. The activists, indeed, had great difficulties in reaching Jews in hiding, and did not begin to act on a larger scale until a year or so later.

From these nuclei of primary contacts, some existing before the war and some formed during the ghetto period, an extensive network of secondary contacts developed as the number of Jews on the Aryan side increased. By the time mass escapes from the ghetto began to take place, towards the end of the Great Deportation in 1942, a sizeable community of Jews in hiding and non-Jews helping and hunting them had arisen quite spontaneously and largely invisibly, eventually involving tens of thousands of non-Jews and providing the means of escape, hiding places, documents and other necessities of life for tens of thousands of Jews.

Because attention has thus far been concentrated on the small group of activists, whose experiences and perceptions have dominated our understanding of the period, it has been difficult for authors to explain, or indeed accept, the existence of large numbers of Jews in hiding in Warsaw. Shmuel Krakowski, for example, describing the notion that there were tens of thousands of Jews in hiding as 'absurd', put the question to me: 'how could there have been so many *melinas* [hiding places], when it was so hard to find places for seventy ghetto fighters who escaped at the end of the [Ghetto] Uprising?'[1] One of the purposes of the present undertaking is to provide an answer to Krakowski's question. The difficulties in finding housing will be addressed in Chapter 3, the numbers involved will be substantiated in Chapter 6, and this chapter will try to explain how there could, indeed, have been so many *melinas*.

The Jewish Milieu

Origins: Jewish Acculturation and Assimilation in Warsaw

The Jewish community of Poland was one of the least assimilated in Europe: most Jews spoke Yiddish, and Polish only as a second language, if at all. Even those whose Polish was fluent usually spoke it with an accent, and most Jews, even those who had perfect Polish, generally regarded themselves as members of a national rather than a religious minority: they were Jews, not Poles, by nationality. Social contacts between the two communities were very limited. One might aptly characterize them by the title of Hugh McLennan's novel about the French and English in Quebec: *Two Solitudes*.

Yet, like all generalizations, this picture masks a considerably more complex reality. With the establishment of the Polish state in 1918, Polish became the language of government and education. With that, the forces that had promoted Jewish assimilation in Western Europe, held back in Poland by 123 years of foreign rule, were finally set in motion. Most Jewish children growing up in the interwar period attended Polish state schools, if only because they were free. There were also private Jewish schools, such as *Nasza Szkoła* (Our School) in Warsaw, in which the language of instruction was Polish. Even in Yiddish- and Hebrew-language schools, Polish as a second language was – for practical reasons as well as by law – compulsory. Anyone under thirty or so at the outbreak of war could therefore speak Polish fluently. Even the older generation had acquired a working knowledge of Polish by then, because they had had to deal with a Polish state for twenty years, and because industrialization and modernization created increasingly complex economic relations. It was still possible, in a city with 360,000 Jews, to live and work entirely in a Yiddish-speaking milieu, but it had become increasingly difficult.

This was acculturation, for the most part, rather than assimilation, of which the litmus test in Poland was the sense of being Polish by nationality. But acculturation is the first step towards assimilation. If the Holocaust had not intervened, it is likely that the Jewish community of Poland would by now have become as completely assimilated (in the Polish sense) as any other modern diaspora community. Whether this inner sense of Polish self-identification would have been matched by acceptance from the Polish side and real integration into Polish society is of course more doubtful.

Assimilation can be defined by three elements. Assimilants: 1) retained the Jewish faith, or abandoned religion altogether (otherwise they were not assimilants but converts); 2) were fully acculturated, not only speaking Polish but considering it their native language; and 3) regarded themselves as Polish by nationality, 'Poles of the Mosaic faith'.

In the 1921 census, 58,021 Varsovians declared themselves to be Jews by religion but of Polish nationality.[2] Ten years later, when the corresponding question was asked about language rather than nationality, some 19,300 Warsaw Jews gave Polish, rather than Yiddish or Hebrew, as their native language.[3] By 1939, their number would have reached about 22,000.

The number of assimilants, despite the seeming precision of the census figures, is hard to estimate. Many traditional Jews, for example, following the long-established policy of 'loyalty to the Crown', would have declared themselves Polish by nationality, though they were decidedly not assimilated. Other respondents may have confused nationality with citizenship. In 1931, on the other hand, responses were affected by political considerations. The four streams of Jewish life in Poland – assimilationist, traditionalist, diasporist and Zionist – were ideologically associated with language, so that a diasporist (Bundist or Folkist) who normally spoke Polish might well have declared for Yiddish to show solidarity. And no Polish Jew could honestly claim to be a native Hebrew-speaker: those who did so were declaring their Zionist loyalties. These political considerations played an especially strong role in the capital, as we can judge from the fact that only 5.5 per cent of Warsaw Jews claimed to be native Polish-speakers, compared with 13.1 per cent in the rest of the country, even though Warsaw was the assimilationist centre of Poland. If we apply the national percentage to the Warsaw Jews, we arrive at about 46,000 native Polish-speakers, and the true number must have been even greater. Eight years later it was likely to have been greater still. We can thus safely suppose that there were at least 50,000 fully acculturated Polish-speaking Jews in Warsaw on the eve of war.

The Jews claiming Polish nationality in 1921 constituted 18.7 per cent of the Jewish population of Warsaw; if this proportion still held in 1939, then their number would have grown to about 72,000 by then. But it is impossible to tell, on the basis of the census data alone, how many of them were acculturated. We may assume, at any rate, that those Polish-speakers who declared their language to be Yiddish or Hebrew for political reasons thereby made a statement of national affiliation, so that it is only among the 22,000 declared Polish-speakers that we should search for assimilants. In fact it is reasonable to assume that, in the politicized atmosphere of the 1930s, declaring for the Polish language was also a political statement, amounting to a declaration of assimilationist sympathies. On this assumption there must have been at least 20,000 Jewish assimilants in Warsaw at the time of the 1931 census, and perhaps 25,000 by 1939.

The overall picture, then, would be this: by 1939 nearly all Warsaw Jews spoke Polish, some 50,000–60,000 were acculturated native Polish-speakers, and, of these, 25,000 or so mainly middle-class Jews were assimilated.

This picture changed somewhat after war broke out. A certain number of Warsaw Jews fled eastwards in 1939–40, most of whom would spend the war in the Soviet Union, while large numbers of refugees from the territories incorporated into the German Reich, mainly from Łódź, flooded into the city. When the ghetto was formed, its population was augmented by still larger numbers of mainly Yiddish-speaking Jews resettled from smaller centres near Warsaw, and later also by Jews from Germany and Czechoslovakia. A few hundred Gypsies were also forced into it.

About 30,000 Jews left the city or were killed in 1939, among whom, pro rata, we should expect to find about 4,500 acculturated Jews and among them about 2,000 assimilants. The losses were eventually more than made up for by the influx of about 100,000 Jews from outside Warsaw, among whom acculturated Jews formed a much smaller proportion; but in absolute numbers there were probably enough to offset those who had been lost. Thus, there would still have been approximately the pre-war numbers of acculturated Jews and assimilants in Warsaw when the ghetto was closed.

Newcomers and poor Yiddish-speaking Jews constituted the great majority of those who died in the ghetto, while the generally well-connected Warsaw assimilants were in a much better position to hold their own. Thus, by the time of the deportations from the ghetto, the assimilants would have dwindled somewhat in number, but not by nearly so much as the unassimilated outsiders. This tendency to concentrate assimilants was accentuated by the deportations themselves. Assimilation, in Poland as elsewhere, was a top-down affair, with the assimilants largely drawn from the bourgeoisie, especially the professional and managerial classes. Such people made up the privileged group that clustered around the Jewish Council, or were otherwise well connected, and despite German expropriations had by and large managed to retain enough assets to buy food and favours. About 12 per cent of the total population of the ghetto remained intact after the first deportation, so that, pro rata, we would expect to find about 5,000–6,000 acculturated and assimilated Jews among them, in addition to 4,000 or so who had stayed out of the ghetto or fled by that time.

We certainly cannot assume that all the assimilants fled, and, as we shall see in the next chapter, the number of Jews who escaped from the ghetto after the deportations was much greater than this. Therefore most of those who escaped from the ghetto were neither assimilated nor acculturated in the strict sense. Nevertheless, their fluency in Polish can be judged from the fact that nearly 94 per cent of the Warsaw testimonies taken down by researchers of the Central Jewish Historical Committee in 1945–46, before the great majority of unassimilated Jews had left the country, are in Polish rather than Yiddish.[4]

What the pre-war census figures do not allow us to deduce is what proportion of unacculturated Warsaw Jews were nevertheless truly bilingual. Since the assimilated and fully acculturated Jews cannot by themselves account for all the Jews who escaped, it would seem that it is to this category that most of the later fugitives belonged. Assimilants and converts escaped first, but the secret city ultimately grew too large to allow us to conclude that the possibilities of flight were limited to these circles alone.

Converts

Converts can be divided into three groups. First there were the old converts, descendants of Jews baptized in the nineteenth century, who no longer counted as Jews under the Nazi 'racial' criteria but in many cases retained sympathy for and ties to the Jewish community. Virtually all of the many prominent families who chose the assimilationist path during the period of 'Polish–Jewish brotherhood' in the 1860s converted in the second or third generation: the Bersons, Blochs, Epsteins, Kronenbergs and Wawelbergs, to name but a few. Second were the new converts, more recently baptized, who were still regarded as Jews under Nazi law but not by the Jewish community or most Poles. As apostates, they were viewed with hostility by most Jews. Jewish history is peppered with prominent converts who turned into persecutors of Jews (Torquemada, for example, was said to have been of Jewish descent), and the stereotype readily formed that all converts were ardent antisemites: supposedly they needed to make a show of antisemitism to demonstrate their loyalty to Poland and to prove that they were no longer Jews. In truth, however, most converts came from liberal and secularized circles: they converted either to marry, or because they reasoned that if they were going to be non-observant Jews, they might as well be non-observant Catholics instead, and save themselves a good deal of trouble.

Though very traditional families would sever all contact with relatives who converted, most converts did not come from such a background. They therefore had both Jewish and non-Jewish family and friends, and whether they elected to enter the ghetto or stay out of it, they served as a vital link between the two communities. Among other things, the two active Catholic churches within the precincts of the ghetto (All Saints' in Grzybowski Square and the Holiest Virgin Mary in Leszno Street), which catered to converts, allowed legal and later clandestine contacts to be maintained across the ghetto wall. Monsignor Marceli Godlewski, the prelate of All Saints', is particularly well known in this connection, even though he was regarded before the war as an ardent antisemite.[5]

The third category of converts was made up of what may be called emergency converts, persons who married willing non-Jews after the outbreak of war to try to get around Nazi anti-Jewish decrees. These converts were viewed with greater sympathy by the Jewish community, and for example, unlike other converts, are under some circumstances accepted as Jews by Yad Vashem.[6] Coming from the assimilant community, they resembled assimilants rather than other converts in the nature of their contacts (that is, they were less ostracized by the Jewish community and had fewer Polish contacts than the older converts did), except that they enjoyed closer connections through their spouses' families.

Solid estimates of the number of converts on the eve of the war are hard to come by, as with the exception only of antisemites in search of scandal neither Polish nor Jewish authors, nor the converts themselves, were anxious to publicize the phenomenon. We are therefore obliged to rely on a study conducted at the turn of the century by the antisemitic writer Teodor Jeske-Choiński, based on Warsaw parish records. Jeske-Choiński counted 146 Jewish converts to Catholicism in 1862–99, as well as 198 converts to Lutheranism and 336 to Calvinism: 680 all told. His polemical purpose was to alarm Polish society by drawing attention to the threat of infiltration by opportunistic converts and to portray the Protestant converts as agents of Germanization. As his figures are hardly alarming, however, they are probably accurate enough.[7]

Conversion to Catholicism in the nineteenth century ordinarily accompanied intermarriage, so that Jeske-Choiński's figures would make for a community of more than a hundred mixed marriages with some 250 children, giving in all about 350 first- or second-generation Catholic converts at the turn of the century. Conversion to the Protestant faiths, on the other hand, was normally a personal statement that did not imply intermarriage: there were few Lutherans or Calvinists to marry in Warsaw. If we allow, nevertheless, for fifty Protestant convert families with 125 children, then the convert community, *circa* 1900, probably stood at about 1,000. These were the converts of the first type, the old converts.

The pace of conversion increased steadily: Jeske-Choiński gives twenty-six Catholic converts in 1862–80 and 120 in 1880–99. If the latter rate had merely been maintained over the next two decades, then the number of first-generation Catholic converts at the moment of Polish independence would have stood at about 380. Alina Cała maintains, however, that in the twentieth century conversion was almost exclusively to Catholicism, with many Protestant converts also changing to the Catholic faith.[8] In that case, the 534 Protestant conversions of

1862–99 should have been matched by an approximately equal number of Catholic conversions between 1900 and 1919, to which could be added the conversion from Protestantism to Catholicism of many of the 534. This would bring the total number of first-generation Catholics at the moment of Polish independence to at least 1,000, with 2,000 or so second-generation converts, and perhaps 500 first- and second-generation Protestants, or 3,500 all together. By 1939 their number would have grown to about 4,000. These were the converts of the second type, the new converts.

In January 1941, according to the Demographic Statistics Division (*Wydział Ewidencji Ludności Żydowskiej* – WELŻ) of the Jewish Council, there were 1,540 Catholic converts in the ghetto; in addition there were 148 Protestants, thirty Orthodox Christians and forty-three of other non-Jewish faiths: 1,761 in all.[9] We may note that the ratio between Catholics and Protestants supports Cała's contention. These cannot have represented all the converts in Warsaw in 1939, let alone in 1941 after hundreds of emergency conversions. It will be shown in the next chapter that some 2,400 Jews according to the Nazi definition stayed out of the ghetto, most of them first- and second-generation converts, which would lead us to the conclusion that the converts in Warsaw when the ghetto was closed numbered about 4,000. Thus, the number of converts of the third type, the emergency converts, seems to have been just enough to make up for the converts who fled to the east in the first two years of the war: pro rata, perhaps 400.

Table 1.1 summarizes the argument so far, in rough figures.

Table 1.1 Characteristics of the Warsaw Jewish and Convert Community, 1939–42

Category	October 1939 Number	%	March 1941 Number	%	September 1942 Number[†]	%
Unacculturated	306,000	84	406,000	87	46,000	77
Acculturated	35,000	10	35,000	8	8,000	13
Assimilated	20,000	6	20,000	4	5,000	8
Converts	4,000	1	4,000	1	1,000	2
Total	365,000	101	465,000	100	60,000	100

[†] Not counting those in hiding.
(Percentages do not necessarily add up to 100 because of rounding errors.)

Secondary Networks

Mixed marriages contracted in Poland by Jews of the educated class were characterized by their outstanding permanence, in contrast to Germany, where the majority of such [...] marriages broke up. [...] It can be taken as axiomatic

that if a Jew had Polish relatives, he could count on their help, even if the family
was antisemitic. Polish antisemites didn't apply racialism where relatives or
friends were concerned. On that score, the old maxim prevailed: every Pole,
even the greatest antisemite, had his own Jew [*swego Moszka*], of whom he was
fond.

Emmanuel Ringelblum[10]

If we assume, for the sake of argument, that half of the 4,000 converts were married to non-Jews (taking into account first-generation and adult second-generation
converts), then the bridging community of which the converts were part would
have included about 2,000 non-Jewish spouses, 4,000 parents-in-law and some
15,000–20,000 Christian members of their extended families. Beyond that were
widening circles of friends and other Christian contacts. Coming from an assimilationist milieu, as I have noted, most converts could keep up relations with Jewish
family members, and had friends and colleagues on both sides of the ghetto wall
as well. Conversely, most assimilants and many acculturated Jews had one or two
relatives who had converted, or had personal or professional relationships with
converts. Between them, then, the 4,000 converts are likely to have had
connections with most of the 20,000 assimilants, many of the 30,000–40,000
acculturated Jews, and perhaps a few thousand of the more traditional Jews as
well. Thus, the converts were at the heart of a community of something like
100,000 people that spanned the ghetto wall.

Assimilants knew or were related to many of the same people as the converts,
and had independent contacts on both sides of the ghetto wall as well. If we suppose that each assimilant had just one independent close contact on each side of
the ghetto wall, then this would have added another 20,000 Jews and 20,000
non-Jews to the bridging community. On these estimates, then, more than 70,000
Jews (including the assimilants and converts themselves) and a similar number of
non-Jews maintained fairly direct, close relationships, in a city where Poles and
Jews on the whole did not mix. To this one could add the occasional contacts and
friendships inevitably formed by acculturated Jews, and even many non-
acculturated Jews, in the years of cohabitation – former teachers, clients, servants,
employees, employers and so on.

As the case study that occupies most of this chapter illustrates, these contacts
were in turn only the nucleus of a still larger network. As Jews in hiding were
passed from hand to hand, the nature of the relationships between them and their
helpers grew ever more tenuous: a helper might be a former neighbour's neighbour, a friend of a cousin's friend, an uncle's former client or a chance-met
stranger. These networks intertwined and reached into every corner of Polish and
Jewish society, and into all social classes and milieus. It is thus likely that even the
most unworldly *Hassid* had a relative who had a friend who knew someone who
had some contacts on the 'other side'.[11]

It thus becomes clear that whatever it was that limited the number of *melinas* available to the Jews, it was not the lack of people – Poles, and Jews with connections – to whom they could potentially turn for help. All the Jews in Warsaw, if they racked their brains, could probably come up with some Polish acquaintance or associate with whom they had been on good terms before the war, or some relative who had such contacts. Similarly, in a city where more than a quarter of the population was Jewish, nearly every Pole had some Jewish colleague, friend or acquaintance. The same can also be said, unfortunately, of the Polish criminal classes and of devoted antisemites. The Jews in hiding were, in short, an integral part of underground Warsaw, for better and for worse, however isolated they may individually have felt.

Of course, not all potential helpers were willing, or able, or had the courage to help, and even if they had all been mobilized, it would not have been possible for them to save all 490,000 Jews who passed through the Warsaw ghetto. But the number of people who actually did escape from the ghetto probably did not exhaust the city's absorptive capacity, nor did it account for all of those who had the necessary contacts. As we shall see in Chapter 2, many Jews were in the midst of making arrangements when they were caught up in the German sweep, or were inhibited from escaping by a variety of factors, including an unwillingness to put their Polish friends at risk. As it turned out, the secret city was largely composed of the Jewish middle class, which was at least acculturated. More Jewish Jews, while not without resources, had to rely on indirect contacts and were thus at the end of a very long queue. Very traditional Jews almost all perished and, as Helena Merenholc remarked, 'the Jewish proletariat was lost'.[12] But the wave of escapes was still swelling when the Ghetto Uprising broke out on 19 April 1943; given another six months or a year, perhaps many of these Jews would have been saved as well.

The Polish Milieu

Beyond personal contacts and friendships, the fate of the Jews on the Aryan side was intimately connected with the more general characteristics of the society into which they had escaped. I do not intend to become involved here in an extensive study of Polish–Jewish relations, which is a subject for another book, but a sketch of the political and ideological conformation of Polish society is certainly in order.

Besides being socially isolated from the Jews, the bulk of Polish society was influenced in its views by the institutionalized antisemitism of the Catholic church and the populist incitement of nationalist politicians, as well as by all manner of ingrained prejudices and superstitions. Lurid antisemitic pamphlets circulated freely during the interwar years, and a sizeable segment of the Catholic and nationalist press mouthed extreme antisemitic propaganda.

The Catholic church, more than any other institution, believed itself to be at war with encroaching secularism, of which it believed the Jews to be the main agents. The church of course did not preach violence, but it did support 'self-defence'. Cardinal Hlond, in a famous 1936 pastoral letter, prefixed an exhortation against anti-Jewish violence and 'slander' with a lengthy list of slanders of his own, holding Jews responsible, *inter alia*, for prostitution, pornography, atheism and Communism, and in the name of 'self-defence' endorsed the Endecja's economic boycott of the Jews.[13]

Among the leading disseminators of antisemitic propaganda was Father Maksymilian Kolbe, later canonized, whose publishing enterprise included the *Mały dziennik* (Little Daily) and the weekly *Rycerz niepokalanej* (Knight of the Immaculate). These two publications were among the most widely read in Poland, and both consistently attacked Jews, Freemasons and other objects of the paranoia of the time. *Mały dziennik,* with the largest circulation of any daily in Poland, enthusiastically promoted the *Protocols of the Elders of Zion*, claimed that Poland was united in an 'anti-Jewish war' (28 December 1937) and told readers among other things that the Talmud allowed Jews to murder non-Jews (8 and 22 January 1939).[14] Kolbe's standing and high moral character, together with the evident popularity of his newspapers, are at odds with any claim that extreme antisemitism was a marginal force in interwar Poland, or imported from abroad, or limited to 'bad Catholics', as some apologists claim. Kolbe does not seem to have been an overt antisemite himself, but by allowing his newspapers to print such rubbish, especially in the inflamed atmosphere of the 1930s, he, like other churchmen, at the very least acted irresponsibly.

As might have been expected, the malice of this propaganda, combined with the credulity and settled prejudices of its readers, caused 'self-defence' to take violent forms from time to time, despite the official position of church and state. This violence was not limited to the uneducated and ignorant. In the interwar era, university students were particularly apt to adopt extremist right-wing postures that glorified violence and vilified the Jews, and in Warsaw much of the anti-Jewish violence was inflicted by gangs of student 'corporatists' (*korporanci*) belonging to the Fascist-style National Radical Camp (ONR). Joining them were razor gangs (*żyletkarze*), composed of ordinary street thugs. Ultimately the anti-Jewish psychosis led to the infamous pogroms in Przytyk (1936), Jedwabne and Radziłów (1941) and Kielce (1946), as well as numerous smaller ones. Jolanta Żyndul counted major outbreaks of antisemitic violence in ninety-seven towns and cities in 1935–37, with fourteen Jews killed and 2,000 injured.[15] Such events, of course, made an appalling impression on Jewish and world opinion, and have continued to colour the country's image to this day.

It is difficult, on the other hand, to remember nowadays that, before the First World War, the Poles had quite a different image abroad. The West in those days tended to think of them as dashing revolutionaries, in the mould of Kościuszko and

Pułaski, after whom streets are named in every larger town in America. The Jews, too, once thought of Poland as an island of tolerance, between reactionary Russia and assimilationist Germany, where they could live their own life in peace. In choosing Hebrew names for their countries, German and Spanish Jews adopted the names of biblical distant lands, Ashkenaz and Sepharad; but the Polish Jews called their country Canaan, the Promised Land. In Yiddish it was simply *der Haym* – the Home.

Images are by definition superficial, and the truth about Poland includes both these realities in some proportion. Towards the end of the nineteenth century the romantic nationalism of Pułaski and Kościuszko yielded to a new, xenophobic form, and by the interwar period Roman Dmowski's National Democracy movement (Endecja), and with it political antisemitism, were solidly entrenched in Polish society. The older and more tolerant tradition survived, however, particularly in the person and circle of Józef Piłsudski, whom the Jews generally viewed with favour. (Adam Czerniaków, chairman of the Warsaw Jewish Council, kept a picture of the Marshal above his desk.) It must be remembered that Piłsudski, not Dmowski, was the dominant political figure of the interwar period and to this day is regarded with a certain reverence in Poland. In addition, the new force of Socialism gained a strong foothold in the country, and the Polish Socialist Party (PPS), then led by Piłsudski, was thought to have been the largest party in Poland on the eve of independence in 1919.

It would not do to draw too romantic a picture of Old Poland, where blood libels and massacres did occur, or to overstate the liberalism of Polish political parties. All agreed that the Jews in some sense constituted a problem for the country, but they disagreed as to its nature and proposed different solutions. To the parties of the right, the problem was that there were too many Jews in Poland: 'a little salt may improve the taste of the soup', Dmowski declared, 'but too much will spoil it.' Dmowski's party believed that the Jews were an obstacle to the economic advancement of the Poles, since they comprised a large segment of the business and professional classes and many of the artisans and craftsmen as well. The Jews had in fact become the pioneers of a new social order by historical accident: their traditional role as middlemen had placed them in a better position than the largely agrarian Poles to take advantage of the new opportunities in a modernizing society. Taking a traditional, static view of society, the Endecja failed to understand that by developing the country's economic life the Jews were creating opportunities for Poles and not destroying them (Dmowski's liberal rivals, the 'Warsaw positivists', understood this point well enough).[16] Nor was the Endecja moved by the fact that the most successful Jewish plutocrats generally assimilated to Polish society and eventually converted: the right viewed assimilants and converts with deep suspicion, as a fifth column of International Jewry. In any case, Dmowski believed that the Jews were too numerous to assimilate. The solution, in his view, was the removal of as many Jews as possible by voluntary emigration, and the introduction of restrictive measures against the rest.

As a national electoral force, the Endecja was far less successful than Piłsudski's Sanacja. It never ruled on its own, but only as part of the centre–right coalition governments of the early twenties, and Dmowski himself never held public office of any kind. But the dominance of the Sanacja owed less to its nebulous political programme than to the Marshal's personal popularity, buttressed by no small measure of electoral manipulation, and as an ideological force the Endeks were unequalled. They were old hands at organizing boycotts of Jewish business, and they successfully promoted the principle of the *numerus clausus* and ghetto benches in institutions of higher education, adoption of the 'Aryan paragraph' excluding Jews from professional associations, the use of nationalization policies to expropriate Jewish businesses, and legislation limiting ritual slaughter. Their rhetoric, like that of the church, was *de facto* an incitement to violence, which moderate Endeks opposed in theory but without much conviction. Radical Endeks proposed the forcible expulsion of the Jews; the mainstream position favoured 'voluntary' emigration, to be encouraged by making it clear to the Jews that they were not wanted. In all these respects it was distinguishable from the ruling party after Piłsudski's death only by the passion of its rhetoric; programmatically, both church and state had embraced the Endek position by 1939.

To the parties of the left, on the other hand, the Jewish problem consisted in the 'separateness' of the Jews: that is to say, their cultural distinctiveness, but also the same concentration in certain economic sectors that exercised the right. Antisemitism, according to their analysis, was in part the result of xenophobia, and in part the 'Socialism of fools', an attempt by the bourgeoisie to split the working class. The solution to the 'Jewish problem' was for the Jews to follow the example of their Western brethren and assimilate, recognizing common class interests. In the meantime, the parties of the Polish left were prepared to co-operate fraternally with their Jewish equivalents, the Bund and Labour Zionists; this co-operation extended not only to joint industrial action and bloc voting in the Sejm and Warsaw City Council, but also to support from the PPS for demonstrations against antisemitic excesses, and armed action by the PPS militia against right-wing extremists.

Remarkably, discussion of the relative strength of these tendencies has most often proceeded without so elementary a tool of political analysis as an electoral table. It is true that interwar Polish election results are hard to interpret: there was a bewildering variety of splinter parties and name changes, and elections were often manipulated. Even if corrections are made for these factors, the fact remains that of course not all supporters of a given party will be in agreement with all of its policies, so that there were no doubt those who voted for the PPS despite rather than because of its opposition to antisemitism. Conversely, there were many centrist, and even some right-wing, voters who were not antisemites: the Polish aristocracy, for example, was traditionally friendly, if patronizing, towards the Jews. Nevertheless, election results are at least a starting point towards quantification and give us a rough idea of the disposition of political forces.

The electoral results most pertinent here are those of municipal elections in Warsaw, which were held three times in the interwar period. These were the results:

Table 1.2 Results of Warsaw Municipal Elections, 1919–39

Party or bloc	Percentage of seats obtained		
	1919	1927	1938
Sanacja	**	13	40
Endecja	51	39	8
ONR	**	**	5
PPS	19	23	27
Jewish parties	23	23	19
Other	7	2	1
Total	100	100	100

After Edward D. Wynot, Jr., *Warsaw between the Two World Wars* (New York: Columbia University Press, 1983) 118–26.
** Party did not exist in these years.

With the governing (from 1926) Sanacja being able to control the city council at best in a weak coalition with the parties of the right, and the PPS the only party willing to join forces with the Jewish bloc, the lines were clearly drawn. In judging the respective strengths of these groupings, there are a number of caveats to be observed. It would be better to have the popular vote rather than the numbers of seats won, but I could find only scattered figures. The 1919 and 1927 elections were held under proportional representation, while a less representative ward system was used in 1938. The 1938 results are affected by gerrymandering and government spending on behalf of the Sanacja, so that these figures overstate the Sanacja's real support and understate that of its opponents: the degree to which this was so can be judged from the fall in the representation of the Jewish parties, by one-sixth of their former seats. The support of the left is also understated for 1927, when the Communist KPP won a remarkable 16 per cent of the popular vote (compared with 18 per cent for the PPS), but was not allowed to take its seats. Thus, the parties of the Polish left had the support of 34 per cent of voters in 1927, while their proportion of seats in 1938 was again lower by about one-sixth. Since the rightward swing of the Sanacja had alienated its left-wing and Jewish supporters, most of whom would have gone to the PPS, the underrepresentation of the PPS was probably greater still. The same rightward swing, however, attracted votes to the government at the expense of the right-wing parties, so that their decline, much greater than one-sixth, is partly real as well as the result of electoral manipulation. Some 18 per cent of Jewish voters voted for Polish parties, almost entirely the Sanacja (in 1927) and the PPS. The following approximate picture can thus be drawn of the electorate in 1938, after making corrections for these various factors:

Table 1.3   Adjusted 1938 Municipal Election Results

Party or bloc	Polish voters (percentage)	Jewish voters (percentage)
Sanacja	38	–
Endecja	14	–
ONR	8	–
PPS	39	18
Jewish parties	–	82
Other	1	–
Total	100	100

Voters were thus sharply polarized along both ethical and political lines. About 60 per cent of Poles voted for parties of the right, but nearly 40 per cent for the left. Jews voted overwhelmingly for Jewish parties, with the PPS the only party that still attracted both Polish and Jewish voters. The parties of the centre were squeezed out altogether, except to the extent that the Sanacja still had a centrist element.

The role of the PPS as a bridge between the Polish and Jewish communities is thus made clear, as well as the party's significance in the city's politics. It was the only major party in Poland with a significant Jewish membership, mostly assimil-ants and converts, and with a branch in the ghetto. One of its representatives in the wartime Government-in-Exile in London, Ludwik Grosfeld, was a Jew; it maintained fraternal ties with the Bund, and its militia had helped fight off anti-semitic attacks by the ONR during the street brawls of the thirties.

The PPS was not the only party that bridged the Polish–Jewish divide. Another was the KPP, which had scored such a success in the 1927 elections. But the KPP was accused of Troskyism and dissolved by the Comintern in 1938; most of its activists were summoned to Moscow, where they were murdered. Its voters either abstained in 1938 or supported the PPS, the Bund or the Labour Zionists. The ghost of the KPP would rise again in 1942, when the Soviet-sponsored Polish Workers' Party (PPR) was formed. The party's pro-Soviet orientation would have alienated many KPP supporters, so its popularity is unlikely ever to have approached the levels reached by the KPP. Thus the PPR remained small, but it would prove to be an important link across the ghetto wall.

In 1939, the centrist and left-wing Pilsudskiites who had been repelled by the Sanacja's turn to the right went on to form the Democratic Party (SD – *Stronnictwo Demokratyczne*), which also had Jewish members and supporters. The party was small, but no instrument is available by which its exact degree of popular support can be judged.

During the war, the Polish underground coalesced around the various political parties, which, however, underwent numerous splits and realignments. The PPS split over the Soviet invasion of Poland in 1939, into the anti-Soviet Freedom-Equality-Independence (WRN) faction, and the left-wing and much smaller Polish Socialists (PS), later the Workers' Party of Polish Socialists (RPPS), which advocated an independent Polish state in alliance with the Soviet Union. In general, the PS maintained close ties with the Bund, and Jewish sources speak highly of it, while WRN was more standoffish. An English-language pamphlet published in September 1943 by its American branch, the Polish Labor Group, is a case in point.[17] The pamphlet contains two pages on the Warsaw Ghetto Uprising, recently in the news, but there is no other mention of the Jews. The next two pages describe the 'battle of the monuments', in which the Germans tore down statues of Polish heroes, and the two pages after that the massacre of 117 Poles in Wawer in 1939. The killing of two million Jews, on the other hand, is passed over in a single sentence. A similar indifference is displayed in the recently published correspondence between WRN leaders in Poland and their representatives in London.[18] The situation of the Jews is mentioned briefly in a report dated June 1942; the next mention of the Jews is in a similar report, a year later. The entire tragedy of the Warsaw Jews, from the start of the Great Deportation in July 1942 until the Ghetto Uprising of April 1943, thus passes without comment in the correspondence of the most pro-Jewish of the major parties in Poland.

What little is said about the Jews in these letters, in the pamphlet mentioned above and in the PPS publications is entirely sympathetic and proper, without antisemitic overtones. In the report of June 1942, for example, we read that:

> The Jews have already in large measure been murdered. Recently the Jews of Cracow have been liquidated, and 'cleansing' units are currently sweeping the Jews out of the smaller towns and townlets. [...] Really one must reach for the strongest measures here, because another half year of this destruction, together with the coming winter with no heat, and the number of victims will have to be counted in the millions.[19]

But that is virtually all that is said on the subject, in a report of four printed pages. The 'strongest measures' recommended are 'retaliation against Germans, particularly in the United States'; but that was rejected in the West as impracticable and immoral. In fact, no organized action on behalf of the Jews was undertaken by WRN until December 1942, when Julian Grobelny of WRN became the chairman of Żegota. Even so, after Grobelny's capture by the Germans in March 1944 several months elapsed before a replacement could be found.

This myopia on the part of WRN should be regarded as evidence of self-absorption rather than of any anti-Jewish bias: the party's credentials as opponents of antisemitism were impeccable, and many of its individual members were very active in helping Jews. Indeed, many of its members were Jews, including the authors of the American pamphlet. WRN was a source of individual contacts for Jews, however, not the nucleus of an organized rescue effort. Like other parties, it tended to extend aid to its comrades within the ghetto, helped to smuggle some of them out and offered them aid on the Aryan side. Individual WRN activists became involved in the organized aid effort from 1943 onwards. But the party as a whole, and its supporters, cannot be said to have exerted itself to an extent appropriate to the circumstances. (There was hardly an institution in Europe or abroad, though, about which the same could not be said.)

In general, Helen Fein's opinion must be confirmed, that even progressive elements of Polish society regarded the Jews as outside their 'universe of obligation', an alien element whose fate was of little concern to Polish society as a whole.[20] This followed from the isolation of the two societies from each other, a situation that was not, as some authors have implied, the result of some Polish policy of apartheid, but had existed for centuries by mutual consent. The advantage of the arrangement to the Jews was that it protected them from assimilation. The disadvantage became apparent when they desperately needed their neighbours' help, and found them, even when friendly, preoccupied with their own affairs.

Thus, the large bloc of left-wing voters in Warsaw, and the large organized party of the left, formed a bridge that was less solid than it seemed. It would certainly be wrong to conclude from the electoral statistics that 40 per cent of the Polish population were sympathetic to the Jews, or even interested in them. Given the difficult housing situation in occupied Warsaw, described in Chapter 3, only a minority even of those who were sympathetic could offer *melinas*. And given the risks involved, only a minority in turn of those who were in a position to offer help had the courage to do so. On the other hand, there were also individuals who had no particular sympathy for Jews, or whose attitude even remained hostile, but for whom the principle of Christian charity, or the strength of personal ties, or the chance to earn some money outweighed both fear and ideology. Further, the anti-semitic trend of the surrounding milieu in some ways worked in favour of the Jews: it made for especially warm relations within the small, beleaguered circle of the Jews and their friends, and it made the Jews more wary and streetwise.

It will be argued in Chapter 3 that 7–9 per cent of the population of Warsaw did become involved in helping Jews, and on the evidence presented so far this does not seem an extravagant claim.

A Case Study

The case study that follows will serve to illustrate the nature and extent of the relationships that crossed the ghetto wall, and will flesh out the case made above.

This study is based on two longer accounts, one Polish and one Jewish, and a number of shorter ones, which, as we shall see, mesh together into a common story. This story is not about people who were part of the organized underground, and whose networks therefore spread, as it were, automatically, through their organizations, but concerns fairly ordinary people, with the sorts of contacts that ordinary people might have: they were people who happened to meet, some of whom happened to survive and happened to write their stories down. We will, in the telling, run into some prominent people and activists, but this should not, by itself, cause us to doubt that this story is typical. When we trace connections, we inevitably find our way to the well-connected. But the nature of these connections is usually unremarkable, even when the people are not. We shall begin, for example, with a national boxing champion, and soon be led to the director of the Warsaw zoo, who later was deeply involved in Żegota. But the link between these men has nothing to do with their membership in an elite (even supposing that boxers and zoo directors tended to move in the same circles) – rather, the boxer had a friend whose father-in-law did business with the zoo. Our two prominent individuals thus immediately lead us to two others, the friend and the father-in-law, who were quite average members of the Jewish middle class, and quite representative of the kind of people who escaped from the ghetto. Both the people we are about to meet, and the relationships between them, are on the whole typical of those reported in the memoirs generally.

Dramatis Personae

Szapse Rotholc was a national boxing champion before the war, and a member of the Bundist *Shtern* sports club. Together with his friend and fellow-boxer **Shmuel Kenigswein**, he became a member of the ghetto police and participated in smuggling, in the process forming contacts with German and Polish policemen and with smugglers on the Polish side.[21] Rotholc's experiences on this front will be described in more detail in the next chapter. Rotholc claims that he used his position as a policeman to help his nephew and several other Jews escape from the ghetto; and he himself, with his immediate family, escaped with the aid of a Pole, another boxer named **Tadeusz Mańkowski**, who was later killed together with Rotholc's wife after a betrayal. Rotholc also had a good Polish friend named **Stanisław Chmielewski**. Kenigswein's father-in-law had been a supplier to the Warsaw zoo, so that Kenigswein knew the zoo's director, **Dr Jan Żabiński**. Both Chmielewski and Żabiński became involved in bringing aid to their friends in the ghetto and later in hiding fugitives on the Aryan side. Chmielewski had twenty-four Jews under his direct care, keeping some in his own flat and helping many others, while Żabiński hid more than twenty-five Jews in the zoo, and again helped many others. Żabiński, in turn, knew the engineer **Feliks Cywiński**, passing a number of people on to him. Cywiński arranged hiding places and documents for dozens of Jews and kept seven in his own flat at Sapieżyńska 19. Cywiński was drawn into these activities by his friend **Jan Bocheński**, who had asked him for help in finding places for two Jewish friends. Both Cywiński and Bocheński sold family land to raise money, which they used to rent four additional apartments where Jews could be hidden. Cywiński and Bocheński are credited with having twenty-six Jews under their direct care, of whom twenty-three survived, including the writer **Rachel Auerbach**, **Barbara Temkin-Berman** (Adolf Berman's wife), and **David Guzik**, director of the Joint.[22] In this way, this network was connected to Jewish activist circles, while Żabiński and Cywiński later also acted in Żegota. They were drawn into the organized aid effort by another friend, the psychologist **Janina Buchholtz-Bukolska**, who in turn was inducted by a fellow-psychologist, **Dr Jadwiga Zawirska**, a friend of the Bermans.[23] Kenigswein, with his family, stayed with both Żabiński and Cywiński; during the Warsaw Uprising in 1944, he became the leader of a Jewish platoon, organized by Cywiński, in the 'Wigry' battalion of the Home Army.[24] Another of the Jews under Cywiński's care, the lawyer **Mieczysław Goldstein**, was passed on to him by **Stefan and Marta Koper**, the caretakers of a building in the right-bank suburb of Praga, who hid thirteen Jews in their flat.[25] It should be noted that in all these cases aid was extended without payment.

Each of these people had further friends and contacts, some of whom have left records of their experiences, so that the description of this network could be extended considerably. Indeed, since the activists were in touch with many thousands of Jews, who in turn had networks of their own, we could probably find our way to all the Jews in hiding if we could trace all of the connections in full. Because only about one per cent of them wrote memoirs, and few are still alive, there are too many gaps in the record to allow such a task to be completed today. Instead of trying to cast the net more widely, therefore, let us instead try to give the picture more depth by looking at a few of these stories in detail.

The 'One-Man Underground Organization': Stanisław Chmielewski

Chmielewski – described by Ber Mark, then director of the ŻIH, as a 'one-man underground organization'[26] – was apparently a homosexual, who was drawn into helping Jews through his relationship with his Jewish lover 'Karol' (**Władysław Bergman**).[27] Early in the war, Chmielewski and Bergman fled to the Soviet-occupied sector; once there, Bergman decided to flee deeper into Soviet territory, while Chmielewski promised to return to Warsaw to look after Bergman's mother Stefania as well as his own. First, though, Chmielewski went to Vilna, where, he maintains, Rotholc was living at the time (Rotholc's account of events seems to make this impossible).[28] In Vilna, Chmielewski associated with the circle of refugees from Warsaw, many of them Jews: 'I had known many of them already, and got to know many others [. . .], becoming sincere friends with them,' he writes.

Late in October 1939, Chmielewski smuggled himself into the German-occupied part of Poland, carrying with him letters and messages from his Jewish friends in Vilna. 'Crossing the border that night', he relates, 'I knew how I would fight against the Hitlerite invaders. Not with weapons, which I did not have, but with a weapon that was given to me at birth: God's commandment, love thy neighbour as thyself. [...] So began my fight with the Nazi invader, the daily battle against Fascist racism.'[29] Thus Chmielewski was moved by idealism as well as personal friendships to devote himself specifically to helping Jews. Perhaps as a homosexual he was also sympathetic to Jews as fellow-victims of persecution, and his own family obligations were few.

The letters that he delivered put Chmielewski in contact with a wider group of Jews, a number of whom he next helped to escape to the Soviet zone. He was also introduced to wider Jewish circles by Mrs Bergman, who drew him into the work of aiding Jewish refugees from Łódź. Chmielewski in turn recruited his own mother, and also a young Polish engineer, Andrzej Szawernowski, who 'throughout the occupation bravely helped me with my daily difficulties', particularly with arranging documents and finding hiding places for the Jews under Chmielewski's care. Chmielewski insists that he also had help from other quarters:

> even the most stubborn 'Polish fascists', from the Camp of Great Poland [OWP] or even the National Radical Camp [ONR], for the most part renounced their youthful ideology, and in an honest, real, brotherly fashion helped first of all me, and later even directly the Jews themselves. The Christian idea, 'love thy neighbour as thyself', eroded the ideology 'beat the Jew'.[30]

There are indeed documented instances of members of the far right who devoted themselves to helping Jews – the case of Jan Mosdorf is well known,[31] and a few other cases will turn up later in this book. In general, however, the far right did not 'renounce its former ideology': its underground press maintained an uninterrupted barrage of antisemitic propaganda, and partisan groups of the NSZ, the military organization of the OWP and ONR, carried on an internecine war against what it regarded as the nation's enemies, including Communists, liberals and Jews. The NSZ carried out a series of assassinations, among others of the Jewish historian Marceli Handelsman, and some of its partisan groups carried out attacks on Jewish partisans. Another organization of the far right, *Miecz i Pług* (Sword and Plough), was widely regarded as collaborationist.

This is not the place for an adjudication of these claims, some of which are contested, but there is at least reason to think that Chmielewski's optimism is misplaced. He accurately reports the contradictory aspects of right-wing Christian ideology that warred in the breasts of such people, but certainly 'love thy neighbour' did not always, or even very often, win out over 'beat the Jew'. These issues are taken up in greater detail in Chapter 4.

With the closing of the ghetto, Chmielewski resolved to maintain contact with his Jewish friends and bring them aid. But as he writes, he agonizes over the moral dilemma with which the enormity of the ghetto presented him:

> Acting almost alone, I could not of course reach most of the prisoners of the ghetto, so that of necessity, of tragic necessity, my aid had to restrict itself to the narrow group of people who were my friends. I knew, in any case, that I was not isolated in my action, I believed that there must be others like me, who had friends among the Jews. This thought and faith gave me strength.

Indeed, there are a number of accounts of Poles who maintained contact with their Jewish friends in the ghetto, and also of Jews who elected to remain outside the ghetto and smuggled food and other necessities in to their relatives. We shall meet more of them in the present case study, and others in the next two chapters. Ringelblum reports that, in the last few days before Christians were excluded from the ghetto, there was 'a mass phenomenon: Poles come to their Jewish friends . . . with packages of food, with flowers'.[32] How many of these people kept up contact later on is hard to say, but certainly some of them did. As a policeman who participated in the illegal traffic through the ghetto gates, Rotholc noticed that

> [t]here were also Poles who went into the ghetto. Polish 'noggins' [*lebki*]' . . . were looked after better and more carefully [by the guards at the gates]. It was taken into account that these Poles who came to the Jews were risking their lives, and this gave rise to respect for them. These Poles also arranged things for the Jews. Jews entrusted them with their fortunes. These Poles brought the Jews money. They took all sorts of things out of the ghetto. Those Jews who didn't have the possibility of smuggling food not seldom got money from Poles, which they used to buy food from the smugglers.[33]

As for the principle of 'charity begins at home' – the 'tragic necessity' that Chmielewski invokes – this, more than anything else, decided who would be first in line for hiding places. Though people with indirect contacts had some chance, the assimilated intelligentsia and political activists – those who knew people like Chmielewski – made up most of those who were saved.

Chmielewski's action during the ghetto period consisted of arranging the sale of his friends' possessions to raise money for them (he could get a better price on the Aryan side than they could in the ghetto), and smuggling food and medicine across to them. In this work, he says, he had the help of a 'small, but faithful and reliable group of friends'. Among these was a German member of the Nazi party, **Erich Horst**, who 'hated Hitler, and did whatever he could and however he could, always with dedication, to save the victims of persecution, Poles and Jews alike'.[34] Horst gave Chmielewski's group access to German gendarmes who could be bribed. Later, Chmielewski found a less expensive and less dangerous method of smuggling. The ghetto's garbagemen, who dumped their refuse outside the ghetto, could be persuaded (for a price) to carry food back with them, concealed in their empty wagons. Still another method was to throw food over the ghetto wall, at prearranged times and places. Chmielewski's mother helped in this work, together with a friend of hers whose daughter-in-law was in the ghetto: here therefore is an example of how the conversionist milieu helped in maintaining such contacts.

With time, contact with the ghetto became more and more difficult and dangerous. Even the court building in Leszno Street, where Jews and Poles could legally mingle, became a favourite place for *łapanki* (hostage-takings and round-ups for forced labour). Furthermore, access to the court building became restricted to those on court business, so that heavy bribes had to be paid to get in.

Money, in general, was the lubricating fluid of all transactions, according to Chmielewski. Now less sanguine about his fellow-countrymen, he complains that 'During the occupation, unfortunately – today we have to be completely honest about this – money decided everything. You could look for sentiment with a candle in your hand. Or you could dream or daydream about it'.[35] Raising money therefore became an increasing problem for Chmielewski, a man of modest means, especially as his work multiplied with the liquidation of the ghetto. He recounts that:

> During that feverish period I was once at a kind of reception. The home was cultured, the company select. [...] It started with cold snacks, prepared in the traditional Polish way; there were two green tables for bridge, and in the living room they were getting ready for a concert. The host was a man of inherited wealth, a member of the typical West-Polish [*poznańsko-wielkopolskiej*] bourgeoisie, the guests included wealthy landowners. *Nota bene*: the hostess was hiding two Jews in her house. One of them was a doctor. Both took an active part in the reception, in the discussion, in the numerous disputes and controversies that usually take place under such circumstances.
>
> This was a typical social gathering of that tragic period, [...] which in effect not only brought together the representatives of the two nations but, the most important thing then, produced a greater or lesser income. Because all the participants in such gatherings [...] had to make a donation to a fund to aid the victims of the ghetto.[36]

Jewish sources do not mention such receptions, but it must be kept in mind that the recorded testimony represents only a small part of the whole reality. It seems, at any rate, that financial help to the Jewish fugitives was not limited to the money officially channelled to the aid organizations by the Government-in-Exile and Jewish groups abroad, but that money was raised within Poland as well. The sale of land by Cywiński and Bocheński has already been mentioned, and other examples will crop up.

While on the subject of the plutocracy, Chmielewski also mentions the Berson family, wealthy bankers long ago converted to Christianity, who nevertheless retained a sympathetic attitude to Jews. Among their philanthropies, for example, was the Bersons' and Baumans' Children's Hospital, which was incorporated into the ghetto. The Bersons maintained two estates, in Boglowice and Leszno. According to Chmielewski, both gave employment and hiding places to Jews who had escaped from the ghetto, and both contributed money and food to the relief of the ghetto. It would be an interesting subject of future research to probe the activities of the old convert community as a whole, a group that was numerically tiny but had considerable wealth.

Besides raising money to cope with the flood of refugees, Chmielewski also needed to recruit more helpers. One of these was a **Dr Karlsbader** of Żelazna 31, a woman who 'gave aid and shelter to many people from the ghetto'; another was a **Mrs Gerzabek** of Natolińska 3: their houses served as temporary shelters for Jewish fugitives. From there, Chmielewski and his friend Szawernowski found them more permanent places.

One of Chmielewski's Jewish friends, the professor of medicine **Dr Leo Płocker**, was assigned to a *placówka* (work detail) outside the ghetto, where he had to perform heavy physical labour for which he was unfit. Chmielewski rescued him from this otherwise probably fatal situation by arranging for him to sneak away from the *placówka* and spend his days with another friend, **Władysław Martyny**. In the evenings, Płocker would rejoin the work party and return to the ghetto. After Płocker escaped from the ghetto, Chmielewski found him a place with Dr Karlsbader, and placed Płocker's wife first with a **Mrs Halicka** and then with a **Mr** and **Mrs Łukasiewicz** in Mokotowska Street.

Mrs Płocker was a concert pianist, a gold-medallist of the Leipzig Conservatory, and of Aryan appearance. She could therefore appear in public, and gave fund-raising concerts, often at the home of a couple called **Andrzejewski**, who had an excellent Bechstein. Chmielewski placed Dr Płocker's mother with yet another friend, a **Mrs Wala**, in Wilcza Street. Chmielewski also placed with Wala some relatives of his lover Władysław Bergman, **Alina Lewinson** and her daughters, **Janina** and **Sophie**. Janina Lewinson, under her married name of Janina Bauman, is the author of *Winter in the Morning,* one of the outstanding memoirs of the period, from which we learn a good deal more about Chmielewski, Wala and many other people. But that is getting ahead of the story.

Chmielewski placed Stefania Bergman somewhere in Wesoła Street, and after that *melina* was 'burnt', with a **Mr** and **Mrs Henrychów** in Kopernika Street. This couple was also looking after a **Mrs Kasman**. Mrs Kasman's daughter-in-law had been caught while hiding and shot, leaving a small son, whom Chmielewski took into his own flat. At that time, he was also hiding Mieczysław Goldstein, the lawyer.

Thus we come full circle, with Chmielewski's network connecting with that of the Kopers, and thereby to Cywinski, Żabinski and the mainstream Polish underground. These various networks on the Polish side arose spontaneously as a result of the personal contacts and humanitarian impulses of such people, and eventually merged into a single large network, connected to the Polish underground and eventually also to the aid agencies when they arose. As it grew beyond its humanitarian nucleus, it came to include, as Chmielewski tells us, those for whom 'money decided everything', and was infiltrated by more sinister elements as well.

Janina Lewinson (Bauman)

Chmielewski's relatively short memoir (twenty-six typed pages) only skims the surface of his wartime activities. Writing a quarter of a century after the events, he admits that he has forgotten the names of many of the people in his circle, and can tell us little more about the Jews in his care. Janina Bauman's memory is more vivid: her extraordinarily detailed account puts the experiences of at least one of the families whom Chmielewski helped under the microscope and provides more details of his activities.

Chmielewski's lover, Władyslaw Bergman, was Bauman's rather distant cousin. Her main 'angel' throughout the occupation, however, was not Chmielewski but 'Aunt Maria' – **Maria Bułat**, her mother's former nanny and her grandparents' housekeeper. Bułat was recognized as a 'Righteous Gentile' in 1993.[37] Sharing a single room with her sister and brother-in-law, Aunt Maria was unable to give shelter to Jews in her own home, but extended help in many other ways. During the ghetto period, she maintained contact with Bauman's family, by telephone, through the courthouse in Leszno Street and also through her brother-in-law, who as an electrician had a pass that allowed him to enter the ghetto freely. He would bring 'letters, money, and all sorts of useful things from her'.[38] In January 1943, Aunt Maria arranged for the Lewinsons – Janina, her mother and her sister – to escape from the ghetto and escorted them to their first *melina*. This was a large flat in the centre of Warsaw belonging to the aristocratic family of Chmielewski's friend, Andrzej Szawernowski.

Eight Poles stayed at the Szawernowskis', as well as four Jews – 'Aunt Maryla' (Stefania Bergman) and the three Lewinsons. Not all the Poles were equally generous or courageous. The Szawernowskis' daughter, **Mrs Simonis**, was nervous about 'keeping cats' (the wartime slang for hiding Jews): she was cool towards them, demanded large payments and refused to take in Jews after the flat had been visited by blackmailers in June 1943. The Szawernowskis themselves, on the other hand, would later take the Lewinsons in without payment, while their daughter was away on holidays.

Forced out of the Szawernowskis' flat by the blackmailers, the Lewinsons next turned to **Zena Ziegler**, the ex-wife of their grandfather's former chauffeur, who was already giving shelter to Janina's uncle **Stefan** and his fiancée, **Jadwiga**. But

Ziegler was a morphine addict, and indiscreetly told her boyfriend, so that the Lewinsons had to find another hiding place after only a few days.

Stefan and Jadwiga found shelter with Ziegler's sister, **Mrs Kulesza**, while Mrs Simonis arranged a temporary place for the Lewinsons – with a prostitute named **Lily** who entertained German soldiers in her flat, and whose brother was a *Reichsdeutsch* working with the railway police (*Bahnschutz*), whose job included catching Jews. Clearly this *melina* was unsuitable, and Aunt Maria next placed them with her sister **Helena**. Helena was not supposed to take such risks because her son was a high-ranking member of the AK, whose arrest could therefore have serious implications for the movement. Again, therefore, the Lewinsons were able to stay for only a few days.

After this, Janina suffered from fever and her normally acute memory becomes blurred. She speaks of wandering on the outskirts of Warsaw, staying in 'somebody's cousin's flat; somebody else's friend's flat'.[39] Chmielewski then came to the rescue, finding a place for her in the city centre. This was a sophisticated, specially constructed hiding place on the burnt-out first floor of a building above a German trading company. Here the porter of a neighbouring building, whom Bauman identifies only as '**Kazik**', and his mother hid 'dozens' of Jews: fifteen were there when the Lewinsons arrived, eight others had just left. Kazik appears to have been middle-class, not the usual sort to be a building porter; Bauman thinks he was a member of the AK, using the porter's job as cover.

It was now the late summer of 1943 and the Lewinsons had lived in at least seven *melinas* in perhaps as many months. The Hotel Polski affair was at its height, and twelve of the other fifteen Jews staying with Kazik, having presumably had equally unsettling experiences, all decided to go there. The Lewinsons also seriously considered it.

Very soon, Kazik's *melina*, too, became 'burnt', when a pair of blackmailers robbed the six remaining people of everything they could find. The Lewinsons found temporary refuge with **Kazik's mother**, who was also looking after a Jewish woman and her baby (Bauman thinks that the child was Kazik's). Kazik now placed the Lewinsons with his friends **Tom** and **Wanda**, who printed underground pamphlets, forged documents and banknotes in their cellar. But Tom was soon arrested on the street. Since such arrests were invariably followed by a house-search, the Lewinsons had to clear out quickly. They returned to the Szawernowskis'. The Szawernowskis could offer a place only until the unsympathetic Mrs Simonis came back from holiday, and the search for a hiding place therefore resumed immediately. Alina Lewinson and her younger daughter, Sophie, were put up in the suburb of Rembertów by another sister of Zena Ziegler's, **Janka Zielińska**, while Janina was placed in another suburb, Radość, with a family whom she calls the **Majewskis**.[40]

The Majewskis proved to be of a type encountered much more often in the accusatory literature than in the memoirs: they required the payment of a large sum in advance, were rude and uncouth, starved Janina and then invented a story that a stranger had been nosing about, in order to get rid of her and keep the money. Janina then joined the rest of her family at the Zielińskis, a family of four. Here, at last, the Lewinsons found some stability, staying for six months until January 1944. Between them they had had to move at least thirteen times in eight months.

Like the Majewskis, the Zieliński household also charged for keeping the Lewinsons, but Bauman writes that the amount was reasonable and they were well looked after. A working-class family, the Zielińskis could not get by during the occupation without supplementing their income by illegal activities. Mrs Zielińska, a midwife, performed abortions and traded on the black market: keeping the Jews, says Bauman, was no more risky and less exhausting. But living with another family at close quarters and under such conditions could not remain just a commercial enterprise:

> for the people who sheltered us our presence also meant more than great danger, nuisance, or extra income. Somehow it affected them, too. It boosted what was noble in them, or what was base. Sometimes it divided the family, at other times it brought the family together in a shared endeavour to help and survive.[41]

Thus Janka generously gave up her double bed to Janina and her mother, sleeping in a single bed with her own daughter while her husband slept with their son.

Eventually, this hiding place, too, was discovered by blackmailers, and after they had been paid off there was no money left. To help out, Aunt Maria sold a plot of land that Janina's grandparents had given her. Chmielewski placed Janina with an elderly woman who was also looking after Stefania Bergman; her mother and sister in the meantime 'were going through terrible ordeals. For various reasons they had to leave one shelter after another, to hide in wardrobes and chests, often to walk along the streets in full daylight'.[42] Since all three had a 'bad' appearance (Chmielewski thinks that the younger daughter, Sophie, could safely pass as a non-Jew, but Bauman thinks otherwise), appearing in public was highly dangerous. They disguised themselves by wearing mourning, but such disguises could often draw the very attention they were meant to deflect. Briefly, they sought refuge in a church, where the priest, suspecting who they were, offered food and consolation.

Chmielewski then found lodgings for all three of them with Mrs Wala, in a space of which Chmielewski and Bauman have different recollections. Chmielewski describes a flat with many rooms running off a central corridor, all of which were sublet to fugitives of various kinds. Bauman describes a single room in which Wala's neighbours expected her to be living alone, so that mere conversation aroused suspicion. Possibly Wala had sublet the rest of her flat and lived only in the small part of it that Bauman describes. At any rate, Wala and her boyfriend Edward were also looking after Stefania Bergman at the time and periodically, in Chmielewski's telling, after many other Jews as well. This *melina*, too, had to be abandoned when Wala died in hospital. Edward tried to keep up her work, but with her death her flat reverted to the city and all the tenants had to leave. Finally, Aunt Maria found a place for them with a neighbour of hers, where they stayed until the 1944 uprising.

Bauman's story, though told with exceptional clarity and detail, is otherwise not untypical of the memoir literature: the constant moving from place to place, the repeated threat of blackmail and denunciation, the problem of money, the dependence on the goodwill of large numbers of people who were essentially strangers, the temptation to join in the Hotel Polski scheme are all quite typical.

The Lewinson family were also rather typical of the assimilated Warsaw intelligentsia. Janina's father was a urologist, one grandfather was also a doctor, the other owned a music shop. Her family adhered nominally to the Jewish faith, but were non-observant and had adopted such Christian customs as putting up a Christmas tree. She received her primary education at *Nasza Szkoła* and then entered a state *gimnazjum*. She was the only Jewish girl in the whole school, the result of the unofficial *numerus clausus* that kept out all but the ablest Jews.

Bauman does not mention any pre-war Christian friends of the family, except to say that some of them visited just before the ghetto was closed. Here, then, we have some further evidence of Ringelblum's 'mass phenomenon', but also an indication that many – probably most – such people did not follow through. For whatever reason, the Lewinsons did not seem to rely on these contacts later on. Instead, their main point of contact with the outside world was through their servants. Domestic labour was cheap in pre-war Poland, and any respectable middle-class family, even one that was not very wealthy, would have a maid or a nanny or a cook. A number of family servants figure in Bauman's story: besides Aunt Maria and Zena Ziegler, there is also Ziegler's husband, a *Volksdeutsch*; a nurse named Sister Franciszka, also a *Volksdeutsch*; and Stefania Bergman's Christian maid, who moved into the ghetto with the family (there were not a few such cases).[43]

Summing up Bauman's story, then: the Lewinsons' beachhead on the Aryan side consisted of the old nanny, Aunt Maria and the chauffeur's ex-wife, Mrs Ziegler. They in turn recruited various friends and relatives. Aunt Maria enlisted her sister Helena, her brother Tadeusz and her brother-in-law, the electrician with a pass for the ghetto. This beachhead was then expanded through the further families, friends and neighbours of these servants. These were working-class Poles, most of whom were honest but for whom looking after Jews was primarily a way of supplementing their income. Chmielewski, who as a cousin's lover was tenuously related to the Lewinsons, acted as another beachhead. In helping the Lewinsons, Chmielewski used contacts with the Polish underground, Andrzej Szawernowski and the porter Kazik. Through the daughter of the aristocratic Szawernowskis, in

turn, the Lewinsons met the *Reichsdeutsch* prostitute Lily; while the contact with
Kazik led to the ill-fated underground printing shop of Tom and Wanda. This was
the structure of the Lewinsons' network on the Aryan side.

On the Jewish side, Bauman mentions thirteen relatives and eleven friends who
were alive and in Warsaw when the ghetto was closed or subsequently. Of these,
two relatives stayed out of the ghetto; seven relatives, five friends and three parents of friends escaped from it, and three relatives died or were deported. We are
not told the fate of the remaining six friends. Thus, at least fifteen out of twenty-
four – nearly two-thirds – either escaped from the ghetto or never entered it. Of
those of whose final fate we are told (excluding Bauman herself), six survived, two
died in the 1944 Warsaw Uprising and four died on the Aryan side before that
uprising. Thus, at least a quarter of this very well-connected group of Jews survived the war, and more than half of those on the Aryan side survived at least until
the uprising in 1944.

Conclusions

It would be premature at this point to draw far-reaching conclusions or try to
estimate numbers; but certain things can already be said on the basis of this case
history. First of all, relying mainly on the testimony of one Polish and one Jewish
witness, we have found our way to more than a hundred Jews, sixty-odd Poles,
four Germans (Chmielewski's helper Erich Horst, one of Bauman's blackmailers,
the prostitute Lily and her brother) and two *Volksdeutsche* (Zena Ziegler's husband
and the nurse, Sister Franciszka). Through Kenigswein and his connection with
Żabiński, we have also arrived at the Polish and Jewish aid organizations, which
ultimately reached thousands of the Jews in hiding. Each of these Jews in turn had,
like Bauman, additional contacts with Poles and other Jews, and the Poles also had
further contacts of their own. Here, then, is how the secret city arose, spontaneously, through personal networks.

Nechama Tec has suggested that Polish helpers of Jews largely thought of
themselves as 'outsiders', a proposition that Michael Marrus finds so self-evident
that he describes it as 'a circular argument'.[44] Some of the people described by
Chmielewski and Bauman and the others were indeed outsiders: Lily the prostitute, Zena Ziegler the morphine addict, Chmielewski the homosexual. And there
is more than a hint that much of Chmielewski's circle was a homosexual underground, helping its fellow victims of Nazi persecution. But the larger network that
these accounts reveal reached into the most extraordinary variety of milieus. It
included the aristocratic Szawernowskis and the working-class Zielińskis, the
extreme right-wing ONR and OWP circles with which Chmielewski was in contact, and also the Communists to whom his friend Dr Płocker belonged. It
included Poles, Germans, *Volksdeutsche* and old Jewish converts, members of the

Polish underground and of the Nazi party, sportsmen and boulevardiers, priests and atheists, servants and masters. It included people of great kindness and nobility, others whose interest was purely mercenary, and (counting the *szmalcowniks*) the vilest of criminals. In short, it reached into every corner of Polish society and involved people of every type.

On the Jewish side, the network may in principle have reached most of the Jews in the ghetto – though Bauman's milieu is assimilated, many other memoirists had relatives who remained traditional – but the principle of 'charity begins at home' ensured that those with the closest contacts had the best chances. There were also many psychological barriers that held back the less assimilated Jews. For many reasons, the community of Jews on the Aryan side consisted almost entirely of assimilated Jews, except for the relatively small group of political and social activists who escaped through the efforts of their organizations.

In the next chapter, we will take up the topic of escape, to show how the secret city arose.

2 Escape

The thirty months of the Warsaw ghetto's existence can be divided into the following periods, each offering different prospects of escape and posing different problems:

1. The closing of the ghetto, from the ghettoization decree of 12 October 1940 until the deadline for resettlement, 15 November. During this period Jews had to decide whether to enter the ghetto or to live illegally outside it.
2. The main ghetto period, from 16 November 1940 until 21 July 1942: the Jews of Warsaw were shut up behind the ghetto walls and many others were forced into the ghetto later, from surrounding towns and then from Germany and Czechoslovakia. In all, some 490,000 Jews lived in the Warsaw ghetto at one time or another. Conditions were grim: 78,000 people died from starvation or disease, and tens of thousands were rounded up for service in labour camps, where the mortality rate was still higher. Contact with the Aryan side was mainly through food-smuggling and other forms of illegal trade. There was a substantial Jewish presence on the Aryan side in connection with this trade, but few Jews left the ghetto with the intention of staying out for good. The main ghetto period can be subdivided into two shorter periods:
   a. Before Hans Frank's decree of 15 October 1941, escape was risky but did not carry the death penalty as a matter of policy.
   b. After Frank's decree, discovery on the Aryan side in principle (not always followed) meant death for the Jew and all 'accomplices and instigators'.
3. The period of the liquidation of the ghetto. Escape was effected on a larger scale, mainly through work parties that worked outside the ghetto and could leave it legally. The liquidation actions stretched over nine months and were carried out in stages:
   a. The *Grossaktion* or Great Deportation, 22 July–12 September 1942: all but 55,000–60,000 Jews were deported to Treblinka and killed. During this *Aktion*

conditions in the ghetto were chaotic, and the true nature of the deportations became known only gradually. Illegal trade all but stopped, and escape was very difficult.

b. The 'shops' period, when the ghetto was divided into German-owned work-shops and, in effect, converted into a labour camp.

    i. Between the Great Deportation and the January *Aktion* (18–22 January 1943), when a further 6,000 Jews were transported to labour camps. The number of escapes diminished, as many people thought the deportations had run their course, at least for the time being.

    ii. From the January *Aktion* to the outbreak of the Ghetto Uprising on 19 April 1943. The ghetto was finally convinced that it was doomed, and the number of escapes increased greatly.

4. The Ghetto Uprising and its aftermath: once fighting started, normal escape routes ceased to exist. Jews escaped through sewers and tunnels; they jumped from the deportation trains or escaped from labour camps, or they hid in the 'wild' ghetto, which had officially been cleared of Jews, and then made their way to the Aryan side, usually at night.

To determine proportions, 224 individual cases have been examined. The results are summarized in Table 2.1.

It will be seen from this table that only a relatively tiny number of people stayed out of the ghetto or escaped before the onset of the deportations in 1942. Although the number of people escaping during the first deportation was much larger, it was still proportionally quite small (the percentage given in the table is calculated on the basis of the ghetto population about halfway through the depor-tation). The bulk of escapes took place only after the end of the deportation, when almost a quarter (22–24 per cent) of the 55,000–60,000 remaining Jews (35,000 living in the ghetto officially and 20,000–25,000 'wild' Jews) managed to get away.[1]

If more than 13,000 Jews escaped from the ghetto after the 1942 deportation, and another 6,000 were deported during the January *Aktion*, then the total number of Jews who remained in the ghetto during the uprising could not have been greater than 41,000, whereas Jürgen Stroop's report on the suppression of the Ghetto Uprising claims to account for 61,000–62,000 Jews: 5,000–6000 'destroyed in explosions or fires' and 56,065 Jews either killed by his men during the uprising or deported afterwards. This discrepancy need not detain us too long, however. German figures concerning the Warsaw ghetto are generally inflated. The number 56,065 is suspiciously palindromic, and its accuracy is clearly spurious: it is the sum of a number of figures that are themselves broad estimates.[2] On the basis of German figures and *Judenrat* estimates, Berenstein and Rutkowski found room for 42,500 fugitives from the ghetto;[3] this number is clearly overstated, but it does show how much uncertainty there is in ghetto

Table 2.1   Time of Escape from Warsaw Ghetto or Arrival on the Aryan side

Category	Number in sample	projected*	Percentage of all escapes and arrivals	of remaining ghetto population
Never entered the Ghetto	19	2,400 ± 1,100	8.5	0.6
Escaped				
before deportations	26	3,250 ± 1,250	11.6	0.8
during first (1942) *Aktion*	48	6,000 ± 1,600	21.4	5.0
between *Aktionen*	20	2,500 ± 1,100	8.9	4.2
between second *Aktion* and Ghetto Uprising	60	7,500 ± 1,700	26.8	12.5
during or after Ghetto Uprising from ghetto	21	2,600 ± 450	9.4	5.2
from train or camp	8	1,000 ± 700	3.6	2.5
Came to Warsaw to hide	22	2,750 ± 1,150	9.8	—
Totals	224	28,000	100.0	5.5[†]

* Error bars at .95 confidence level. Overall total has been estimated independently (see Chapter 6).
† Of total ghetto population (490,000).

population figures. The estimates given here – nearly 23,000 escapees and more than 5,000 who stayed out or came to Warsaw to hide – are based on the direct evidence presented in Chapter 6, and are certainly more reliable than Stroop's braggadocio.

Staying Out: The Formation of the Ghetto

At the time of the establishment of the ghetto, the number of Jews on the Aryan side was negligible. Even totally assimilated Jews and also converted Jews preferred to live in the ghetto for fear of punishment. In the Aryan sector there remained a very small group of people of Jewish origin who were linked by family ties to Polish surroundings and who did not have the courage to wear the Jewish armband.

Adolf Berman[4]

The Jews in Warsaw [. . .] could be divided into two categories: those who, from the first moment [. . .] as a matter of principle sabotaged all decrees applying to Jews, ignoring the threat of disproportionately heavy punishments, and exposing themselves at the same time to criticism from their fellow victims of persecution; and those who 'risked' themselves only at the time of the final liquidation [. . .] or shortly before.

'Citizen Frajnd'[5]

One of the most serious errors [. . .] was the hostile attitude to the acquisition of 'Aryan papers.' Until the time of the big deportations this was regarded as a kind of desertion. The consequence of this attitude was that during the most tragic period there were not enough workers on the 'Aryan side' and there was not even the minimum point of support outside the walled-in ghettos.

Michal Borwicz[6]

Waldemar Schön, director of the Resettlement Office for the Warsaw District and the first Commissioner for the Jewish Residential District, reported that he had been forced to mount a 'great police operation' on 16 November 1940 to round up 11,130 Jews who had remained outside the district.[7] Like Stroop's figures, and other figures in Schön's report, this one is no doubt inflated in the service of his own prestige. Still, the report is not altogether an invention, and it seems reasonable to suppose that a substantial number of Jews did remain outside the ghetto for the moment. It would also be entirely uncharacteristic for such a *razzia* to have caught all its intended victims, especially since it took place only in certain districts. Viewing the round-up from the other side, Citizen Frajnd at any rate was not impressed. 'Fortunately', he writes, 'the hunters had not yet attained the perfection that they would reach in three years' time, so that there were relatively few victims.'[8]

In most instances, Jews who missed the 15 November deadline for moving into the ghetto probably did not mean to evade the ghettoization decree: they had simply been unable to find quarters inside the designated district in time. And final details of the ghetto boundary were not published until 14 November, when some Jews suddenly found themselves on the wrong side of the boundary. Wrangles over certain streets (Graniczna and Biała) continued until well past the deadline, so that resettlement continued even into the first week or two of the ghetto's existence.[9] Schön's 'great police operation' was thus carried out in an atmosphere of considerable confusion, and largely entrapped the victims of that confusion rather than genuine evaders. Even those who escaped Schön's round-up over the next few days eventually moved into the ghetto voluntarily, by and large. As we have seen, something like 2,400 remained.

Every Jew who stayed outside the ghetto was highly acculturated, and usually a convert. Only highly acculturated Jews were motivated to live on the Aryan side, and capable of surviving 'on the surface' by passing as non-Jews. No case has turned up of a Jew staying on the Aryan side in order to live in hiding, 'under the surface'. But because it was obviously dangerous to defy German decrees, most acculturated Jews and even converts did not stay outside: other exceptional circumstances had to be present as well.

In most cases, the decision to pass as a non-Jew was made before the ghettoization decree was published, and remaining outside the ghetto was merely a further consequence of this decision. When it did not follow from the resolve to 'sabotage all German decrees', as in Frajnd's case, the decision to pass as a non-Jew was usually forced as a result of entering into a mixed marriage after the occupation began: there was a rash of such marriages, mainly in the hope of evading anti-Jewish measures. Since marriages between Jews and Aryans were illegal under the Nuremberg Laws, the Jewish spouse – and often close relatives as well – had to establish a false identity.[10] Other factors such as youth and a sense of adventure, weak links to the Jewish community and limited Jewish family ties,[11] a strong attachment to a non-Jewish spouse or companion[12] and good connections with the Polish underground[13] were often also present.

Bearing in mind that people who stayed out of the ghetto had to survive on the Aryan side for more than four years before liberation, we might surmise that projections based on survivor testimony could well understate the case. To test this possibility, the fate of eight such people was determined from third-person reports. Three of them survived,[14] one entered the ghetto after being harassed by her Christian neighbours and died there,[15] one was killed in the Warsaw Uprising of 1944[16] and three died on the Aryan side.[17] The sample is too small for any firm conclusions to be drawn, but at any rate it would seem that survival on the Aryan side for such a long time, though far from certain, was possible. Three survivors out of eight represents about the same proportion as the overall survival rate (41 per cent) calculated in Chapter 6, so that there is no definite reason to suppose that the Jews who stayed out are underrepresented. Perhaps the greater risk that these Jews ran by spending a long time in hiding was offset by their closer integration into Polish society and their greater familiarity, during the more dangerous period later on, with conditions on the Aryan side and with the techniques of survival.

The Main Ghetto Period: 16 November 1940–21 July 1942

1 The Porous Wall

Unlike the ghettos in many other cities in Poland, the 'Jewish Residential District' in Warsaw was centrally located and could not easily be isolated from the rest of the city. The German authorities had been aware of this problem, and had initially considered building the ghetto 'on the outskirts of the city, namely embracing the districts of Koło and Wola in the West of the city and Grochów in the East', according to Schön. But they had to take into account the 'special and extremely complex conditions in the city of Warsaw'. 'The point was made', wrote Schön, 'that the creation of a ghetto would cause considerable disruption to industry and business. Since eighty percent of the artisans were Jews, one could not place them under siege for they were indispensable.' Here then was an early victory for the 'productionists', as Christopher Browning has called the Germans who wanted to exploit Jewish labour, over the 'attritionists', to whom the ghettos were a means of extermination. The decision to create the ghetto was thus delayed; in the meantime, the pre-war Jewish neighbourhood was declared a 'quarantine district' (*Seuchensperrgebiet*), apparently because the Nazis believed their own propaganda that the Jews were 'immune carriers' of typhus. As if by way of commentary on this propaganda, construction of a wall to isolate the 'quarantine district' began on April Fool's Day in 1940.

Paradoxically, the Nazis' eagerness to seal off the Jews contributed to the decision not to create a completely isolated ghetto: the wall represented a certain commitment, and the delay caused by building it created an atmosphere of haste, even panic, later on. When the decision to create a closed ghetto was made, on 20 August 1940, it was decided to leave the Jews where they were. Economic factors were invoked, but the fear of typhus may have decided the issue:

> hermetically sealed Jewish ghettos should not be created, but rather Jewish residential districts which permitted economic links with the surrounding Aryan area, which would be vital to the survival of the Jewish residential district. [. . .] The creation of a ghetto at the edge of the city would have taken four to five months in view of the need to regroup nearly 600,000 people. However, the resettlement measures had to be completed by 15 November [. . .] since experience showed that the winter months saw an increase in epidemics.[18]

The ghetto was thus essentially coextensive with the city's traditional Jewish area, in the very heart of Warsaw: its borders started two blocks west of Marszałkowska Street and two blocks north of Jerusalem Avenue, the city's two most important streets. No fewer than five tram lines transected the ghetto. The wall itself was makeshift in character:

> The Jewish Residential District is separated from the rest of the city by the utilization of existing walls and by walling up streets, windows, doors and gaps between buildings. The walls are three metres high and are raised a further metre by the barbed wire placed on top. They are also guarded by motorized and mounted police patrols.[19]

It was punctured by twenty-two gates, soon reduced to fifteen; at each gate was a *Wache* or sentry-post, manned in principle by one German gendarme (of the 304th *Ordnungspolizei* battalion), one Polish 'Blue' policeman, and one member of the *Jüdische Ordnungsdienst* (Jewish Order Service), the ghetto police. There continued to be some legal traffic across the ghetto wall: 'Passes are issued for passage in and out of the ghetto for essential purposes', as Schön wrote, though the number of such passes was sharply curtailed in time. All trade across the wall was supposed to be handled by a new agency, the *Transferstelle*; all other commercial traffic was forbidden. Nevertheless:

> Smuggling began at the very moment that the Jewish area of residence was established [...] It was calculated that the officially supplied rations did not cover even 10 percent of normal requirements. If one had wanted really to restrict oneself to the official rations then the entire population of the ghetto would have had to die out in a very short time.[20]

In fact, not only food was smuggled: an extraordinarily varied underground economy soon sprang up, much of it based on trading illegally with the Aryan side. This trade is important here for two main reasons: first, that in connection with it methods of crossing the ghetto wall were developed which also served, mainly at a later time, for smuggling people and arms; and second, that to understand why people decided to leave the ghetto or stay there we must also understand the possibilities, on the one hand, of escape from the ghetto, and, on the other, of survival within it. Both these possibilities depended crucially on smuggling and the underground economy that it sustained.

The means of physically crossing the ghetto wall were as numerous as human ingenuity could devise; among them were:

1. Trams. Each tram on the five lines that traversed the ghetto stopped at an entrance gate on its way into the ghetto, where it was boarded by a Blue policeman. The tram would then pass through the ghetto, stopping only at the exit gate, where the policeman would alight and report to a German gendarme. At certain points, however, these trams had to slow down for sharp turns, where people could jump on or off the open cars. Bags of food or other goods could also be thrown to or snatched from confederates within the ghetto as the trams went by. The conductor and policeman would usually have to be bribed – Dawid Białogród says that 2 zł was the normal tariff[21] – and any Polish passengers would have to be counted upon for their discretion. Jack Eisner, himself one of the child smugglers who used this technique, describes it in detail.[22] Białogród later escaped from the ghetto in this way, together with his wife and child.

2. **Other conveyances.** Various other vehicles could enter and leave the ghetto with official permission. People could cling to the underside of fire engines or refuse carts as they left the ghetto. Food was regularly smuggled in by the ghetto's garbage collectors:

> The garbagemen smuggled from the beginning of the ghetto's existence. [...]
> They took the garbage to a dump in Wolska [Street]. When they left the ghetto,
> things being exported would be hidden under the garbage, and on the way
> back they would buy some hay and rye for their horses. Under this [...] they
> would hide food.[23]

Another technique: a cart would enter the ghetto drawn by two horses, and leave with only one.

A private ambulance service offered passage out of the ghetto for a price, and hearses ostensibly carrying the bodies of converts for burial in Christian cemeteries could carry the living instead. In these cases, the Germans' fear of disease could be exploited: dropping the word 'typhus' would discourage a closer search. People could also hide aboard trucks legally carrying goods into or out of the ghetto, the guards having been bribed not to search them too thoroughly.

3. **Legal passes.** A certain number of Poles had businesses within the ghetto or other legal reasons for being there. The priests of the two functioning Catholic churches within the ghetto, All Saints' in Grzybowski Place and the Holiest Virgin Mary in Leszno Street, could pass freely in and out of the ghetto. The director of the Warsaw zoo, Jan Żabiński, obtained an appointment as inspector of trees and could enter the ghetto to carry out his duties, as could various municipal workers, and rent and tax collectors. Polish owners and managers of enterprises within the ghetto, as well as their Polish workers, could similarly pass in and out. Officials of the welfare agency RGO were allowed to visit the Pawiak prison within the ghetto. Jews already living on the Aryan side could get passes on various pretexts: A.P., for example, was able to visit her relatives by claiming that she was having a dress made by a seamstress in the ghetto. Jacob Celemenski, a courier for the Bund, was equipped with Aryan documents and a range of forged passes, identifying him as an electrician or municipal worker. A few Jews who were not living 'on documents' also had passes to leave the ghetto: for example, Marek Edelman, at the time an orderly at the Bersons' and Baumans' Children's Hospital, routinely carried laboratory samples for analysis. In time, however, the number of passes was greatly reduced, and all passes were cancelled when the deportations started.

4. **The courts.** Though officially on the Aryan side, the main court building in Leszno Street was entirely surrounded by the ghetto. Access from the Aryan side

was provided through its back entrance, by means of a narrow passage along Biała Street – the buildings on both sides of which were in the ghetto – which connected it to Mirowski Place on the Aryan side. Since both Poles and Jews could be involved in court proceedings, they were allowed to mingle freely within the building, though Jews had to wear their Star-of-David armbands. In principle, special passes were needed, but enforcement was lax and a bribe could generally deal with any difficulties. A Polish woman, H.Z., describes how she smuggled food into the ghetto through the courts: she would enter the building from the Aryan side, carrying full shopping bags, and go into a stairwell. There she would put on an armband and then go out on the ghetto side. On the way out, she would reverse the procedure.[24] The same technique could easily be used to leave the ghetto for good: Eugenia Rolnicka, for example, escaped from the ghetto in this way in May 1941.[25] Though access to the court building was progressively tightened, this escape route remained available for at least a few people even after the deportations began, until the building was zoned out of the ghetto in mid-August 1942.

The court was not the only building that allowed access to the Aryan side. The municipal offices in Długa Street also had entrances on both sides of the wall, and until the Germans got wind of it the concierges would allow people in and out of the ghetto for 'a few zlotys'. A pharmacy in Dzika Street was also accessible from both sides, and the pharmacist would allow anyone through who could state a good reason.[26]

5. '*Mety*'. Large-scale smuggling was most commonly carried out at the so-called *mety* (singular: *meta*) or 'hideouts', places where the ghetto boundary was formed by internal walls in adjacent buildings. In such places holes could be knocked in the shared walls, or smuggling could be carried on across the rooftops. Liquids and grains could be poured down drainpipes. Diana Kagan writes that she regularly visited her relatives in the ghetto by entering and leaving through such adjacent buildings, jumping from one rooftop to another.[27]

6. **Gęsia Street Market.** This was actually located in a lane running from Gęsia to Niska Street, where open trade was carried on between Jews selling used clothing and other goods and Christian buyers who were allowed to enter the ghetto for this purpose. The Gęsia Street market was closed down at the start of the deportations.

7. **Over, under and through the wall.** Child smugglers in particular made their way in and out of the ghetto through holes in the ghetto wall, which were filled in with loose bricks when not in use. In certain places, a proper wall had not been built and the ghetto was separated from the Aryan side only by a wooden fence or barbed wire: the emaciated children could easily (though not without risk) slip through the

wire or past a loosened plank. Food and goods could also be thrown to confederates on the other side, or the wall could be scaled, with lookouts keeping watch on both sides. In the secluded remoter reaches of the Jewish cemetery, no lookouts were needed: there, smugglers could climb unobserved into the neighbouring Powązki Christian cemetery or the Evangelical cemetery. But the Jewish cemetery was separated from the rest of the ghetto by its own wall. Contraband moving in or out had to pass through the Okopowa Street gate, which was often manned by the infamous 'Frankenstein' (a particularly sadistic German guard so named, apparently, for his resemblance to Boris Karloff). This smuggling was accomplished by undertakers from the Pinkert firm, who hid the smuggled goods in special compartments in their coffins.[28] Smuggling at the cemetery wall was one of the few channels that remained available after the deportations, during the 'shops' period.

8. The ghetto gates. The policemen guarding the gates could often be bribed or distracted, and occasionally turned a blind eye out of goodwill. Szapse Rotholc offers the following description of smuggling at the gates, worth quoting at length partly for its colourful character, and partly for the light it casts on this form of smuggling, particularly on the relations between Jewish and German policemen. It helps also to answer the argument recently made popular by Daniel Goldhagen: here are some of 'Hitler's willing executioners', closely observed by a Jewish eyewitness:

> If you sensed that a new gendarme was prepared to talk to a Jewish policeman, if he let you stand next to him, that meant he'd be good for a bribe. There were different kinds of gendarmes. They were from different places. If you had a gendarme from Austria, he'd offer on his own to help with the smuggling. The worst were the gendarmes from Germany.
>
> We often talked politics with the gendarmes. Sometimes a gendarme would express a sort of sympathy. In 1942–3 [during the deportations] you would often say to one of those gendarmes, 'What good is your sympathy? The next time you come on duty I'll be dead.' That kind of gendarme would be glad to see you alive the next time. If you asked him, 'Where are your seven million German Communists?' a gendarme like that might say, 'You don't know what's going on underneath my uniform.' That kind of gendarme wouldn't take any money for helping with the smuggling. That kind of conversation could happen in the later period.
>
> Most often gendarmes broke down and made friends with Jewish policemen during conversations about family. If you got them onto the subject of their families you could easily lead them. Some of them would tell you about letters they'd got from their families, where they'd been told about the deaths of their dearest ones. At a moment like that a gendarme would lose interest in everything and would say, 'Everything is shit already, do what you want.'[29]

Goldhagen claims that the 'willing executioners' acted sadistically towards Jews because they had been culturally programmed with 'eliminationist antisemitism'. But according to Rotholc, 'Quite a few gendarmes said that the battle with the Jews is only politics but they hate the Poles from the heart.'

Once relations had been established, not only food and goods could be smuggled through the gates.

> There were 'players' [*grajkowkie* – Jewish policemen involved in smuggling] who [with the help of] 'their' gendarmes would rarely let contraband through but mainly let people [...] go back and forth. This lasted for the whole time the ghetto existed until [the last period] when letting people through to the Aryan side assumed an entirely different character. [...] These 'players' we called noggin-men [*łebkarze*].[30]

Rotholc says little about the Polish policemen at the ghetto gates, except that they would demand their share of the bribes and were generally dissatisfied with what they received. We can infer that, though self-interested, they could usually be counted on to co-operate. Polish policemen later became involved, sometimes, in leading people out of the ghetto and in making arrangements on the Aryan side. On the other hand, as we shall see in Chapter 4, they were also charged with hunting down Jews in hiding, a duty that some of them carried out zealously. Others found a profitable occupation in collaborating with *szmalcowniks* to extort money from Jews.

In short, all three police forces contained people of various kinds, from those who abused their power, to those who were officious in their duties, to honest and decent men. The Germans, having the most power, could commit the most extreme abuses, and of course through the routine exercise of their duties ensured the starvation and ultimate destruction of the ghetto. But having the most power to harm, they also had the most power to help. One thing is certain: without those policemen who did retain their humanity, including some of the 'ordinary Germans' of the 304th Orpo battalion, the ghetto could not have been kept alive through smuggling, and the 'Greatest Escape' could not have taken place.

9. Work parties. Groups called 'placements' (*placówki*) left the ghetto every day to carry out jobs of various kinds outside the ghetto; there were also Polish *placówki* within the ghetto. Members of these work parties could smuggle goods out with them to sell on the Aryan side, and could smuggle in food on the way back. The quantities that could be smuggled in this way were small, and the number of work parties was also quite limited at first. *Placówki* assumed much greater importance after the liquidation of the ghetto started, however, when most other methods of smuggling stopped. A significant development during the months leading up to the liquidation action in July 1942 was a sharp increase in the number of Jewish *placówki*, owing to labour shortages on the Polish side (in turn created by the round-ups of tens of thousands of Poles for forced labour in Germany: this was one of the many ways in which the irrationality of the Nazi system created opportunities for the Jews). The number of Jews employed in these work parties rose from 700 in March 1942 to 1,700 in April and 3,000 in May.[31] *Placówki* continued to operate until the end of the ghetto's existence, and even – in the form of small work camps on the Aryan side – after its destruction. They proved to be by far the most important channel of escape. Jews wanting to escape in this way would join a work party, bribing the overseer and the policemen at the gates to miscount the workers and turn a blind eye to the extra clothing they were wearing and to anything they were carrying. (The bribes would not always save the escaping Jews from a trip to the *Wache*, however, where they could expect to be beaten and have their money and valuables confiscated. In this way the policemen not only increased their profits but presumably salved their consciences for having taken bribes.) Once on the other side, the Jews would then take off their armbands and slip away. This is what Rotholc means when he says that in the final period letting people through at the gates 'assumed an entirely different character'.

10. Sewers and tunnels. This method was rarely used during the main ghetto period, but became more important shortly before and during the Ghetto Uprising. Several tunnels were constructed by the Revisionist ŻZW to help smuggle arms in.[32] Their own fighters left the ghetto through the tunnel under Muranowska Street, which was also discovered fortuitously by a handful of others after the defeat of the uprising. The story of the escape of seventy of the ŻOB ghetto fighters through the sewers is well known, and a handful of memoirists also say they got out in this way. Occasionally small quantities of goods, including firearms for the ghetto fighters, were also smuggled by this method.

The Autumn and Winter of 1941–42: Measures to Combat Smuggling; the Development of the Ghetto Economy

To combat smuggling, the authorities adopted a series of increasingly severe measures, which had a marked effect on the problem of leaving the ghetto. I have mentioned that passes were increasingly curtailed and finally cancelled altogether. The ghetto boundaries were changed in October and November 1941 to eliminate adjacent Aryan and non-Aryan houses. Usually the whole city block would be zoned out of the ghetto, with the wall rebuilt to run along the length of the street behind it, taking up the sidewalk on the Jewish side. The number of gates was reduced still further, and the guard was strengthened. Lightning raids were carried out at known smuggling points, and German and Polish police patrols circulated outside the ghetto wall; on one occasion, a hundred Jewish policemen were executed for their part in the smuggling. The tram lines were re-routed or closed.

The Catholic churches in the ghetto were shut down. None of these measures succeeded in stopping the illegal commerce, leading to a ghetto joke reported by
Ringelblum: 'Three things are invincible: the German Army, the British Navy, and
Jewish smuggling'. Further steps to isolate the ghetto preceded the start of the liquidation action: most (but not all) of the telephones in the ghetto were discon-
nected, the number of gates was reduced yet again, and all remaining non-Jews
were forced to leave, except for managers of German enterprises.

The most significant of these steps was Hans Frank's decree of 15 October 1941,
which read in part:

1. Jews who leave their designated districts without authorization will be subject
   to the death penalty. The same penalty will apply to those who consciously
   give such Jews hiding places.
2. Instigators and accomplices are subject to the same penalties as perpetrators,
   and an attempted act will be punished in the same way as an accomplished one.
   In less serious cases imprisonment or imprisonment with heavy labour may be
   imposed.[33]

On 10 November, this was reinforced by a still more draconian order from the
Governor of the Warsaw District, Dr Ludwig Fischer:

Recently, Jews who have left their designated district have in numerous verifi-
able cases been responsible for the spread of spotted fever. In order to forestall
the resulting danger to the population, the Governor General has decreed that
a Jew who leaves his designated district without authorization will be subject
to the death penalty.

The same penalty will apply to anyone who consciously gives help to such a
Jew (for example, by making available a night's lodging, food, offering transportation of any kind, etc).

I draw the attention of the entire population of the Warsaw District to this
new administrative resolution, since from now on it will be applied with mer-
ciless severity.[34]

Fischer's version of the decree makes no mention of 'less serious cases', and
extends the death penalty to various minor acts, not only giving Jews hiding
places.

After the publication of these decrees – which were widely posted around the
city, especially near the ghetto – the number of escapes decreased markedly, with
only half as many over the next nine months as in the previous eleven. But fear
for their own safety was not the main factor that dissuaded Jews from fleeing –
indeed, Dawid Białogród, for one, decided that crossing the wall once and for all
would be safer than continuing to smuggle.[35] As the case studies discussed below

demonstrate, people who escaped during the main ghetto period generally did so only if they were facing an acute personal crisis that seemed to make survival in the ghetto impossible; and in such cases, the degree of risk that they would face on the 'other side' was hardly relevant. On the other hand, Jews were reluctant to put their friends in danger. Karol Popower writes: 'We had Polish friends [. . .] who had long been trying to persuade us [to leave the ghetto] and had invited us to stay with them, but we had kept putting it off because we didn't want to be a burden on them.'[36] People who were prepared to take such risks could in any case probably help more effectively, and certainly more safely, by smuggling food in than by trying to smuggle their friends out. Finally, during this same period, under the 'productionist' administration of the new Ghetto Commissioner, Heinz Auerswald, there was a marked improvement in the ghetto's economy and a slight decline in the death rate. This probably had far more effect in reducing the number of escapes than Frank's and Fischer's decrees.

It is possible that before these decrees survival was statistically more likely outside the ghetto than within it. But the prospects were not the same for everyone. The ghetto's flourishing underground economy provided at least a thin living for those who were able to find a place in it, and a few even became wealthy. At worst, the Jewish upper and middle classes were able to sustain themselves by selling off their belongings: it was the poor who were overwhelmingly the victims of starvation and disease. The *Judenrat* estimated at the end of 1941 that the average ghetto resident consumed 1,125 calories daily, enough to sustain life; but there were great inequalities. Officials of the *Judenrat* received 1,665 calories a day, shopkeepers 1,429, unemployed members of the middle class 1,395, workers in German workshops 1,229, refugees (that is, Jews who had been forcibly moved into the Warsaw ghetto, and who lived in shelters provided by the *Judenrat*) only 805, and street beggars 785.[37] The last two groups, together with orphans, made up the bulk of the ghetto's mortality.[38] But these were primarily unassimilated, Yiddish-speaking Jews, with few social contacts among Poles who might have provided hiding places and no prospects at all of being able to live 'on the surface' by passing as Poles. The refugees, even when assimilated, were strangers to Warsaw and had even fewer contacts, either directly or through Jewish assimilants in the ghetto.

The poor, out of desperation, did cross the ghetto wall, not to find hiding places but in search of food: their children became the ghetto's celebrated child smugglers. This sort of smuggling, without benefit of bribed policemen or contacts on the Polish side, was by far the riskiest. Emaciated ghetto children in their torn and shabby clothes were also easily recognized, and thus especially vulnerable on the Aryan side. The following is a characteristic anecdote, from a Jewish woman, A.P., who had stayed outside the ghetto.

One evening I was returning home from my work in the city later than normal. In order to get home I had to cross a large bridge as we were living on the east bank of the Vistula river, which parted us from the city. I was in the middle of the bridge which was quite empty at this late hour according to the imposed curfew. Only a lonely SS patrolman was walking slowly on the other side of the bridge.

Suddenly a tiny shadow nearing the SS man emerged from the opposite direction. The shadow grew bigger and bigger and I could recognize in this little pathetic figure a small boy walking towards the SS man. I could only guess that this was a Jewish boy. He was around ten years old, very thin and dark haired. [...] No child living in the Polish district would be allowed out on the street at this hour. This boy in his hunt after some bread was probably delayed in returning home [...] This boy on the bridge, he was a brave one, he dared to go out of the ghetto to bring some food maybe for his sick parents or small brothers or sisters. They waited in vain.

The little boy was now nearer the SS man, who suddenly without uttering a word, without asking the boy any questions, seized him by the collar and threw him into the dark and turbulent waters of the Vistula. The boy did not even have time to utter a sound.[39]

A similar story is told by another Jewish woman who was living on the Aryan side:

At the corner of Jerusalem Avenue and Krucza Street, a Jewish child sat, a little skeleton, four or five years old, as in India. People wouldn't give him money, but would put a bun in his hand. An elegant German came by, opened a sewer-grating, took the child, and threw him into the sewer. I can't forget this picture.[40]

If the Germans could recognize these children as Jews, then Polish policemen or *szmalcowniks*, with their greater sensitivity to the nuances that distinguished Poles from Polish Jews, could certainly do so.

Despite these risks – not to mention the risk of crossing and re-crossing the wall – the child smugglers continued their activity in order to support their families. When they no longer had a connection with the ghetto – after their families had died or been killed – they often stayed on the Aryan side for good.

If the poor were forced into desperate measures, the relatively affluent Jews who did escape later on could survive in the ghetto by selling off personal possessions or managing some source of income in order to pay for food at black-market prices. Only relatively marginal dangers such as typhus or deportation to a labour camp remained, and there were greater risks on the Aryan side. Escape from the ghetto in any case solved nothing, only adding the problems of an illegal exist-ence to all the other difficulties that Jews faced. Even in purely economic terms, life was by no means easier outside the ghetto than within it. Food prices might have been lower on the Aryan side, but fugitives characteristically had to pay exorbitantly high rents and pay off the *szmalcowniks*, and their prospects of earning money were uncertain. Therefore, even in hindsight, the rational course of action for most Jews before 22 July 1942 was to try to stay alive in the ghetto rather than risk life on the outside.

2 Escape during the Main Ghetto Period

Those few Jews who nevertheless did escape during this period had certain characteristics in common. First of all, nearly all those who escaped lived 'on the surface'; life 'under the surface' could be contemplated only by Jews with very good Polish friends who were prepared to provide all material needs, as well as a hiding place, without charge. Under any other circumstances, life in confinement was depressing, expensive and dangerous. Even in the best case, it was impossible to earn a living, or to help relatives left behind in the ghetto, while living 'under the surface'. Therefore, nearly all of those who escaped during this period had what the ghetto believed to be the essential prerequisites for life 'on the surface' – 'good looks' and good Polish. Whether these characteristics were actually essential for survival will be considered in the next chapter; for now it is enough to note that this was the general belief. A second common characteristic was some form of pre-existing contact with the Aryan side, either through illegal trade or through Polish friends who had stayed in touch. Those who escaped had therefore either some experience in moving about freely on the Aryan side, or friends upon whom they could rely. A third characteristic was that nearly all those who escaped during the main ghetto period faced some personal crisis which, they felt, made survival in the ghetto impossible.

Not all of these factors were present in all cases: for example, a few Jews escaped from the ghetto without having any contacts on the Aryan side. Diana Kagan, who left shortly after the ghetto was closed, seems to have been quite self-sufficient at first, although she mentions a number of Polish helpers later on. She moved to Mińsk Mazowiecki, forty kilometres from Warsaw, where she lived on 'Aryan papers' and supported herself as a municipal worker. Thirteen-year-old Szlama Rotter and his younger brother smuggled to support their father, who died of hunger, however, after both boys fell ill with typhus. Having no way to support themselves within the ghetto, they then escaped to the Aryan side and lived in attics, begging food during the day. Subsequently they left Warsaw for the countryside, where Szlama survived by going from village to village doing odd jobs. He became separated from his brother and does not know what happened to him.[41]

In most respects, even the Rotters conform to the usual pattern: they had 'good looks' (as Szlama puts it, 'We didn't have a Jewish physiognomy'), enough knowledge of Polish Catholic customs to be able to recite Catholic prayers on demand, and Szlama had good enough Polish to be able to live with a Polish peasant for a year apparently without being suspected. They faced a crisis, precipitated by the death of their father. Although they lacked personal contacts on the Aryan side, they were used to being there. The need for identity documents was normally an obstacle to such self-reliant escape, but as children the Rotters were not required to carry them. Probably for this reason, children such as the celebrated 'Cigarette-Sellers of Three Crosses Square'[42] would eventually constitute a sizeable proportion of those who simply fled and lived by their wits.

3 Ominous Signs: The Spring and Summer of 1942

By mid-1942, the Jews of Warsaw had been hearing reports of massacres and liquidations of ghettos for nearly a year and had, of course, been apprehensive about their fate from the moment of the German invasion of Poland. Chaim Kaplan wrote on the first day of the war: 'Wherever Hitler's foot treads, there is no hope for the Jewish people. Hitler, may his name be blotted out, threatened in one of his speeches that if war comes the Jews of Europe will be exterminated.'[43] Concrete reports of massacres had been arriving in the ghetto for many months before the liquidation action began. An echo of the *Einsatzgruppen* massacres is found in Kaplan's diary on 2 February 1942:

> It is reported that the Führer has decided to rid Europe of our whole people by simply having them shot to death. [...] You just take thousands of people to the outskirts of a city and shoot to kill; [...] The reports are bloodcurdling: In Vilna 40,000 Jews were shot to death.[44]

Kaplan, moreover, had reason to believe that these were not isolated incidents but part of a larger plan:

> The day before yesterday we read the speech the Führer delivered celebrating January 30, 1933, when he boasted that his prophecy was beginning to come true. Had he not stated that if war erupted in Europe, the Jewish race would be annihilated? This process has begun and will continue until the end is achieved.[45]

In the same month, Jacob Grojanowski had escaped from the death camp in Chełmno, reached Warsaw and reported in detail on the camp's operations.[46] Rumours of an expulsion from Warsaw had also been circulating for months: for example, on 2 November 1941 Kaplan expressed the fear that Hans Frank's recent visit to Warsaw portended the expulsion of the Jews.[47] On 2 February 1942 he added: 'Heretofore we were afraid of expulsion. Now we are afraid of death.'

When the Final Solution began in earnest, in the spring of 1942, reports of the destruction of Jewish communities began to trickle in. On 22 March Kaplan mentions the liquidation of the Jewish communities of Lublin and Równo, and on the following day reports that Jews are being deported from Lvov at the rate of 1,100 daily.[48] On 26 March, Abraham Lewin noted that the Jewish communities in Wąwolnica, Słonim, Nowogródek and Izbica had been destroyed.[49] A report in the Oneg Shabbat archive, dated 5 May, lists details of the liquidation of Jewish communities of Wąwolnica (22 March), Mielnik (23 March), Rejowiec (7 April) and Dubienka on the Bug (13 April).[50]

But the information received in Warsaw was mixed, and however obvious the pattern of events might appear in hindsight, it was not so obvious at the time. Some of the rumours that reached Warsaw were untrue: Kaplan reports as a 'definitely established fact' that the ghetto in Łódź had been liquidated, but for 'a meager remnant'.[51] It was said that German Jews being relocated in Warsaw (another aspect of the Final Solution) would be allowed to settle in the Aryan quarter, and that the Warsaw ghetto would be cleared to make way for German civilians whose homes had been bombed out.[52] When stories were broadly true, they were often ambiguous or mistaken on points of detail. The Oneg Shabbat report of 5 May states that the Jews of Wąwolnica had been sent 'to an unknown destination' (in quotation marks in the original), while in Rejowiec 200 Jews had been massacred and the rest 'driven in the direction of Bełżec'; but there is no indication that the significance of this destination was understood.[53] Those who tried to hide were said to have been sent to a labour camp in Krochowice; others were supposedly taken to Chełm and released. The population of Mielnik was said to have been destined for 'immediate resettlement in the eastern regions of the General Government', and the detail was added that they had been relocated to 'Dubienka on the Bug, as well as to other localities in that region'. And these reports, qualified as they are, are mixed with less dramatic stories about the Jewish communities of Szczebrzeszyn, Międzyrzec Podlaski, Grodzisko and several others. Resettlement actions of various kinds, directed against Poles as well as Jews, were in any case old news: they had been taking place sporadically since the occupation began, especially in the territories incorporated into the Reich and in the Lublin region.

Until now, furthermore, German actions, though barbaric, had at least had some comprehensible motive behind them: to concentrate the Jewish population in the larger centres, the better to control them and exploit their labour; to clear certain areas for colonization; to prevent the spread of infectious diseases supposedly carried by the Jews; to remove unproductive elements. The harsh, uncompromising utilitarianism of the Nazis, together with their antisemitic prejudices, seemed to account for such actions, which were in any case not yet aimed at total extermination. In Vilna, 40,000 had been killed, but 10,000 had survived to be confined in a ghetto. Jewish leaders in Łódź, the second-largest ghetto, were proud of their achievement in putting the ghetto to work: by making the ghetto useful to the war effort, they believed, they had insured it against destruction. Moreover, they seemed to be right: after a wave of deportations in the spring, directed against the ghetto's social margins, things seemed to have settled down, and on 1 July there were still more than 100,000 Jews in the Łódź ghetto (the bulk of them would survive another two years until their ghetto was finally liquidated in July 1944).[54] As to Warsaw itself, deportations had not yet reached the city, and the optimists believed that they never would. The Germans might move with impunity against remote provincial towns, they argued, but would never dare destroy the largest and most prominent Jewish community in Europe.

It was therefore difficult for the Jews of the ghetto – even those as well informed as the Oneg Shabbat circle – to form a complete picture of the unfolding events or to assess them accurately. Kaplan, in a calmer moment, wrote: 'I must confess it was careless of me to put on paper rumours which were born of certain moods and were not based on solid facts.'[55] And it was also difficult to work out the reasons for the deportations. There was little alternative, in the end, to believing that the Germans were behaving rationally, and the 'work to live' strategy of the Jewish leadership in Łódź was in practice adopted by all the other Jewish Councils as well. Most of the ghetto's inhabitants followed same reasoning, and struggled, not to escape, but to have themselves counted among the productive rather than the unproductive.

The First Liquidation Action, 22 July–12 September 1942

> The date when the 'resettlement action began', 22 July 1942, marks the beginning of mass Jewish crossing to the Aryan side.
>
> Emmanuel Ringelblum[56]

On 22 July 1942 the Warsaw *Judenrat* was informed that 'all Jewish persons living in Warsaw, regardless of age and sex, will be resettled in the East'. The deportees were to take food for three days and 15 kilograms of personal baggage, including (pointedly) 'all valuables such as gold, jewellery, money, etc.'. Exemptions were granted to *Judenrat* members and employees, the ghetto police, hospital staff and patients, people in German employment or fit to work, and their wives and children.[57]

This was the opening blow of what is variously called the first *Aktion*, the *Grossaktion* or the Great Deportation of the Jews from Warsaw. It was part of Operation Reinhard, the German plan to destroy the entire Jewish population of the General Government, but by degrees, so as to soften the blow to German war production and economic interests. Himmler's order of 19 July to Friedrich-Wilhelm Krüger, Higher SS and Police leader for the General Government, specified that 'from December 31, 1942, no persons of Jewish origin may remain within the [General Government], unless they are in the collection camps in Warsaw, Kraków, Częstochowa, Radom and Lublin'.[58] All work requiring Jewish labour was to be concentrated in these 'collection camps'. The Warsaw ghetto was in effect to be converted into a work camp, and all 'unproductive elements' were to be taken to the death camp of Treblinka and gassed. In Warsaw the operation started on the day that the Treblinka camp was completed and ended, after 270,000 Jews had been killed, on 12 September, Rosh Hashanah. In January 1943, Himmler then ordered the remnant of the ghetto to be transferred to labour camps in the Lublin area (Majdanek, Trawniki, Poniatowa and others), making Warsaw *judenrein*. This was carried out in two stages: the second *Aktion* of January 1943, in which 6,000 Jews were transferred or killed, and the third *Aktion* in April, which was interrupted but not stopped by the ghetto revolt. Finally, all Jews in the Lublin labour camps were murdered in the 'Harvest Festival' of 3 November 1943.

All of this was, of course, unknown to the Jews on 22 July. Kaplan's interpretation of the deportation order is probably characteristic: despite his earlier speculations, he now speaks merely of 'a whole community of 400,000 people condemned to exile'.[59] The next day, he writes that 'in comparison with the Lublin expulsion we have before us a liberal document',[60] noting the various classes of exemption. It took some time for the ghetto to work out that 'resettlement in the east' actually meant transportation to a death camp, and longer still for the implication to sink in that the liquidation of the entire ghetto was intended.

Accurate information may have been available fairly quickly. According to Bundist sources, the Bund courier Zalman Friedrich left the ghetto on 23 July to see where the trains were going. Their destination, he learned from Polish railwaymen, was a camp near Treblinka station that was obviously too small to accommodate the thousands of people being taken there each day. He also learned that no food was being delivered to the camp, that the trains returned empty and that civilians were not allowed to enter the station. Subsequently, he met two escapees from the camp who described just what was going on. The Bund activist Jacob Celemenski maintains that Friedrich returned with this information on the 27th, and that it was published in the Bund newspaper *Shturm* on the following day.[61] (According to Israel Gutman, however, Friedrich left the ghetto 'at the beginning of August' and the article appeared in another Bundist newspaper, *Oyf der Vakh*, only on 20 September. But not all of the ghetto's underground press has been preserved.)[62]

Even if Celemenski's account is correct, the story did not circulate widely, or perhaps was simply disbelieved. Chaim Kaplan wrote on 1 August, four days before he himself was taken: 'We have no information about the fate of those who have been expelled. When one falls into the hands of the Nazis he falls into the abyss.'[63] Lewin refers to 'Treblinka (the place of execution?)' on 6 August, his source of information apparently being an official of the *Judenrat*.[64] Not until 9 August does he write that 'it is clear to us that 99 percent of those transported are being taken to their deaths'. On 11 August:

[Hirsch] Smolar [...] was told that those deported, or if they are deported, to Tr., are going to their 'death'. [...] In Warsaw there is a Jew by the name of Slawa who has brought reports of Treblinka. Fifteen kilometres before the station at Treblinka the Germans take over the train. When people get out of the train they are beaten viciously. Then they are driven into huge barracks. For five minutes heart-rending screams are heard, then silence. The bodies that are taken out are swollen horribly.[65]

However, again these stories had the character of rumours – Lewin's description contains a number of inaccuracies – and were not always believed. There were other rumours as well. On 16 August Lewin wrote: 'Rumours have reached me again that letters have allegedly arrived from the deportees saying they are working in the area of Siedlce and conditions are not bad.'[66] In fact, it seems that some letters and postcards were received: Gutman speculates that some had been sent by Jews who had managed to escape from the trains, while Jews arriving at Treblinka had been forced to write others to dictation.[67] These shreds of evidence were enough: wishful thinking did the rest.

But it was not only wishful thinking that impeded the spread of information: many Jews were simply too preoccupied with their own daily struggle for survival to pay much attention to such questions. It took still longer to work out that the various classes of exemption were illusory, an exercise in divide-and-rule: one supposedly exempted group after another lost its privileged status in the course of the *Aktion*. In the end even the bulk of the ghetto police, who had been forced to carry out the 'resettlement' under the threat that they and their families would meet the same fate, were packed off, with the rest, in a special shipment on 21 September (Yom Kippur).

The illusion created by the exemptions was a powerful one. For example, Adam Starkopf formed a plan to leave the ghetto with his wife and child early during the *Aktion*; but

[w]hen I revealed this plan to my father and to Pela's parents, they were horrified. It was insane, they said, to take such chances with Pela and the baby. They begged our neighbours and friends to talk us out of our madness. One of my neighbours tried to impress upon me that instead of exposing my family to the perils of the unknown I should concentrate on obtaining a legitimate work permit [...]. Once I had a job [in a German factory] I could be certain that the Germans would not deport me and my family, and I would not be risking the lives of my wife and child.[68]

A lucrative trade developed in work certificates (*Ausweise*), and, since the wives of exempt men were also exempt, a wave of fictitious marriages took place. Crude hideouts began to be built, in which Jews hoped to evade the round-ups. And for the first time there is evidence, not only from Starkopf but from many other diaries and memoirs as well, that among all these alternatives the idea of escaping from the ghetto was also beginning to occur to people on a broader scale.

The barriers to escape were formidable, however. The deportation action had been carefully prepared, as we have seen, and paths out of the ghetto had been systematically blocked off. An anonymous child smuggler writes that '[d]uring the action it was impossible to cross, because the walls were solidly guarded by Ukrainians and Latvians', and that 'the German and Polish police organized raids on the Aryan side and caught a lot of our friends'.[69] Two German gendarmes were now posted at each of the ghetto gates, so that each 'friendly' policeman was accompanied by another whose attitude could only be guessed at. Smuggling ceased on the day the deportation started, not only because it was harder than ever to leave the ghetto, but because the smugglers, like everyone else, were preoccupied with evading capture. The price of food therefore rose astronomically – on 27 July Kaplan reported a price of 60 zł for a loaf of bread,[70] seven times higher than on the Aryan side, five times higher than a few days earlier in the ghetto – and the ghetto economy was disrupted, leaving only those who worked for one of the German 'shops', and thus had a valid *Ausweis*, with any means of earning a living or any legal security. Those who had not gone hungry hitherto now faced starvation, or a struggle for food even more formidable than the one they had waged over the past two years. This, together with the scramble to evade the round-ups and anxieties over relatives who had been captured, was what principally occupied their time and energies.

Escape during the Great Aktion

Despite these difficulties, a few thousand Jews did manage to get away during the *Aktion*. One group that had little trouble leaving the ghetto for good was the small band of child smugglers who were orphaned by the *Aktion*. Like the children who had escaped earlier, they no longer had strong ties to the ghetto, were practised at getting in and out, and were used to moving about freely on the Aryan side. They also knew each other, and were able to form mutually supporting circles. They survived on the Aryan side by begging or petty trade and sleeping rough.[71] The best-known account of these children's lives is Joseph Ziemian's memoir, *The Cigarette-Sellers of Three Crosses Square*.[72]

For adults, leaving the ghetto was more complicated. Jews who wanted to live 'on the surface' needed to have false identity documents; if they planned to live in hiding, they needed a suitable *melina* on the Aryan side. Either way, they needed to have a friend and protector outside the ghetto, either a friendly Pole or a Jew already established there, who could make the necessary arrangements. Jews were generally reluctant to leave without their families, whereas it was especially difficult to make arrangements for larger groups. Forced to choose single individuals, families would often send out adult children, if they had 'good looks' and Polish contacts, with the idea that after they had established themselves they would bring the rest of the family out. Younger children were often sent ahead. As one remembered: 'In July or August 1942 my sister and I went out to the Aryan side to Poles on Krochmalna (for money). By degrees the whole family moved there (this took a week).'[73] Parents who felt unable to leave the ghetto sent their children to be looked after by Polish families, usually after making large advance payments. In some cases, the Polish families involved later sent such children back to the ghetto, either because they looked 'too Jewish' and were hence felt to pose too much risk, or because the parents had been deported and could no longer pay. To encourage this trend (and because the ghetto's existing orphanages had been emptied in the course of the *Aktion*), the Germans set up a special showcase orphanage in Dzika Street which accumulated some 200 children, many of whom had been returned from the Aryan side. The children were given decent clothing and extra rations, and were placed in the care of Jewish staff who tended them with sympathetic care. The Dzika Street orphanage was then liquidated, children and staff alike, during the second *Aktion* in January.[74]

The role in organizing escape played by the 'bridging community' of converts and Poles in mixed marriages is illustrated by the testimony of Dr Jan Kuciński:

When [. . .] the German authorities announced the so-called 'resettlement' of the Jewish population to the east, I realized perfectly well what this smelled of. [. . .] I quickly began looking around for a means of getting out of the ghetto. Since I had very little money, the matter looked less than jolly for me. But [. . .] by chance, I learnt that in one of the German factories on the territory of the ghetto [. . .] a Pole named Mr Kauczyński was employed in a management position. He was the elder brother of a [school] friend of mine [. . .]. Later this Kauczyński [. . .] had married a Jewish woman [. . .] and settled in Łódź. Now, suddenly, he had shown up in the ghetto. I went to him and, mentioning our pre-war acquaintance, asked for help. He immediately expressed willingness to help me, but there was a problem with my child. He advised me to get the child out through the courts and he would simply add me to the work brigade leaving the ghetto daily for the Aryan side, and there I'd be able to get away. And that's what I did. At the end of July, my son was taken in by the Aryan wife of Kazimierz Grossman, the director of the firm where I worked before the war [. . .] and I left on 2 September.[75]

As this example shows, Jews wanting to escape could sometimes rely on quite remote and indirect connections with the convert community, though everything of course depended on the decency and courage of those who were approached.

Dr Kuciński, as it happened, could meet face to face with the man who helped him, but this was an exceptional case. Arrangements were usually made by

telephone, which, strangely, remained in operation even during the Ghetto
Uprising. Was this an oversight? Or was it felt that telephone contact was
convenient for the Germans themselves? Were there practical difficulties, or
obstruction by Polish telephone workers? Or did the Germans simply not care what
the people in the ghetto got up to, since they were doomed anyway? Whatever the
reason, though the number of telephones was severely reduced, they were still
available at key points. In addition, there were experts in the ghetto who could
hook up telephones illegally even in private homes and underground bunkers.[76]

The psychological barriers to escape diminished as the *Aktion* proceeded. One
by one, the illusions and false hopes fell away and more and more Jews, finding
themselves alone, no longer had family ties to keep them in the ghetto or compli-
cate the problem of leaving. Practical barriers, too, were overcome. As the number
of Jews already established on the Aryan side increased, those who had escaped
could often make arrangements for others, and the techniques and channels of
escape became perfected with time. Thus the number of escapes increased steadily
towards the end of the first *Aktion*, even as the ghetto population dwindled.

The 'Shops' Period

> We are the tiny remnant of the greatest Jewish community in the world.
> Diary of Abraham Lewin, 11 September 1942[77]

The first *Aktion* not only resulted in the destruction of most of the population of
the ghetto, but also wrought a fundamental change in the structure and function
of the ghetto, once more altering the nature of the problem confronting the Jews,
requiring new adaptations and affecting both the prospects and the means of
escape. What had been a relatively autonomous community with its own government was now a shrunken remnant, the *Restghetto*, divided into a set of mutually
isolated labour camps. These served privately owned German workshops (called
'shops' in the ghetto jargon, using the English word) and were controlled by the
SS. Geographically, the *Restghetto* was divided into a small northern section, called
the Central Ghetto, and the much larger area that had been depopulated by the
Aktion, called the 'wild ghetto', within which several of the shops formed enclaves.
The 'wild ghetto' was also the area of operations of the *Werterfassung*, whose task
was to salvage the property of the deported Jews for the Reich and to rehabilitate
their homes for occupation by Aryans. Jews were confined to the territories of the
individual 'shops', each in principle a housing block or a set of contiguous housing blocks, in which Jews lived and worked. They were forbidden to appear in the
streets except in work parties under guard. Administratively, the *Restghetto* came
under the control of the *Judenreferat* of the Warsaw Gestapo, headed by the very
junior *Untersturmführer-SS* (Sublieutenant) Karl Brandt; but the real power in the

ghetto was the Project Reinhard team (*Einsatzstab Reinhard*), whose task was not the management of the ghetto but its liquidation. After its chairman, Adam Czerniaków, committed suicide on the second day of the *Aktion,* the Jewish Council became a powerless rump. Most of its various agencies and departments were dissolved, the Order Service was reduced to 300 men, and police functions passed to the *Werkschutz* (Works Police), consisting mainly of former members of the Order Service but employed by the shop owners.

Apart from the remnant of the Jewish Council and Order Service, only those employed in the shops, by the *Werterfassung,* or in the *placówki* were supposed to remain in the ghetto: these were the 35,000 or so Jews who had been registered and received 'numbers for life' in the final stage of the *Aktion,* the so-called 'cauldron' (*kocioł*) of 6–12 September. But in addition there were a large number of 'illegals', or 'wild' Jews, who had managed to evade the deportation and lived in hiding within the ghetto. Their number has been estimated as 20,000–25,000, from which it would follow that 55,000–60,000 Jews remained in the *Restghetto* all told.[78] Since we now know that the number of people who escaped from the ghetto during the 'shops' period must have been considerably greater than previously thought, it may be necessary to revise this estimate upwards.

Adaptation to these new conditions included ways of getting about, despite the prohibitions on movement and the barbed-wire boundaries between the 'shops'. Gradually, the *Restghetto* developed a veritable rabbit's warren of underground passages. Holes were knocked in the cellar walls of adjacent buildings, tunnels were dug under streets, and ultimately it became possible to travel considerable distances within the *Restghetto* without coming to the surface.

The black-market economy continued to exist – without it, the 'wild' Jews could not have survived – but in a different form. Its engine now was *szaber,* aptly described by Abraham Lewin as 'looting from the looters';[79] that is to say, *Werterfassung* workers would 'steal' Jewish property they were supposed to be reclaiming, smuggle it back to their housing blocks, and the *placówkarze* would then smuggle it out to the Aryan side and sell it (at preposterously low prices, as Lewin noted). The proceeds were used to buy food on the Aryan side, which the *placówkarze* smuggled back into the ghetto.[80]

Leaving the ghetto during the 'shops' period was accomplished almost entirely through the *placówki:* usually Jews attached themselves to Jewish work groups leaving the ghetto for work in the morning, but sometimes also to Polish work groups as they returned to the Aryan side in the evening. The general procedure was much the same as before, except that it might first be necessary to traverse the ghetto illegally to reach the work group's assembly point. People did this either through the underground passages, or by attaching themselves to work groups moving about within the ghetto, or with the help of the *Werkschutz.* As before, arrangements had to be made and bribes paid; the trade in *szaber* largely paid for it all.

Besides the *placówki*, a new method of escape was developed during this period. Once the *Aktion* was finished, certain categories of pass were restored, allowing some Jews to leave the ghetto, but a new regulation required them to be accompanied by an Aryan *Begleiter* (companion).[81] *Begleiters* could readily be bribed, providing Germans with an easy source of income and Jews with an easy way of leaving the ghetto: Chaskielewicz even says that his parents were escorted out of the ghetto by a member of the *Einsatzstab Reinhard*, who was very polite and wished them good luck.[82] Escapes that were not accomplished through *placówki* or *Begleiters* were managed during this period by scaling the wall, or by bribing a guard and walking out through one of the gates. This last method was the riskiest, however, as the gates were beset by whole armies of *szmalcowniks*. Leaving through tunnels and sewers was still uncommon, and the courts, trams and *mety* were no longer available.

The introduction of the regulation concerning *Begleiters*, without considering the uses to which it could be put or placing any controls on it, was symptomatic of the chaotic nature of the German administration during the 'shops' period. That so junior a man as Brandt was placed in control of the ghetto shows how little the SS were now concerned either with the economic production of the *Restghetto* or its internal affairs. Brandt was no match for the resourcefulness and ingenuity of the Warsaw Jews, and it proved quite easy to bamboozle him in various ways. Considerable numbers of Jews were shot for appearing in the streets illegally,[83] but no real effort was made to root out the 'wild' Jews, and the underground communications network seems never to have come to his attention. Indeed, Brandt agreed to let air-raid shelters (!) be built within the ghetto, allowing cement and other supplies to be brought in for this purpose. That despite the tighter controls the underground trade continued to flourish, and Jews now managed to escape in droves, was in great part thanks to Brandt's incompetence (or was it perhaps sabotage?). But for the same reason, seemingly realistic alternatives to escape also presented themselves.

Alternatives to Escape: 'Bunkers' within the Ghetto

The 'air-raid shelters' that Brandt allowed to be built were actually thousands of bunkers, many connected by the network of underground passages, in which Jews hoped to be able to hide out until liberation. Rudimentary shelters or bunkers had existed since the first days of the ghetto, when they were used mainly to hide valuables and trade-goods from German 'requisitions'. The number and variety of shelters had multiplied during the first *Aktion*, when people had used them to evade capture. When the *Aktion* was over, construction efforts were redoubled. On 24 December 1942 Ringelblum wrote:

a new series of hiding places began [to be built] after the selection [of 6–12 September], when ghetto life had settled down somewhat. [...] But these are entirely different places from those built in the summer, during the action. First of all, they had to be adapted to winter conditions. Secondly, they were furnished so as to make it possible to survive in them for several months. The idea behind these hiding places was as follows: if they will liquidate all the Jews of Warsaw, then we will go down into the shelters and stay there until liberation.[84]

By the time the Ghetto Uprising broke out the following April, the network of shelters and underground passageways was so extensive that the entire population of the ghetto could disappear into it. Although the hope of surviving until liberation was too optimistic, this underground city proved to be a formidable redoubt, in which the ghetto fighters were able to hold out for nearly a month. Its construction, in only seven months, must be rated as one of the most extraordinary coups of the Second World War.

Those historians who have stressed the ghetto's preparations for armed resistance during this period have sometimes characterized the construction of bunkers as part of these preparations.[85] In fact, as we can see from Ringelblum's contemporary testimony, the underlying intention was evasion rather than resistance: the chief alternative to the construction of bunkers in the ghetto was escape to the Aryan side. The whole of the contemporary record attests to the fact that most of the ghetto's Jews at that time vacillated between these two alternatives, with only a small minority of mainly young people thinking about armed resistance. As the ghetto fighter Simcha Rotem put it candidly: 'Our environment wasn't very encouraging. The relatively few Jews left in the ghetto were generally not enthusiastic about our operations. Thus the ŻOB was in a double underground, hiding from the Germans and from most of the Jews as well.'[86] The choice between the two forms of evasion was by no means clear-cut, and contemporary observers differed widely in their assessments. Stefan Ernest wrote:

> There is a dilemma: here or there? Should we build shelters here, hiding-places with supplies to last for weeks, or should we go over the wall? It is an insoluble problem. There, on the other side of the wall, you need money – either money or friends. On that side, one false step, one piece of blackmail, can overturn all the careful planning for hiding for weeks or months. Not to mention more dramatic circumstances. And to leave aside a whole mass of unbelievable difficulties connected with 'getting settled'.[87]

Despite these difficulties, he added, '[t]he few telephones in the ghetto are constantly besieged; whoever can, whoever has a chance, crosses. Going out beyond the walls is becoming a mass phenomenon and is increasing every day.' But he still felt that 'in comparison with the general numbers, these are only individual cases. Others [...], and they are naturally the overwhelming majority, [...] dig in where they are: shelters, hiding places, hideouts. Those who passively await a miracle or death are in the minority.'[88] Weighing in the balance, on the other hand, were a great number of technical difficulties in building and concealing bunkers within the ghetto, which are described at length by Ringelblum.[89] Taking these difficulties into account, the Bund activist Adina Blady-Szwajger believed that most decided in favour of escape: 'Those who had friends on the Aryan side, or who had a lot of money, looked for a way of getting out of the ghetto; others built themselves hideouts in cellars [...]. But there were very few of these; the majority thought about hiding on the Aryan side.'[90]

Compromise solutions were also sought:

> people make arrangements ahead of time with a Christian who, while the Jews are hiding, is supposed to supply them with everything they need. In some 'shops' hiding places are built so that they have an underground connection with the Aryan side. That is possible only in 'shops' bordering on the Aryan side. To that end, they build underground tunnels leading to a Christian's cellar on the Aryan side.[91]

The parents of Noemi Szac-Wajnkranc had another idea in mind when they hid in a bunker during the 'cauldron': 'if they add our street to the Aryan district, we'll come out and make do somehow'.[92]

Flight to the Aryan side, formerly (as we have seen) regarded as a kind of betrayal, now became not only respectable but was even seen as a form of active resistance:

> Everyone I talk to says the same thing: 'We shouldn't have allowed the deportation to happen. We should have gone out into the street, set fire to everything, blown up the walls and fled to the other side. The Germans would have taken their revenge. It would have cost tens of thousands of victims, but not 300,000. And now we are ashamed, for ourselves and in front of the whole world, that our policy of compliance has proved worthless.[93]

Thus the ghetto did not necessarily see hard-and-fast distinctions between resistance and evasion, honour and survival; nor were people generally 'paralysed', as Hilberg would have it; but they mulled over practicalities and tactical considerations, and tried to decide between the available alternatives, as people generally do.

Contemporary Perceptions of Escape

We have observed, on the basis of memoir evidence, that most escapes from the ghetto took place during the 'shops' period, and that a considerable proportion of the remaining ghetto population – nearly a quarter – succeeded in escaping. Such a large exodus naturally found an echo in contemporary accounts. We have already seen that Ernest and Blady-Szwajger were impressed by the magnitude of the phenomenon, though they differ in their overall assessment. Here are Abraham Lewin's observations in October 1942:

> The Jews dream of escaping to the Aryan side, to the Poles, or to the 'East' in the area of Białystok. Each day someone leaves the shop secretly and gets out of the town. [...] Friends around me are having photographs made and are trying to negotiate papers of various kinds, *Kennkarten*, and are preparing to leave Warsaw. I, having no money, do not involve myself with these matters.[94]

This entry was made in the early part of the 'shops' period, when the number of escapes had in fact initially diminished somewhat.

As I have mentioned, our perceptions have hitherto been shaped by those of the ghetto fighters and other activists, who believed escape to be very difficult, if not impossible. Ringelblum, like Lewin, believed that it was possible only for the rich: 'Some – the wealthier ones – began going over to the other side',[95] or the corrupt: 'a hundred men from "number 13" [13 Leszno Street, headquarters of the 'profiteering' 'office for combatting usury and speculation', known in the ghetto as the 'Jewish Gestapo'], who caught people, are on the other side. Their headquarters are on Litewska, Szternfeld is their chief.'[96] He took a negative view of prospects on the Aryan side:

> The Poles have been reminded of the regulation prescribing the death penalty for helping Jews. Very weak activity of progressive organizations. So far [only] for individuals. [...] Bands of *szmalcowniks* hold court outside the wall. [...] The Polish intelligentsia quake with fear and do not want to take in their Jewish friends; an exception is the idealistic element. From the start of the deportation to the end of October 150 Jews have been caught on the other side.[97]

And: 'Divide and conquer. They have poisoned relations between Jews and Poles and have made all help from the other side impossible.'[98] Despite all that, he added that 'it was estimated that over a period of several months, hundreds of people left the ghetto daily by means of the work posts'[99] – an estimate that indeed seems considerably exaggerated. If, as proposed in Table 2.1, about 10,000 people escaped in the seven months between 12 September 1942 and 18 April 1943, then the average daily number of escapes was only forty-six, rather than 'hundreds'; and even in the most active period, the ninety days between 18 January and 18 April, the 7,500 escapes still amounted to only eighty-three people daily. Put another way, one or two people slipping away from each *placówka* on each of its forays to the 'other side' would both fit with contemporary reports and easily account for escape on the scale observed.

Ringelblum's view therefore was inconsistent: according to his numerical estimate, a very large number of Jews were escaping, yet he maintains that escape was difficult and almost impossible, only for the favoured few. Had he lived to polish and refine his work, he would no doubt have reconciled these inconsistencies.[100]

We can see, then, that contemporary observers had some inkling of the magnitude of what was going on, but because it took the form of a trickle over a period of months rather than a sudden flood, it was difficult to appreciate its true dimensions. The belief that escape was limited to the rich and those with good connections was entirely rational, but it was the product of *a priori* reasoning and not observation. The reality was that many, perhaps most, of the surviving Jews had enough direct or indirect connections with the Polish side, that in time they might have been able to find their way safely out of the ghetto. During this final period, the belief that escape was nearly impossible was in many cases a bigger obstacle than any reality to which it may have corresponded.

German Responses to Escape

The Germans were of course aware that people were escaping, and took appropriate steps. The simplest of these were propaganda and persuasion. Eugenia Szajn-Lewin writes:

> The resettlement staff has its spies. They know that Jews are escaping and hiding among the Poles. Brand[t], head of the [...] *Vernichtungskommando*, makes a speech: the Jews are to work, workers will stay where they are, and those who hide on the Aryan side will be betrayed by Poles in any case.
>
> There's a good deal of truth in this. On the Aryan side there are specially organized groups of agents, who are helped by the Polish 'Blue' police. Jews are starting to come back from the Aryan side. There is no way to make it over there; people lack money to pay off the blackmailers.[101]

Jews caught outside the ghetto were offered an 'amnesty': on 1 November a decree announced the establishment of six ghettos in the Warsaw District and gave Jews in hiding until 1 December to report to one of them. While this 'amnesty' was in force, Jews who were caught were returned to the ghetto instead of being killed. At first they were kept at Żelazna 103, the offices of the *Werterfassung*. When this facility proved inadequate, they were moved to the Gęsia Street prison. Those who were not put to work in the *Werterfassung* were then transported to the Lublin-area work camps in January and eventually killed there.

Escape during the 'Shops' Period: Case Studies

Ringelblum writes that the standard bribe to the foreman of a *placówka* was only 50–100 zł: roughly, in today's money, $7–15. But money was needed for all sorts of other things as well: 'You had to pay to go with them, and it was very expensive. The foreman ... had to bribe the gendarmes at the gate, who would then miscount those leaving, and, of course, he wanted something for himself as well.'[102] These expenses were only the beginning, as many memoirists attest. Ringelblum's conclusion that escape was only for the rich therefore seems well founded; but then how was it possible for so many people to escape?

Noemi Szac-Wajnkranc and her husband began to think about escaping during the 'cauldron'. After her husband had had to rescue her twice from the *Umschlagplatz* (by bribing policemen), he arranged for her to leave with a *placówka*: 'For a few hundred złotys the group's director takes a few non-workers who want to cross the "border".'[103] She wore several changes of clothes, a common expedient, and some items of jewellery that she intended to sell to support herself. But no arrangements had been made on the other side. Once at the workplace, a luggage factory, Szac-Wajnkranc began telephoning friends, but everyone was afraid to talk to her. She became depressed, contrasting her situation with that of her fellow-workers: 'There are people here who come every day, waiting for acquaintances who are supposed to come for them, take them to a pre-arranged dwelling, deliver documents to them; some have already spent huge sums on this. No, I think to myself, I'll never manage.'[104]

Nevertheless she managed to make contact with Alina K., a Polish woman to whom Szac-Wajnkranc and her husband had signed over their factory to save it from expropriation by the Nazis. K. had maintained contact with them for a time in the ghetto; subsequently the factory's equipment had been 'requisitioned' by the Germans – or perhaps, as Szac-Wajnkrantz suspects, appropriated by K. At any rate, at that point contact had been lost. K. was now disconcerted to hear from Szac-Wajnkrantz. She did not offer to take her in, but instead sent a Mr S. to see her. Szac-Wajnkranc 'naïvely' (in her words) told him everything – to his astonishment, as he had been told merely to appraise her jewellery and had no idea that she was Jewish. He offered to escort her to a friend's house and look into having documents made. In this haphazard way, Szac-Wajnkranc managed to establish herself on the Aryan side; her husband followed two days later, though we are not given details.

Eugenia Szajn-Lewin describes how two of her relatives escaped:

Józek and his wife [Anna] worked in an SS *placówka* on the Aryan side, in the old Soviet embassy. [...] They lived there, in barracks [...] from the first days of the action. They didn't experience the nightmare of the deportations. Their director, an SS man named Schmedke, cared about his people. He was strange, different from the other SS-men. During the 'cauldron' [...] he went there [i.e. to the part of the ghetto where the 'cauldron' action took place] to rescue the father and brother of one of his workers. [...] Schmedke turned a blind eye to their extra income. Anna, like the others, traded. She would come to the ghetto under the protection of a soldier, buy Jewish clothing practically for nothing, and sell it at a profit to Poles.

Just before 11 November [...] Schmedke declared that he would have to reduce the staff of the *placówka*. Anna and Józek were on the elimination list. Schmedke said he would personally escort them to the *Werterfassung*, [...] where they would get jobs. [...] But Józek, Anna and their friend Jadzia didn't believe him. [...] At nine o'clock in the morning, they jumped out of a high second-storey window straight into the arms of the astonished passers-by in Poznańska Street.[105]

Jadzia was a former dancer and had many friends, but each would put the group up for a single night only. Jadzia eventually found a more permanent place, but not before Józek had become discouraged and returned to the ghetto. Soon after, Anna and Jadzia were betrayed; the January *Aktion* got under way, and they were taken to the *Umschlagplatz*. There, Anna 'shouted and fought with the Germans' and was shot dead. Schmedke rescued Jadzia and led her back out to the Aryan side.

This example, first of all, documents an extraordinary case of an SS man who helped Jews, and without being bribed. This was not the only such case: for example, Elkana Ahlen writes of a Polish-speaking Silesian SS man named Karol Porchet who supervised a dentistry *placówka*, the *Zahnstation*, whom Ahlen describes as a 'regular guy' (*równy chłop*).[106] Second, it shows again that escape was possible without money, advance preparations, or good contacts on the Aryan side; but it also shows the risks of such a venture.

Examples like this could be multiplied, but one more will suffice:

An old friend from university days came up to me. [...] He gave me 200 złotys. He said: 'What are you sitting here for? Tomorrow morning at five o'clock, go to the corner of Żelazna Street and give these 200 zł to the German who guards the gate there. He'll either shoot you or let you through.' [...] I went. The German took the money and didn't even look around. [...]

I knew well where my friends lived. [...] But I was dazed. It's hard for me to describe my state at that moment. I remember walking along some overpass. [...] [S]ome man in a worker's outfit came up to me and asked if I'd escaped from the ghetto. I didn't know about *szmalcowniks* then, or perhaps it had slipped my mind. I said yes. To that he said: 'Then come with me, ma'am. After the war we'll need educated people.' [...] He lived in two rooms with his wife and two children. I lived with them for two weeks.[107]

These examples of unprepared escape raise the question of why more Jews did not simply 'give it a go' in a similar manner, once they realized that the alternative was almost certain death. Those with a great deal of money and good friends on the other side were no doubt better placed, but three of the five people just mentioned did survive, and they are by no means the only ones.

A matter that gave rise to much controversy, and continues to do so, was an offer by the Catholic church to hide Jewish children in convents. On 14 December 1942 Ringelblum commented as follows:

The priests want to rescue Jewish children. Certain circles have lately been discussing the matter of saving a certain number (several hundred) of Jewish children by placing them in convents in all corners of the country.

What has inclined the clergy to this? There are three contributing reasons. First of all: hunting little souls. The Catholic clergy have always taken advantage of difficult moments in the life of the Jews (pogroms, expulsions etc) to win over adults and children. The present moment no doubt plays the most important role, although the clergy give assurances that they have no intention of christening Jewish children whom they take into their institutions.

Second: a factor of a material nature. For every Jewish child it will be necessary to pay, for a year in advance, 600 zł a month. That's a fairly good transaction for the convents. Feeding them will be very cheap, since they have their own lands and estates. Parents of wealthy children will pay double, to pay for poor children whose parents are not in a position to cover this sum.

Third: the factor of prestige. The Polish clergy have so far done very little to rescue Jews from the slaughter, deportation. In connection with protests spreading throughout the world against the mass murder of the Polish Jews, the rescue of a few hundred Jews may serve to testify that they have done everything they could to rescue Jews, especially Jewish children.

I have taken part in a discussion among intellectuals on this subject. One said categorically that he was against it. Despite the fact that, in accordance with our wishes, children between ten and fourteen will be taken into the convents, they will after all come under the influence of the priests and will sooner or later accept baptism. [...] He felt that we should follow in the footsteps of our ancestors and die in the name of our faith. [...]

Others maintained: [...] a basic knowledge of our history teaches that not death in the name of our faith was the reality, but the opposite: marranism – pretended Christianity. The Jews always adapted themselves to the most difficult circumstances, always managed to survived the most difficult times. Taking a small number of Jews over [to the other side] will preserve the creators of a new generation of Jews. We must not take away the right to life of this new generation. [...]

[Still] others [...] agreed that one ought to proceed in this way, but without the approval of the representatives of Jewish society. People save themselves in various ways, let the action of the convents bear an individual character.[108]

The last position seems to have won out; at any rate, there is little evidence in the historical record of an organized effort from either the Jewish or the Polish side to help Jews escape – with the exception only of the activists themselves, a few hundred of whom got out with the aid of their organizations. Catholic organizations did help hundreds of Jewish children on an individual basis, once they had been sent out of the ghetto; whether they could have saved more if this offer had been taken up must remain moot.

The terms in which this debate was couched are somewhat disturbing to modern sensibilities: among other things, the phrase 'looking a gift horse in the mouth' springs to mind. Ringelblum's conjectures about the motives of the Catholic church are not entirely without foundation – we shall see evidence of conversionist motives in Chapter 4 – but Jewish intellectuals could surely have taken a less jaundiced view when the lives of children were at stake. To be fair, Ringelblum himself refused an offer to smuggle him and other Zionist leaders to Hungary with the dismissive remark that 'the concept of duty no longer means what it used to'.[109] These were men of a certain generation, in wartime, when nation was all, the individual nothing and self-sacrifice the order of the day. But to disdain an offer to save children on similar grounds is surely more dubious. The Jewish leadership protested mightily when it judged shipments of arms from the Polish underground to be inadequate, but was content to grumble in private about the inadequacy of institutional rescue efforts, which they clearly mistrusted. In sum, the fate of individuals was not on their minds.

Escape after January 1943

After the January *Aktion*, any remaining hopes of long-term survival in the ghetto evaporated. There is a paradox here: we now know that the *Aktion* of 18–21 January, probably ordered by Himmler when he visited the ghetto on 11 January, was meant as a limited operation to remove 8,000 people, taking them not to Treblinka and death but mainly to labour camps, as part of the project of transferring the 'shops' and their production to the Lublin area. Shortly before the *Aktion*, the owners of the 'shops' had appealed to their workers to volunteer for transportation to Lublin, assuring them that they could work and survive there; a group of eight Jewish workers were brought back from Lublin to testify to the decent conditions. But the Jews no longer trusted such assurances; and in the long run, of course, they were right. When German police and their Ukrainian and Baltic auxiliaries entered the ghetto on 18 January, it was widely assumed that the final liquidation of the ghetto was at hand. The resistance movement as yet had virtually no weapons, but a few members of ŻOB opened fire with pistols and word of this daring act spread rapidly through the ghetto. When the *Aktion* was stopped on 21 January, only 6,000 Jews having been taken, the ghetto reasoned, *post hoc ergo propter hoc*, that the Germans had been frightened off by the resistance. No one doubted that they would be back, however, and sooner rather than later. It was at this point, therefore, that the greatest wave of escapes began.

By this time the ghetto had adapted itself to the new conditions, and the methods of escape had become well oiled. Stefan Chaskielewicz writes: 'At the end of January 1943, when I was leaving the ghetto together with my parents, the act of crossing to the Aryan side was no longer difficult. Germans keeping watch at the gates or so-called *Wachen* could be bribed, drank too much and were altogether depraved.'[110] As the number of escapes multiplied, it became increasingly possible for Jews to rely on Jewish friends and relatives already established on the Aryan side:

Although I was born and educated in Warsaw, I didn't have any Polish friends on whom I could count for help and support on the Aryan side. On the other hand, my brother-in-law, who left the ghetto in October 1942, had possibilities of setting himself up on the Aryan side. He was the one who decided to get me out of the ghetto. His plan was realized on 15 January 1943, as follows: he gave me the address of a tailor's shop in the ghetto, bordering on the Aryan side [...]. To this shop a sizeable group of Aryans would come to work every morning, and go back every evening to their homes on the Aryan side. I spent a whole day in this establishment. I can remember a small but characteristic detail. Someone sewed a fur collar onto my winter coat [since furs had been confiscated from Jews and a coat with a missing collar would be conspicuous] [...]. In the evening, I left with a column of these workers [...]. After the group broke up – a friend of my brother-in-law's piloted me, a Jew, but with very good looks and living at that time on the Aryan side – I was led to a house near the ghetto [...].[111]

Irma Morgenstern was helped to escape by a Jew posing as a Polish peasant, whom she identifies only as 'Mr Antopolski'. As a Pole, Antopolski could pass in and out of the ghetto fairly freely, and according to Morgenstern was able to rescue a number of Jewish children, especially girls. Antopolski had a confederate, a Polish policeman named Eliasz Pietruszko, who managed Morgenstern's escape in February 1943 and kept her as his own daughter. Pietruszko was supposed to have got her parents and brother out as well, but these plans came to naught.[112]

Again, contacts were sometimes formed in an impromptu fashion. Thus Tadeusz Grundland, Morgenstern's future husband, established contact with his main helper while working in a *placówka*, unloading coal for trains at Warsaw's Eastern Station. In March 1943 he was approached by a Mr Broniak, who told him that he was willing to take him in and had built a shelter. Grundland took advantage of this offer, and stayed with the Broniaks in the right-bank suburb of Bródno until liberation.[113]

Even in this final period, there was still some resistance to the idea of leaving the ghetto. Michał Line had made arrangements well in advance, and had got some members of his family out, but he delayed leaving the ghetto himself. As the manager of a Jewish factory, he feared that his departure would cause closure of the factory and the deportation of all the workers. Therefore he stayed until the Ghetto Uprising.[114]

Activists began leaving at this time as well, as preparations for armed resistance intensified. Blady-Szwajger was assigned to work on the Aryan side by her party, the Bund. She describes the deliberations that led to her departure from the ghetto, at the end of January 1943:

> Marek [Edelman] explained that I had 'good' looks – I had blonde hair and blue eyes –, that I had no accent when I spoke Polish, which meant I could walk around the town freely, and that I would be of more use to them there than here; but it still seemed to me that it would be simply desertion, and that they would die here, and I might survive there, and that I couldn't do it [...] Then Abrasza Blum joined in. [...] He didn't speak much, he just smiled with that serene smile of his and said that it had to be done. And that it wouldn't be safe at all. But we had to have people over there who would take care of various things. [...] After all, our weapons came from the other side, he said.[115]

Most of the activists who left in connection with preparations for armed resistance had not meant to stay on the Aryan side permanently, but were caught there by the outbreak of the Ghetto Uprising. But Leon Feiner had established himself as the Bund's permanent representative on the Aryan side early in 1942, staying with the Polish actor Aleksander Zelwerowicz. Adolf Berman took up the corresponding post for the ŻKN shortly after its formation in October 1942. The liquidation of the ghetto's orphanages had made his position as director of CENTOS redundant, and as a psychologist he had good professional contacts with Polish colleagues. In each of these cases, the activist was leaving on party business, and the party therefore paid the bribes and made the arrangements.

In these examples I have emphasized some rather exceptional phenomena: decent SS men, escape without prior preparations, escape through very indirect contacts. It should be understood that these cases are not the norm: the great majority of escapees relied on networks like those described in Chapter 1. I have stressed the exceptions here, giving numerous examples, to make the point that these were not freak events that can be safely ignored. Only a minority of people left the ghetto in these ways, but enough of them to demonstrate that possibilities of escape did exist even for people who lacked some or all of the supposed prerequisites – 'good looks', good contacts, money and so forth. But of course having all these things did help a great deal.

Escape during and after the Ghetto Uprising

With the outbreak of the Ghetto Uprising on 19 April, the ghetto once again became hermetically sealed. Nearby streets on the Aryan side were emptied, machine-guns were set up at strategic points on the ghetto wall, the gates stopped functioning altogether. The vast majority of the remaining ghetto population disappeared into their well-prepared bunkers and virtually all traffic with the Aryan side stopped. Only the sewers and the tunnels remained as channels of communication; but the sewers were a maze, requiring a guide – an experienced sewage worker – for safe navigation; while very few people were aware of the existence, let alone the location, of the tunnels. Jews remaining in the ghetto could do no more than hide, wait and hope. After a few days' fighting, the Germans adopted the tactic of systematically burning the ghetto to the ground, block by block. After an area had been burnt out, it was searched by policemen with dogs, often accompanied by Jewish informers who knew where the bunkers were located. These individuals co-operated in the forlorn hope that their own lives would be spared. But 'a certain number of bunkers' as Janina Baran explains, 'were not engulfed in flames, nor discovered. The people in them, mainly at night and with the help of an organized action, crossed the wall to the Aryan side.'[116] There is regrettably no historical evidence of an organized action, but there are several accounts of individuals and small groups escaping in this way.

As the advancing flames and smoke threatened their bunkers, some Jews made their way at night or through underground passages to other hiding places, in the 'wild' ghetto or in areas that had already been burnt and searched. There they could hold out for some time, scavenging from the homes of Jews who had been killed, and could eventually make their way out of the ghetto. Most of those who escaped in this way waited until the Ghetto Uprising was over, when the ghetto wall was no longer guarded and people could steal out under cover of night. One or two stragglers, however, managed to hold out in the ghetto until the outbreak of the 1944 Warsaw Uprising. But the great majority of the remaining inhabitants did not escape. Those who did not succumb to the smoke and flames came out of hiding and were taken to the *Umschlagplatz* and thence to the Lublin camps.

On 28 April, the Germans again declared one of their 'amnesties', offering to transport all those who surrendered voluntarily to the labour camp at Poniatowa. Michał Line, whose workshop had by now ceased to exist, had spent nine days with his daughter and Maria, his future second wife, sitting in complete darkness in a cramped and stifling bunker at Leszno 76. The Lines decided to take advantage of this 'amnesty' and gave themselves up; but as they were waiting to be loaded onto trucks, Maria was seized with misgivings and told Line she would not go to Poniatowa.

And then Line, not hesitating, moved in the direction of the *Wache*. [...] The *Wache* was strongly guarded by German gendarmes, Polish police and police agents. Line went up to a group of German soldiers and said, 'Let five people through!' They didn't shoot him. They looked at him with stunned expressions. They remained silent. A couple of gendarmes left. Two remained. Then Line said, almost as if giving an order: *Retten Sie drei Seelen!* [Save three souls!]. One of them answered, *aber schnell!* [but be quick!]. And by that miracle, so hard to believe, they managed to get out of hell.[117]

The success of this audacious move, in light of the evidence we have reviewed concerning the behaviour of the German gendarmes, may lead one to wonder whether this really was such a miraculous outcome – surprising and improbable, certainly, but not altogether unprecedented – and once again, whether many lives might not have been saved if more people had been prepared to 'give it a go'.

Escape through *placówki* was still possible during the Ghetto Uprising, but only in the case of permanent workposts that were not caught up in the fighting. Zofia Goldfarb-Bachniak[118] worked in the *Werterfassung* until the outbreak of the Ghetto Uprising. Her father died as a ghetto fighter, the last of her thirty close relatives to have remained alive. On 23 April she was assigned, together with a group of artisans and mechanics, to the same Ostbahn labour camp in Bródno from which Michał Grundland had escaped. She worked there until 13 July when, a few days before the camp was dissolved, she managed to slip away.

Still another method of survival, the most improbable of all, was to be incarcerated in a German prison. Israel Hochberg[119] was an inmate of the Pawiak prison, in the grounds of the ghetto. He survived there until he managed to escape in February 1944. As we shall see, other prisoners in the Pawiak were rescued in August 1944 when the Warsaw Uprising broke out.

Escape from Camps and Trains

The deportees from Warsaw, especially those who were taken to labour camps, still had slight chances of escape. Small numbers of Jews escaped from camps and trains even during the first two *Aktionen*, but this form of escape assumed the greatest importance during and after the Ghetto Uprising, when the deportations were exclusively to the labour camps near Lublin.

The cattle cars that took Jews to the camps moved slowly and stopped on sidings often to let higher-priority traffic pass. The 50-kilometre trip to Treblinka could easily take several hours; the journey to Lublin could take much longer.[120] The wagons themselves were equipped with small windows strung with barbed wire, but the wire could be removed or filed through, and anyone small and agile enough could jump out. Alternatively, the doors could be prised open. Jumping from the trains was dangerous, of course: not only physically, but because each train included one or two wagons with roof-mounted booths, manned by guards with machine-guns. It was therefore safest to make the attempt while the train was moving, the faster the better. Not only youth and agility were required, then, but also a fair bit of nerve. George Pfeffer, who was deported to Majdanek after the Ghetto Uprising, writes that there were 150 people in his wagon, of whom 'some' escaped through the windows, despite the difficulties. He himself did not, because he had his wife and son with him.[121] In the testimonies reviewed here, Stanisław Laskowski (Antypolski)[122] escaped from a train; so did Marian Berland[123] and Irena Mikelberg's sister.[124] Ringelblum had earlier heard of such instances; he wrote in October 1942: 'They escaped from a wagon! Those with experience. Young men. One escaped twice. Organized eight jumpers.'[125]

Escape from concentration camps was more difficult, and was further inhibited by the principle of collective responsibility, which the authorities freely applied. At Majdanek, writes Pfeffer, 'comrade-prisoners watched each other even more assiduously than the SS men, for, according to the regulations, if a prisoner attempted to escape, every second prisoner-worker in the unit would be hanged.'[126] But Pfeffer reasoned that all the prisoners at Majdanek were doomed in any case. He had the good fortune to be given a job in the camp kitchen, and by selling favours to other prisoners was able to accumulate 1,700 zł. He used this money to 'organize' civilian clothes and to bribe his way onto a *placówka* working outside the camp grounds. He walked off the worksite by posing as a Polish worker, then made his way back to Warsaw over the space of several weeks.

Majdanek was a proper concentration camp, one of the worst, from which escape was indeed difficult. The same cannot be said of some of the labour camps nearby. Janina Baran found herself in the camp at Poniatowa, where the Többens 'shop' had been relocated. In order to convince his 13,000 workers that they were safe with him, Többens equipped the camp with a well-staffed hospital and even a kindergarten, and security at the camp was quite lax. 'At first', writes Baran,

> escape from this camp presented almost no difficulty. And so many Jews did escape. The escapes were both organized and 'loose'. In the first days of May, whole caravans of people went from there to Warsaw. Often Soviet partisans would come to the camp at night and try to talk the Jews into escaping, but unfortunately these people were so blinded or discouraged that no one wanted to make the move. [...] Why people didn't escape [...] can only be explained by the fact that some had nowhere to go, others were discouraged – for them it was all the same – and others no doubt believed Többens.[127]

The Poniatowa camp was liquidated in November as part of the 'Harvest Festival'. Baran herself managed to escape before then. She writes that 'our escape was organized by a Jewish fighting group that had been on the Aryan side the whole time after the deportation action in the ghetto'; but she provides no details, and the identity of this Jewish group is unknown.

The best-known case of escape from a labour camp after the Ghetto Uprising is that of Emmanuel Ringelblum. Ringelblum escaped from the ghetto, with his wife and son, in February 1943. He returned to the ghetto just before the uprising broke out and was caught up in it. He was then transported to Trawniki, whence he managed to smuggle a letter to Warsaw in July 1943. Shortly after this letter was received, he was rescued from the camp by the young Polish activist Teodor Pajewski and Emilka Kossower of the ŻKN.

With the exception of the two last cases, and of getting its own activists out, the Jewish underground played almost no role in the flight of the Warsaw Jews to the Aryan side, which had overwhelmingly an individual and spontaneous character. Yithak Zuckerman writes, somewhat defensively:

> we didn't have to be convinced that one of the essential things for us was to rescue Jews; we all knew that. However, the essential function of the Jewish Fighting Organization was to organize Jews for war wherever possible. [...] [T]here were Jewish remnants in various places. What did we want to do with those Jews? We couldn't bring them to Warsaw because we didn't have any place to hide them. [...] Very few were brought to Warsaw; and each one of them is known by name, like Ringelblum and [Jonas] Turkow. Every person was important, but it was symbolic and you could count them on your fingers, there were so few of them. Nevertheless, there were some tens of thousands more Jews, even in the two camps of Poniatów [sic] and Trawniki.[128]

Zuckerman also claims that plans had been discussed with the Polish underground which came to naught:

> there were still concentration camps and we encouraged the spirit of uprising in them. ... The Poles lied; they didn't set up contact stations as they promised. We didn't have the power to set them up. The stations were needed for shelter and passage in case inmates escaped from the concentration camps before they were executed.[129]
>
> [U]ntil September 1943 [...] we were trying to construct a joint plan to rescue young people from the Poniatów and Trawniki camps, where we formed groups of the Jewish Fighting Organization. They promised to help but they didn't keep their promise.[130]

Zuckerman finally alludes to the difficulty of escape:

> You could escape from the camps, but you had to know where to go, you needed some base, some assistance, some friendly village, hut, forest. Where

could a Jew escape? What happened to the Jews who escaped from Treblinka? After all, hundreds did escape and only a few dozen arrived from Treblinka! Sometimes there are such naïve and absurd questions. You can't convey the 'climate', and the 'geography' of Poland in those days. You simply can't describe the relations between Jews and non-Jews, everything that threatened the Jew in that period! As an individual, a Jew might still have a chance to escape from Poniatów or Trawniki; but when there were dozens or hundreds of people, someone had to prepare the escape.[131]

This was an activist's view, and is the received wisdom. But as we have seen, individual Jews did escape, without help; they did make it back to Warsaw – even from Treblinka – and some of them did survive. Zuckerman's view is similar to that of Pinchas Freudiger, cited in the Introduction, and the answer is the same: perhaps only a few dozen out of hundreds who escaped from Treblinka survived; but among those who did not escape, there were no survivors at all.

Conclusions

Normally, leaving the ghetto required friendly contacts with Poles of the sort documented in Chapter 1, though increasingly these contacts were indirect, through friends and family members or through Jews already established on the Aryan side. Probably most of the Jews of Warsaw enjoyed contacts of this kind. Normally, leaving the ghetto needed arrangements to be made in advance, to have documents made up and at least a temporary *melina* on the 'other side'. Normally, money was needed to bribe policemen and foremen of work parties, to pay off *szmalcowniks* and to pay for accommodation and food. The perception of many people in the ghetto was that all these things were prerequisites, so that escape was only for the rich, the well-connected, the blond and blue-eyed, with good Polish and good friends: certainly, therefore, for only a small minority, and not for ordinary Jews.

Yet there were people with none of these attributes who escaped successfully, and nearly everyone was missing an element or two. The sheer volume of escapes, especially after January 1943, was such that we ought to conclude that despite the assimilationist and middle-class character of most of the fugitives, some at least were indeed ordinary Jews with no special resources, who happened to have a willing Polish friend, acquaintance, colleague or former servant, or who were related to someone who did, or who were prepared simply to 'give it a go'.

The wave of escapes was showing no signs of abating when the Ghetto Uprising broke out: if escapes had continued at the same rate for another six months, half of the Jews of the *Restghetto* might have fled; if the Germans had tried to leave the 'shops' in operation until late in 1944, as they did in Łódź, they might have found their entire labour force gone. As was so often the case in the Holocaust, it was above all German timing and intentions that determined the outcome; all other influences have to be put in that context.

We cannot know, of course, whether the rate at which escapes took place between January and April 1943 could have been sustained. Most likely not, since limiting factors would eventually have come into play. But with escape still accelerating when the possibilities were cut off, we can only speculate as to what those limiting factors might have been. In any case, the scale of this 'greatest escape', without equal in occupied Europe, suggests that we should be looking to explain its success, not its failure.

Warsaw was unique in many respects: the size of the Jewish community and its degree of assimilation – modest by Western standards, but unusual for Poland; the centrality of the ghetto and its many links with the Aryan side; the vigour of the smuggling operation, the channels and contacts that it created, and its corrupting effect on the various police forces; the size of the city; the peculiar course of the liquidation operations, stretching over nearly a year with many stops and starts. All these factors made escape possible on a larger scale than anywhere else. The suddenness of the 1942 *Aktion* ensured that most Jews were ensnared before they could react, but it also stripped the remainder of their illusions, which Jews elsewhere continued to entertain.

Survivors have in conversation urged on me the conclusion, often found in activist memoirs, that many more Jews could have escaped but for the inhospitable conditions on the Aryan side – the 'climate' and 'geography' of which 'Antek' Zuckerman writes. But in truth the decision to escape could not have depended on these considerations. Whatever impressions they might have retained, the Jews could not have known what awaited them in that other world, from which they had become so estranged during their two-and-a-half years behind the ghetto wall and which they were now about to rejoin.

3   The Secret City

Introduction

> Here it was as if nothing had happened in the last two years. Trolleys, automobiles, bicycles raced along; businesses were open; children headed for school; women carried fresh bread and other provisions. The contrast with the ghetto was startling. It was another world, a world teeming with life.
>
> Vladka Meed[1]

> I was privileged to be in the Aryan quarter after being separated from it for nearly two years. [...] The Aryan quarter is like a cemetery. There is no life and no traffic in it. In the stores there is not a living soul. Everywhere there is cleanliness, but it is the cleanliness of a ghost town.
>
> Chaim Kaplan[2]

Appearances, as these two quotations show, can deceive. These contrasting reports are, first of all, a lesson in the relativity of perception: Kaplan's brief visit to the Aryan side – under police escort, to testify in a trial – came before the Great Deportation, when the ghetto was still inhumanly crowded; Meed escaped during the 'shops' period, when the ghetto had largely been emptied.

But there is more to the psychology of these impressions than such figure–ground effects. Helena Merenholc, herself a psychologist, reflected on her own perceptions:

> I walked along the streets and it was normal. That was my first impression. I was in a daze. It seemed to me that I was a free person. When, in the ghetto, I had looked out of my window at people on the Aryan side, it had seemed to me that they must be happy. The perceptions of prisoners .... After all, I knew

very well what a tragedy was being played out in Warsaw, in the whole of occupied Poland. But the shadow of the ghetto followed me.[3]

This reaction, echoed in many memoirs, was the product of wishful thinking – the hope that salvation was at hand, the premature anticipation of real freedom. Where Kaplan wanted to believe (not unreasonably, in view of their economic importance) that Warsaw could not survive cut off from the Jews, Merenholc, after the deportations, knew that the Jews could not survive cut off from Warsaw. She wanted to see life and hope 'over there'.

In reality, 'over there' was (as Merenholc points out) a city under a particularly severe form of Nazi occupation, where, though material conditions were much better than those in the ghetto and there was no threat of imminent annihilation, there was still poverty, overcrowding and terror. In some ways, even, life was worse on the Aryan side: in particular, political repression was harsher and more direct. (That is why there were reportedly members of the Polish underground hiding out in the ghetto, some of whom were caught in the round-ups and sent to Treblinka 'by mistake'.) The Nazis controlled the Jews by means of the ghetto wall, behind which they rarely ventured, but they ruled Aryan Warsaw through police terror. Better or worse, the Aryan side in any case posed its own problems and threats, different from those of the ghetto, which the fugitives had to master if they were to survive.

Life in Aryan Warsaw

The conditions created in Warsaw by the five-year Hitlerite occupation were characterized among other things by an extraordinarily large crowd of people 'in hiding'. It can boldly be said that never yet in the world has there existed a city which for such a long time led such a decidedly double life. On the surface, in the case of controls, demands for documents, personal searches: nothing but loyal citizens of the General Government, [...] working directly or indirectly [...] for the victory of the 'Greater Reich' [...] . In reality – the most rebellious, the most stubbornly perverse city, made up almost wholly of people for whom any closer contact with the police could have a fatal end.

Of course, the concept of people in hiding took in extremely varied groups of people. So, for example, an agent of the underground might have to hide [...]; but equally an agent of the Gestapo, fearing a well-deserved bullet. An unregistered officer [of the Polish Army] might be in hiding, or a 'tradesman' with excessively complicated business interests; so might an unemployed worker who had ignored numerous summonses from the *Arbeitsamt*, and a 'Blue' policeman caught attempting blackmail or taking a bribe. Finally a Jew might be hiding, regardless of his religion, if any, and a too-well-known *macher* who fabricated false documents.

But where for some people hiding might amount to spending a few days or a dozen nights away from home, as a last alternative to leaving for the provinces, for others it consisted of a battle for the right to live, painful in its constancy and killing in its apparent hopelessness, and grew to the dimensions of a problem so complicated, and endlessly becoming ever more complicated, that it required no small sturdiness of soul and no little invention to last till the end [...].

Understandably, it was the Jews in hiding who always had to conquer the greatest difficulties.

Citizen Frajnd[4]

As we saw in the previous chapter, the Jews on the Aryan side were at first – in 1940 and 1941 – few in number, well integrated into Polish society and for the most part had well-established 'Aryan' identities. Many of them were regarded as Jews only by the German authorities. They formed only a small part of the clandestine community then living in Warsaw, and did not attract particular attention. The *szmalcowniks* and corrupt policemen had plenty of Jewish smugglers and Polish black-marketeers to prey upon, and paid little attention to the handful of Jews in hiding. Those Jews who elected to stay out of the ghetto not only saved themselves the difficult and dangerous task of escaping from it, but also never lost touch with the Aryan side, which consequently never became an alien world to them. They were able to adapt gradually to the increasing controls imposed by the occupation authorities, and thus create and maintain convincing Aryan personas. Yet despite these advantages, the risks that they faced gradually became greater and greater, as Frajnd says, and they had to endure these risks for more than four years. In the long run, therefore, it cannot be said that they chose the soft option.

It seemed at first surprisingly easy for a Jew to live on the Aryan side: it was not always even necessary to establish a false identity. Frajnd, for one, continued to live under his own name, even though it was Jewish-sounding; he writes that he was 'automatically' treated as an Aryan: 'without an armband, in the Aryan district, where was there any reason for doubt?'[5] Identity documents were only a small inconvenience at this early stage: the Germans had not yet got around to issuing their own and relied on the pre-war Polish ones. Not only did the Polish underground have an ample supply of blank forms and authentic official stamps and seals, together with authentic pre-war officials who could contribute their own authentic signatures, but the city administration quickly managed to convince the Germans to issue 'temporary' documents to replace ones that had supposedly been lost or destroyed in 1939. Such documents required only the sworn statements of the applicant and two witnesses.[6]

The documentation problem was not so straightforward as it appeared at first, however. As Frajnd observes:

> The Germans, through the whole time of their rule in Warsaw, aimed step by step, by means of interlocking decrees, to create a reporting and documentation system that would render any kind of machinations impossible and that would locate every single inhabitant of the city with appropriate precision.[7]

The Germans inherited not only identity documents but also certain other aspects of this system from the pre-war Polish government. All residents of Warsaw who lived in housing blocks – the vast majority – were registered in their buildings' tenancy records as well as the municipal records office (*Wydział Ewidencji Ludowej*). In addition, all Catholics, the quick and the dead, were represented in parish birth, baptismal, marriage and death registers. A forged identity document by itself might pass muster in the event of simple street check, but if someone fell under suspicion, the authorities would begin to delve into this whole web of documentation. Therefore, there were 'solid' documents, properly backed up, and 'bogus' (*lipne*) documents, lacking the proper backing, which offered little protection.

Setting yourself up as a *homo novus* required not only the creation of a new identity but also the severing of all ties to the old, tainted one. Therefore you had to move. Your former self could then vanish, while the new self registered in the normal way in the new quarters. Changing addresses in principle involved the following procedure: you had to de-register at the registry office in the old district, receiving a coupon in return. You then registered with the building manager at the new place, again receiving a coupon. Both coupons then had to be taken to the local registry office, within a certain grace period, as proof of registration. Thus, your entire residential history could in theory be traced back to the beginning of the occupation. To break the chain of evidence, it was necessary to have a forged de-registration coupon, and this needed to have backing in the files of the registry office. The Polish underground had infiltrated the registry offices, so that it was usually possible to find a clerk who would plant the necessary records, possibly even without payment.[8] Alternatively, you could claim to have lost the coupon: a zealous clerk (but there were few such) would then get in touch with the appropriate registry office; an alert clerk (the majority) would spot the chance to boost his income and 'make a mistake' for a *Góral* (a 500-złoty note, which bore the portrait of a Góral, a native of the Carpathian mountains). You then had to hope that no one would spot the error and investigate it later on.

Far easier, no more unsafe in the event of an encounter with the authorities and better from the point of view of anyone who really wanted to live a secret existence, was to bribe the building manager to allow you to stay unofficially, unregistered. Whatever complications living unregistered might cause with the authorities – you could always claim that you had only just moved in and had not had time to register – registering brought a far more pressing danger, which was that some blackmailer, having learnt your name, would be able to trace you to your home through the municipal records. (The most serious blackmailers were police agents, who had routine access to these records.) Addresses, for all those living in hiding, were a matter of the utmost secrecy:

> Jews on the Aryan side have to act like real conspirators. No one knows their addresses. One brother does not know the address of the other, children do not know the addresses of their parents. [...] It is forbidden to write down the addresses – they must be learnt by heart or put down in some code form.[9]

The need to maintain this kind of secrecy, and at the same time to have one's documents in order, represented a circle that was never really squared. The saving grace was that because many people in Warsaw were living underground, living unregistered did not by itself betray someone as a Jew. But that did not guarantee safety: 'Poket went to the Aryan side, and the very next day the house where he was staying was searched. They were looking for political suspects. He wasn't registered and they took him.'[10]

Parish records presented a somewhat easier problem. At first, the usual expedient was to claim as your birth-parish some locality in the Soviet-occupied zone, or else a church known to have been destroyed in 1939. Authentic-looking birth certificates could be forged, sometimes with the help of priests from those parts who had brought their parish seals with them. But the authorities soon realized what was going on, and it was not long before such exotic birthplaces came to attract suspicion instead of allaying it. In any case, the eastern parishes came under German control in the summer of 1941, and those who had relied on this form of disguise were suddenly open to exposure.

A better procedure was to have the necessary parish records created or altered. This needed a friendly priest, but there were a number of such men working for the Polish underground, assuming you had some contact with it.[11] Otherwise, you could approach a parish priest individually – recalling that many Catholic Poles had good reason to conceal their identity, this did not necessarily mean owning up to being Jewish – or else you could assume the identity of some real person known to be dead or out of the country. If the person was dead, the death record would have to be removed from the parish register.

In the course of 1941, new complications arose. The authorities introduced compulsory labour for all Poles aged eighteen to sixty and Jews aged fourteen to sixty, creating a new agency, the *Arbeitsamt* (Labour Office) and introducing new forms of identification. The first of these was the *Ausweis*, issued by the employer and held by the employee; this was followed in mid-year by the *Arbeitskarte*, issued by the *Arbeitsamt* and held by the employer, who returned it to the *Arbeitsamt* on termination of employment. The employee also received a certificate (*Bescheinigung*) from the *Arbeitsamt* as evidence that an *Arbeitskarte* was on file. Without these documents as evidence of employment, you could be seized for forced labour, possibly in Germany or in a concentration camp, or be taken as a hostage and shot. Street round-ups for these purposes were a daily occurrence in occupied Warsaw.

Frajnd describes the consequences of the new measures for Jews in hiding:

> The *Arbeitskarte* was obligatory for every working Aryan, so that the forms that had to be filled in to receive it required you to state over your own signature that you were an Aryan and of Aryan descent. [. . .] I had friends who turned back at this point [. . . .] These forms also demanded – merciful God, what they demanded! Four full pages of legal foolscap, they required confirmation by the [building] manager, and the municipal registry office, of the petitioner's place of residence. Here lay the whole difficulty, and here for the first time one had to pass the test of skill in cheating the Hitlerite administration. It wasn't a simple matter. To get a statement from the building manager and the registry office meant tearing down the previously erected protective wall, giving up a safe hiding place, coming out of the shadow into full sunlight, into the middle of the road. [. . .] And the designated deadline meant in addition having to hurry [. . . .] And so I had to register in turn with my building manager, who was keeping me unregistered for a small payment [. . .]; receive from him the corresponding form for the municipal registry office, give my employer the [newly registered] address, and then move out and live somewhere unregistered. How easy it is to say! [. . .] But how hard, how terribly onerous it was to arrange all this: to find a new home, answering all needs, that gave some kind of guarantee of safety; to find people ready to put up an unregistered person [. . .]; to find someone who would organize things at the registry office and do it honestly, and with all that, to watch the deadline, to hand in all the papers at the same time as everyone else so as not to stand out from the crowd.[12]

Further complications were not long in coming. The German identity document or *Kennkarte* was introduced throughout the General Government by Hans Frank's decree of 6 June 1941, although delaying tactics by Polish clerks ensured that implementation dragged on well into 1943. All non-Germans over the age of fifteen were required to obtain a *Kennkarte* through their local record offices, in much the same way as the *Arbeitskarte*. The *Kennkarte* bore a serial number and a fingerprint as well as the name, address and photograph of the bearer. Once again, however, a loophole was provided in the form of a provision for lost or destroyed documents, so that a *Kennkarte* could in practice be obtained, like the 'temporary' Polish documents, on the oath of two witnesses. As Tomasz Szarota points out, the consequence was that a golden opportunity arose once again to obtain quite official documents for entirely fictitious people, an opportunity of which the Polish underground made the fullest use.[13] 'It turned out', writes Aurelia

Wyleżyńska, 'that everyone had lost [their original documents], or nearly everyone, at any rate everyone who was … "with it".'[14] By a fortunate coincidence, the introduction of the *Kennkarte* stretched over precisely the time when the largest number of escapes from the ghetto was taking place, so that the minting of large numbers of identity documents for the fugitives could go wholly unnoticed among the mass registration of the entire population of Warsaw.

Document production was carried out by many private entrepreneurs, and also by the 'legalization' or 'passport' cells (*paszportówki*) of the Polish underground, each political party having its own. The scale of the operation, and also of the number of people in hiding, can be gathered from an estimate made by the Gestapo and *Arbeitsamt* in the summer of 1943 that 15 per cent of *Kennkarten* and 25 per cent of *Arbeitskarten* were forged.[15] If this was true, it meant that as many as 170,000 adults were concealing their identities in some way, certainly good camouflage for 28,000 Jews.

It was scarcely necessary to forge *Kennkarten* since they could be obtained legally in such a simple way. But Jews emerging from the seclusion of the ghetto, disoriented and often with no way of contacting official sources, were frequently tricked into paying exorbitant sums for crude forgeries with no supporting documentation. As a general rule, the more documents cost, the less they were worth. Forged *Kennkarten* were at best a temporary expedient, allowing time for proper documentation to be generated. The legalization cells therefore concentrated on forging the supporting documents required to obtain a *Kennkarte* and an *Arbeitskarte*, and took care, through their agents, to ensure that fictitious documentation was inserted into the files of the *Arbeitsamt* and the records office. Best of all, these services (which were meant for the Polish underground, not specifically for Jews) were usually entirely free, apart from perhaps two or three thousand złotys to pay the necessary bribes. Jews themselves rarely had direct contacts with the underground, but many of the Poles who helped them were involved with these circles, or could reach them with relative ease. There was, at least at first, some resistance from the *paszportówki* to providing forged documents for people who were thought to look very Jewish, on the grounds that obvious forgeries might compromise the security of the whole operation, but as the forgers gained confidence these objections faded away. An honest helper could therefore generally arrange top-quality documents at little or no cost; most memoirists who mention documents seem to have arranged them in this way.

After Żegota was created at the end of 1942, it developed its own legalization cell, which provided this service specifically for Jews. According to Marek Arczyński, who headed this effort, the cell generated 50,000 documents between the end of 1942 and the outbreak of the Warsaw Uprising, on average fifty and eventually one hundred per day, 'of which 80 per cent got into the hands of Jews'. 30,000–45,000 zł per month – about 10 per cent of Żegota's budget – was assigned for this purpose, therefore 20–30 zł per document, enough to pay for materials and perhaps the occasional bribe. Arczyński writes that his cell produced the following types of documents: '*Kennkarten, Arbeitskarten, Ausweise,* identity documents for officials (including functionaries of the SS and Gestapo), birth certificates, death records, marriage certificates, registration-card coupons, passes and the most varied certificates and printed items.'[16]

Setting up these paper walls was only the beginning of solving the identity problem, however. A Jew in hiding was unable to live a normal life, however good the documents, and therefore fictional identities invariably clashed with realities. A fictional former address could be listed at the registry office, but what if no one at that address could remember the fictional Mrs X? And what if she herself could not even describe the building, or name the porter or any of the residents? Most Jews could not work normally, for fear of betraying their identity through daily contact with Poles; therefore their *Ausweis* and *Arbeitskarte* were also often not backed by reality. There were employers who, usually for payment, carried imaginary workers on their employment rolls, all of them people in hiding on a false *Ausweis*. But when you were under suspicion, an investigator might telephone the employer and, for example, ask to speak to you, or ask the employer to explain what you were doing in the street during normal working hours. The employer would now have to be both co-operative and quick-witted for disaster to be averted.

Not only residence and employment could trip a suspect up, but the whole web of normal life. A suspect could be asked about family and friends, for example; the assumed identity would therefore have to include a plausible family history, which could be checked in the records. For this reason, the most solid documents were those belonging to a real person with a real family, the details of which could be memorized. But the investigator, if conscientious enough, could then contact these supposed family members. It would come as a shock to them that a long-dead relative had suddenly come back to life; and even if they had the wits and sympathy to realize what was going on, they could hardly (for example) provide an accurate description of someone they had never met. A simpler method was to claim that all your family members were dead, but that in turn aroused suspicion. In short, no form of documentation could provide absolute safety.

In practice, however, interrogations of suspected Jews rarely followed such complicated paths. In the case of men, the simplest check was removal of the trousers: if the physical evidence was there, no ordinary documentation would avail. There were, however, three courses of action open to circumcised men (not all men who were Jewish under the Nuremberg Laws were circumcised).[17] The first and easiest was to obtain a medical certificate stating that the individual had undergone surgical circumcision, a procedure used to correct phimosis (abnormal development of the foreskin) or in certain cases of venereal disease. The second was to undergo plastic surgery to restore the foreskin: a small group of doctors carried out these skin-grafts (Citizen Frajnd was one of the patients), but the results were unsatisfactory as the surgical scars were easy to detect.[18] The third – an expedient open to a few Jews with the right contacts – was to pass as a Muslim or Karaite, since both groups practise circumcision.

There was a small Muslim community in Poland, descended from Tartars who had fought as Polish allies against the Teutonic Knights in the fifteenth century; there were enough of them in Warsaw to support a mosque. Their organization, the Union of Tartar-Muslims (*Związek Tatarów-Mahometan*), had its own document-forging operation and instructed Jewish fugitives in the principles of Islam.[19] As to the Karaites, a sect that had broken away from mainstream Judaism in the eighth century, an attempt was made to save Jews through forged Karaite certificates in Vilna, the main Karaite centre in Poland, but no similar effort was mounted in Warsaw. So tiny was the Karaite community in Warsaw – a few dozen families – that the practical possibilities of surviving in this way were small. Helena Szereszewska knew two married couples who had Karaite papers and so were exempted from wearing the Jewish armband, but they did not survive.[20] Karaite communities in Poland were forced to provide lists of their members, and anyone with Karaite papers who was not on these lists was an easy target. Besides, the legal status of the Karaites continued to be a matter of debate within Nazi circles throughout the war, so there could be no certainty even if the documents stood up.[21]

Most circumcised men did none of these things, but simply hoped that they would never be examined in this way. Sometimes a confident offer to display the evidence would convince the examiner, who would decline out of embarrassment. If a doctor carried out the examination he would, if he was decent, simply lie, or write out a certificate of surgical circumcision. But not all doctors were decent. Julien Hirshaut writes that he was examined at Gestapo headquarters in Szucha Avenue by a German doctor, who turned a blind eye and certified him as an Aryan. He was then sent as a Pole to the Pawiak, where the Polish prison doctor wrote a report to the Gestapo classifying him as a Jew. Fortunately, another Pole, Leon Wanat, who worked in the prison office, intercepted the report and altered Hirshaut's file.[22]

Women were less easy to identify. The standard method was to quiz the suspect on aspects of the Catholic religion. Alina Margolis-Edelman describes how she and a friend were questioned by an officer of the Blue police:

'Well, OK, we'll do an exam', he said. And to me: 'Pray'.

I blessed my nanny. I knew all the church prayers and songs. I started the 'Our Father'. He listened and interrupted.

'And now, miss' – he turned to Zosia –, 'have you been to Holy Communion?'

'Yes', said Zosia.

'Well then, tell me. How big is the wafer that the priest gives you during Communion?'

Zosia pointed to the palm of her hand. We were done for.

'And you're a Jewess too' – he added, looking at me – 'only smarter'.[23]

Such an interrogation could be carried out by any Catholic, but sometimes a priest was called in. The record of the Catholic church in providing forged documents and hiding places, the latter chiefly for children, was generally an admirable one; but not all priests were equally admirable, and some could be found who were prepared to rule on a suspect's Aryanness, knowing the consequences of a negative ruling.

Thus far, the discussion has concerned the problem of identity *vis-à-vis* the authorities; that is, once a Jew had fallen into their hands. But still more complex and burdensome was the business of keeping up an 'Aryan' identity in everyday life. For a Jew 'on the surface', this required playing a role twenty-four hours a day – literally:

'Mr Piotrkowski', the Ukrainian with whom Lorek was staying said to me, 'what has gotten into you, sending me this yid to stay here?'

I feigned surprise and outrage, but to no avail.

'This guy was shouting in his sleep and talking Yiddish! So I gave him a little fright and he took himself off.'[24]

The problem that caused Jews the most anxiety, and was taken to be the *sine qua non* of living 'on the surface', was physical appearance. As Ringelblum explained:

Only individuals with so-called 'good' – that is, Aryan – appearance can survive 'on the surface'. [...] In the Ghetto, 'studies' were carried out in order to establish by what features a Jew or Jewess can be recognized. The results of the 'studies', these incessant discussions in the Ghetto, were as follows: a Jew can be recognized by his nose, hair and eyes.[25]

Memoirists often express the entirely irrational belief that Poles – by implication nearly all Poles – look like the Nazi stereotype of an Aryan. An anonymous author writes: 'I had a Jewish face by Polish standards, the Poles being blond and blue-eyed for the most part. I had dark brown hair, dark skin and green eyes'.[26] Despite these disabilities, the author lived 'on the surface' and survived.

Nazi racial stereotypes thus seem to have found their way into the wartime consciousness of many Jews, despite their manifest silliness (they were lampooned in a well-known wartime joke: the ideal Aryan should be blond, like Hitler, tall, like Goebbels, and physically fit, like Göring). As I write this, I happen to have to hand a group photograph of a Swedish choir. Of these thirty-nine 'Nordic' singers, nine are blond, twelve are black-haired and the rest have dark brown or grey hair. This sort of diversity, which is really characteristic of all European populations, gave the

1. Page 2 of a ŻKN recipient register in the handwriting of Barbara Berman.

2. List of twenty-two ŻKN aid recipients showing names, places and dates of birth, pre-war places of residence, professions and amounts received. The children Rutti Feldman and Paweł Kraus (nos. 20 and 21) are from Czechoslovakia; Sura Rodzynek (no. 5) is 'presently working in Germany'.

Marzec 1934 d.c.Aniela/

121.Maryla Grossowa	osób 1
122.Bensteinowa	1
123.J.Radoszyn	1
124.Ruffowie	2
125.Rubzowie	2
126.Z.Grinbaumowa	1
127.Paulina Landsberg	1
128.Kabakowa	1
129.Olga Ader z rodz.	3.
130.Natalia Greniewska	1
131.Antonina Diamand	1
132. Adw.Jan Disel z rodz.	3
133. Mel.Wasserman	1
134.Puszetowa z córką	2
135.Doc.Brokman	1
136.Sew.Kahane	1
137.Germanowie	3
138.Bilaner	1
139.Smietański	1
140.Celińska	1
141.Józefa Kahane	1
142.Natan Lewy	2
143.Goldbergowie	2
144.Szydłowerowa	1
145.Ratowie	3
146.Gans z rodziną	3
147.Sal Jussym	1
148.Janina Kolberg	1
149.Józef Neumark	1
150.Rozalia Wenig	1
151.Gordonówna	1
152.J.Grossmanowie	2
153.Dr.Königsbein z rodz.	3
154.Aniela Kohn z dzieć.	2
155.Majerowiczowie	2
156.Małolet.Lewkowicz	1
157.Dr.Flora Herzog	1
158.Dawidsonowie	3
159.Grywińska	1
160.Salomon Fridman z rodz.	3
161.Tadeusz Chorążycki	1
162.Alek.Kohn	1
163.Ida Brauner	1
164.Fran.Szwarc	1
165.Stef.Halberstadt	1
166.Regina Herzog	1
167.Holzerowa z dzieck.	2
168.Halberstein z żoną	2
169. Blumowie	3
170.Jadwiga Korngold	1
171.Salomea Fridman z dzieć.	3
172 Akser	1
173.Dr.Kreps	1
174.Dr.Katzner	1
175.Dr.Gotlibowa	1
176.Garlinkiel	1

Łącznie osób 296

Dodatkowi.

Adw.Kleinchauerowa	zł. 1000.-
Doc.Erl chówna	1000.-
" Brokman	1000.-
Dr.Marc.Landzberg	2000.-
Tadeusz Silberberg/chor/	2000.-
Dr.Zyg.Lilintal	2000.-
Jabłonkówna	500.-
An.Muszkat	500.-
Goldsoblowie	1000.-
Żeltowa	1000.-
Dr.Eliasberg	500.-
M.Reyman	1500.-
Wiklinowa	1000.-
Birnowa	5000.-
Rozenberg Irena	500.-
Dr.R.Bornstein	1000.-
Rathowie	1000.-
Lud.Pinskier /choroba/	1000.-

Razem	23500.-
Prezent	960.-

Łącznie	24460.-

Wypłaciłam 296 osób.a 500zł. 148.000.-
dodatkowi j.w. 24.460.-

Łącznie 172.460

Otrzymałama 170.000.-

Niedobór wynosi 2.460

Ponadto otrzymałam i wypłaciłam

Na chleb do obozu 12.000.-
Dla Zygmunta Grossa 2.000.-
Anny Margolis do rozdziału 4.500.-
----

3. Fragment of Bund recipient list for March 1944 (coded as 1934), for recipients under the care of the activist Aniela Sternberg.

4. (*above*) The psychologist Dr Adolf Berman was head of the Orphan Care Central (CENTOS) in the Warsaw ghetto. When the ghetto's orphanages were liquidated, he escaped from the ghetto and became chairman of the ŻKN in 'Aryan' Warsaw as well as its representative on the Jewish Co-ordinating Committee (ŻKK) and the Council to Aid Jews (*Żegota*). He died in Israel in 1978.
5. (*above right*) Dr Leon Feiner was the Bund's representative on the Aryan side, as well as on the ŻKK and on *Żegota's* governing council. He died of cancer shortly after liberation.

6. (*below*) Hirsch Wasser, a Left Labour Zionist activist from Łódź who fled to the Warsaw ghetto in the first days of the war. He became the secretary of the Oneg Shabbat archive in the Warsaw ghetto and later of the ŻKN on the 'Aryan side'. He died in 1980 in Israel.
7. (*below right*) Maurycy Herling-Grudziński, a Jewish lawyer, was a member of the Polish Home Army who headed the 'Felicja' cell of *Żegota*. He hid 500 Jews on his estate in Boernerów, near Warsaw – an outstanding example of how Jews who had established themselves 'on the Aryan side' in turn helped others. Defying orders, Herling-Grudziński preserved Felicja's receipts, the only *Żegota* recipient records to survive.

8. Smuggling food into the Warsaw ghetto: a clandestine photograph of smugglers at a *meta* or smuggling-point. The man at the top of the wall is probably a Polish smuggler, handing bags down to Jewish confederates within the ghetto, while lookouts watch for policemen. This was one of the many ways by which German plans to isolate the ghetto were defeated.

9. Policemen at the gate of the Jewish cemetery. Two Polish 'Blue' policemen (first and fourth from the left), a German gendarme (third from the left), and three Jewish policemen with a Jewish woman. This was the gate at which the notorious gendarme nicknamed 'Frankenstein' often served.

30. Convent girls on an outing, spring 1942. Two of them are Jewish: Ursula Pfeiffer (bottom left, facing camera) and Lidia Sicarz (face scratched out). The nun Sister Zofia (here beside Lidia) scratched out Lidia's face, fearing that the photograph might endanger the convent because Lidia looked 'too Jewish'.

31. Zofja and Alicja Fajnsztejn. Fourteen-year-old Alicja had 'good looks' and lived under the false name of Jadwiga Kapińska; she and her younger sister Zofja, here dressed for her First Communion, lived with Helena Biczyk, her grandmother's maid, and Helena's husband, Józef, the superintendent of a building owned by the Fajnsztejns. The Biczyks also eventually took in the girls' parents, Izaak and Malka; the whole family survived.

12. A Jew emerges from a hiding place beneath his underground bunker after its capture by German troops during the Warsaw Ghetto Uprising. Thousands of bunkers like this one were built in the final months of the ghetto's existence; they provided the main alternative to escaping to the Aryan side.

13. Bunker 'Krysia', drawn by Orna Jagur, one of only two occupants of the bunker who survived. Built underneath a glass house belonging to the market gardener Mieczysław Wolski, the bunker contained two rows of three-tiered bunks, a long table and benches, a stove and a toilet bucket. Emmanuel Ringelblum was hidden here with his wife and son, together with thirty-five other Jews.

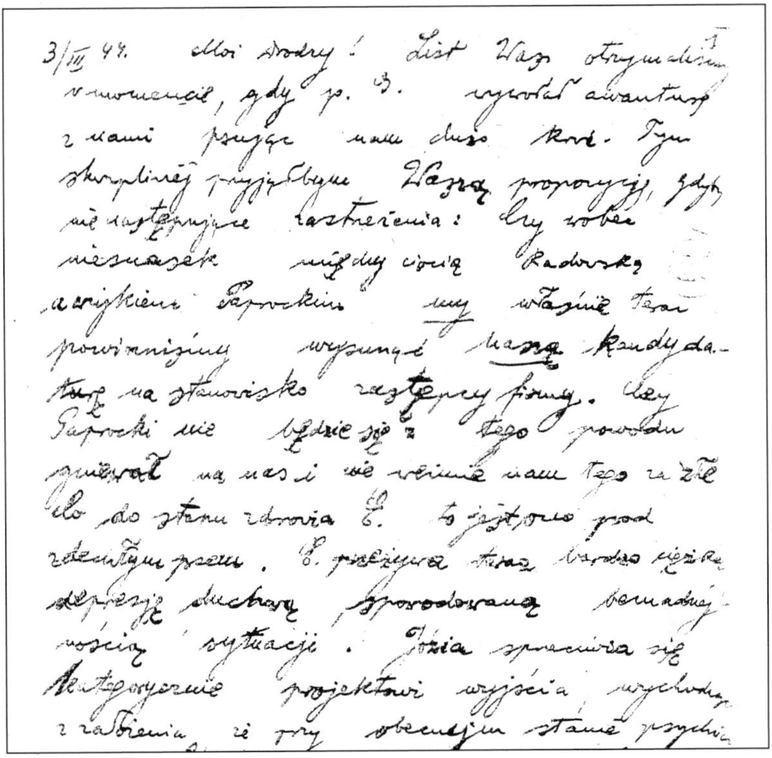
3/III 44. Moi drodzy! List Wasz otrzymaliśmy
w momencie, gdy p. B. wywołał awanturę
z nami psując nam dużo krwi. Tym
skwapliwiej przyjęlibyśmy Waszą propozycję, gdyby
nie następujące zastrzeżenia: Gdy wobec
niesnasek między ciocią Radowską
a wujkiem Saprockim my właśnie teraz
powinniśmy wysunąć naszą kandyda-
turę na stanowisko zastępcy firmy. Wuj
Saprocki nie będzie się z tego powodu
gniewał na nas i nie weźmie nam tego za złe
Co do stanu zdrowia E. to jest ono pod
zdecydowanym psem. E. przeżywa teraz bardzo ciężką
depresję duchową spowodowaną beznadziej-
nością sytuacji. Józia sprzeciwia się
kategorycznie projektowi wyjścia, wychodząc
z założenia, że przy obecnym stanie psychi-

4. Fragment of a letter from Emmanuel Ringelblum to Adolf Berman, written in bunker 'Krysia' on 3 March 1944, four days before it was discovered. Writing in coded language, Ringelblum turns down an offer from Berman to set him up as the Left Labour Zionist representative on some body (possibly the 'National Committee for the Homeland', the provisional Communist government, then being organized in Warsaw), for personal and political reasons.

5. (a) (*left*) Itzhak Katznelson, Yiddish-language poet and educator, member of the Zionist youth group Dror Hehalutz, author of the *Song of the Murdered Jewish People.* (b) (*right*) Israel Kanal, a ghetto policeman and member of the Jewish Combat Organization, who carried out the attempted assassination of the head of the ghetto police, Józef Szeryński. Katznelson and Kanal were among the 3,500 Jews who volunteered for the 'Hotel Polski' scheme in 1943, on the expectation that they would be exchanged for Germans interned abroad. Both were subsequently killed in Auschwitz.

16. Rose Guterman-Zar and her brother Benek Guterman in 'Aryan' Warsaw in 1943. Rose escaped from th ghetto in Piotrków Trybunalski in April 1940 and came to Warsaw, where she lived under false papers and acted as a courier for the Zionist underground. Benek joined her later; both survived the war.

17. Funeral of Bund activist Regina Klepfisz in the Christian cemetery in Bródno. Regina was the sister of Michał Klepfisz, who died a hero's death in the Warsaw Ghetto Uprising. Third from the left is his widow, Róża Perczykof-Klepfisz. Second from the left is Anna Wąchalska, and in the centre, her sister Maria Sawicka, Polish activists in the Council to Aid Jews (Żegota). The man standing next to Sawicka is unidentified; the other people present are Jews passing as Poles.

Nazi 'racial experts' all the evidence they needed to support their numerous prejudices: for example: 'The Poles: a thin germanic layer, underneath frightful material'.[27] Thus the Nazis themselves, though they had clear ideas about what Jews looked like, did not assume that anyone who deviated from the Aryan stereotype must be Jewish. Several memoirists agree that Germans were 'poor physiognomists'. (Poles were rather better at detecting Jewish traits, but as we shall see, they were not guided by physical characteristics.)

Perhaps more to the point, since the wave of Frankist conversions in the eighteenth century there had been a small but steady influx of Jewish converts into Polish society, and there were thousands of Poles whose Jewish origins were just beyond the reach of the Nazi racial laws. Whether for this reason, or simply because 'Jewish appearance' is largely a myth, even those who looked 'typically Jewish' were not always Jews. Ludwik Landau noted that 'People with a Jewish appearance are hunted on the streets – it seems that more than one person, having nothing at all to do with Jews, has paid with his life for his "suspicious" appearance'.[28] This of course was small comfort to those who 'fell in' because they really were Jews. But the Polish police, at least, soon became aware that they were arresting 'innocents', and began to be more cautious about checking documents. The Warsaw police chief cautioned his men as early as January 1942 that Poles were being arrested as suspected Jews (see p. 147). No doubt for this reason, the Blue police did not carry out German orders to shoot Jews on the spot; rather, people suspected of being Jewish were imprisoned and investigated further. This gave Jews an additional chance for survival, if their documents were good enough to pass the test or if a friendly Pole came forward to vouch for them. A Jewish appearance, at any rate, was not decisive.

Attempts at camouflage could backfire. 'In practice', writes Ringelblum, 'it turned out that platinum blondes gave rise to more suspicion than brunettes', and he repeats a ghetto joke: 'A Jew on the Aryan side can be recognized by a moustache, high boots, and a *Kennkarte*.'[29] Michael Zylberberg encountered a blackmailer who, after being paid off, offered him some friendly advice: among other things, to shave off his 'Polish-looking' moustache.[30]

A much better approach turned out to be simple chutzpah. Thus, Renia Brus tells of a friend who 'looked like a whole synagogue'[31] but went about freely, reasoning – apparently correctly – that no *szmalcownik* or police agent would believe that such a Jewish-looking Jew would dare to show his face.[32] Conversely, lack of confidence was a giveaway. Chaskielewicz writes:

I quickly worked out while walking around the city that Jewish descent is mainly noticeable in passers-by not as a result of this or that appearance but by the uncertainty with which they looked around. I could recognize Jews [...] easily through the fear that characterized their glances. People who had even typically Jewish features did not stand out from the crowd of passers-by if they looked and behaved calmly and confidently. So boldness and self-confidence were essential.[33]

Thus, if a Jew could move about confidently and behave like a Pole – for example, responding to attempted extortion by threatening to call the police – then 'bad looks' and many other disabilities could be overcome. But under the circumstances this required extraordinary discipline and self-control.

A more decisive factor that could identify a Jew was language: many Jews spoke Polish imperfectly or with a characteristic accent, and even someone whose Polish was perfect might let slip a characteristically Jewish expression or turn of phrase. Chaskielewicz, for example, once recognized a man as a Jew because he asked, 'What street are you from?', where a Pole would have asked, 'What district are you from?'[34] Like all the other problems, the language problem could be overcome with ingenuity or boldness. Among the activists, both 'Antek' Zuckerman and Jacob Celemenski are said to have had atrocious accents in Polish; nevertheless both of them moved about for the most part 'on the surface' – Celemenski was a courier for the Bund throughout the ghetto period – simply by acting self-assured and saying as little as possible. Another expedient was to pretend to be deaf and dumb. But this was a hard act to keep up, and made you conspicuous. For good measure, therefore, Samuel Willenberg's father, a portrait painter by profession, deflected suspicion by specializing in custom portraits of that famous non-Aryan, Jesus.[35]

At the other extreme, Jewishness could be suspected if someone's Polish was 'too good': many assimilationist Jews had a rather exalted image of Polishness and the Polish language, and spoke the language of Mickiewicz and Prus rather than the language of the street. Class differences could sharpen these distinctions, too: many Jews were forced to find work where they could – for example, as domestic servants – and if they were of middle-class origin then their language and manners would stand out sharply. But circumstances also forced many middle-class Poles into similar occupations. Chaskielewicz worked for a time in a bakery, where he was taken to be a member of the Polish underground hiding out from the authorities. To reinforce this camouflage, he cultivated the Warsaw street dialect and avoided 'excessively correct Polish and excessively high-brow [*inteligenckich*] expressions'.[36] (I wonder, though, whether a Polish intellectual in a similar position would have gone through the same contortions, and whether Chaskielewicz's attempts to play the street tough would not themselves have attracted attention. Wheels within wheels.)

Many minor cultural differences could identify a Jew. A man who failed to remove his hat in church would be guilty of a particularly glaring error, for example. Polish Catholics celebrate their *imieniny* (patron saint's day), and naturally know the date of their own *imieniny*, those of their friends and close relatives and all the most common ones as well. The least religious of Catholic Poles can recite the 'Our Father' and the 'Hail Mary', and knows how to behave in church. Outside of religious customs, Jews generally did not share the Polish taste for vodka and might find it particularly difficult to down the harsh wartime *bimber* (moonshine). Jewish women working in the home might not know how to make traditional Polish dishes, or might have no idea what to do with a piece of pork. The list of such subtle differences could be extended indefinitely.

Suffice it to say that many Poles seemed to have an uncanny 'nose' for Jewish characteristics. Helena Szereszewska's daughter Marysia, who considered herself completely assimilated and moved about freely, once saw some lemons (almost unobtainable in wartime) on a market stall. Out of curiosity, she asked the price, and when the stall-keeper named an astronomical sum she exclaimed 'Jezus, Maria!', as a Polish Catholic would. To which the stallkeeper replied: 'You've known them such a short time, missy, and already you're on first-name terms.' How did she know? Marysia had no idea.[37]

The problems mentioned thus far arose from established differences between Poles and Jews; others were the result of the specific circumstances of the German occupation. Jews had been isolated in the ghetto for two years, and emerged into an unfamiliar world. They no longer knew the price of a tram ticket, for example. As we saw in the previous chapter, Jews had been forced to surrender their furs at the end of 1941, so that to wear a winter coat from which a fur collar was visibly missing would be suspicious. (On the other hand, many Jewish coats were sold to Poles as *szaber* during the last phase of the ghetto, so that there were presumably not a few Poles wearing such coats as well.) After two years spent in the hell of the ghetto, and having lost many close relatives and friends, Jews were frequently depressed and despondent; they could be recognized notoriously by their 'sad eyes' (for which various cures were found: one man, says Ringelblum, darted angry glances at everyone; others wore sunglasses). Neglect of appearance frequently accompanies depression, and the same *szmalcownik* who told Michael Zylberberg to shave off his moustache also advised him to clean his shoes. (Middle-class Poles, on the other hand, made a point of dressing well, to avoid giving satisfaction to the Germans: this was part of the policy of maintaining a 'stiff posture towards the occupier'.)

Jews living 'on the surface' could easily be recognized by building porters or neighbours. The porter Stefan Giemza writes of a certain family: 'I could tell at once they were Jews. No one came to see them. They didn't get any letters.'[38] (A service sometimes provided by Poles was therefore simply to drop in to see their Jewish friends from time to time.) In a city where early curfews were enforced, evening social life revolved around the courtyard, building or staircase (the typical Warsaw residential complex consisted of four housing blocks clustered about a central courtyard, from which one or more gateways opened onto the street and numerous staircases led to the upper floors). Alicja Kaczyńska describes this social life: 'Tenants visited each other, wandering from floor to floor, talking about the day's events, sharing news about the political situation, often playing bridge.

but you always know more people by sight than seems possible. Besides friends and acquaintances whose faces readily come to mind, there are colleagues or fellow-employees; students, teachers, employers or subordinates; former landladies, tenants or neighbours; ex-clients, tradesmen and professional people with whom you have dealt; servants (most middle-class families in Warsaw had a maid, at least) and friends' servants; and if you are regular in your habits, then perhaps also tram conductors, newspaper vendors, shopkeepers and so on. An average person can be recognized by hundreds of people – friends, enemies, strangers. Though even that number is a drop in the ocean of a city like Warsaw, you would still rub shoulders with thousands of people every day, especially in a crowded city where everyone had to walk or travel by tram. Even if only one person in 10,000 knows you, if 300 different people see you in the street every day then someone is likely to recognize you about once a month.

Most Jews 'on the surface' were recognized on the street at one time or another by people who knew that they were Jews, and, most likely, most non-Jews recognized a few Jews (as Kaczyńska did). It was, indeed, not uncommon for Jews themselves to recognize each other in the streets, and there were even certain cafés where, in complete disregard of all conspiratorial principles but out of a desperate need for respite and companionship, they would congregate. Michael Zylberberg, for example, mentions having recognized both Adolf and Barbara Berman in public places in Aryan Warsaw, and having run into a pre-war Jewish acquaintance aboard a bus. He adds:

Jews in hiding often met by chance in the streets, restaurants and churches. In Sewerynów Street you would find the Catholic Community Centre of St Joseph, which had a well-patronized restaurant. The fact that it was in a quiet side street and the service by the nuns was so pleasant attracted many Jews to the place. [...] It was known to nearly all the Jews hidden in Warsaw, and offered an hour's respite from the cruel outside.[44]

Adina Blady-Szwajgier and Vladka Meed both describe a coffee-house at which Jewish activists met, at Miodowa 24.[45] Another, anonymous memoirist describes a restaurant at Grójecka 1, the *Stara Gospoda* (Old Inn), that became an asylum for Jews. He also points out that to prevent fraternization, Germans were not allowed to enter Polish establishments, an added attraction of such havens.[46] These chance encounters and nascent signs of a community life should not be too surprising: the Jews made up, after all, about 2 per cent of the population in 1943–44, about the same proportion as in London today.

If Jews were often recognized, how often were they denounced? Denunciation must be underreported in the memoir literature, since we must assume that most people who were denounced did not survive; therefore we have to use indirect methods to arrive at an estimate. As a starting point, let us take a story with a happy ending. Anna Lanota recounts that her cousin was spotted in a crowded tram by a former fellow-student at Warsaw University:

> He recognized her at once and started shouting at the top of his voice, 'That's a Jewess! Catch that Jewess!' She quickly got off the tram and, as quickly as she could manage [she was lame], walked away and mingled with the crowd. And the whole time he ran after her shouting, 'Catch the Jewess!' She wasn't caught, but it shows you about this man's attitude.[47]

Here, Lanota's cousin was unmasked in front of a crowd of randomly assorted strangers, any one of whom could have obeyed the student's cry of 'Catch the Jewess'; but none of them did so. What conclusions can we draw?

Let us defer, for the moment, considerations of crowd dynamics and leadership, which do not seem to apply to this situation: the student's attempt at leadership was ineffectual (and unopposed), and there is no indication that the members of the crowd interacted with each other in any way. They reacted, rather, as individuals, each of whom had to make a decision whether or not to interfere with her flight. Since the crowd was apparently a random sample of the Warsaw population, we have here, as it were, an impromptu Gallup poll of popular attitudes to denouncing Jews.

Activists often say, as Vladka Meed did about a friend of hers, that 'if they had known she was Jewish, they surely would have betrayed her' (see below). Jonas Turkow wrote: 'how large was the number of good Poles? So small was this minority that it was almost drowned in an ocean of ill will.'[48] In his diary, Mordechai Tenenbaum described the Poles as 'a nation of hooligans, which rejoices in having Hitler "purge" Poland of the Jews'.[49] If these opinions are correct, then Lanota's cousin must have been incredibly lucky to escape. But let us put the activists' beliefs to the test.

We do not know how many people were in this crowd; let us suppose that it consisted of only 50 people (a crowded tram would hold at least that number, and there were more people in the street, but let us be conservative). Let us further assume that one of Tenenbaum's 'hooligans' would be only too happy to grab a lame Jewish woman being chased by a fellow-hooligan. What, then, are the chances that a group of 50 randomly selected Poles will include not a single hooligan, if, let us say, even half of all Poles meet this description? Mathematically, it would be like throwing all heads in a toss of 50 coins: the odds work out to more than a quadrillion to one against. In short, if as many as half of the Poles had really been 'hooligans', Lanota's cousin's escape would have been not just lucky, but miraculous.

On the other hand, the student in this story was certainly a hooligan by this definition, so that our 'Gallup poll', if it is representative, points to perhaps 1 hooligan in 50 (or perhaps 100, or 200: it would help to know the size of the crowd). What if 1 Pole in 50 was that kind of person? In that case, the chances of escaping in such a situation work out, on the above assumptions, to about 1 in 3.[50] This removes her survival from the realm of the miraculous, and allows us to attribute it to mere good luck. In other words, the experience of Lanota's cousin is more consistent with the supposition that there were a small number of 'hooligans' among the Polish population – perhaps 1 or 2 per cent – than with the broad generalizations that Tenenbaum, Turkow and Meed make. If these generalizations were correct, quite simply no one would have survived. For all the Jews in hiding faced multiple threats of this kind, whether all at once at the hands of a crowd, as in this case, or, more usually, one after another at the hands of individual Poles.

As an example of the latter kind of experience, let us consider the case of Dawid Glat. A Dr Eichhorn, who took down Glat's testimony after the war, describes Glat thus: 'very handsome, curly hair, Jewish eyes, despite that was not taken for a Jew'.[51] But when we read his deposition we find that in fact he was 'taken for a Jew' several times. Glat lived 'on the surface' after his escape from the ghetto in December 1941 and ended the war in the camps as an Aryan, so that his ordeal on the Aryan side lasted three and a half years. Glat recounts a number of threatening episodes. On one occasion he was rescued from three blackmailers by a member of the German *Feldgendarmerie*, who accepted his Aryan documents and sent the blackmailers on their way. Another time, a Ukrainian policeman threatened to carry out a check to see if he was Jewish. 'I expressed satisfaction over this,' Glat says, 'and it saved my life', for the policeman let him go. Later, a sub-tenant in his flat, 'suspecting I was Jewish, started to steal from me systematically'. When the landlady sided with Glat and evicted the sub-tenant, the latter threatened to denounce him to the Gestapo. But, Glat says, 'keeping my cool, I stayed in bed until noon, and that completely disoriented her'. Later, he was arrested as a suspected member of the Polish underground, and from August 1943 to the end of the war was in Majdanek, Auschwitz, Buchenwald and other camps. In Auschwitz, a Polish prisoner tried to denounce him as a Jew to some Luftwaffe men, but they ignored him; the Pole then drew a Jewish star on Glat's camp uniform and wrote down his prisoner number, threatening to report him to the camp office. Glat managed to get himself transferred to another *Kommando* and so evaded further denunciation.

Glat thus describes four attempted denunciations in three and a half years, but as a Jew with evidently 'bad looks', and living 'on the surface' the whole time, he must have encountered hundreds of people who, like the sub-tenant, the blackmailers and his fellow prisoner, had their suspicions about him. With luck and presence of mind, Glat, like Lanota's cousin, managed to escape several threatening situations; but if the propensity of Poles to denounce Jews was anywhere near as high as the activists supposed, then Glat would have had hundreds of such encounters, not just four, and his survival would again have been miraculous.

An appropriate metaphor to describe such serial or simultaneous threats is that of 'running the gauntlet': someone who is forced to run a gauntlet might be lucky enough to dodge a few of the blows aimed at him; but running the whole gauntlet unscathed must be more than a matter of luck. Lanota dodged, figuratively, the student's attempt to denounce her, and Glat dodged four separate denunciation attempts, but all the other bystanders who might have struck at them held back their blows. Nearly everyone who survived in hiding has similar stories to tell. Indeed, 'running the gauntlet' is an apt metaphor for the whole experience of the Jews on the Aryan side, and proves useful again and again in this book. Each of the Jews of the secret city faced one potentially deadly risk after another, and had to survive them all to come out alive. Thus the cases of Glat and Lanota's cousin are not at all exceptional or unusual, let alone miraculous.

The multiplication of risk involved in running the gauntlet may be called the 'gauntlet effect': though the number of 'hooligans' who were prepared to betray Jews was small, Jews in hiding had so many encounters with them that their overall chances of survival were significantly diminished. Conversely, the fact that the Jews' chances of survival were not good is not an indication that there were large numbers of hooligans: quite a small number sufficed. It will be estimated in Chapter 6 that about one in every seven of the Jews of the secret city died as a result of betrayal or denunciation by Poles, or directly at their hands. The number of 'hooligans' will be estimated at about 3,000, or about 0.3 per cent of the population. The 'gauntlet effect' helps to explain why so few people could do so much damage.

Two broad conclusions can be drawn: first, that though hostility to the Jews was widespread, few people were rabid enough to want to send people to their deaths; but second, that even a few malicious people could cause enormous harm to a small and vulnerable minority, particularly in an atmosphere of widespread hostility. Crowds such as the one encountered by Lanota's cousin were generally passive rather than friendly: while no one tried to catch her, if someone had caught her it is unlikely that anyone would have come to her aid. We will encounter a few more cases of Jews being exposed in front of crowds of people, who turn out to behave variously. On occasion, a debate will break out over whether the Jew should be turned over to the authorities or not, and the crowd will be divided on the issue. The hooligans thus had their passive sympathisers, and were not ostracized for their activities.

The issue of crowd passivity has received considerable scholarly attention since the case of Kitty Genovese, who was raped and murdered in New York in 1964 in full view of hundreds of people in nearby tenement buildings, none of whom even called the police. Initial explanations centred upon the alienation of modern urban life, which allegedly causes people to become callous and indifferent, while more sophisticated later models have proposed such mechanisms as 'diffusion of responsibility' (everyone assumes that someone else has already called the police;

no one feels personally responsible).[52] A possible reading of the case of Lanota's cousin is that it was like the Kitty Genovese case in reverse: people who might have been inclined to 'catch the Jewess' might have refrained from acting because they assumed that someone else would catch her. According to the 'diffusion of responsibility' interpretation, the larger the crowd, the more diffuse the responsibility, and hence the less likely it becomes that anyone will act, one way or the other. This interpretation cannot be applied to the serial risks that Dawid Glat faced, in common with most other Jews in hiding; it is therefore of limited value in explaining how so many Jews managed to run the gauntlet successfully but it might have been one factor in a complex equation.

Another factor that worked on crowds was fear: standing out from the crowd could be dangerous in occupied Poland. That is of course why Jews who witnessed such scenes did not intervene themselves. Conversely, however, crowds in Warsaw were canny enough to realize that someone who raised the cry of 'catch the Jew' might easily be a German provocateur, and that the 'Jew' might turn out to be a member of the Polish underground. Here again Jews benefited from the camouflage provided by the large number of non-Jews who were in situations similar to their own. There were thus many things that influenced the behaviour of crowds, but in one way or another they all encouraged a passivity which could work for or against the Jews. A crowd's passivity could be broken, however, if a leader emerged: then the crowd would often follow. Although leadership did not play a role in the cases just discussed, it will figure in other examples that we shall encounter later on, and the more diffuse leadership role of the Polish underground, the Catholic church, the political parties and the underground press, together with the central question of antisemitism, will be discussed at some length in the next chapters.

In summary, then, the chance that a Jew who was exposed in public would be betrayed was the product of many different factors. Jews were right to fear exposure, but the amount of risk involved in such encounters cannot be reliably inferred either from the degree of their fear, nor in any simple way from an assessment of the balance between friendly and hostile attitudes. We can only say that all the Jews in hiding 'ran the gauntlet' and that many if not most of them came out alive. Neither the Jewish activists' most pessimistic conclusions, nor the more sanguine conclusions that are put forward by the Polish activists are borne out by this fact.

Housing

To understand the problems that Jews faced in finding *melinas*, we must begin by understanding the general housing situation in the city into which they had escaped. Pre-war Warsaw was a poor and overcrowded city, with a population of 1.25 million crammed into only 661,000 residential rooms – about 1.9 people per room.[53] A substantial part of the population, 36.9 per cent in the 1931 census, lived in single rooms, which constituted 42.7 per cent of the city's dwellings. The housing situation was worsened by the bombing in 1939, which destroyed 78,000 rooms, nearly one eighth of the housing stock. Population losses due to war deaths and the flight of refugees from the city were soon more than made up for: most of the refugees returned once the fighting was over, and other refugees streamed into Warsaw from the Polish territories incorporated into the Reich. In addition, the city had to make room for increasing numbers of Germans, who naturally helped themselves to the best and least-crowded areas. The non-Jewish population grew as follows:

Table 3.1   Non-Jewish Population of Warsaw, 1940–43

	June 1940	December 1941	November 1943
Poles	895,000	907,279	974,765
Germans*	8,000	16,200	28,012
Other	10,000	17,321	1,894
Total	913,000	940,800	1,004,671

* Includes *Reichsdeutsche*, *Volksdeutsche* and *Stammdeutsche*. Excludes about 50,000 occupation troops quartered in barracks.
Source: T. Szarota, *Okupowanej Warszawy dzień powszedni*, 67–70.

The pre-war non-Jewish population was about 890,000.

Adding 393,300 Jews to the total for June 1940, we arrive at a total city population, shortly before the creation of the ghetto, of 1,306,300, for whom there were 582,940 rooms, an overall density of 2.24 people per room. The closing of the ghetto segregated 139,644 rooms behind the ghetto wall, giving a population density in the ghetto of 2.94 people per room, rising to 3.29 people per room when the ghetto reached its peak population of 460,000 in March 1941. The segregation of the ghetto in turn left 443,296 rooms for some 920,000 non-Jews, or 2.08 people per room. Thus, though housing was certainly scarcer in the ghetto than on the Aryan side, the difference was not so great as we might suppose.[54]

Readers who are familiar with the story of the Warsaw ghetto may be surprised by these figures for the ghetto's population density, which are much lower than those usually cited. Most authors derive their information from a report on the closing of the ghetto by the German Resettlement Commissioner, Waldemar Schön, who calculated the ghetto's population density at six to seven people per room, on the basis of 27,000 dwellings of two-and-a-half rooms each, thus 67,500 rooms in all.[55] But these calculations are mistaken. Besides being careless with his figures, it is also likely that Schön confused the number of dwellings reported by the Jewish Council (61,295) with the number of rooms, and so divided (67,500 rooms ÷ 2.5 = 27,000 dwellings) where he should have multiplied (61,295 dwellings × 2.28 = 139,644 rooms).

There are many reasons why Schön's report should have aroused suspicion, even without looking into the provenance of his figures. For example, he grossly exaggerated the number of Jews in the ghetto (according to him, between 470,000 and 590,000). His report is also internally inconsistent. Schön maintained that 115,000 Poles had left the designated district to make way for 138,000 Jews; he would therefore have us believe that a net increase of 23,000 people, less than 6 per cent, could have tripled the population density in the Jewish district. Independent estimates put the number of Poles displaced at only 70,000 so that, once again, Schön is boasting: his figures allowed him to claim that his resettlement operation had involved a quarter of a million people. Even so, the net inflow of Jews was only 68,000, not nearly enough to balance the books.

Despite the manifest absurdity of Schön's figures, they have generally been accepted uncritically. Raul Hilberg, for example, who is generally more careful in his use of German documents, gives a population density of 7.2 people per room in the ghetto and 4.1 on the Aryan side (at least getting the proportions right, but these are the correct figures per dwelling, not per room).[56] Israel Gutman, who should certainly know better, repeats Schön's figures without correction, even adding that 'calculations made after the war' point to a still higher density.[57] Similar figures are repeated in nearly every book about the Warsaw ghetto.[58] The notion that several families were squeezed into each room has made its way into the popular image of the ghetto: those who have seen *Schindler's List* may recall the scene – treated quite humorously – in which one family after another troops into a ghetto apartment.[59] Hollywood will take liberties, of course. But that so many eminent historians have been taken in should serve as a warning against the martyrological tendency that exists in the Holocaust literature and the distortions and blind spots to which it gives rise. The reality of the Warsaw ghetto was awful enough; there is no need to exaggerate.

Having said that, it should be added that if population density is measured in people per hectare instead of per room, then the ghetto was indeed fantastically overcrowded: it held 1,017 people per hectare, compared with sixty-seven for the rest of the city.[60] For the sake of comparison, Manhattan has about 290 inhabitants per hectare. The daytime population of the City of London is estimated at 330,000 in an area of 299 hectares, a density of 1,104 people per hectare.[61] This may help visualize the scene in the ghetto: it was as crowded, all the time, as the centre of a major city during rush hour. The overcrowding did not come about mainly because huge numbers of people were packed into the ghetto, but rather because all non-residential space was excluded from it, including parkland, commercial areas and even the Jewish cemetery. The great density per hectare in the ghetto created an enormous congestion of pedestrian traffic, contributing to an oppressive feeling of crowding and deprivation whose psychological dimension has been admirably described by Barbara Engelking.[62] The present chapter, however, is less concerned with psychology than with the practical aspects of finding housing on the Aryan side, and here it is chiefly necessary to note that Jews contemplating escape could not, despite appearances, expect to find abundant accommodation on the 'other side', even by contrast with the ghetto.

The housing situation, as described so far, can be summarized as follows:

Table 3.2   Population Densities in Warsaw during the Initial Ghetto Period, November 1940–March 1941

	People per room	People per dwelling
Germans	1.1	3.4
Jews (ghetto)	2.9 increasing to 3.3	6.7 increasing to 7.5
Poles and others	2.1	4.1

Where there was demand, supply arose to match it. New housing stock became available through the conversion of non-residential space (offices and warehouses), and to a much greater extent through a phenomenon characteristic of wartime Warsaw, the subdivision of rooms by partitions or curtains. By the end of 1941, the number of dwellings had increased slightly, from to 284,000 to 286,000 (presumably the result of the conversion of non-residential space), but the number of rooms had increased from 582,940 to about 620,000, mostly as a result of subdivision.[63]

A much bigger source of new housing on the Aryan side was the progressive shrinkage of the ghetto. At the end of the 1942 *Aktion*, the *Restghetto* had in all only 428 of the 1,483 buildings that had belonged to the ghetto when it was closed, housing 35,000 people officially and almost as many 'wild' Jews. These buildings comprised about 17,700 dwellings of 40,300 rooms, giving a density of perhaps 1.74 people per room. The remaining 1,055 buildings, containing about 43,600 dwellings and nearly 100,000 rooms, were eventually made available to the Polish population. Consequently, the number of rooms available to Poles and others increased to 536,000, or perhaps 565,000 once room subdivision and reclamation are taken into account. By January 1943, when the major wave of escapes from the ghetto began, the number of non-Germans on the Aryan side was about 957,000 (by extrapolation), which means that the population density of the Polish areas at that point was also about 1.7 people per room.

In purely numerical terms, then, the housing situation in the city into which the bulk of the Jewish fugitives emerged was, after many ups and downs, about the same as that inside the ghetto; in both cases it was slightly better than before the war. The city's housing crisis had been solved Nazi-style, by the murder of one-quarter of the population.

The Demographics of the Aryan Side

But statistics, as ever, do not tell the whole story. On the face of it, there was a slow and steady growth in the Polish population, met by housing reclaimed from the ghetto, but this characterization masks a situation of considerable turmoil. For one thing, the mortality rate grew steadily:

Table 3.3   Mortality Rates outside the Ghetto in Warsaw, 1938–43

	Deaths			
	Non-Jews		Jews	
Year	Number	Per thousand	Number	Per thousand
1938	10,208	11.4	3,680	10.2
1939	22,760	25.4	8,408	23.4
1940	17,976	22.6	8,342	20.3
1941	19,226	20.2	*	*
1942	19,258	19.5	*	*
1943	17,125	17.6	3,400[†]	125.9

* Insufficient data. [†] Pro rata, on the basis of 6,800 deaths on the Aryan side in total (see Chapter 6).
Source: Szarota, *Okupowanej* 78–9 *et passim.*

From this we can calculate that there were about 30,000 more deaths in 1939–40 than we would expect on the basis of the 1938 figures, about 20,500 Poles and 9,500 Jews. Of these, 10,000 Poles and 3,000 Jews died as a result of military action in 1939; the rest, 10,500 Poles and 6,500 Jews, as a result of German terror and poor living conditions. This was the situation when the ghetto was closed.

By the end of 1942, about 74,000 Poles had died from all causes since the beginning of the war, and an equal number had been taken for forced labour in Germany. Some of these were volunteers driven by poverty and unemployment, but most were simply pressganged, in the round-ups that were an everyday feature of life in the capital. A modest number of people – 19,991 between November 1941 and May 1943 – registered their departure from the city after having been permanent residents; at least an equal number, probably, left without registering.[64] All told, therefore, easily 200,000 non-Jews who had lived in Warsaw before or during the war were no longer there by mid-1943. Thus, more than a fifth of the city's non-Jewish population had either been killed or had left under more or less abnormal circumstances. Taking into account family members affected by this dislocation, we may assume that most of the city's population was in some distress as a result.

The birth rate was not nearly enough to make up for deaths and outflows, let alone to account for the observed net increase in population. In 1940–42, 31, 662 live births were recorded among Poles in Warsaw, an average of 10,554 annually, compared with 13,104 in 1938.[65] This no doubt reflects poor sanitary conditions, poor nutrition and the distressed state of families in general. Further evidence is provided by the precipitous increase in infant mortality, generally a reliable index of living and sanitary conditions. The 584 infant deaths recorded in the first five months of 1941 – pro rata, 1,409 for the year[66] – meant that some 13 per cent of newborns died in their first year, a statistic that few third-world countries could match today. A report by the Delegatura in 1942 estimated infant deaths at one-fifth of live births, and maintained that the situation was worsening.[67] Tuberculosis – another indicator of poor sanitary conditions – accounted for 23 per cent of all deaths in 1943, more than twice the pre-war proportion.[68]

The substantial net increase in the non-Jewish population, despite losses of this magnitude, is therefore evidence of a very considerable influx of population, largely of refugees displaced by the various German resettlement programmes. The net increase amounted to 61,575 between November 1941 and May 1943, so that the gross inflow must have been about a quarter of a million people.[69] During the same period, 143,972 people registered with the municipal authorities as temporary residents (not counting 69,945 hotel guests) and 17,611 as permanent residents; in addition, many people lived unregistered.[70] It can be seen, therefore, that large numbers of people – certainly tens of thousands at any given moment – were constantly seeking accommodation. The addition of many thousands of new dwellings through the shrinking of the ghetto brought only temporary relief: by the end of September 1943, according to the Polish-language 'reptile' (German-sponsored) newspaper *Nowy Kurier Warszawski*, 14,423 families – at four persons per family, nearly 60,000 people – were seeking lodgings through the municipal accommodations office.[71] Despite the doubtful source, these statistics are probably accurate enough as far as they go; but there were of course many others who made arrangements privately, including the hundreds of Jews in hiding who at any given moment found themselves homeless because of blackmail or for other reasons. They could hardly register with an official agency.

Thus, despite the statistical easing of the housing situation in 1943 (the decline in density from 2.1 to 1.7 people per room), the shortage of housing was in fact more severe than ever. The space that had statistically become available largely consisted of rooms vacated by people who had died, fled or been deported, in dwellings occupied by their families, which were given up to strangers only with the greatest reluctance. The authorities therefore set quotas, forcing families in 'under-utilized' dwellings to accept billets. A decree issued in the autumn of 1943 required a three-room dwelling to accommodate at least five people, and a four-room dwelling at least seven people.[72]

The consequence of this situation for Jews escaping from the ghetto was not really that space was unavailable – thanks to billeting, subletting, the subdivision of rooms and the conversion of non-residential space, it was not hard to find accommodation of some sort – but that privacy was difficult to achieve. Both the *Herrenvolk*, who craved privacy, and the Jews, who needed it desperately, thus faced an acute housing crisis.

Housing the Jews: The Search for Melinas

The kind of accommodation that Jews needed depended on whether they were living 'on the surface' or 'under the surface'. Jews living 'under the surface' needed strict isolation, or else to share accommodation with trustworthy non-Jews. Of those who lived in isolation, a few were in purpose-built 'bunkers' such as 'Krysia' (a codename for *kryjówka*, hideout), which was located under a greenhouse on the suburban property of the market gardener Mieczysław Wolski at Grójecka 81.[73] Emmanuel Ringelblum, who was one of its inhabitants, described the conditions there:

> As for Krysia, her situation is as follows: in 28 square metres, thirty-eight people. There are fourteen bunks in which thirty-four people sleep, meaning that in some very crowded bunks there are three people (in ours, for example – Uri [Ringelblum's son] sleeps at our feet). The other four people sleep in camp cots or beds scattered around. [...] The food supply isn't bad, but the crowding is indescribable. Fleas and bedbugs on top of it all.[74]

Orna Jagur, who left the bunker shortly before it was discovered on 3 March 1944, had the following first impression:

> A wave of hot, stuffy air struck me. From below there poured out a stench made up of mildew mixed with sweat, stale clothing, and uneaten food. [...]
> Some of the inhabitants of the shelter were lying on the bunks, sunken in darkness, the rest were sitting at the tables. Because of the heat, the men were half-naked, wearing only pyjama bottoms. Their faces were pale, tired. They had fear and unease in their eyes, their voices were nervous and strained.[75]

Ringelblum's wife, Judit, commented on the psychological effects of these conditions in a letter to Adolf Berman in November 1943: 'Here a terrible depression reigns – an indefinite prison term. Awful hopelessness. Perhaps you can cheer us up with general news and maybe we could arrange for the last of our nearest to be with us'.[76] These were the conditions in what was considered to be an exceptionally good *melina*.

The Bund also had a bunker, of 24 square metres according to Ringelblum, in which a group of party activists were hidden. A few other 'bunkers', on a smaller scale, were built by sympathetic Poles such as Mr and Mrs Broniak, mentioned in the previous chapter.[77] Some bunkers were in buildings reclaimed from the ghetto, and had been built by Jews trying to evade the round-ups. Other Jews lived in spaces of whose existence or residential use the authorities were unaware. Recall, for example, 'Kazik's' *melina* from Chapter 1, where Janina Bauman, her mother and sister were hidden for a time on the burnt-out first floor of a building, above a trading company, converted into a *melina* by a member of the Polish underground. They shared this space with fifteen other Jews; eight others had just left.[78] Other accounts mention attics, cellars, broom closets, even a photographic darkroom.

Another type of *melina* consisted of a flat or room with a separate entrance, set aside for the purpose of hiding Jews. As we have seen, such completely private spaces were hard to find. Żegota had a housing section that tried to arrange accommodation of this kind for Jews, but with limited success. The Jewish aid organizations were also able to achieve little in this field; that is why the ŻKN had such difficulty in finding places for seventy surviving ghetto fighters, at a time when the number of Jews in hiding was at its peak. Nevertheless some places were found. The seventy fighters left the ghetto on 10 May 1943 and were taken temporarily to the Łomianki woods, where they were helped by a chance-met local peasant who brought them food. Tuvia Borzykowski, one of the seventy, writes in his diary-cum-memoir: 'We also had the problem of finding hiding places in Warsaw for the sick and for those who had to remain in the city to work with the Jewish National Committee and the Coordinating Committee [...]. All those arrangements were concluded by May 19; then we cleared out of the woods.' In a diary entry for 17 May, he writes: 'Today, we left the tomianki woods and went to the "Aryan" side of Warsaw.' Thus the fighters' stay in Łomianki lasted only about a week. Most of them went on to the Wyszków woods nearby, to join a partisan group of the communist People's Army; Borzykowski, Marek Folman and Simcha Rotem returned to Warsaw, where they stayed in a *melina* operated by a Jewish woman masquerading as a Pole.[79] There were also private individuals who undertook initiatives to provide separate housing for Jews: we noted a number of examples in Chapter 1, such as the engineer Feliks Cywiński and his partner Jan Bocheński, who sold family-owned land in order to pay for four flats in which twenty-six Jews could be hidden.[80]

In all the kinds of *melinas* mentioned so far, it was absolutely necessary for a non-Jew, or sometimes a Jew living 'on the surface',[81] to build or provide the shelter and to act as a link with the outside world. Jews living in isolation had to be supplied with food and other necessities. For example, if the space was not designed for human habitation, some sort of makeshift toilet facility had to be provided, often simply a bucket, which then had to be emptied periodically. If the space was a normal room or flat, then someone had to provide 'cover', that is, to own or rent it and give the appearance of living there.

The most common recourse for Jews living 'under the surface' was to live with Aryans, who would necessarily have to be aware of their guests' identities. Precautions then had to be taken to conceal the arrangements from visitors and other tenants. In some cases, Poles who were hiding Jews were known to deflect suspicion by loudly voicing antisemitic opinions.[82] Suspicion could be aroused in many ways: for example, if a landlady, supposedly a woman living by herself, was regularly seen bringing home large amounts of food, or if she hung out washing that was clearly not hers. Thus, clothes had to be dried indoors; shopping was done often and in small quantities. It was wise, also, not to visit the same shops too often, which made shopping difficult and time-consuming. Conversations had to be conducted in whispers. To put her neighbours off the scent, one Polish woman made a point of leaving the door of her flat open for part of the day 'to air it', so that curious neighbours could see for themselves that there was no one hiding there: in the meantime, the Jewish family she was keeping had to hide in a cupboard. When guests came, the Jews would tiptoe from one room to another while the guests were shown around the flat according to a pre-arranged plan.[83] It would be interesting to know whether people who were hiding non-Jews, such as members of the underground, felt the need to take similar measures. Most likely not.

Even with the most careful precautions, however, Jews in a *melina* of this kind were likely to betray their presence sooner or later. Visitors might notice some small detail out of place. Neighbours might hear coughing, sneezing, snoring or the crying of a small child. Then the neighbours would start to talk, and the gossip might reach the ears of blackmailers or police agents, or one of the neighbours might approach the porter and threaten to denounce him if the Jews were not removed. Occasionally, a neighbour might actually denounce the Jews, though this was uncommon. (Among other things, denunciation would also mean betraying the Polish landlord, a serious breach of the wartime code of solidarity. Conversely, though, Jews could find themselves caught in the middle of some personal vendetta and be denounced precisely because someone wanted to strike at their Polish carers: Nathan Gross, for example, was threatened by a feud of this kind.[84]) Alternatively, rumours might reach the landlord that suspicious people were nosing about, or he might simply become nervous. In any of these cases, the *melina* would be 'burnt', and the Jews would be abruptly faced with the problem of finding a new one.

Jews living 'under the surface' who had lost their *melina* had few options if their friends could not find them another one very quickly. Sometimes friends who were afraid or not in a position to offer long-term shelter would put them up for a night or two, giving them time to organize something. Otherwise they could give up the clandestine life altogether. The most tempting such opportunity came at the time of the Hotel Polski affair (see chapter 4); alternatively, they could return to the ghetto while it still existed, or go to another ghetto that had not yet been liquidated, or they could make their way to the labour camps at Trawniki or Poniatowa. All of these alternatives involved trusting the Germans, clearly an act of desperation. Faced with this dead end, some people committed suicide or, what amounted to the same thing, simply turned themselves in to the police.

Objectively, the best chance of survival for a Jew with nowhere to go was to try life 'on the surface': that is, to trust the Poles rather than the Germans. Many of those in hiding in fact lived both 'on' and 'under' the surface at various times. Coming out of hiding in this way required strong nerves and self-assurance, or an optimistic outlook on life; but for those who could steel themselves for it, it offered a broader range of options.

Jews living 'on the surface' could rent rooms or flats in the same way as anyone else, assuming that they could convince landlords of their Aryanness. Nathan Gross describes the problem:

> My fellow-tribesmen who have survived the Hitlerite hell, you know how you have to go about renting a flat, you know how you have to pretend that you aren't in a hurry, though today, or at the latest tomorrow, you'll be without a roof over your head. You know the suspicious glances, the questions meant to trip you up, the demands for references![85]

It was better, if possible, to find a landlord who would knowingly shelter a Jew. When the underground organizations found housing for Jews, they felt it both necessary on ethical grounds to make the landlord aware of the risk, and desirable for practical reasons for the landlord to be forewarned and therefore forearmed.[86] Activists also needed to sound out landlords to make sure that they were not hostile.

Non-Jewish activists could approach landlords openly without much risk to themselves, but Jews acting on their own generally did not dare to reveal themselves to complete strangers. Therefore when Jews found accommodation on their own account they generally did not disclose their identities. But living with an uninitiated landlord could be nerve-racking: the tenants could never be sure that landlords would not guess their secret, or what their reaction would be if they did. Someone living 'on the surface' with strangers also had nowhere private to go where it would be possible to drop the act and be oneself even for a moment.

But we have also noted that it was hard for Jews to conceal their identity for very long, and this was especially true in the intimate circumstances of a subtenancy in a shared or subdivided room. Therefore, most landlords no doubt formed their suspicions sooner or later. For that reason, even Jews living 'on the surface' preferred to find places to live through their network of contacts rather than by public means.

Children generally had to live 'on the surface', apart from the fortunate few who could stay hidden with their parents. Most were placed in convents or orphanages, or were taken in by Polish families. It was very difficult to find a place 'under the surface' for a Jewish child who, it was feared, would grow restless in hiding and lack the self-control to keep quiet when necessary. Therefore nearly all children in hiding were represented as Catholics – orphans, or the children of some real or imaginary relatives. Żegota activists have estimated that 500 Jewish children were hidden in convents in the Warsaw area, another 200 at the Father Boduen Orphanage and 500 more in orphanages operated by the RGO.[87] In all, about 7,000 children were sent into hiding; most of them were placed with Catholic families. But there were problems:

> The matter of children isn't easy. It's especially hard with a boy. After all he has his Jewish mark. The Poles are afraid. [. . .]
> You have to pay in advance, to the end of the war, because if the parents are killed [. . .][88]

> Herszkowicz is crying. [. . .] Two days ago they sent their child to some Poles, but today they have brought it back to the ghetto. They don't want to keep it, it looks too Jewish.[89]

(As readers may recall from the previous chapter, so many children were returned from the Aryan side that the Germans set up a special orphanage in Dzika Street to accommodate them.)

Children whose appearance was acceptable still, like adults, had to learn an appropriate behavioural repertoire. Especially if staying in a religious institution, they had to be taught the catechism and the basic prayers. They had to be taught to give appropriate answers to questions – for example, in response to 'What was your name before it was Marysia Kowalska?', the child had to learn to insist that she had always been called Marysia Kowalska, and to 'Where are your real parents?', to insist that she had no other parents besides her foster parents. These rules were learnt so well that they proved an obstacle to reclaiming younger children after the war.[90]

A small group of children lived 'on the surface' in a very literal sense, living on the street and supporting themselves through begging or, like the cigarette-sellers of Three Crosses Square, by petty trade. These were mainly the child smugglers of the ghetto period, who had got out of the ghetto by their well-tried paths and now lived by their wits.

The experiences of the twenty-odd cigarette-sellers have been described in a moving and well-known memoir by Joseph Ziemian, an activist working with the Jewish National Committee, who made contact with the children and found them shelter. Ziemian writes:

> After their escape from the Warsaw ghetto they led an independent life on the 'Aryan' side. Condemned to death, baited and hunted at every turn, they knew how to find ways to fight their way through the jungle created by the occupation. They knew how to defend themselves and fight for existence, they knew – in contrast to many adults – how to help each other mutually.[91]

Astonishingly, nearly all these children survived. Ziemian lists twenty-one survivors, at least one of whom has written his own memoir.[92] Besides the cigarette-sellers, Marek Edelman mentions a group of eight children who survived by hiding in the ruins of the royal palace, bombed in 1939, and there are other individual accounts.[93] Perhaps in all a hundred or so Jewish children lived on the street in Aryan Warsaw.

Finally, some adult Jews also lived on the street, hiding in bombed-out buildings, sleeping in attics, cellars or stairwells, begging or stealing food. Ringelblum believed that this was the norm: 'A Jew who has lost his flat will not find shelter anywhere, even for a day or two. He has to hide in the ruins of bombed buildings or in open fields, with his life in danger until he finds a flat, which costs more every day.'[94] This kind of life could not be kept up for long, especially in winter; it was usually a short-term expedient, while Aryan friends worked out something else. Such Jews were, of course, terribly exposed – if nothing else, they could be arrested for violating the curfew – and it must be assumed that most did not survive. At any rate, there is very little trace of them in the memoirs.

Though they were not usually forced out onto the street, Jews did face an ordeal every time a *melina* was 'burnt', which happened very often. Janina Bauman lists fifteen *melinas* during the eighteen months that she and her family were in hiding, and some people moved even more often. The longer memoirs note an average of 7.5 *melinas* (more on this below). But these facts lead to a conclusion somewhat different from Ringelblum's. Here is another gauntlet that the Jews had to run, and the same logic applies as before: if the prospects of finding a place to live had been as slim as Ringelblum believed, then the chances of several thousand people surviving all these dangers and ending the war in one piece would have been infinitesimal.

The activist circles from which Ringelblum got his information tended to see mainly the problem cases; people who had their own resources preferred not to involve outsiders, even Jewish organizations, which might after all have been infiltrated by the police. In fact, Jews could negotiate such dangerous passages successfully again and again because they were part of the spontaneous, conspiratorial, protective secret city, with its network of Gentile helpers and other Jews in hiding, which meant that most Jews could minimize their contacts with the dangerous outside world. Activists, on the other hand, who had more people under their care than their personal contacts could handle, were forced to deal with strangers.

The Bund activist Adina Blady-Szwajger writes:

So many addresses – where did we get all those addresses from? Someone once asked me, and I didn't know. Maybe from notices in the entrances to the blocks of flats advertising rooms to let? Or, rather, more often, through the network of contacts with people who were 'sure'. Whenever we went to an address, we never knew for certain whether it was genuine, or a trap, whether on leaving such a place we wouldn't meet the police, and whether the lives of the people we had lodged there would be safe.[95]

People finding accommodation for themselves were faced with the same dilemma, and so again preferred, when they could, to use their networks. In one way or another, therefore, they generally stayed with people who knew or guessed that they were Jews.

Thus, although Jews living 'under the surface' were completely dependent on non-Jewish helpers, those living 'on the surface' were not really much less dependent: they needed help to arrange the escape from the ghetto, to procure documents, to provide the initial *pied-à-terre* on the Aryan side and emergency *melinas* afterwards, to hold and sell possessions, to lend money, to ransom or vouch for them if they were arrested and to arrange all sorts of other details. Even the most self-reliant Jews, living 'on the surface' and vastly experienced, like Citizen Frajnd, found it indispensable to have at least a few people to whom they could turn in an emergency, who would put them up for a day or two while arrangements were made, organize new documents and so on.

In any case, the distinction between 'on the surface' and 'under the surface' is not hard and fast, since most people had mixed experiences. For example, a family might be living 'under the surface', but one or two members with 'good looks' might go about freely: in such cases, the *melina* was really 'under the surface', though some of the people in it were in effect living 'on the surface'. Children, too, lived 'on the surface', but almost always under the care of people who knew that they were Jewish. In the case of adults living 'on the surface' in rented accommodation, too, the question hinges on whether the landlord knew his tenant's identity: if he did, then he was essentially in the same position as if he were providing a *melina* 'under the surface'. The situation was slightly easier since he did not have to conceal the tenant from neighbours or visitors; but on the other hand, Jews who went about freely were more likely to attract blackmailers. *Melinas* were thus 'burnt' with equal frequency, whether they were 'on' or 'under' the surface, and represented about the same degree of risk to all involved.

How often were Jews hidden for money, and how often out of humanitarian motives? And what moral conclusions ought to be drawn? Nechama Tec reports that of 535 helpers about whom her informants offered information on payment arrangements, eighty-six or 16 per cent helped solely for money. Of these, fourteen robbed their tenants and thirteen broke their promises (absolute numbers calculated on the basis of the percentages given by Tec). Thus, only twenty-seven landlords out of 535, or 5 per cent, behaved dishonestly towards their tenants. However, some selective perceptions are at work here. The ratio of helpers to people helped in Tec's sample is less than 2:1, whereas the average memoir lists about seven different *melinas*. It would seem, therefore, that payment details are mentioned only about a third of the time. Once again, then, we probably have a case of 'the dog that didn't bark in the night'. Since human perception, memory and storytelling conventions all conspire to weed out the everyday cases and emphasize the extraordinary ones, we are likely to be hearing mainly about exceptions: on the one hand the altruists, and on the other hand the cheats and robbers. If the missing two-thirds represent the 'normal' cases – probably the honest, paid landlords – then instead of 84 per cent altruists, 11 per cent who were honest but paid and 5 per cent who cheated or robbed, the true proportions might be something like 28 per cent altruists, 70 per cent who were honest but paid, and 2 per cent who cheated or robbed. But this is entirely speculative. At any rate, it is apparent that the dishonest landlords were in the small minority.[96]

This line of reasoning is reinforced by a number of other pieces of evidence. We have observed that most *melinas* were found through personal contacts, that is, by trustworthy people who in turn approached others they thought they could trust. The secret city was thus not composed of a random cross-section of the Warsaw population, but was a self-selecting conspiracy of decent and honest people. There was a criminal element as well, it is true. But there was no large-scale enterprise involved in hiding Jews, on the model of the smuggling during the ghetto period: when it was done for money it was done mostly by people who were trying to supplement their incomes or make ends meet. It was therefore an activity that offered too little profit, for the risk involved, to attract major criminals, though there were, as we shall see, some individual exceptions. As to the moral value of paid assistance, it might be observed that help for money is still help: we do not begrudge the doctor his fee. And people who helped Jews were risking their lives.

The fact of the death penalty for helping Jews has been a central point of discussion between Poles and Jews, and warrants some discussion here. Some defenders of the Polish record claim that the death penalty, which was not normal policy in other countries, was proof of a special Polish inclination to help Jews, which the Germans allegedly felt they needed extraordinary measures to counter. But in truth the death penalty was a standard feature of Nazi decrees in the General Government. On 31 October 1939, in the first month of the German occupation, Governor-General Hans Frank issued a Decree for the Combating of Violent Acts, which provided among other things that 'Whoever incites or encourages disobedience to the decrees or regulations of the German authorities is subject to the death penalty' and 'Instigators and helpers will be punished in the same way as perpetrators, an attempted act will be punished in the same way as a completed act.' Other paragraphs of the decree provide the death penalty for the possession of weapons, sabotage, arson, violence against Germans, conspiracy to commit any of these acts and failure to notify the authorities immediately on hearing of someone's intention to commit any of these acts.[97] This decree, clearly aimed at the Polish underground, set the pattern for other decrees in the years to come. The corresponding decree about hiding Jews, issued on 15 October 1941, was cited in Chapter 2 but is repeated here for convenience:

Jews who, without permission, leave the district to which they have been confined are subject to the death penalty. People who deliberately offer a hiding place to such Jews are also liable to the same punishment.

Instigators and helpers are subject to the same punishment as perpetrators; an attempted act will be punished in the same way as a completed act. In less serious cases the punishment may be imprisonment with hard labour or imprisonment.[98]

The similarity of wording is striking.

In practice, the occupation authorities did not hold themselves to any laws. Jews were killed for leaving the ghetto long before the 1941 decree, and Poles were routinely and summarily killed for such things as violating the curfew, owning a radio, possessing underground pamphlets, performing abortions or trading illegally.

Hiding Jews for money was therefore no riskier than many other ways of earning a living – or, indeed, than simply living. Kazimierz Brandys wrote:

Death threatened for bacon and gold, for weapons and false papers, for evading registration, for a radio and for Jews. The wits said that they were afraid only of sentences higher than death; to them the death penalty was like a prewar jaywalking ticket. Over the city there hung a deadly absurdity.[99]

It is currently estimated that about 700 Poles were executed for hiding Jews, a negligible proportion of the 1,800,000 Poles who died under Nazi occupation. If, as Teresa Prekerowa has estimated, at least 160,000 Poles were involved in hiding Jews, then the chances of being killed for hiding a Jew were about one in 230, whereas one Pole in fifteen was killed in all. On the face of it, then, people who were hiding Jews were much safer than other Poles! But this would be a specious conclusion, since those who hid Jews ran most of the other risks as well, and for a longer time. It works out that during the period of mass hiding an average Pole had a 2.2 per cent chance of being killed, while for those who hid Jews the chance increased to 2.6 per cent, nearly one-fifth higher. But many other activities were much riskier.

Still, selling buns in the street was not the same as taking the source of danger into your home and living with it twenty-four hours a day. Yad Vashem, at any rate, will recognize helpers as 'Righteous Gentiles' even if money was charged, provided that the sums were not extortionate and the Jews were not exploited or mistreated.[100] It was perfectly reasonable to expect Jews to contribute to their own upkeep if they could, and many poor families simply had no choice. Help extended without payment, or not conditional on payment or other considerations, was of course unambiguously altruistic and admirable.

Can we form an impression of the extent of such help? An analysis of thirty *melinas* reveals that 122 Jews were hidden in them all together, at the times for which we have descriptions of them, an average of four Jews per *melina* at any one time. Sixty-eight Gentiles (sixty-seven Poles and one German) were involved in providing the *melinas*, 2.3 per *melina*. Jews in hiding were continually moving from one *melina* to another as each one was 'burnt'; in the cases for which full information is available, each Jew moved an average of 7.5 times. In general, *melinas* were not reused once 'burnt': landlords would become too nervous, and prudence would dictate at least waiting for things to cool down. Only two of the thirty melinas were reused after they had been 'burnt'. If this was typical, it would follow that the average Jew in hiding lived in seven different *melinas*.

With these estimates to hand, we can put forward the following tentative conclusions. First, given that the average population of Jews in hiding (from October 1942 to August 1944) was about 20,000, it would follow that some 5,000 *melinas* were needed to house them at any one time, tended by 11,500 helpers. The total number of *melinas* needed over the whole period would have been seven times higher, therefore 35,000, tended by about 80,500 helpers. Not all of the latter would be aware that they were helping Jews, though many who were not told explicitly must have guessed. Impressionistically, let us say that some three-quarters of helpers were told or guessed; therefore, some 60,000 people were involved in consciously providing hiding places for Jews. This fits well with Ringelblum's estimate of 40,000–60,000.[101]

Providing a hiding place was the most difficult and dangerous form of help, but the average memoir also lists numerous people who offered other kinds of substantial help. It must be appreciated that in such an overcrowded city many people of courage and goodwill were simply not in a position to offer the necessary space or privacy for a *melina*, but could perhaps organize a place with friends, provide emergency shelter for a day or two, arrange to have documents made, hold property for safekeeping or arrange its sale, offer or arrange a job, give or lend money, organize escape from the ghetto, escort Jews safely to their *melinas* and so forth. In many memoirs there is a 'guardian angel', who hovers in the background and offers assistance when required. Such a figure, for example, was Janina Bauman's 'Aunt' Maria, or Helena and Mieczysław Tarwid, who performed many services for Bernard Mandelkern and his wife.[102] Nor should we forget those other background figures, the members of the Polish underground who operated the 'legalization' cells or worked in the city records offices, the postal workers who routinely intercepted letters addressed to the Gestapo and so saved many people from denunciation (among them Emmanuel Ringelblum), doctors whose discretion could be relied upon and who tended to the sick, and of course those in their hundreds who worked for the aid organizations and distributed money to those in hiding. Other forms of help could be enumerated at great length. Zofia Kubar's memoir, for instance, lists nine such incidental helpers, among them her former headmistress, Maria Uklejska, a reformed antisemite, who provided a haven that Kubar could visit and where she could feel at home, and helped in many other ways; Szczęsny Dobrowolski, who arranged her escape from the ghetto and her documents; Cesia Sczypińska, who befriended her and made various arrangements; Janek Nowak, who was afraid to put her up himself but arranged for her to stay with his girlfriend; a tram driver named Jaś Grabowski, who got her to a reliable doctor when she broke her leg; and the doctor, a Dr Trojanowski, probably one of the two 'Righteous Gentiles' by that name.[103]

How many such people there were is very difficult to say. In most memoirs, nearly as many secondary helpers as *melina*-providers are mentioned, and there were also others in the background of whom the Jews were unaware, such as the people involved in 'legalization'. On the other hand, there must be considerable overlap between cases (activists who distributed money or provided documents could each easily have helped hundreds of Jews, someone who was offering incidental help to one Jew might have been hiding others), and not all helpers (for example, clerks in registry offices) were necessarily aware that they were acting on behalf of Jews. Still, we would probably be estimating conservatively if we put the number of secondary helpers at between 10,000 and 30,000 – between one-sixth and one-half as many as provided hiding places – and therefore the total number of helpers at between 70,000 and 90,000.

This broad range arises not only as a result of the uncertainty of the estimates, but also because of the rather hazy boundary between genuine help and simple decency. Peleg-Mariańska met a man after the war who claimed that he had helped her, simply because he had known who she was and not denounced her: we can safely exclude such silence from the category of genuine help. But what of those who offered a meal, a lift, gave directions, said a few encouraging words? Yad Vashem limits recognition as 'Righteous among Nations' to those who helped repeatedly or over a long period. Here, however, we are not trying to decide how many 'Righteous Gentiles' there might have been in Warsaw, but how many people helped in one way or another, without for the moment worrying about how they might be classified. As a rule of thumb, included in the above estimate are those who helped in ways sufficiently notable to warrant mention in the memoirs, and those who worked in the background in ways that have been well documented. If we were to include people who offered minor kindnesses, the number might be two or three times larger; if we were to exclude those who helped for money alone, it might be smaller by 20,000–30,000.[104]

Money and Jobs

Jews living 'on the surface' could sometimes support themselves by working, though that was not easy even for non-Jews. In June 1941, the living expenses of a working-class family of four were estimated at 489 zł per month, compared with 152 zł. before the war. Official wages, meanwhile, were fixed at 1.16 zł per hour for skilled workers, 0.72 zł and 0.58 zł for semi-skilled and unskilled workers. Women, regardless of skill, were paid 0.46 zł. Boys under sixteen earned 0.29 zł. and girls 0.23 zł. A skilled worker working sixty hours per week could therefore earn at most about 300 zł per month. His wife, working similar hours, could contribute no more than 120 zł.[105] Even with their children working such Dickensian hours, therefore, it could well be impossible for a family to make ends meet at the official wages. There was a wartime joke:

> Janek and Franek meet in the street.
> Janek: How are you? Are you working?
> Franek: Yes, I have a job
> Janek: And your wife, is she working?
> Franek: Yes, full time.
> Janek: What about your son?
> Franek: He's working too.
> Janek: My God, what do you live on?

To which Franek replies that, thank God, his daughter is unemployed, so she can support the whole family. Small wonder, then, that Ludwig Fischer complained that Polish workers often absented themselves for one or two days a week to deal on the black market.[106] In response to this problem, the official rates were raised on 28 December 1942 – to 1.32 zł per hour for skilled men.[107]

Fischer also complained, on the other hand, that there was a labour shortage in Warsaw, with 5,000 jobs unfilled in May 1942 and a shortage of 10,000 hands to carry out earthworks.[108] The liquidation of the ghetto and the large-scale round-ups of Poles for forced labour in Germany only made things worse. Thus, a black market developed for labour, as for everything else, and jobs could be found paying much more than the official wages. Even so, most families supplemented their income with some sort of illegal dealing: black-marketeering, bribe-taking, forging documents, selling adulterated food, hiding Jews for money or blackmailing them. The criminal margin of society expanded under the pressure of wartime conditions, and every sort of theft and swindle flourished. In one confidence game, a swindler would approach a Jewish family, claiming to have information about relatives who were supposedly safe in hiding somewhere but needed money to survive. The swindler might offer personal information about the relatives, perhaps taken from a letter that the relatives had thrown from a deportation train; or the letter itself might be offered as proof. The swindler would offer to take the money to them, and of course would never be seen again. Another swindle involved plans to smuggle Jews to Hungary, Slovakia or Sweden – a few Jews really did manage to reach safety by those routes – for which the organizer would need money for expenses and bribes. Again, the swindler would vanish once the money had been paid. The ghetto had provided a rich source of income through smuggling; its liquidation left hundreds, probably thousands of Poles without a decent source of income. But it also left them with experience in Jewish matters and in dodging the law, and with a large pool of fugitives whom they could prey on or help. Some people did both.

Rents were similarly fixed at pre-war rates, in theory. Fischer reported that rental income in the Aryan sector in July 1941 amounted to 3,545,700 zł, 84.1 per cent of the amount owed; in the ghetto, 1,727,350 zł, 56.3 per cent of the amount owed.[109] On this basis, it can be calculated that average monthly rents were nominally 9.50 zł per room on the Aryan side and 22 zł in the ghetto. But in practice, market prices reached much higher levels. The 'reptile' *New Warsaw Courier* reported that the price for the most modest accommodation was 150 zł per month as early as March 1940,[110] and it exceeded 300 zł or even 500 zł in 1943 and 1944. To live illegally, unregistered, also involved bribing the building manager, so that all the many classes of people living underground found life expensive. As always, it was worse for the Jews, for whom landlords had to run additional risks, and who were vulnerable to exploitation.

The typical monthly price for room and board of a Jewish child placed with a Christian family, in 1943–44, ran to 2,000 zł and more. Ringelblum claims still higher prices: 'the cost of keeping a child on the Aryan side in the summer of 1942 [...] was [already] very high, about 100 złoty a day',[111] and 'While in January of this year [1943] it was possible to find a flat with board for a hundred złoty per person per day, now they are asking for two hundred or more.'[112] However, a number of letters have been preserved in the Berman archive from Jews asking for aid from the ŻKN, often outlining their writers' material circumstances. Where these mention concrete sums, somewhat lower figures predominate. For example:

Aaron Fajgenblum, M.A., escaped from the camp at Lipowa 7 in Lublin
I, Bela Fajgenblum
My little sister Rachela Kapłan
Our expenses are as follows:
For rent we pay, for my husband, for myself and for my sister –   3,000 zł
Food costs us –   3,000 zł
Or, all together –   6,000 zł.[113]

In this case (from an undated letter, probably written in mid-1944), room and board came to 2,000 zł per person per month, or about 67 zł per day. From another letter:

Warsaw, 16.V.44
There are six of us, of whom three are not working.
Maria Gibiańska – home seamstress, earns up to 40 zł per day, with her sixteen-year-old son, for whom she pays 3,000 zł per month. Alina Wdowińska, seamstress, earns 1,500–2,000 zł [per month], bears the cost of room and board

for herself and her mother-in-law, Adela Wdowińska, in the amount of 3,500 zł a month. Mulużna, a governess, out of her [monthly] salary of 400 zł pays room and board for her eight-year-old daughter Alina, 2,000 zł per month.

We ask urgently for help, because we have already sold nearly everything, and we will not be in a position to hold out.[114]

Here the daily rate works out at 78 zł per person.

We may note that Gibiańska and Wdowińska earned money at black-market rates, perhaps 5–10 zł per hour, many times the official rate for women. Even so, they could not begin to make ends meet. Many Jews could not earn money at all; women working as domestics, the most common occupation, earned much less than this.

Such rents seemed outrageous to people who had been separated from the Aryan side for two years: the same kind of black market for accommodation did not exist in the ghetto, and Jews had been accustomed to paying the official rates. But by the time these letters were written, the cost-of-living index had reached sixty-seven times its pre-war level, and the amount required to equal the pre-war income of an unskilled worker was therefore about 7,500 zł per month.[115] Thus 6,000–9,000 zł per month for room and board for a family of three was steep but not wholly unreasonable. Whether it should be considered exploitative depends on the landlord's actions if rent payments could not be met.

The unavoidable gap between earnings and expenses was usually filled, as the second letter indicates, by selling belongings. Most Jews who escaped from the ghetto took with them whatever valuables they still had, sewn into their clothing or otherwise hidden, or else they counted on Christian friends to whom they had entrusted property or goods before the ghetto was closed. Such material reserves were the difference between life and death for thousands of Jews. They were unfortunately also a target for the dishonest and unscrupulous. 'Jews have gold' was a popular motto of the time, implying that they could easily be separated from it, and that anyone who did not take advantage of the opportunity was a fool. This theme will be taken up again in due course.

Besides working and selling goods, Jews living 'on the surface' had a number of other ways to raise money. They could seek financial help from Gentile friends, for example. Thus Mandelkern collected debts owed to his father (which the debtors were under no legal obligation to pay). Chaskielewicz proposed to sell some of his family's real estate to a friend, who instead lent him a large sum, to be paid back after the war. This was obviously a high-risk loan. But in the event Chaskielewicz survived, while the property was destroyed in the 1944 uprising.

Jews could earn a decent living by operating on the black market: many traded with the ghetto while it still existed; afterwards, some (for example, Michael Zylberberg and Nechama Tec) bought and sold goods on the Aryan side. As we have noted, some of the surviving child smugglers got by by selling cigarettes or newspapers on the street. All forms of street trade were risky, because of the constant exposure to *szmalcowniks*, and because the German and Blue police carried on a sporadic war against it. Those rounded up were routinely shot, held as hostages or sent to concentration camps.

The official answer to unemployment was to go to the *Arbeitsamt* and volunteer for work in Germany. Poles avoided this recourse if they possibly could, but it had its attractions for Jews. Germans were generally not sensitive to the many nuances of language and behaviour that distinguished Polish Jews from non-Jews, so that it was much easier to pass as a Pole in Germany than in Poland. Volunteering for work in Germany involved undergoing a medical examination, an obvious problem for circumcised men. But this could be evaded in the usual ways, or if the examining doctor was friendly or could be bribed. Alternatively, the volunteer could send someone to the examination in his place. Conditions for forced labourers in Germany were often unpleasant, but the main worry, apart from Allied bombing raids, was denunciation by Polish fellow-workers. A friend of Vladka Meed's who had gone to Germany told her after the war: 'If they had had the slightest inkling of my identity they would surely have denounced me'.[116] But that was jumping to conclusions. We will look more closely in Chapter 5 at the experiences of Jews who found themselves in labour camps as Aryans; for now, it will be enough to note that here is another example of 'running the gauntlet' which some Jews did survive.

Those living 'under the surface' had very limited possibilities of earning money. They could work from home like the seamstresses mentioned above. Chaskielewicz describes a Jew who worked alone in a photographic laboratory and slept there. Chaskielewicz himself, during his time 'under the surface', collated and folded underground newspapers. Nechama Tec's family baked buns, which Tec (the only one of the family who could 'pass') sold on the street. One of Helena Szereszewska's daughters was given room and board in exchange for caring for the landlady's mentally disturbed sister. Others performed domestic work or tutored children, although these were relatively risky occupations for Jews 'under the surface': they would have to be hidden from visitors, and children might talk.

Finally, Jews could rely on charity, at least in the short run. Jews 'on the surface' could resort to the doss-houses and soup-kitchens provided for Poles by the RGO, or seek sanctuary in a church or convent. Such stop-gaps could tide Jews over for a few days while they found a new *melina* or a job.

The form of help that figures most prominently in the post-war literature is of course that extended by Żegota and the other underground aid agencies, whose functioning is described more fully in Chapter 5. The sums provided were modest – in principle, 500 zł per month, at times cut down to 400 or even 300 zł, although extra money could be paid in exceptional circumstances. These donations provided only a fraction of the amount needed for even a modest living, and at best eased rather than solved the fugitives' problems. In any case, organized aid reached only about a third of the Jews in hiding, and reached them rather late in the day.

Other Problems

Numerous everyday problems caused difficulties, especially for Jews living 'under the surface'. Jews living 'on the surface' who fell ill could go to hospital or see doctors in the same way as anyone else, although circumcised men had to consider that a medical examination or nursing care might reveal their identity. Arranging medical care for Jews 'under the surface' who fell ill was difficult. A trustworthy physician had to be found, and a hospital visit was out of the question. The Committee of Democratic and Socialist Physicians offered aid to Jews in hiding, but contacting it required connections with one of the aid agencies, which again most Jews did not have, or not until a very late date. For the most part, Jews who fell ill 'under the surface' either recovered naturally or died.

Jewish children were born on the Aryan side, but doctors and midwives were rarely available to assist. Feliks Cywiński writes that he had to deliver a child to a Jewish woman in hiding himself.[117] A bigger problem was the care of the infant, especially if mother and child had to live under the surface. Various solutions were found. They could move to the countryside where, with houses far apart, a child's crying might go unnoticed. In other cases, newborns were taken in by Polish families or sent to orphanages. Naturally, under the circumstances, childbirth was not such a frequent event; but if the birth rate among Jews in hiding was even half of that among the Poles, then some 200 Jewish children would have started their lives in Aryan Warsaw.

Rather more Jews, 800 or so, died of natural causes while in hiding. It was not entirely impossible to arrange a Jewish funeral for them, but most Jews who had been living 'on the surface' were given a Christian burial, under their Aryan names. In the case of a death 'under the surface', the trickiest problem was removing the body of the deceased without attracting attention, especially if other Jews were still living in the *melina*. If a corpse could not be smuggled out of the house, it was buried in the cellar or, in the countryside, in the garden.

Life in Aryan Warsaw: In Conclusion

Jews escaping from the ghetto were faced with life in an impoverished and over-crowded city, in which general living conditions were poor, and which was under the control of a harsh occupying régime. This régime tried to tighten its control over the whole population through a network of documentation and other means, as well as through terror. Jews in hiding faced many challenges, which often resulted in betrayal and death, and life in hiding, especially 'under the surface', was nerve-racking and often involved very difficult physical conditions. On the positive side, the Jews were not the only people in hiding, and they benefited from underground documentation factories set up for, and camouflage provided by, other fugitives. Above all, they benefited from the protection of that self-selecting, spontaneously arising network of mainly honest and decent people who, together with the Jews themselves, constituted the secret city.

But the secret city was also a city beset with enemies, and the next chapter will consider its attackers.

4 The City under Siege

Where the previous chapter described the life of the secret city, this chapter will consider in greater detail the forces that threatened it.

Threats from the German Side

Jews on the Aryan side were threatened not only by terror directed specifically at them, but also by the general terror against the Polish population. Street round-ups for forced labour in Germany, a threat in the early part of the war, had largely subsided by the time the great wave of escapes from the ghetto took place, but at the same time assassinations and acts of sabotage by the Polish underground increased, bringing German reprisals in which Jews could easily be caught up. Thousands of street executions took place in 1943–44, and house searches were very frequent as well. In the largest such operation, on Good Friday 1944, about a third of the district of Żoliborz was surrounded and combed, building by building; Ludwik Landau also notes a rash of such operations in July 1943. Searches of individual buildings were a daily occurrence.

Terror directed specifically against the Jews took various forms. These included measures to prevent the escape of Jews, such as flooding the sewers, using a combination of intimidation and rewards to induce the Poles to hand Jews over, offering various 'amnesties' to induce the Jews to surrender, forcing Jews who had been caught to act as stalking-horses to catch other Jews, and, most important, the Hotel Polski trap.

The Hotel Polski

Jewish organizations abroad, notably RELICO, the Relief Committee of the World Jewish Congress in Switzerland, had tried for some time (and with some success) to rescue Jews from occupied Europe by arranging passports and visas, mostly to certain Latin American countries that were prepared to offer citizenship *in absentia*. If a parcel of land was bought in someone's name, these governments were prepared to issue a letter called a *promesa,* undertaking to issue a passport on receipt of the proper documentation. Sometimes consuls agreed to issue entry visas; in other cases visas or passports were simply forged.

When a large number of such documents arrived in Warsaw, meant for Jews who had already been killed, the German authorities spotted a chance to set a trap. In June 1943, just after the final liquidation of the ghetto, a group of about 100 Jews was transferred from Pawiak prison to a small hotel, the Hotel Royal, where they were well treated. At the same time it was put about that these documents could be bought, as the Germans were not interested in the identity of individual Jews but needed a suitable number of people to exchange for Germans interned abroad (there was indeed such a programme, called the 'Exchange Action', though nothing came of it in the end). Anyone volunteering for this scheme would be allowed to live legally in the hotel until the exchange could be arranged. The response was greater than expected, and soon a hotel was dedicated to the purpose, the Hotel Polski at Długa 29.

The credibility of the scheme was enhanced by the fact that huge sums were asked, though it turned out that payment could be waived if a volunteer lacked the necessary means. It was further enhanced by the fact that some prominent Jewish personalities endorsed it, among them the head of the Joint Distribution Committee in Warsaw, David Guzik (Daniel Kaftor), and his deputy, Józef Gitler-Barski. In addition, news of the happy fate of foreign Jews previously deported to the transit camp in Vittel had spread among the Jewish community, even while the ghetto was still in existence. Once more, wishful thinking did the rest.

The Hotel Polski accumulated guests throughout the summer of 1943, becoming full to overflowing. Some had bought the foreign documents; others were 'wild' Jews, who came to the hotel because their *melinas* had been 'burnt' and supported themselves by carrying on all sorts of business with the Jews who were there legally. Then two shipments, totalling about 3,000 people,[1] departed via Pawiak prison for Vittel and Bergen-Belsen, whence almost all were eventually deported to Auschwitz and killed. A few hundred, mostly 'wild' Jews who remained in the Hotel Polski after these deportations were sent direct to Auschwitz to be gassed, or were shot within the precincts of the Pawiak. All told, of the perhaps 3,500 people who fell into the Hotel Polski trap, only one or two hundred survived.

As I have noted, the sheer number of victims helps to verify that there was indeed a large number of Jews in hiding, and the fact that such a large proportion of the fugitives volunteered for it – about one in seven – also shows the efficiency of the communication networks that connected the Jews in hiding, as well as the extraordinary attractiveness of the scheme.

The Hotel Polski affair raises a perplexing question: why – after the Ghetto Uprising, after the complete liquidation of the ghetto, after the truth about Treblinka was known – did so many Jews allow themselves to trust the Germans? Various authors have characterized the Hotel Polski as an 'island of hope', a 'ray of light' and so on. If it was perceived this way by the victims, then they must have believed that their havens on the Aryan side were not islands of hope or rays of light. In short, given a choice between trusting Poles who had shown good faith or a proven gang of murderers, a good proportion of the Jews in hiding opted for the latter.

With the exception of the 'wild' Jews, the victims were far from the most desperate. It cost a great deal of money to buy into the plan – an Engineer Sołowiejczyk was asked for 300,000 zł, for example[2] – and many of the victims gave up quite good *melinas*. We may, for instance, once more recall 'Kazik's' *melina* from Chapter 1, where the Lewinsons were staying, at no cost, in a spacious area above a shop, in which they could move about freely outside business hours and which was equipped with an emergency shelter and an electric alarm to warn of approaching strangers.[3] In every respect this was an ideal situation, the sort of *melina* that thousands of Jews dreamt of having. Yet twelve of the fifteen Jews who were staying there when the Lewinsons arrived went to the Hotel Polski, and the Lewinsons seriously considered it. Similarly, the scheme took in the educated, the politically sophisticated and the well-connected: not only Guzik and Gitler-Barski, but also the poet Yitzhak Katznelson; the writers Hillel Seidman and Yehoshua Perle; one of the leaders of the Left Labour Zionists, Natan Buksbaum; the community activist Nathan Eck; the Bund militiaman Simcha Solnik; the Tsukunft activist Leib Szpichler; Hela Schüpper-Rufeisen of Akiba; several members of the ŻOB command including Israel Kanal and Eliezer Geller; ŻZW commander Simcha Korngold, and many others. Guzik smelt a rat and escaped in time, but the others, including Guzik's family, refused to give up their places in the scheme and went to the camps. Perhaps being well connected helped, however: of this group, Gitler-Barski, Eck, Schüpper-Rufeisen, Korngold and Seidman survived (as did Engineer Sołowiejczyk).[4]

Clearly it is an oversimplification to attribute the 'psychosis' of the Hotel Polski to the difficulties of life on the Aryan side or the attractions of the scheme itself. No rational calculation could lead there. Adina Blady-Szwajger took her husband to the Hotel Polski, at his wish and against her better judgment; she believes his impulse was suicidal.[5] And this may give us the necessary clue. A woman with a long history of suicide attempts once told me that when she had made up her mind to kill herself, she felt completely at peace. Perhaps the Nazis, who often showed astonishing insight into the psychology of their victims, understood this. They offered what the best *melina* could not: a few months of serenity and apparently normal life. Their victims swallowed the offer like a drug.

After the Hotel Polski, German efforts to trap Jews subsided. As we have seen, the Germans seemed to have believed that there were only 5,000–6,000 Jews in hiding in Warsaw: once they had trapped 3,500 of them they must have thought that they had nearly the lot. This intelligence failure on the part of the Germans was a tribute to the secret city's success in staying secret, and to the conspiratorial solidarity within Polish society that made it possible. The authorities next tried bribery, but without much success. Franz Konrad, the head of the *Werterfassung*, testified after the war that 'for denouncing and delivering a Jew alive in Warsaw outside the ghetto through the Polish Police, the informer received a payment of 20 per cent of the captured property. Nevertheless, this was taken advantage of in only rare cases.'[6] Naturally: why would a blackmailer settle for 20 per cent when he could get 100 per cent by blackmailing the victim himself? Thus, if walls of solidarity separated the decent Poles from the Germans, the blackmailers were equally separated from them by walls of greed. Still, Jews were caught: only in 'rare cases' by denunciation, more often as Aryans or in house searches directed at the Polish underground, most often by the Blue police and *Kripo*, who were obeying German orders.

Threats from the Polish Side

Despite their overwhelming strength in Poland, the Germans could not have succeeded in ferreting out Jews to the extent that they did without Polish ferrets. The same is true, of course, of their efforts to penetrate the Polish underground, of which the outstanding success was the arrest on 30 June 1943 of the commander-in-chief of the Home Army, Stefan 'Grot' Rowecki. The two were, indeed, not unconnected. Konrad described how Polish agents had helped with the seizure of Jewish property in the first days of the occupation. He commented that, by giving these helpers a large share of the loot, 'the Gestapo was able to reward its agents well [...] In this way the Gestapo laid the foundation for a large organization of these people, which later provided the Germans with valuable espionage services against the attempts of the Polish population to [...] defeat the hated German intruder'.[7]

On the whole, Polish commentators have taken pride in Poland's record as the 'country without a Quisling'. Collaborators are popularly identified with the *Volksdeutsche*, and were held in contempt by Polish society. Others have maintained that such collaborators were 'the dregs of society – not Polish, not Jewish and not German, but general human scum, which serves any master',[8] or, alternatively, 'extremists of the near-fascist elements on the extreme Right'.[9] One of the tasks of this section will be to determine whether this sanguine picture is correct. In addition, I shall try to catalogue and characterize the various kinds of threats that beset the Jews from the Polish side – denouncers, the Blue police, the various police agents and spies, and assorted kinds of rogues and thieves – and, as ever, try to estimate the numbers of people involved.

'Three Warsaws'

The Delegatura produced a report in mid-1942 entitled 'Three Warsaws', which estimated that 25 per cent of the population belonged to 'the proper, underground, heroic, fighting Warsaw', 70 per cent to the 'Warsaw of Mr and Mrs Kowalski', passive and wanting only to survive the war, and 5 per cent to 'shameful Warsaw' which 'plays, hustles, does small deals with the occupier, gambles in the casinos, dresses well, eats in the pre-war way, throws money away by fistfuls, [and] doesn't long for the war to end'. According to a clandestine survey carried out for the Polish underground by the city administration [!] in the autumn of 1942, 25–30 per cent of the population of Aryan Warsaw were 'ready for action at any moment', about 60 per cent were 'passive' and 10 per cent belonged to the 'dregs of society, entirely harmful from the point of view of our interests'. On the basis of this and other information, Szarota estimates in absolute numbers that of the adult and adolescent non-Jewish population of Warsaw, 180,000 people were actively engaged in underground work, 360,000–420,000 were passive and 30,000–60,000 had an 'anti-citizen and anti-patriotic' attitude.[10] The methodology behind these figures is somewhat doubtful; but whether or not they are precisely right, the broad picture is no doubt accurate enough.

There were also Three Warsaws from the Jewish point of view. On the one hand, there was the network of supporters who made up the bulk of the secret city; on the other, its criminal element: the various kinds of *szmalcowniks*, denouncers, the Blue police and so on. In between were the great majority, who stood outside the secret city and were only vaguely aware of its existence. Whatever they thought of the Jews, they neither actively harmed nor helped them.

Were these two methods of triage identical? That is to say, was the 'proper, underground, heroic, fighting Warsaw' uniformly on the side of the Jews? Were the *szmalcowniks* and so on drawn exclusively from 'the dregs of society'? And were the inert majority the ordinary Warsaw of 'Mr and Mrs Kowalski'? We have a partial answer from the case histories presented in Chapter 1, where we saw that the networks on which the Jews depended for their survival reached into every corner of Polish society, from prostitutes and drug addicts to servants and working-class families to intellectuals and aristocrats. We shall keep these questions in mind as we run through the catalogue of crimes against the Jews and identify and characterize their perpetrators.

Denunciation and the Threat of Denunciation

Denunciation of all kinds was a popular sport in occupied Poland, as Jan T. Gross has shown.[11] In some cases money was the motive, that is to say, some people denounced Jews in order to collect the reward that was offered. But as we have seen, such cases were relatively rare, since it was more lucrative to blackmail Jews than denounce them. A blackmailer could also square his actions more easily with his conscience, since, after all, he was not directly causing his victim's death. The threat of denunciation was the blackmailer's weapon, but like a mugger's gun it was not meant to be used. This weapon also had other uses: for example, nervous tenants, afraid of collective reprisals, could threaten denunciation as a way of forcing Jews to leave their building.

Actual, rather than threatened, denunciation was an entirely different matter. It was usually done anonymously, therefore not for gain but for personal or ideological reasons. Gross has written of the 'privatization of the state' in totalitarian societies, by which he means that to increase the general terror the totalitarian state makes its police apparatus available to citizens to pursue private vendettas.[12] Jews could be denounced not only by personal enemies or antisemites, but also, as I have noted, by people with grudges against their Polish protectors.

Very occasionally, we have reliable eyewitness testimony to an act of denunciation. Zofia Kubar befriended a certain Lena, 'an elegant, pretty woman in her thirties', from the landed gentry, who was 'charming, very intelligent and well read'. Lena's brother owned an estate in the outlying town of Radość, where he lived with their mother. Through Lena, the mother agreed to take in a Mrs Górska, a Jewish woman living 'on the surface', as a housekeeper. Later, she also took to feeding a Jewish couple who were hiding in the forest nearby. Kubar recounts what Mrs Górska told her:

> one day [...] Lena's brother returned earlier than usual and caught the Jews taking their meal. In a rage, he locked them in a room and phoned the police. [...] In no time, the German gendarmes arrived and took the Jews outside. About fifteen minutes later, Mrs Górska heard several shots. The next day she learned that the Germans had ordered a peasant in a neighbouring cottage to take the corpses away and bury them somewhere.[13]

Kazimierz Moczarski, chief prosecutor of the underground courts in Warsaw, incidentally mentions 'the owner of a villa in Radość' as one of the *szmalcowniks* tried and sentenced to death by the Polish underground.[14]

There were other such Jekyll-and-Hyde families. Here is a note from the file that Adolf Berman maintained on such people:

Stefanja [*sic*] Rosner, Raszyńska 3 apt. 2, works in the gendarmerie in Leszno Street. Has caused more than a dozen [*kilkanaście*] blackmails against Jews. [...] Has more than once declared that she wants to exterminate a large number of Jews but doesn't always succeed. An exceptionally dangerous individual. With her lives her sister, Halina Rosner, an entirely different character. Good, honest, helps many Jews. One needs to be careful not to make a mistake.[15]

We have in these cases a clue as to some of the motives behind denunciation. Rosner was motivated by greed – Berman notes that she 'was a great pauper, now she wants for nothing'[16] – but obviously the desire to 'exterminate a large number of Jews' was the product of an antisemitic ideology. In the case of the villa owner, the motive seems (at least on this occasion) to have been purely antisemitic, without the element of greed. He gained nothing by his actions, and if he had merely been afraid of reprisals he could have made the Jews leave instead of having them killed. That the same family could contain, in two sisters or in a mother and son, two such radically different personalities – one prepared selflessly to help, the other a cold-blooded murderer – shows how questionable are all generalizations about class, nationality, religion and so on, as determinants of character and behaviour. In these two cases, a family of paupers and one of wealth and refinement both contained exactly the same extremes of nobility and depravity.

The Blue Police

The Polish Police, commonly called the Blue or uniformed police in order to avoid using the term 'Polish', has played a most lamentable role in the extermination of the Jews of Poland. The uniformed police has been an enthusiastic executor of all the German directives regarding the Jews.

Emmanuel Ringelblum[17]

Popular antipathy to the police long predated the war: Poland was a country where for 123 years state power had lain in hostile hands, and even the interwar period was mostly characterized by authoritarian governments which sometimes used the police as a means of repression. As a matter of habit, most people preferred not to have too much to do with the police, and co-operation with it was regarded as a kind of betrayal.

Since policemen were regarded with suspicion and mistrust, the police force attracted men of often dubious character and generally of a rather low educational and intellectual standard. Their easy corruptibility was also well established before the war. Frequently such men were antisemites: this was a police force that had shown no great inclination to intervene in such affairs as the notorious Przytyk pogrom of 1936, and its post-war successor, the *Milicja*, made up largely of the same men, was actively involved in inciting the still more notorious Kielce pogrom of 1946.[18] The police in the capital may, however, have been of a higher standard than was to be found in the provinces.

The Blue police were pressed into service by the Germans in 1939: the men were ordered to report for duty on pain of reprisals against their families. The force was placed under control of the *Schutzpolizei* (*Schupo*), and the top positions were filled by Germans. In due course, the lower echelons came increasingly to be composed of wartime volunteers – overt collaborationists, then, many of them *Volksdeutsche*. It was used for ordinary policing duties, but also to guard the ghetto gates and to flush out Jews in hiding. It was deployed in the suppression of the Warsaw Ghetto Uprising, when several of its members were wounded and one gave his life *für Volk und Führer*. It was also used against the Polish underground, to combat illegal trade and to round up Poles as hostages or for forced labour.

In general, then, the Blue police was regarded by contemporaries, Poles and Jews alike as an unreservedly collaborationist force, differing from the German gendarmerie only in being somewhat easier to bribe. The Polish underground carried out numerous assassinations of particularly odious or prominent policemen: most notably, Alexander Reszczyński, the police commandant in Warsaw, was assassinated by the communist People's Guard in March 1943.

But this is not the whole story. Unbeknownst to most contemporaries, the Blue police were heavily infiltrated by the Polish underground. Reszczyński, for example, worked in AK (Home Army) counterintelligence, so that the AK were quite upset by his assassination.[19] Itzhak Zuckerman also reports that the ghetto fighters received accurate intelligence information from the Blue police, via the Polish underground, through nightly telephone calls.[20] Whatever their reasons for collaborating, almost none of the Blue policemen served the Germans out of ideological zeal. So, for example, German attempts to recruit a Polish police battalion to be used against Soviet partisans ended in fiasco.[21] Evidently it was one thing to enjoy special privileges and the chance to get rich from bribes, while living at home; it was quite another to be sent to distant parts to risk your life for the hated occupier.

The Blue Police in Warsaw

On the eve of war, the State Police in Warsaw comprised seventy-two officers and 2,962 men. By the beginning of 1940, their numbers had dropped to sixty-one and 2,786 respectively, but by April 1942, with the addition of nearly 400 new recruits, the same sixty-one officers found themselves in command of 3,172 men. Thus about 12 per cent of the men were volunteers, while 88 per cent (the pre-war contingent) were more or less unwilling conscripts. There were also twenty-eight officers and 1,605 men in the Warsaw District outside the city, of whom, if the same proportion holds, about 200 were volunteers.[22] In addition to these uniformed forces, there were several hundred plainclothes members of the pre-war State Prosecution Service. These men were placed under the direction of the German Criminal Police (*Kripo*) and were called the 'Polish *Kripo*'. In the Warsaw District, they numbered 778 in July 1940 and 878 in April 1942, so that at least 100 had signed up after the war began. The manpower of the Polish police forces in the Warsaw District, at the time the Jews emerged from the ghettos in 1942–43, was therefore, all told, about 6,000 officers and men, including some 700 volunteers, 100 of them in plain clothes. Two-thirds were stationed in the city proper.[23]

The German authorities in Warsaw never entirely trusted the Blue police, and kept them under close supervision. In combat against illegal trade, Fischer wrote, 'unfortunately, the Polish uniformed police often behaved very passively, so that the supervising German officer had to intervene energetically'.[24] As to measures against the Jews, we have seen that a Blue policeman was posted at every entry gate to the ghetto, but with a German gendarme to keep an eye on him. The *Schupo* commander for the Warsaw District, a Colonel Jarke, dressed down a group of Blue policemen in August 1941 as follows:

Despite my repeated orders that the Polish policemen serving in the ghetto and at entry gates are responsible for maintaining order, and in that connection should use arms where necessary, there are cases when the German police are forced to use arms while the Polish police behave passively and do not act. In the future, every time the German police use arms, if it is shown that the Polish police did not act previously, I shall punish the Polish policemen on duty there with all the means at my disposal.[25]

We have seen that when the German gendarme at one of the ghetto gates agreed to accept a bribe, the Blue policeman could be counted on to follow suit. We have also seen that when the liquidation of the ghetto began, the authorities seemed to find it necessary to replace the Blue policemen with Germans. The Blue police were not used to round up Jews during the deportation actions in Warsaw; instead, Ukrainian and Baltic auxiliaries were imported for the purpose. Did this mean that the Blue police were not trusted to do their duty? Or merely that the *Einsatz Reinhard* had its own methods and personnel? Blue policemen were used for the round-ups in some smaller centres, where no ghetto police were available, and in Warsaw they were posted at intervals outside the ghetto walls, to catch escapees. They were also pressed into service during house searches, and every policeman was expected to arrest any Jew who came to his attention on the Aryan side.

On 10 December 1942, the Blue police were ordered to shoot summarily any Jew caught on the Aryan side without authorization; shortly thereafter, each commissariat was ordered to return a monthly report showing the number of Jews arrested and the number shot. According to Adam Hempel, the surviving records show only small numbers arrested and none shot.[26] Nevertheless, there were some men who carried out their duties zealously, even overzealously. Reszczyński complained in January 1942: 'There are cases when the Polish police has uncritically arrested Poles, suspecting them of Jewish descent, and imprisoned them, even though it is possible to ascertain on the spot that the accusation is unfounded. Such conduct is inadmissible and demands the immediate intervention of the district commandants.'[27] Can one read into this a hint that the Blue police should be lax in verifying documents? For otherwise, how was it possible to 'ascertain on the spot that the accusation is unfounded', without lengthy investigations? Or were the police to understand by this that they should carry out a physical examination of male suspects? We can only guess what this instruction meant, and how it was received.

The Blue Police and Blackmail

It was not in collaborating with the Germans that the Blue police posed the greatest threat to the Jews, however, but rather in their freelance activities. Blackmailers – the most dangerous kind of *szmalcowniks* – were very often *Kripo* men, or were accompanied by uniformed policemen. Policemen, perhaps those who had once supplemented their incomes with bribes taken from food-smugglers, now found a lucrative substitute in extorting money from Jews in hiding. Such instances are found very frequently in the memoirs.

Policemen, like *szmalcowniks,* were generally interested in money and not in causing the death of their victims. Therefore, even a Jew who had been arrested and taken to a police station was not necessarily lost. Janina Drutowska, for example, was arrested twice.[28] She spent thirteen days in a 'death cell' at *Kripo* headquarters, Aleje Ujazdowskie 8, and was freed in return for a large bribe. Later, she was denounced and imprisoned in Częstochowa, and freed again on the basis of her landlady's sworn statement. Naturally, such cases are exceptional: most people who fell into the hands of the police (on the evidence, one or two dozen a day)[29] perished.

In many cases, Blue policemen justified their behaviour by invoking the staple propositions of native Polish antisemitic ideology: the Jews are enemies of Poland, are part of the *Żydokomuna* or Jewish–Communist conspiracy, 'the whole world suffers because of the Jews' (as a Blue Police blackmailer told Nathan Gross).[30] Whether these beliefs were the motivation or merely the rationalization for these men's actions is open to discussion.

There are, on the other hand, cases of Blue policemen who used their position to help Jews.[31] In general, Blue policemen, who had passes allowing them to enter the ghetto freely, often played an important role as messengers and go-betweens in arranging escapes from the ghetto: we noted several instances in the previous chapter.

The behaviour of the Blue police, in short, is difficult to characterize unambiguously. Each policeman acted according to his own character and conscience, and as with Polish society as a whole, their behaviour ranged from the basest to the most noble. The police force was sprinkled with volunteers and collaborators, but consisted for the most part of the ordinary pre-war force. To which of the 'Three Warsaws' did they belong? Some, surely – on either the Polish or the Jewish scale – to each of the three.

Szmalcowniks

Can some reasonable estimate be made of the number of these criminals, and can anything be said about their provenance and motives?

Nearly every Jewish memoir or testimony of any length mentions encounters with *szmalcowniks*, and most often several such encounters. Even the most assimilated and best-integrated Jews seem to have drawn their attention: Citizen Frajnd, for example, was victimized three times. The average number of Jews in hiding over the two years when the *szmalcowniks* were most active was about 20,000, so that there were something like 50,000 to 100,000 encounters all told, or about 2,000–4,000 per month.

How many victims might one *szmalcownik* gang find in a month? For the moment, let us defer discussion of the less numerous but more dangerous blackmailers, many of them police agents, and concentrate on the street extortionists. It is curious, first of all, that there was a kind of going rate for extortion. In a way, street extortion represented an open market: the *szmalcownik* was selling a commodity, non-denunciation, whose price was negotiated with the victim. As in any negotiation, both sides were under pressure. The extortionist knew that if he had to carry out his threat and denounce his victim he would have to have dealings with the police, an uncomfortable prospect for a street spiv. If that happened, he would at best have to settle for the small reward offered by the Germans, and might find even that appropriated by the policeman whom he summoned. Finally, what the extortionist was doing was illegal, since a citizen's duty was to report Jewish fugitives to the authorities, not profit from them himself; therefore, an extortionist who carried out his threat might find himself reciprocally denounced by his victim, or arrested on the policeman's own initiative. Nathan Gross, for instance, recounts the story of two tram drivers who decided to dabble in extortion. Unfortunately for them, they happened to choose a non-Jewish woman as their victim. She complained to the police, and the pair were arrested and imprisoned.[32] Hence, the extortionist, too, had good reason to avoid complications: all things considered, it was therefore in his interest not to be too greedy. Thus, there was a kind of market price, which the extortionist asked and potential victims made sure they carried.

We have some idea from the memoirs of the kinds of sums that were demanded: Citizen Frajnd, for example, says that the standard ransom was 500 zł in 1941, but that a demand for 20,000–30,000 zł would not have raised an eyebrow in 1943. Frajnd himself was forced to pay 6,000 zł to a four-man gang in 1943, a price he regarded as modest. Two extortionists similarly demanded 3,000 zł from Vladka Meed in December 1942.[33] Such relatively small amounts seem to be the norm: the large sums mentioned by Frajnd would have been typical in encounters with blackmailers who sought Jews out in their homes, but not on the street. Impressionistically, an average street encounter would cost about 2,500 zł per extortionist early in 1944, or about 10,000 zł for a gang of four. The latter amount represented some five months' keep for a Jew, a huge sum that few people carried, so that the larger gangs probably averaged a little less – perhaps 1,500 or 2,000 zł each.

But *szmalcowniks* were reputed to be earning a good living from their trade, and 2,000–2,500 zł by then was hardly a princely sum. As we have noted, in May 1944 it took a monthly income of 7,500 zł to maintain the standard of living of an unskilled worker before the war. To make anything that could be described as a good living, therefore, the average extortionist must have needed to find at least three or four victims a month.

On this admittedly shaky basis (but no better method of estimating is available), we might calculate that the 2,000–4,000 instances of extortion per month, each involving a gang numbering from one or two individuals up to whole swarms of adolescents, would mean that there were perhaps a few hundred or as many as 1,000 gangs, perhaps 3,000–4,000 people all told. Ringelblum wrote of *szmalcowniks* 'in their hundreds and maybe even thousands':[34] we cannot improve very much on his impression.

Blackmailers were less common than extortionists: their trade offered big money, but involved some research and planning, and therefore intelligence and organization. Besides, many were police agents or worked with policemen as allies, which again was not to the taste of ordinary street criminals. *Kripo* had been infiltrated by the Polish underground, which managed to accumulate some information about these agents, and this led to a few prosecutions and death sentences against them. The Polish civil underground courts came into existence at the end of 1942, and meted out their first death sentences in January 1943. The first sentence against a *szmalcownik* in Warsaw, one Borys Pilnik, was passed on 7 July and carried out on 25 August.

A fragment from Pilnik's notebook has been preserved. Pilnik, who had infiltrated the Polish underground and was therefore as much of a threat to Poles as to Jews, lists about thirty 'customers', of whom nine are noted as Jews.[35] We will come back to him shortly. More information is available from three other sources. First, five notices were published in the underground press announcing the execution of blackmailers. Second, there is a deposition by Kazimierz Moczarski,[36] who from the autumn of 1943 until 1 August 1944 was the director of the prosecution branch of the underground Special Courts in Warsaw, concerning the cases that came to his attention. Third, there was Adolf Berman's file on *szmalcowniks*. Finally, there is a single letter of denunciation in the Żegota archive, against a Jewish woman who allegedly fraternized with SS men. The information contained in these files is variable in quantity and quality; but there is enough to establish a few basic facts about some of the cases, on the assumption that the allegations are true. These facts are tabulated in Table 4.1.

Table 4.1 Characteristics of Known and Suspected Warsaw Blackmailers and Police Agents

| | | Ethnicity | | |
Organizational affiliation	Polish	*Volksdeutsch*	Jewish	Total
None or unknown	25	–	–	25
Blue police	4	–	–	4
Plainclothes police*	13	–	–	13
Other German organizations**	2	2	1	5
Total	44	2	1	47

* Kripo, Gestapo.
** Orpo, SA.

We can see from this that the supposition, popular in Poland, that blackmailers and police agents were drawn mainly from the *Volksdeutsche*, or included substantial numbers of Jewish turncoats, is quite mistaken. In fact, the ethnic proportions almost exactly mirror those of the population as a whole. Second, despite the bias towards police informers because of the sources from which these cases are drawn, the figures suggest that most blackmailers were freelancers rather than police agents.

Blackmailers demanded much bigger sums than those paid to street *szmalcowniks*, sometimes stripping their victims completely. According to Pilnik's notebook, Jerzy Pakulski and his wife, Salomea, had paid him 50,000 zł. Janina Drutowska was accosted by a blackmailer accompanied by a Blue policeman; the price demanded (late in 1942 or early in 1943) was 10,000 zł. But most often, blackmailers simply demanded everything, and were prepared to turn the *melina* upside-down to find it. This was the experience of Janina Bauman, her mother and sister, and three other Jews, when they were robbed by a Pole and a uniformed German. Since it represented the entire remaining wealth and means of support for six people, the haul might have been worth hundreds of thousands of złotys.[37]

Not only did blackmailers demand huge sums, but their appearance meant that a *melina* was 'burnt': if the victims did not quickly find new accommodation, the blackmailers could return, and if the Jews had nothing to pay them with, they might be turned over to the police. Thus, where extortionists were usually no more than petty thieves, an irritant rather than a real threat, an encounter with blackmailers could leave a Jew destitute, homeless and desperate. Those who had good

Polish friends to whom they could turn could generally manage somehow; others were driven to desperate measures. Many – about 600, according to the statistics developed in Chapter 6 – returned to the ghetto, while it still existed, or found their way to the labour camps in Trawniki or Poniatowa; others joined the 'wild' Jews who congregated at the Hotel Polski; still others wandered the streets until they were caught. Some committed suicide,[38] or turned themselves in. One way or another, in the end they died. To be left destitute and homeless was usually tantamount to a death sentence, so that those who robbed Jews of their last pennies can also be counted among the murderers.

There is a bizarre footnote to the story of Borys Pilnik, who went by the name 'Bogusław' and was nicknamed 'bloody Bogusław' by the AK. He was known to Stefan Chaskielewicz as the owner of a photographic workshop, and had given shelter to Chaskielewicz and his parents, as well as another Jew. Bogusław had frequently visited them in their *melina*, bringing news and copies of underground newspapers; according to Chaskielewicz, he had always been cheerful and had helped to keep up their spirits. A few days before Bogusław was executed, Chaskielewicz had mentioned to him that his money had run out and that he would have to take a job, whereupon Bogusław took out a large amount of money – perhaps the 50,000 zł he had extorted from the Pakulskis – and gave Chaskielewicz the equivalent of a month's salary, telling him that to expose himself at work would be too dangerous. Chaskielewicz thought highly of Bogusław, and writes that he still cannot understand the affair. Was it a case of mistaken identity? Were he and his parents being set up as Pilnik's next victims? (Pilnik was executed on 25 August, and the Chaskielewicz family were robbed by three blackmailers on 6 September: could they have been Pilnik's gang?) Or was Pilnik, 'like many other collaborators and criminals', playing a double game, ensuring that if the Germans lost the war there would be people who would vouch for him? To these speculations by Chaskielewicz, one might add some others: possibly Pilnik believed that by merely extorting money from Jews, instead of doing his job and turning them in, he was actually doing good, and deserved to be paid for it. Perhaps in handing some of his take over to Chaskielewicz he thought of himself as a kind of Robin Hood. Or possibly he had a deviant, Jekyll-and-Hyde personality; or he was a sadist who enjoyed toying with his victims; or, like many antisemites, he hated Jews in the abstract but was capable of sincere friendship towards individual Jews. There are no doubt other possibilities as well.

The story of another *agent provocateur*, a certain Stefan Machai, is recounted by Vladka Meed. Machai seems to have infiltrated the entire organized effort to aid Jews through his *entrée* as the landlord of the prominent Bundist Michał Klepfisz, whom he had known before the war. Machai put up Klepfisz, Meed and several others in his flat at Górnośląska 3, which became a regular meeting place for the Bund activists. He was directly involved with Klepfisz and Arieh Wilner in smuggling arms into the ghetto. Machai had been an unskilled labourer and worked during the war as a rickshaw-puller. Evidently the temptation of earning an easy living became too much for him, and he also had a weakness for drink. Somehow he drifted into *Kripo* circles and was seen carousing with known secret policemen. These contacts sometimes proved useful to the Bund, since he could arrange bribes for people's release; but when there was a wave of arrests of Jews in hiding, including Klepfisz, and very nearly Meed as well, and when Machai was suddenly seen to be living a life of ease, the obvious conclusions were drawn. Eventually Machai was killed – by the Germans themselves, Meed believes, because he had outlived his usefulness.[39]

In both these cases – really, the only police agents of whom we have any sort of intimate picture – we gather some inkling of how blackmailers found their prey, what sort of people they were and what motivated them. Neither Pilnik nor Machai seems to have been an antisemite. Machai was simply weak, greedy and rather stupid; Pilnik was probably a typical confidence-man, clever, unscrupulous and two-faced. Both, certainly, were part of the 'Third Warsaw', the 'shameful Warsaw' of the Delegatura report, yet their relationship with the Jews was paradoxical.

Other Forms of Robbery and Exploitation

To avoid being left destitute by blackmailers, or to keep their property from being 'Aryanized' by the Germans, many Jews left goods for safekeeping with friendly Poles, or signed assets over on the understanding that they would be returned after the war. But this left them open to more genteel forms of robbery. Many people who would never have dreamt of accosting anyone on the street and demanding money, let alone collaborating with the police, nevertheless found reasons why they should simply appropriate the property that had been left in their care. In most cases the rightful owners had perished in Treblinka, and the trustees could therefore help themselves with a relatively clear conscience. Who would know or care, after all? And were they not entitled to some compensation for the inconvenience and the risks they had run? One can imagine their shock, then, when some ghost from the ghetto turned up on their doorstep. They might well feel it unfair, when their neighbours had come into some handsome 'post-Jewish' furniture, dinner services, furs or even entire businesses worth millions of złotys, that 'their' Jews had survived. Besides, as everyone knew, the Jews had accumulated their wealth on the backs of the Poles, and had used it as an instrument of economic domination. According to pre-war legend, the Jews were in the habit of taunting Poles with the saying *ulice wasze, kamienice nasze* ('the streets are yours, the houses ours'). To appropriate Jewish property was therefore not really theft but an act of national restitution. And 'the Jews have gold'. Thus, 'economic antisemitism' could provide respectable people with a rationalization for robbery. In other cases, this kind of theft was merely a matter of human weakness. People yielded to temptation, selling a trinket here and there. After all, everyone had to live; after all, they were entitled to something for their trouble. Before they knew it, everything had been frittered away. For example, Michael Zylberberg entrusted a substantial sum to a Polish friend, who gambled it away in a German-run casino. Zylberberg says that the man had helped him in many ways, and that he bore him no grudge.[40]

Whatever the reason, there were many apparently respectable, honest and upright citizens, people whom the Jews had trusted and regarded as friends, who certainly saw themselves as part of the 'proper, underground, heroic, fighting Warsaw', but who, whether out of malice or weakness, were not above depriving Jews of their means of subsistence and leaving them penniless on the street. Such people were more respectable than blackmailers, but just as dangerous and unscrupulous.

Another form of theft was practised by landlords who first agreed to take Jews in, in return for a lump-sum advance payment, and then turned them out, or even denounced them, after pocketing the money. Or else they would keep the Jews, but starve, abuse or exploit them; or keep demanding larger and larger sums, and evict them when they could no longer pay. Rent increases were not in themselves unreasonable, in view of the severe inflation, but a decent landlord would make allowances for his tenants' ability to pay, and if they ran out of money would at least try to make alternative arrangements for them rather than pushing them out onto the street, or worse.

Jewish activists who tried to find housing for their fellow Jews often ran into difficulties of this kind. Their own personal networks were inadequate to cope with the numbers of people whom they had under their care, so they had to rely on commercial contacts. Their perspective was also distorted by what might be called the 'social worker's complex': it was the worst cases that tended to come to their attention, giving them a jaundiced view of Polish society as a whole. Also, as politically engaged Jews, they had a more politicized and therefore probably more negative view of the Poles than did other Jews in hiding, who were mostly members of the assimilated intelligentsia. Because the activists were also the most articulate and wrote most of the early post-war accounts – and also because it was their point of view that filtered through to Ringelblum in his bunker – their views have tended to prevail. Reading these accounts, one has the impression that dishonesty and deceit were the norm. Vladka Meed is especially scathing:

> Some Jews had smuggled money into the 'Aryan Sector' in the hope that this reserve would tide them over. They even made plans for the future, placing their trust in Gentile friends with whom they had kept in touch. In most cases, their plans were eventually thwarted and their money vanished, together with their confidence in their Polish neighbours. The assimilated Jewish intelligentsia [...] were transformed into distressed, bewildered paupers.[41]

Is 'in most cases' justified? Certainly, many memoirists complain of having been cheated,[42] while only a few mention positive experiences.[43] As an example of the latter, Bernard Mandelkern says that his father's business partnership entrusted its affairs to a young Pole named Ludwik Golecki, who before the war had a reputation as an antisemite but who behaved honestly and later helped Mandelkern a great deal. Mandelkern was also surprised when he came to Warsaw and approached a Mr Zaorski, who had owed his father money: though Mandelkern had thought of him, too, as an antisemite, Zaorski acknowledged and paid back his debt, which he was under no legal obligation to do.[44]

But in truth, most memoirists do not comment on the matter at all. What are we to make of this prevailing silence? Perhaps the clue lies in the two cases referred to by Mandelkern: they are mentioned because of their incongruity, because two antisemites had behaved in an unexpected manner. Here, I believe, is another example of the 'dog that did not bark in the night': that people tend to note what is notable and remember what is memorable, and to filter out what is mundane and therefore typical. We have noted that nearly every memoir contains accounts of encounters with *szmalcowniks*. One might assume, therefore, that people who had been robbed not only of a few thousand złotys but of all their possessions, and not by a stranger but by a trusted friend, would be all the more sure to put their complaints on record. Thus, the silence of most memoirs on the subject should be taken again as evidence that extreme behaviour was the exception rather than the rule, that in most cases people whom Jews had chosen specifically because they believed them to be honest and decent behaved as one would expect, that is to say, honestly and decently.

Antisemitic Rhetoric and Propaganda

The final sort of threat from the Polish side that we shall consider took the form of words rather than deeds. Evidence about the attitudes of Poles during the occupation comes from three sources: overheard remarks reported by Jewish and non-Jewish witnesses; the underground press in all its variety; and assessments and situation reports by the Polish underground authorities.

It is easy to establish that occupied Poland was awash with antisemitic material, both verbal and written, quite beyond what originated with the Germans. I should like here to register scepticism, however, over the claim by some authors that Nazi anti-Jewish propaganda 'fell on fertile ground' in Poland. There was no shortage of such propaganda in pre-war Poland, and those who believed it had no need of the Nazi version, while those who paid no attention to native antisemitism were hardly likely to swallow it when it came from the enemy. Such accusations are polemical, serving on the one hand to tar Polish antisemites with the brush of Nazi collaboration, and on the other to exculpate Polish society by portraying antisemitism as an alien influence. Much more influential than Nazi propaganda was the stream of abuse that continued to pour forth from a segment of the Polish underground press, representing an entirely native form of the ideology. Three things remain to be determined: first, what proportion of the population held such views; second, since there are many kinds and degrees of antisemitism, what exactly their views were; and third, whether these verbal expressions represented 'just talk' or posed a concrete threat to the Jews in hiding.

Words Overheard

The least reliable evidence, of course, concerns the spoken word. Ringelblum collected a series of remarks, overheard at the time of the Ghetto Uprising and relayed to him:

> A pious old granny: 'In Holy Week, the Jews tormented Christ. In Holy Week, the Germans are tormenting the Jews.' A seventy-year-old priest: 'It's very good that this happened. The Jews had a great military force in the ghetto. If they hadn't turned it on the Germans, they would have turned it on us.' A conversation in a tram: 'They're burning the little Jew-boys [Żydki], but the big Yids [Żydy] in America rule and after the war they'll rule over us.' [...] A member of the ONR formulated his credo on the April action briefly and concisely: 'The Jews: when you burn them, it still isn't enough.' Another cannibal put it even more briefly: 'The bedbugs are burning.'[45]

Ringelblum is repeating hearsay, but there is considerable direct evidence of reactions of this kind. For example, Luba Bat arrived in Warsaw from Vilna at the time of the uprising. Hearing explosions, she asked a woman working in her garden if there was a fire. 'What are you talking about, fire?' the woman replied. 'The Jews are being barbecued.'[46] Irene Urdang du Tour was on a bus during the uprising, and writes that she had difficulty in keeping herself from crying 'when everybody [on the bus] kept saying, "great, the Jews are burning alive, they deserve it."'[47] Mandelkern writes: 'One evening, the residents of the apartment building I was staying in gathered to watch the flames of the burning ghetto. One man laughed aloud and said, "The bedbugs are on fire. The Germans are doing a great job." Nobody in the group reacted one way or another to that remark.'[48] A woman interviewed by Barbara Engelking related her experience with the family with which she was hiding:

> We sat down to Easter breakfast, [...] outside the window you could see smoke. Someone said 'that's the ghetto burning'. To that, our hostess's sister, who knew who we were, said 'how good that those Jewish bedbugs will burn up'. It surprised me a bit that she would talk like that in our presence.[49]

(Professor Jerzy Tomaszewski believes that 'the bedbugs are burning' should be taken literally: there was an infestation of bedbugs in Warsaw at the time which was generally believed to have originated in the ghetto. Even so ...)

Examples like these could be multiplied. Ringelblum acknowledges that there were also expressions of compassion and concern, but he is convinced that 'in general the antisemitic note predominated, the satisfaction that Warsaw has at last become *judenfrei*.'[50]

Another contemporary Jewish observer, Ludwik Landau, registered the events somewhat differently. He wrote in his diary on 21 April:

> The emotional attitudes to this battle are various: whereas some people express sympathy towards the heroically resisting victims of Hitlerism, others combine it with an antisemitism that makes an exceptionally evil impression at such a moment; whereas the majority, I dare say, regard it with the attitude of a neutral observer. But even among the neutrally or inimically disposed there appears a certain tone of acknowledgment, and everywhere there is a lively and even avid interest.'[51]

Vladka Meed, who is ordinarily very critical of the Poles, does not mention hearing malicious or negative remarks during the uprising. Instead, she reports that the Poles were astonished that the supposedly cowardly and passive Jews were defending themselves, were convinced that there must be Polish officers involved, and 'observed [the] toll of the hated Germans with grim pleasure'. She adds that 'before long the admiration and excitement of the Poles was replaced by a gnawing apprehension. "What's next now?" the Poles wondered. "Will the Germans turn on us also?"'[52] Chaskielewicz goes further. He writes that he did not hear a single voice approving what the Germans did or casting aspersions on the ghetto fighters, and adds:

> All people ever tell me about is some passenger on a tram who loudly expressed his satisfaction that there won't be any more Jews in Warsaw. [...] In the evenings my neighbours would go out on the roof of the building, to watch the smoke of the burning buildings in the ghetto. I was there too. People were terrified, and said that 'when they finish with the Jews, they'll start on us.'[53]

Itzhak Zuckerman had a still more positive impression:

> We can say that the Polish street in those days was pro-Jewish. I'm not talking about fringe groups, who were thrilled that the *Zhids* were burned in the ghetto. Even though the simple Pole tended to be antisemitic, what was happening in the ghetto roused extraordinary respect for the Jewish fighters.[54]

To my mind, this range of responses – admiration for the fighters, delight that the Germans' nose was being bloodied, the fear and self-interest reported by Chaskielewicz and Meed, leavened with antisemitic stereotypes about the cowardliness of the Jews and surprise over their ability to fight – seems far more congruent with normal expectations than the extremes of baseness and nobility reported by Ringelblum and some eyewitnesses. Once again, contemporary accounts tended to note what was notable, remember what was memorable and filter out the ordinary responses.

Other factors were operative as well. It was easier in the atmosphere of the time for the hostile rather than the sympathetic voices to be heard. In many situations it was unwise to draw attention by openly voicing support for an illegal group: you did not hear loud public declarations of support for the AK, though you also did not hear it being denounced. Undoubtedly, most sensible people kept their views to themselves: in general, those who voice their opinions loudly in public tend to include a disproportionate number of cranks and bigots, and the ears of witnesses were tuned to sounds and not silences.

The people who made such remarks remained strangers, and we can know little about them beyond these broad inferences. But Jews in hiding got to know the people among whom they were living quite well, so that on the basis of their observations we can make qualitative and more nuanced judgments about individual motivations, and about the attitudes of the 'Three Warsaws' towards the Jews.

Adina Blady-Szwajger knew a well-to-do family for which two of her colleagues were working as mothers' helpers. The family did not know that the girls were Jewish. To provide Blady-Szwajger with a cover so that she could visit her friends, family members were 'told as much about me as was necessary to awake in them the desire to fulfil their patriotic duty, by helping a messenger from the Home Army who was in danger'. Certainly, then, this family belonged to the 'proper, underground, heroic, fighting Warsaw', willing to risk their lives for their country. Blady-Szwajger's friends were flies on the wall: 'They were treated as members of the family, they ate with the family, and they had to listen to the constant complaints about Jews who had no scruples about putting at risk the lives of decent people.' Blady-Szwajger adds caustically: 'It was a "patriotic" and extremely right-wing family, a combination making for the greatest philistinism one can imagine.[55]

It should be noted, however, that well-hidden Jews also were not enthusiastic about being put at risk by other Jews. Luba Bat was hiding with a former teacher of hers, when a friend knocked on the door and asked to stay:

I said, 'For heaven's sake, how can you say such a thing? I'm here at the mercy of this old sick woman.' He said: 'But I have no place where to go and I'm not going to move.' I said: 'For heaven's sake, do you realize that it's terribly unethical what you're doing?'[56]

Her landlady let the friend stay for a few days while she made other arrangements for him.

Bernard Mandelkern was working as a gardener at the home of Mieczysław Tarwid, a high-ranking officer of the Blue police and Mandelkern's main benefactor. One evening, Tarwid entertained three guests, a former high official in the Ministry of Defence, a former judge and a colleague of Tarwid's from the Polish embassy in Paris. Mandelkern was introduced to them, but 'apparently the classy visitors did not care about the "hired hand", and they paid no attention to his presence'. All were involved in the underground and talked about former friends who had been arrested. The ministry official promised that 'The Germans will pay for all that. [. . .] We will not be like the Jews. We will fight and the Germans will have to respect us.' Here again, then, are representatives of the 'proper, underground, heroic, fighting Warsaw', and again members of the upper classes.

The conversation having thus come round to the Jews, each of the visitors expressed his opinion. The judge:

> In retrospect, and in the light of the Nazi philosophies and their cruelties, I conclude that our own Polish anti-Semitism, of which I was part, was a sort of easy way out – looking for scapegoats. To my understanding now, our anti-Semitism was more our fault than that of the Jews.

Tarwid: 'No member of the human race deserves what they did to the Jews. Besides that, my opinion is that the Jews have no more faults, or virtues for that matter, than the rest of humankind on this planet.' To which the diplomat replied, 'Well said!' But the ministry official held to his pre-war views: 'I still don't think I'll miss the Jews. I only miss my Jewish doctor. My wife and I had such confidence in him. He was a good diagnostician. Poor Dr Mitler, they killed him in the Pawiak.'[57]

We have already noted the pre-war saying that 'every Pole has his Jew'. Indeed, the same is true of antisemites in general: even Hitler is supposed to have had a soft spot for his parents' Jewish physician. The ministry official is an illustration of the type, a man who hates the abstract Jew but not necessarily the actual Jew. As another example, Nechama Tec and her family stayed for money with an avidly antisemitic Polish family, which nevertheless evolved ties of friendship with them and told them that they were 'not like other Jews'.[58]

Mandelkern's wife had a more unpleasant 'fly-on-the-wall' experience. She was working as a servant with a wealthy family, the Zgierskis, who had been told that she was a member of the underground who had fled her home town to hide in Warsaw. One Sunday:

> After the church service, they had guests for lunch and as I brought the dishes to the table all I could hear them talking about was Jews, Jews, and Jews again.

The derogatory remarks and laughter had no end. And all that from people who belong to the elite of Polish society! All this time they were addressing each other as 'Count so' and 'Countess so-and-so'. [...] All the ten or eleven people present gave *credit* to the Germans for liquidating the Jews. The most vitriolic opinions were voiced by the Catholic priest.[59]

It seems, then, that wealth, social status, patriotism, piety and dedication to the Polish cause – membership of the heroic 'first Warsaw' – did not guarantee decency towards the Jews.

Antisemitism in the Underground Press

Easier to gauge than overheard remarks are opinions expressed in the underground press, of which a useful selection has been published by Paweł Szapiro.[60] Szapiro's selection includes only comments on the Ghetto Uprising, but these stretch well into 1944 and serve as a reasonable guide to the range of attitudes represented.

Three things need to be said at the outset: first, that the underground press of all political persuasions devoted very little space to Jewish matters, one way or the other; second, that explicitly antisemitic commentary was limited to the right-wing press; third, that at the time of the uprising itself, the press was nearly united in its admiration of the ghetto fighters, and that overt antisemitism began to creep back in only later. During the uprising, the antisemitic note took the form largely of surprise at the fact that the Jews were offering active resistance and conde-scending remarks about the supposed failings of Jewish culture that had caused the Jews to go 'like sheep to the slaughter'. Finally, it should be added that the present purpose is to identify 'threats from the Polish side' and not to present a balanced assessment of Polish attitudes. The procedure will therefore be to single out articles with antisemitic content, and only afterwards to try to evaluate their overall significance.

Some pre-war antisemites concluded that, since the great majority of Jews had been killed off by the Germans, Poland no longer had a Jewish problem, so that it was now permissible to show compassion towards the remnant. The National Party, however, urged continuing vigilance:

Sometimes we are reminded of the existence of survivors in hiding of this once all-powerful minority, to whom as heirs of this estimable pre-war tradition 'we should extend all possible aid' [an allusion to Sikorski's radio appeal of 4 May 1943] [....]

In percentage terms, we now [July 1943] have more or less the same number of Jews as pre-war Germany, and yet we regard the Jewish question as nearly solved, whereas in Germany [...] it was not regarded so noncha-lantly! [...]

[After the war, the Jews] will play the role of the avant-garde of the Red Army, the role of organizers and leaders of the Communist revolution. For this assignment the remnants of the Jews hiding out in our country are preparing themselves most diligently. [...]

We will wholeheartedly condemn the bestiality of the Hitlerite villains, but we will not cease the economic and political battle with Jewry, [or be] softened by the crocodile tears of Jewish financiers and politicians seeking to impose their authority on us.[61]

The same newspaper had, while the Ghetto Uprising was still under way, referred to the Jews' 'hundredfold-deserved fate'.[62]

Even *Prawda Młodych*, the youth organ of the FOP (*Front Odrodzenia Polski*), edited by Władysław Bartoszewski and with most of the programmatic material contributed by Zofia Kossak-Szczucka – both of whom have been recognized as Righteous Gentiles and were centrally involved in the organized effort to aid Jews – contributed the following nasty and paranoid commentary:

The Jews fed parasitically on the body of the nations of Europe, universally hated and despised. They fought against everything, but only underhandedly, never openly, never with arms in their hands. They were the cause, the motor, of three-quarters of the wars fought in Europe [...], but they most diligently erased the traces of their influence.[63]

After this, the article praised the Jews for their new-found fighting abilities and urged Poles to help the survivors, but readers could take away what they wanted from it.

Even the official press got in on the act on occasion. In a notorious article entitled 'The Ghetto Uprising Seen in its Proper Light', *Ajencja A*, the organ of *Antyk*, the anti-Communist section of the AK, declared that the great majority of Jews, 'in their racially based materialism', had declined to participate in the revolt; that the active elements had been the Bund and the Communists, who aimed to prepare themselves for 'a blood-bath directed against the Poles', and that the uprising had been a good thing since it had led to 'the premature liquidation of one of the armed positions of the Communists'.[64] This article was widely reprinted.

It must be stressed again that this sort of rhetoric emanated only from the right-wing press, and that even on the right attitudes were by no means uniform. Nevertheless, the National Party was one of the four major parties in wartime Poland, and not the most radical on the right. *Walka*, the newspaper in which the first of the above extracts appeared, had a circulation of 10,000–20,000[65] (therefore, Szapiro estimates, 100,000–200,000 readers), and there were about two dozen smaller publications of a similar or more extreme character. Probably the larger part of the capital's population, then, regularly read this sort of material.

'Just Words?'

What was the concrete effect of the overheard antisemitic remarks and the continuing flow of antisemitic propaganda that emanated from the underground press? Most antisemites did nothing to harm the Jews and, indeed, are not infrequently found among the helpers, Kossak-Szczucka being the most prominent example. Nechama Tec writes of the 'Rare Case of the Anti-Semitic Helper',[66] but her rare cases consist of prominent antisemites like Kossak-Szczucka or ONR leader Jan Mosdorf. In her own memoirs, on the other hand, she describes being hidden by an antisemitic working-class family, and examples of this sort are very frequent in the memoir literature. In some cases, such people were antisemites of the traditional Christian sort, in whom antipathy towards Jews was outweighed by other tenets of their religion that inclined them to charity and self-sacrifice. In others, the Jews whom they helped were old friends or even relatives, so that personal ties proved stronger than generic prejudices. In still other cases, help was extended purely for financial reasons, though even then personal ties often developed through close cohabitation. The more sophisticated and politically conscious antisemites – Kossak-Szczucka is an example – were concerned lest it be thought that Poland approved of German methods. Kossak-Szczucka, in addition, had openly conversionist motives:

> [Our] help cannot be limited exclusively to material succour. At the same time, spiritual help must reach them. Prayer for the dying, letting them know that out of their present suffering they can create a great sacrificial pyre hastening their rebirth, removing from the once-chosen nation the burden of their anathema, teaching the Jews that through the force of desire they can be saved in the face of death craving baptism and the true faith.[67]

There were thus antisemitic reasons for helping Jews.

Concerning those who harmed Jews, on the other hand, Teresa Prekerowa has said: 'The crimes mentioned here did not, as is sometimes suggested, stem from anti-semitism. Greed was the motive, and anyone sufficiently defenceless could have fallen victim.'[68] No doubt greed is one of the motives for any kind of robbery. But we have seen that when challenged, the criminals more than once invoked conventional antisemitic stereotypes, including, occasionally, traditional Christian antisemitism. Elkana Ahlen, a dental technician who before the war worked in a practice that served a seminary, says that he was blackmailed and handed over to the Gestapo by one of the seminarians.[69] Mordechai Peleg encountered two men, father and son, Seventh-Day Adventists as he believed. Of the father, he writes that 'all he read was the Bible, particularly the Old Testament'. The son boasted of extorting money from Jews, and tried to talk Peleg (of course not knowing that he was Jewish) into joining him. When Peleg asked the father what he thought of his son's activities, he replied: 'but it clearly says here in the Old Testament that the Jews must perish for their sins. The Jewish prophets themselves have said it!'[70]

The hostility to Jews often and openly expressed by individuals of all social classes, from the pulpit and in the right-wing press – whether or not it constituted mainstream opinion – served to encourage such people and to persuade them that what they were doing was morally acceptable and even a patriotic act. The anti-German solidarity that otherwise united Polish society was much weaker where the Jews were concerned, and people who would not have dreamt of informing on members of the Polish underground, or even Polish street traders, considered the Jews to be fair game. As Michał Borwicz has observed, such elements

> profited ... not only from the protection of the occupying power (which was a matter of course) but also from the 'moral' cover that was offered them by certain Polish groups of the extreme right, all the more dangerous and harmful for the fact that they claimed to be part of the underground and even – the resistance.[71]

I would amend this only by adding that they *were* indeed part of the underground and the resistance.

Finally, the Jews were singled out as victims. There were, of course, a few genuine collaborators like 'bloody Bogusław' who preyed on Poles and Jews alike, and Poles who kept Jews also had reason to fear policemen and *szmalcowniks*. Such cases were the exception rather than the rule, however, and one does not hear complaints about Poles being victimized by swarms of such people. In short, the line between greed and antisemitism cannot be so conveniently drawn.

Verbal expressions of antisemitism served to intensify the terror that the Jews felt, and this in turn increased their vulnerability. We have seen that it was mainly by fear and uncertainty that Jews living 'on the surface' betrayed themselves, and the numerous expressions of hatred, in overheard remarks as well as in the underground press, helped to heighten this fear and uncertainty. 'Just words' could also kill.

Conclusions

The Jews faced numerous threats and problems on the Aryan side; seen cumulatively, they seem overwhelming and appear to justify fully the conclusions of many authors that survival for Jews in hiding was well-nigh impossible. The statistics developed in Chapter 6 will show that these conclusions were mistaken: survival was not only possible but actually not unlikely, despite the gauntlet that all the Jewish fugitives had to run. The practical problems of documentation, housing and so on could be and were overcome. The German and Polish hunters could be and were evaded. Above all, survival on the Aryan side would not have been possible without an army of Poles and also some Germans, who actively took Jews under their protection at the risk of their lives. I have estimated the number of these helpers at between 70,000 and 90,000, or about one-twelfth of the city's population.

There was at the same time an element that was malignantly antisemitic, or criminal, or both, which presented the Jews with a range of threats, from 'just words' to active collaboration with the enemy. We have seen that both pro- and anti-Jewish attitudes and actions cut across all social classes and all the 'Three Warsaws', and even divided families.

Yet the bark of the Polish antisemite was worse than his bite: the relatively low attrition rate deduced in Chapter 6 is testimony to that. I have pointed out various examples of the 'gauntlet effect': most Jews were recognized or exposed as Jews many times (witness the universality of encounters with *szmalcowniks*), and anyone who recognized a Jew might have betrayed him. The fact that many Jews ran the gauntlet successfully shows that few people, even if they hated Jews in principle or wanted to extract money from them, were prepared to go so far as to send them to their deaths.

Another effect that has been stressed is that of the 'dog that did not bark in the night', the natural tendency of untrained observers to pay attention to what is exceptional rather than what is representative. This is reflected in the historiography, which tends to focus on the extreme cases: people who risked their lives to help Jews, on the one hand; rabid antisemites and collaborators on the other. 'Mr and Mrs Kowalski' might not have liked Jews and might have felt nervous about having them next door in the face of German threats, but in situations where Jews faced immediate danger, they tended to be neutral or even passively protective.

One reason for distorted post-war perspectives is that much of our knowledge and many of our beliefs about this period come from Jewish activists, whose situation was not at all typical. Activists tended to come into contact mainly with problem cases, were forced to seek helpers on the open market since their own contacts were soon exhausted and moved in small circles in which everyone knew everyone else. Consequently, they tended to underestimate the amount of spontaneous help that was extended to the Jews, overestimate the dangers facing them, and, because they were politically engaged, largely in anti-assimilationist parties, they often had a jaundiced view of Polish society.

These observations should not be taken as cause for complacency or self-congratulation on the Polish side. A nation is not a moral agent, and collective attributions of credit or blame are wholly inappropriate. But every nation contains good and bad people, and also ideological trends that can be characterized as good and bad. The actions of many thousands of people in Warsaw were wholly noble and admirable, but large and respectable segments of the Polish population engaged in ugly and irresponsible rhetoric, which encouraged criminal behaviour ranging from theft to murder, damaged the morale of the Jews in hiding and added to their burdens. The 'First Warsaw', the nation's moral and political leadership, was regrettably not always on the side of decency and honour when it came to the Jews.

Despite all dangers and difficulties, most of the Jews who evaded the deportations and avoided the trap of the Hotel Polski managed to survive their two years in hiding. This success is above all the result of the secret city that existed in Warsaw during the German occupation – not only that of the Jews, but that of the broader society as well. The existence of 'an extraordinarily large crowd of people in hiding', as Citizen Frajnd put it, meant that a well-honed document-forging operation existed, and that Jews had the benefit of some protective camouflage. Finally, the networks to which Jews had access, which arose spontaneously and through personal contacts, meant that the Jews in hiding were neither so alone nor so helpless as they often felt themselves to be. Philip Hallie has spoken of the 5,000 inhabitants of Le Chambon-sur-Lignon, who rescued an equal number of Jews, as forming a 'conspiracy of goodness'. The secret city was larger and more complex, and its inhabitants had various and sometimes mixed motives. It did, however, consist of mainly decent and honest people, who were not a random sample of the wider population but formed a self-selecting, protective network. They were a conspiracy, let us say, sometimes of goodness, but generally at least of decency. Because this conspiracy existed, despite everything else, nearly 70 per cent of those who avoided the Hotel Polski lived until the Warsaw Uprising, when their story once again enters a new chapter.

5　The Warsaw Uprising and its Aftermath

Introduction

The outbreak of the Warsaw Uprising on 1 August 1944 brought the secret city to an end. The whole army of *szmalcowniks* and Blue policemen disappeared overnight, together with the German apparatus of repression that had given rise to them. Within days, Jewish prisoners in the Pawiak, the Gęsia Street prison and other German facilities were liberated by the insurgents. Gradually, Jews came out of hiding and were able to live, for a few weeks, as free citizens in a free (though not free of hostility) society. The operations of the aid organizations were disrupted by the uprising, and resumed afterwards in a fragmentary way. Many Jews who had relied on the support of these agencies were thus thrown onto their own resources, or forced to seek charity from the insurgent authorities. Of course, the uprising also placed the lives of all citizens in danger. In short, the outbreak of the uprising presented Jews with yet another new set of conditions and challenges to their survival, but at last also with a new opportunity to strike a blow against the common enemy.

As Jan T. Gross has suggested,[1] the Warsaw Uprising represents an opportunity to study Polish–Jewish relations under conditions when direct German pressure was absent but people were still under the influence of wartime conditions and mores. What we learn about the attitudes of Polish society under these circumstances will cast a great deal of light on its conduct over the previous five years, for which, because everyone was leading a double life, accurate information is harder to gather. Here, we shall encounter many situations in which Jews lived openly as Jews, and met with unforced responses from their neighbours, good and bad.

The Course of the Uprising

Within the first few days of the uprising the insurgents had mastered about half of left-bank Warsaw, but their territory was split into five separate enclaves. The largest took in most of the central part of the city, including the city centre, the Old City to the north of it, parts of Koło, Wola and Powązki to the west, and Ochota to the south. Outside this central cenclave they also held Żoliborz in the north, most of Mokotów in the south, the riverside district (Powiśle) to the east and an area in the southeast taking in the suburbs of Sielce, Czerniaków, and Sadyba. Insurgents in several other districts, including Praga on the right bank, engaged in sporadic actions in the first few days, but then withdrew for the most part to more strongly held areas. The right bank fell to the Soviets on 15 September.

The Germans on the other hand held the administrative district, wedged between the city centre, the Old City and the river; the 'German Residential District' to the southeast; about half of Mokotów; all the bridges over the Vistula; and broad bands of territory elsewhere. Jerusalem Avenue, the main east–west artery and a vital link between the northern and southern parts of the city, was largely in the hands of the insurgents, but the Germans held both ends of this straight, wide street and could direct murderous machine-gun and artillery fire along its length. None of the German-held areas was isolated: even the adminis-trative district, though surrounded on three sides and with its back to the river, could maintain contact with Praga across Kierbedź bridge; and by the time the Soviets took Praga, the Germans had the Old City and a clear run to the north. The insurgents had hoped to take the Warsaw garrison by surprise in the first few days, and to capture the bridges, the airport and various other strategic points. In the event, they failed to achieve a single one of these objectives, and the Germans were left with a commanding strategic position as well as an overwhelming supe-riority in manpower and equipment.

The insurgents were now doomed to gradual defeat, from which only the intervention of the Red Army could have saved them. Such intervention was not forthcoming, for reasons that remain controversial. In the meantime, the German authorities decided to put the insurrection down with the utmost severity, '*pour décourager les autres*'. Accordingly, Waffen-SS rather than Wehrmacht forces were mobilized, including some especially chosen for their depravity: a battalion com-manded by Oskar Dirlewanger, consisting of reprieved criminals who fought because the alternative was the gallows, and the notorious RONA (Russian National Liberation Army), made up of renegade Russian POWs, whose chief interests were rape, plunder and vodka. Given a free hand by Himmler, these forces proceeded to reduce the districts of Wola and Ochota, murdering 40,000 inhabitants and raping every woman they could find. Atrocities of this sort were not confined to districts won back from the insurgents: Marymont, which had not risen, was subjected to an intense bombardment on 1 August, and on the next day, RONA and SS troops entering the district threw grenades into crowded bomb shelters, or pulled people out of shelters and shot them. Many similar incidents occurred in other districts as they were reconquered.[2]

Deliberate atrocities apart, the German reconquest of the city was conducted without regard for civilian life: tanks advanced with groups of civilian hostages chained to them; snipers shot people at random; the insurgent districts were bombarded by artillery and aircraft, with the liberal use of incendiaries, and one by one were turned into rubble; civilians in captured areas, when not massacred out of hand, were often evacuated through combat areas without any care being taken for their safety. These methods, no less ruthless than those that had been used against the ghetto, also proved no less successful. Wola and Ochota fell by 11 August. The Old City was abandoned on 2 September. Czerniaków held out until the 23rd, Mokotów until the 26th, Żoliborz capitulated on the 30th, and the city centre, finally, on 2 October, bringing the uprising to an end.

The main body of fighters on the Polish side belonged to the AK. They were supplemented by units of the AL and of the RPPS combat organization, the Polish People's Army (PAL). The AK also incorporated individual members of the NSZ, as well as units of the Socialist Combat Organization (SOB), the military wing of the PPS–WRN. The fighters numbered altogether about 42,000, half of whom fell in action. Including civilians, the number of deaths is variously estimated at between 150,000 and 250,000[3] – possibly half the population of the insurgent areas and a quarter of the overall Polish population of Warsaw.

As the suppression of the uprising proceeded, the Germans set about systematically removing the remaining civilian population. Railway repair yards in the town of Pruszków, twenty kilometres west of Warsaw, were converted into a transit camp. Smaller camps were also set up in the Warsaw suburb of Ursus, in Piastów and in Zakroczym to the northwest. During their period of functioning, from 5 August until 7 October, these camps processed 350,617 people, according to official German figures (more, according to Polish estimates[4]). Their disposition was as shown in Map 5.1. Polish sources add that '*kilkanaście tysięy*' (between 11,000 and 19,000) of this number passed through Ursus or Piastów rather than Pruszków (and 800 through Zakroczym); that some 50,000 people managed to escape from the trains or columns of march on the way to the camps; and that 60,000 of those sent 'to work in the Reich' were put in concentration camps.[5] Once emptied, the city was systematically destroyed, using flame-throwers and bulldozers. Any survivors encountered in the ruins as this work progressed were shot on sight. When Soviet troops finally crossed the Vistula on 17 January, they found that 80 per cent of the city's buildings had been destroyed, and that hiding in bunkers among the rubble were some 200 Jews.

The Jewish Experience of the Warsaw Uprising

The experiences of Jews during and after the uprising depended largely on where they found themselves when it broke out. The most fortunate were those who had been hiding on the right bank, for whom the war was over on 15 September. Even here there were atrocities, though, as the Germans rounded up civilian labour brigades prior to withdrawing. Some unfortunates, caught in these round-ups, were force-marched back into the inferno, and now faced the prospect of surviving nine months in German captivity; a few, in the process, were exposed or denounced as Jews and shot on the spot. Other Jews, hiding in more distant left-bank suburbs, or in towns and villages outside Warsaw, were not affected by the military operations and atrocities, but merely had to hold out for another four months under conditions they had already endured for nearly two years.

As it happened, however, the great majority of *melinas* were in areas that were caught up in the uprising (see Map 5.1). There was a great concentration in areas where the liquidation of the ghetto had made new housing available, especially in what had been the Small Ghetto. Further concentrations were to be found in the streets to the south of the Small Ghetto, in areas near the university, and in Żoliborz, where the Warsaw Housing Co-operative, run by the PPS, provided many hiding places.[6] These were all areas inhabited by the Polish intelligentsia, and hence where the Polish underground was strong. All were involved in the fighting.[7]

In addition to this geographical concentration, there were, as usual, special dangers to which only the Jews were exposed, arising mainly from the attitudes of some Poles: these will be taken up shortly. All these factors would suggest a high rate of Jewish mortality in the uprising. On the other hand, few *melinas* were located in Wola, Ochota or Marymont, where the worst massacres occurred, and relatively few in the Old City, which was completely destroyed in the fighting. Since Jews made up about 1.5–2 per cent of the Warsaw population at the outbreak of the uprising, other things being equal one would expect between 2,250 and 5,000 Jewish victims. Other things were of course not equal, but it is difficult to know without further information whether, on balance, these various factors worked for the Jews or against them.

Working out how many Jewish victims the 1944 uprising claimed is not a straightforward matter, and will be deferred until Chapter 6. It will be proposed on the basis of various strands of evidence that about 4,500 Jews died in the uprising and 900 afterwards. As with other estimates presented in this book, these are 'measures of central tendency' and should be understood as involving an undefinable amount of uncertainty: numbers in this range simply yield the most consistent overall picture.

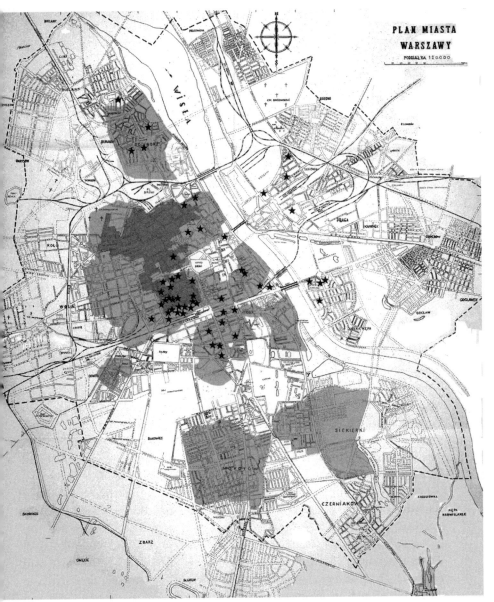

Map 5.1 Locations of *melinas* in relation to the ghetto and areas held by insurgents in the Warsaw Uprising

Notes:
1. The area shown in light grey represents all territory in these districts that was ever in the insurgents' hands after the situation stabilized on 3 August. The whole area was never held at any one time.
2. Outlying and right-bank areas held by the insurgents are not shown.
3. The area shown in dark grey is the ghetto in its original boundaries.
4. Location of *melinas* indicated by ★

We should conclude, then, that in general the factors that worked against Jewish survival in the uprising outweighed those that favoured it, since the number of victims was near the high end of the *pro rata* expectations. It remains to be determined, then, to what extent this unfavourable experience was due to the unfortunate geographic concentration of the Jews, and to what extent to continuing threats from the Polish side.

Jewish Perceptions of the Uprising

The Jews were divided as usual among the optimists and the pessimists.

'Antek' Zuckerman[8]

Jews who found themselves in the insurgent areas had first of all to decide whether to come out of hiding and, if they did, whether to reveal their Jewish identities. Most Jews living 'on the surface' saw no reason to expose themselves in this way. Chaskielewicz, for instance, writes: 'I had no intention, even for a moment, of revealing myself as a Jew.'[9] Those who had been living in hiding generally stayed hidden, but were gradually forced into the open by enemy shelling and the need to find food. The decision to give up a secure and hard-won *melina* did not come easily. George Pfeffer, for example, reports that his group debated for several days whether they should risk showing themselves, despite the risk posed by the bombardment. On the fifth day of the uprising they decided to come out, and no sooner had they reached the ground floor of their building than the flat in which they had been staying was destroyed by a bomb. 'We mingled with neighbours from our apartment building,' Pfeffer writes. 'We told them we had come from a bombed-out house in another block. We didn't want to get the widow [their landlady] in trouble.'[10] Marian Berland reports a similar debate. His landlady (speaking in a peasant dialect) told his group that 'They says on the street that they picks out Jews, and anyone they catches, they kills.' To which her husband added: 'Leave if ye wants [. . .], but if ye leaves, I'll not let yer back in. [. . .] I doesn't want people laughing at me because I was hiding Jews'.[11] Accordingly they stayed in their *melina*, until an insurgent patrol discovered them on the third day and escorted them to (relative) safety.

Under the circumstances, such circumspection was clearly wise; but again it must be asked whether appearance matched reality. The experiences and impressions of Jews caught up in the uprising were in fact extremely varied, reflecting a range of responses similar to that which we observed at the time of the ghetto uprising, except of course that the Jews were not now the focal point of the events. The general atmosphere changed as the fortunes of the uprising unfolded: at first euphoria and fellow-feeling, gradually giving way to anxiety and paranoia, and finally to bitterness and despair.

Tuvia Borzykowski describes the heady atmosphere of the first days of the uprising:

It was not enough to carry the joy within yourself, so everyone sought out people to share their impressions with [...] Anyone who did not participate directly in the uprising or help it in some way was regarded as not a true patriot. On their way to and from their positions, [the soldiers] were ringed by scores of people [...] Women would bring bread and water [...], and cooked for the soldiers.

In conversations among the Polish population you heard no word of opposition to the uprising and no resentment about their own sons and daughters who volunteered for the uprising and risked their own lives. In conversations, Polish mothers and fathers boasted: I have a son in the uprising, I have two sons on the barricades, and so on.[12]

This headiness affected many Jews as well:

What a golden memory and dream it is for me! Joy and the feeling of freedom replaced the fear of slavery and death. [...] Ethnic relations were in every respect friendly: I was treated with the same respect as Polish girls. I, an eleven-year-old brat [smarkula], was promoted to Pani [the polite form of address].[13]

Nor was this an idiosyncrasy or limited to children. Despite his cautious decision not to reveal himself, Chaskielewicz, then a man of 30, had similar feelings:

the start of the uprising produced in me a calmness and almost complete disappearance of fear. [...] I was in danger in the same way as all the other inhabitants of Warsaw. Now even coming out in public didn't lead to certain death. Now, despite everything, for the inhabitants of Warsaw who surrounded me I was one of them, and not someone especially marked out. Maybe for that reason I remember the Warsaw Uprising as an adventure.[14]

Some Jews who came out into the open also reported a similar atmosphere of solidarity. 'Antek' Zuckerman writes:

When I was in the Old City I didn't sense antisemitism even once, neither from the civilian population nor from the AK; the opposite was true. The AL admired us and the AK showed us camaraderie. We were with them on the barricades and my comrades can testify to the fact that not once did we hear a hint of antisemitism.[15]

Cywia Lubetkin adds:

> The Poles in the Old City received us in the same way as you yourselves
> would have greeted Jewish fighters who were still alive after the slaughter. I
> have in mind mainly the leaders, members of the High Command. There was
> a splendid, really pioneer group there. We were told, for example, that since
> there were only a few dozen members of ZOB left, it wouldn't be right for us
> to die in a Polish uprising. The duty of the Poles was to do everything they
> could to make sure that we survived. Therefore we were given assignments
> that didn't directly threaten our lives. We didn't accept this proposition. We
> had joined the uprising to fight. But the cordial reception greatly improved
> our morale.[16]

Not all of Zuckerman's and Lubetkin's comrades concur. Marek Edelman, who
served in the same platoon, writes that 'the AK stood me up against the wall several times, because ... the gendarmerie in the Old City was ONR, pure
Falanga.'[17] It may be relevant that Edelman has a stereotypically Jewish appearance, while 'Antek' did not; but that was not always a factor. Efraim Krasucki
writes:

> In our [AK] company in the Old City, there were more than a dozen Jews with
> a distinctly semitic appearance, but no one paid any attention to that. There was
> no case when someone like that was singled out or ill-treated. As to myself and
> my friend, A. Rotrubin, even though our commander, Capt. Kalinowski, knew
> of our origins, he singled us out only in a positive way. [...] When [one day] he
> needed two trustworthy people to escort [...] officials on some important
> mission, he chose me and Rotrubin.[18]

Similarly, Henryk Poznański, a Jewish member of the 'Parasol' battalion, was
chosen to guide the AK high command through the sewers on 25–26 September.
(When the ZOB high command made its way to Zoliborz from the Old City, conversely, it was escorted by a Polish guide.) Henryk Lederman and David Goldman,
who had acquired a good knowledge of the sewer system during the Ghetto
Uprising, also acted as guides.[19] None of these Jewish guides survived the uprising; all were decorated posthumously.

But some Jews viewed this 'positive discrimination' differently: 'the Jewish
insurgents in the *Armia Krajowa* units suffered persecution from their Polish
comrades. The Poles assigned them to the most dangerous missions and the most
difficult tasks – and on occasion shot them in the back.'[20] Zbigniew Grabowski's
recollections provide a specific instance. He starts with the characteristic
observations:

For me, the uprising was the most important and happiest moment of my life. I was euphoric, choked up with freedom, my red-and-white armband, and the longed-for battle with the enemy. [. . .]

But even in the uprising I had not the slightest desire to reveal my identity, because I remembered [the looks I had received from my comrades.][21]

He continues:

[In mid-September] I was building fortifications at the corner of Marszałkowska Street and Jerusalem Avenue [in the city centre . . .] A sergeant of the AK – also wearing an armband – came up to me, [. . .] and, pulling out his pistol shouted: 'You, Jew: the Germans didn't finish you off, but I'll finish you off.' Fortunately he was drunk, and I was half his age. I managed to run off into the ruins, and his shots missed me. But he did shoot!'[22]

On another occasion:

Three impoverished young men in torn clothes joined our group, saying that they were Jews who had survived and wanted to take part in the battle against the Germans. The AK lieutenant directing our work [. . .] immediately gave them a very dangerous assignment, explaining himself as follows: 'Show that, even though you're Jews, you aren't cowards. After all, your life as Jews isn't worth very much, so don't be afraid of death. You've survived thanks to us, so now you can go first; maybe it'll save some of the other boys.'[23]

Grabowski attributes this 'groundless feeling of superiority' to 'the German example and propaganda'. It could, he feels, 'appear in people who were otherwise brave and apparently decent.'[24]

Atrocities: The Prosta Street Massacre

Among the 'brave and apparently decent' was an AK unit commanded by Capt Wacław Stykowski ('Hal') , which

had beautiful pages to its credit, bloody and often successful encounters with the Germans. Numbering several hundred insurgents, it would lose 20–50 per cent of its manpower in battle, after which it would replenish itself quite quickly. It was therefore characterized equally by great dedication and a fluid and somewhat random composition.[25]

This unit was responsible for the defence of the block within the city centre bounded by Walicòw, Prosta, Twarda, Ciepła and Ceglana streets. An unsigned relation in the Berman archive tells the following story:

On the 11 September 1944 at 3pm, several insurrectionists of the Armia Krajowa came to Prosta 4. There they ran across three men, Jews, standing in front of the house, completely at ease, since this area was free of Germans, entirely mastered by the Poles. The Jews had a well-hidden bunker there, next to which there was a cellar of which they took advantage in moments of relative safety. They always stayed in the bunker at night. The insurrectionists were AK fighters, under the name 'The Gathering of the Valiant' [*Zgromadzenie Chrobrych*]. They asked the Jews for their documents, and on seeing their nationality, expressed satisfaction and interest in their fate. They asked sympathetically where they were hiding, whether they had weapons, how many there were and so on. The Jews answered them with great confidence, [and] not guessing what sign [of the zodiac] these insurrectionists were under, led them to the above-mentioned cellar, where they introduced them to their companions. After a cordial farewell, the AK men left.

At 9 pm on the same day, eight of them came [back], well armed, under the command of Cpl Osloja, the boxer Karolak and the brothers Krawczyk ([*alias*] Mucha). They encountered sixteen people. The rest were in the bunker. Under the pretext that they were taking them to their command-post, they led the unarmed men out of the cellar. The women and children remained, accompanied by one of the AK men. The other [AK men] led the [Jews] to the front of the building, lined them up against the wall and, after searching them thoroughly, Cpl Osloja spoke. He said briefly: 'You son-of-a-whore Yids, you're waiting for the Soviets to come. They'll come, but you won't live to see them.' He finished, and a shower of shots rained down. Only two men managed to run away, disappearing into the darkness between the ruins. They survived.

After throwing the bodies of the murdered men into a nearby shell-hole, the AK men returned to the cellar, where they completed their criminal aim by raping and abusing the women. The despairing cries of the women, calling for help, could be heard until 4am. In the morning, people who tried to look out of the bunker found only dead bodies.

Several of those who were still alive managed to report these events to the command-post. They were received coolly, listened to with irony and mockery. By contrast, the leadership showed a dangerous interest in where the remaining Jews were hiding. The delegates returned home in fear. The victims of the crime were:

The lawyer Jerzy Gutman, his wife [Melania] and their ten-year-old son [Ryszard].

Ignacy Bursztyn, his wife [Estera], their thirteen-year-old daughter [Noemi] and the wife's sister [Anka Knaster].

Cesia Akierman [sister of Ignacy Bursztyn] with her seventeen-year-old daughter [Estera or Marysia],

and three other women and two men whose names are unknown to me. [Tadeusz Orlański, Tecia Szklar, the dentist Szenfeld and his wife, and a 10-year-old girl, name unknown.][26]

A number of other accounts of this massacre are extant;[27] the above version is presented out of historical interest, because it has not been published before, because it is fairly full and concise and because it makes allegations that have not appeared elsewhere. But it is problematic in many respects. No entirely first-hand account is available, simply because no one except the perpetrators witnessed all the events. Most likely, this account is a compilation by one of the members of the ŻKN staff, an attempt at 'instant history'. In its description of the general course of events, and in the reported number of victims (fourteen or fifteen) and their names, it agrees with other accounts, but beyond that there are numerous discrepancies. The names Karolak and Krawczyk do not appear elsewhere, nor does the detail that the women's cries for help went unheeded through the night.[28] According to the Polish historian Michał Cichy, the commander's name was Ostoja, not Osloja, he was not a corporal but a sublieutenant, and he was not the commander of this unit. His speech is quoted, with slightly different wording, by Henryk Bursztyn, who was an eyewitness to events in the bunker but did not see what happened on the street; Bursztyn also misspells Ostoja's name in the same way, so that he is no doubt the source for the Berman report. In that case, the wording 'You son-of-a-whore Yids' is an embellishment; according to Bursztyn, Ostoja said 'Gentlemen'. No other version reports this speech at all. On the other hand, an eyewitness account of the shooting by one of the survivors, Janek Celnik, tells a completely different story:

> When we left the gate of Prosta 4, we were told to lay our identity documents in a pile, and they took everything else out of our pockets themselves, keeping the better things for themselves. [...] Then they took us one by one for questioning, where we had to answer the following questions in a whisper: Are there any holes around here where Jews are hiding? Do we know where any other Jews are hiding? Where [else] have we been hiding during the war? Do we have any connection with other Jews? [...]
>
> After we had all been questioned, we were ordered to march in a group in the direction of Żelazna and Pańska Streets, towards open ground. One by one, they began picking us off. [...] I started to run [...] I managed to get about 50 metres, [but] one man chased me, shooting from his revolver. I was

hit in the shoulder-blade and fell down. He caught up to me and, standing over me, fired about seven shots, of which three hit me, one in the neck, two in the shoulder-blade. [. . .] After a while, he came back to make sure I was dead.[29]

We can therefore reject the story of Cpl Ostoja and his speech as fanciful. The names of the perpetrators would not, of course, have been known to the victims, and it does not appear from the prosecutorial records that Ostoja took part in the massacre at all. His name has probably been borrowed for the story because there was a rumour in the area that he had killed a Jewish boy.

Jewish sources agree that the massacre was carried out by the 'Chrobry [Valiant] battalion', but the men mentioned were under Stykowski's command, whereas the Chrobry (actually Chrobry II) battalion controlled a neighbouring sector.[30] Far from being the unit implicated in the massacre, it was Chrobry II that discovered and reported the crime, and its commander, Capt Wacław Zagórski ('Leszek'), has published an account of it.[31] Zagórski confirms the number of women killed, and adds that they had been robbed as well as raped; in addition, he confirms in general terms the attitude at Stykowski's command-post reported above, and adds that when Stykowski was informed of the massacre, he reacted by saying: 'If they're dead, then they won't run away. Anyway, what business is it of ours? Better come inside, it's time for a snack.'[32]

From Cichy's research, based mainly on the preserved records of the AK's investigation of the affair, we learn that the squad that carried out the massacre (consisting of eight or ten men) appears to have been headed by Cpl Mucha, who was not named Krawczyk: rather Mucha ('Fly') was his real name as well as his *nom-de-guerre*. He and several other members of his squad were known from the ghetto period as *szmalcowniks* and dealers in *bimber* (home-made vodka). A witness from another platoon in Stykowski's battalion says that Mucha's squad carried out special assignments on orders from Stykowski, and they seem to have carried out murders on their own initiative as well. Shortly before the Prosta Street massacre they shot a member of Chrobry II, accusing him of having been a Blue policeman who took bribes, and afterwards they seem also to have murdered one of their own men, a Cpl Unrug. According to an investigator's report dated 21 September 1944, Stykowski's people were claiming that Unrug had killed the Jews in order to loot them. Supposedly, on discovering the bodies and looted gold in Unrug's possession, one of the patrol, a man called Kotek ('Kitten'), was so overcome with disgust that he 'reflexively' shot Unrug, after which he, Mucha, and two others buried him in the ghetto. Then the recovered loot was turned over to a Capt Sęp ('Vulture'). On 21 September, 'Hal' arrested one of his men, 'Francuz' ('Frenchman'), for looting; part of the evidence was that 'Francuz' was frequently seen in the company of a Jew. The report ends with the recommendation that 'Francuz' and Mucha be executed.[33] In Cichy's opinion, this story was concocted by Stykowski in order to muddy the waters.[34]

Stykowski's battalion generally had a poor reputation among the surrounding population. After their group had discovered the remains at Prosta 4, one of the Chrobry II men, Czesław Kuczera, reportedly said to Zagórski:

> Listen, Leszek: I'll bet my life it's those bastards from 'Hal' that did it. They've already shot more than one lad and buried him in the yard outside their gate. Everyone knows, but they're afraid. They say that's their 'martial law', the sons-of-bitches. Anyone who doesn't carry out an order, and fast, gets it. He can have a trial later, when he's chewing earth.[35]

We thus have the picture of Stykowski as a kind of gangster-warlord, ruling his area through terror, with Mucha's squad and perhaps some other men serving as his Tontons Macoute.

Zagórski, together with his battalion's Jewish doctor, Roman Bornstein, brought the Prosta Street massacre to the attention of the AK high command: Bornstein even gained an audience with Gen Antoni Chruściel ('Monter'), AK commander for the Warsaw region and *de facto* leader of the uprising. Bornstein reports that 'it made a strong impression on him. He was outraged. He told the gendarmerie to start an investigation immediately [and that the] guilty parties should be court-martialled.'[36]

The investigation was soon derailed, however. Besides concocting cock-and-bull stories to deflect suspicion, Stykowski's men were able to intimidate eyewitnesses, one of whom fled from a hospital rather than risk testifying. Others, who identified Mucha and Unrug as among the perpetrators, declined to make depositions. Antisemites within AK counterintelligence theorized that the massacre had been carried out by the Jews themselves, either for robbery or to discredit the AK, while Stykowski himself claimed that it had been done by Ukrainians, *Volksdeutsche*, or Communists, masquerading as AK men. The uprising ended before a trial could be held, and no prosecution was undertaken after the war, even though the records had been preserved. In the end no one was convicted of anything.[37] Stykowski, for his valour during the uprising, was later awarded Poland's highest military decoration, the *Virtuti Militari*.

Other Atrocities

The massacre at Prosta 4 is not the only atrocity against the Jews that can be laid at the door of Stykowski's group; indeed, the unit seems to have carried out a veritable Jew-hunt near its precincts. Dawid Zimler claims to know of seventeen Jews massacred by this unit, members of which also arrested and beat him; most likely,

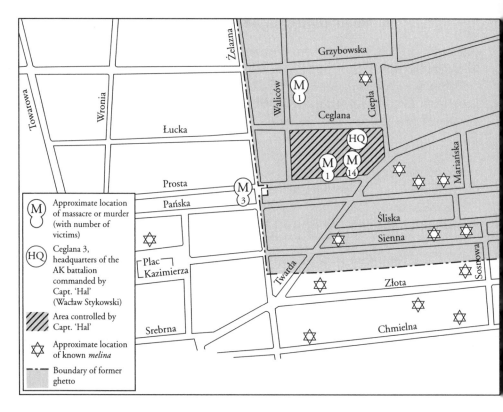

Map 5.2 Murders and massacres of Jews near the area controlled by Capt 'Hal'

this number includes the Prosta Street victims.[38] Simcha Rotem recounts that the ghetto fighter Jurek Grossberg was shot by an AK patrol in the street near Pańska 5: Pańska is one street south of Prosta[39] (see Map 5.2). And Bronka Zonabend writes:

> At the time of the uprising, I was living at Pańska 78 as an Aryan. In my apartment on the fourth floor I was hiding my brother-in-law, who had a very semitic appearance. Despite constant bombardment and several fires above us, I didn't dare take him down to the cellar, since the atmosphere during the uprising was such that he could have been killed if he had come out into the open.
>
> On 5 September [...] I was sitting in the shelter in our building and I witnessed the following scenes: into the cellar through underground passages from Żelazna Street came three AK men, fully armed and with grenades at their sides. They were leading three Jews, two men and a woman, shaking with fear. The woman was wringing her hands with despair. [The Jews] gave me the impression of people sentenced to death. The AK men turned to the [air-raid] warden, shouting, demanding that he show them where Jews were hidden,

threatening that he would be held responsible for hiding them. The warden, Zygmunt Żukowski, a personally decent man who knew that I was hiding someone, [. . .] assured them that there were no Jews in the building. In view of that, the AK men cleared out of our cellar and went for a good 'walkabout', repeating the same procedure in the neighbouring buildings. I didn't have the possibility of checking what happened to the Jews that they were leading around, but everyone said they were shot.[40]

Vladka Meed relates the following:

On the fifth day of the uprising several Jews sought refuge from the German bombardments [in a building at the corner of Żelazna and Chmielna streets, four streets south of Prosta [. . .] Three of them, with distinctly Jewish features, were detained by an insurgent guard of the [AK]. Despite their insistence that they were Jews, the Polish guard took them into custody on the charge that they were German spies. While they were being searched [. . .], several other uniformed and armed men entered and beat them, declaring there would be no place for Jews in liberated Poland. Two of the Jews [. . .] managed to jump out of a window under a hail of bullets. [. . .] The third, Yeshieh Solomon, was killed on the spot [. . .][41]

There are also allegations of individual murders carried out by members of this battalion, for example the Jewish boy whom Lt Ostoja was said to have killed. Another Jew, named Jagodziński, was taken away from Prosta 4 or 6 on 23 August and never seen again. On 8 or 11 September, a Jewish convert named Sokołowska was dragged out of her shelter in Waliców Street; her body was discovered later by her brother-in-law (presumably not Jewish), who in turn was murdered by three AK men on 11 September. If these allegations are correct, then at least twenty-two Jews and three non-Jews were massacred by these men, and possibly many more. It was especially unfortunate that they reigned over an area that had been part of the Small Ghetto, and was particularly heavily inhabited by Jewish fugitives.

Stykowski's group was the main, but not the only perpetrator of crimes against the Jews. Zonabend continues her relation:

Besides that I can verify that none of the Jews I knew dropped his cover during the uprising, since that was regarded as dangerous. Because there were cases when the AK gendarmerie arrested Jews on the excuse that they had false documents. One of my neighbours, a Pole, was stopped on the street because he looked like a Jew. Only the intervention of some acquaintance, who testified that this man was a Pole, caused him to be released.

In the paranoid atmosphere that began to develop as the uprising faltered, suspicions and accusations multiplied wildly. The main AK organ, *Biuletyn informacyjny*, noted on 6 September that

> [o]ne of the serious dangers for the fighting city might be the epidemic of suspicions and false alarms. [...] It is not permissible to make thoughtless, unverified accusations, for example about shooting from windows, [or] spying. In today's mood of excitement and fervour [*zawziętość*], every frivolous accusation can cause a serious wrong, often costing a human life.[42]

'Antek' Zuckerman relates, for example, the case of a young Jew living 'under the surface' whose landlord would leave him locked in during the day – a common practice, which helped allay suspicion. The landlord was unfortunately unable to get back home when the uprising broke out, and the young man was left locked in the flat with dwindling supplies of food. After a few days, he shouted and banged on the door, attracting the attention of some of his neighbours, who then broke into the flat. Paying no attention to his explanations, they took him to the local police post, where he was summarily executed.[43]

Jews were particularly apt to find themselves suspected of working for the Germans – how else had they survived? Almost anything was enough to trigger suspicion: that a Jew had a rifle (though the rifle had been issued by the AK); that he had a list of Jewish names on him, clearly therefore of Gestapo informers (though he was a Żegota activist, and the names were those of Jews to whom he had been distributing aid); that he was seen on a rooftop, supposedly giving signals to the Germans (though he was actually putting out fires).[44] Sometimes no excuse was needed: Chaim Goldstein reported seeing a Jew writhing on the ground after being shot by an AK man, who said as he holstered his gun: 'To hell with him, he was a Jew.' After the perpetrator had walked away, another AK men standing nearby said apologetically to Goldstein: 'I couldn't do anything. He wasn't from my platoon.' On another occasion, Goldstein saw two of his fellow-prisoners from the Gęsia Street prison, still wearing prison clothing, murdered on the barricades by two Poles shouting 'Jews, Jews, s.o.b.s' and 'We don't need Jews! They should all be wiped out!' Other Poles surrounded the perpetrators and 'dragged them away'. But Goldstein believes that there were others: 'Many Poles have begun a Jew-hunt on the barricades. And for a long time cries of "Death to the Jews!" mingle with the joyous cries of the insurgents as all of us watch the enemy retreat.'[45]

In all, several dozen Jews are known to have been murdered by Poles during the uprising, and there may of course have been other cases that remain undiscovered. Crimes of this kind tend to be explained by Polish authors as the outcome of wartime demoralization and anarchy. Teresa Prekerowa, for example, writes that:

Any wartime period, as is known, is criminogenic, accustoms people to force and crimes, creates the conviction that might is right [...] No army in the world has ever completely protected itself from demoralization, no society is made up only of noble people. Negative attitudes therefore had to be evident in Warsaw in September–October 1944.[46]

This is all very well, and goes a long way towards explaining the gangsterism of Stykowski's men, directed (so it seems) against Poles as well as Jews, but it does not explain why most of their victims were Jews, killed, not in the course of robbery or to enforce 'martial law', but only because they were Jews. On the evidence, these criminals were only a small minority of the city's population and the AK: but they were an extraordinarily malignant minority, and the Jews, who were also a small minority, were extraordinarily vulnerable to them. As we saw in Chapter 4, this element cut across the 'Three Warsaws'; it cut across class lines and could include people who were otherwise decent, even heroic: Stykowski's men, as we have seen, distinguished themselves on the barricades, and no doubt many of the other killers who wore AK armbands were valiant in battle as well. A patriotic outlook and a willingness to sacrifice one's life for Poland were not at all incompatible with virulent antisemitism; in fact, as we have seen, even the moderate right defined the Jews as enemies of Poland.

For this reason, the AK was not, and could not be, effective at dealing with the problem of anti-Jewish violence during the uprising. Brave, dedicated, experienced fighters could not easily be sacrificed for the sake of civilian justice; with tens and hundreds of thousands perishing in the flames, a few dozen victims of atrocities were of little account. Chrusciel may indeed have been outraged by the Prosta 4 massacre – we also have the testimonies cited above to the very positive attitude to Jewish fighters among some of the AK High Command – but key subordinates knew how to protect their own. The insurgent gendarmerie and Security Corps were in any case only weakly in control, not having the resources of a peacetime police force and with many able-bodied men on the barricades. They counted on patriotic solidarity to restrain crime. This was more or less successful when it came to ordinary crime, though there was banditry nevertheless, which supports Prekerowa's proposition. But it was not ordinary bandits who committed most of the crimes against the Jews. Those who would explain away these crimes as merely an aspect of the general anarchy during the uprising fail to take into account, first of all, the vastly greater incidence, proportionally, of crimes against Jews than against non-Jews, and, second, the well-documented and particular character of these crimes and of the people who committed them. If we suppose, conservatively, that 'only' thirty Jews were killed by Polish hands during the uprising, then for crimes against Poles to assume similar proportions we should have to speak of 1,500 murders. If the AL, PAL, AK and NSZ had murdered each other on this scale, we would be justified in speaking of a civil war. Such a conflict did indeed ensue after the war, and some 30,000 people were killed in it, but during the Warsaw Uprising the various underground armies fought as allies against the common enemy. Paradoxically, in an uprising whose real purpose was to keep Poland out of Communist hands, Communists were not killed as Communists, but Jews were.

Of course, not all Polish patriots reasoned in this way. That there was a struggle between two conceptions of patriotism can be illustrated by an example. Dawid Zimler describes the situation that developed after he had been arrested by a group of Stykowski's men, who were looking for a place to finish him off:

> A crowd gathered on the street, and from some people's mouths objections were heard that one ought not to murder Jews now, that that was work worthy of the Germans, and not honest Poles. But the lieutenant said that he had received an order that had to be carried out. At that moment a captain appeared, a grey-haired gentleman, who began persuading them that it would be a shame and disgrace for us Poles to kill a Jew who had been hiding from the German villains for several years.[47]

The authority of the older man had its effect, and Zimler was freed. But the bulk of the crowd seem to have stayed neutral in this confrontation, apparently not quite sure where their loyalties should lie.

The sickness at the heart of wartime Polish culture, then, nurtured before the war by the church and nationalist politicians, did not take the form of mass violence against the Jews, but rather of an uncertainty in situations where people's moral obligations should have been clear, which led to a paralysis that gave extremists like Stykowski's group a free hand. The sabotage of the investigation against Stykowski and the lukewarm way in which it was carried out also points to another problem: that even the most extreme and murderous antisemite was still *swój* ('one of us'), and entitled to solidarity and protection, as he would not have been had his victim been Polish. Another illustration: I spoke with a Pole, P., who had hidden a Jewish friend in his own home for more than a year. P. told me how he managed to have his friend smuggled out of the ghetto: he arranged for another Pole, the manager of an enterprise in the ghetto, to lead his friend out and escort him to a safe apartment, where P. came to meet him. When P. arrived, his friend told him that once in the apartment the manager had robbed him of all his money. I asked P. whether he had reported this incident to the Polish underground – P. was very well connected, since the chief prosecutor of the underground courts was his cousin – and P. was taken aback: evidently in fifty years this idea had never occurred to him.

Criminality was a marginal phenomenon, and most Jews were unaffected by these events. Most memoirists do not mention them, and 'Antek' Zuckerman, for one, says that he did not hear of them until after the war.[48] It would also be wrong to ascribe the activities of a relatively small group of thugs and fanatics to the whole of the AK, to the AK as an organization or to the Polish population as a whole. The bulk of the killings that we know about can be laid at the door of a single renegade unit, and the rest were carried out by isolated individuals. There were almost certainly fewer than a hundred Jew-killers out of 42,000 armed men, and most likely fewer than fifty. If many or most of them were in the AK, it was because only the insurgents had weapons, and because the political, antisemitic right had its place within the broad AK spectrum.

Still, such explanations seem hollow. A lesson all societies need to learn from the Holocaust is that they have a special responsibility to protect small and vulnerable minorities, and to prevent hatred and lies about them from proliferating. This was a responsibility almost unknown to the moral and political leadership of Poland at that time, at whose door Jews not unnaturally tend to lay the ultimate responsibility for such crimes. We might perhaps let Chaim Goldstein have the last word:

> I think of the part that Jews took in the uprising led by Bór-Komorowski and the attitude of the Polish fighters towards them. I see Jewish fighters murdered by their own comrades-in-arms – killed purely and simply because they are Jews. The memory of this has a profound influence on me and weakens the sense of comradeship I have for the Poles in the Resistance movement. Of course I realize that the majority of Polish fighters were loyal and friendly towards us: the Jew-killers were only a small minority. Nevertheless, [...] the memory of these killers fills me with anger and pain.[49]

Jewish Participation in the Uprising

The commander of the Jewish platoon of 'Zośka' battalion, Capt W. Miciuta, paid tribute to his men after the war: 'I carry in my heart the memory of those Jewish soldiers of ours, who behaved extraordinarily, heroically. An old officer does not use the word "heroism" for nothing. They carried out assignments, volunteered, were ready to die at any moment.'[50] Most Jews took an active part in the uprising if they could, though few had access to arms. Women generally worked as couriers, often carrying messages under fire. There were also many Jewish doctors in the insurgent units; Bornstein is only the most prominent example. Other Jews, like those from George Pfeffer's *melina*, were put to work building barricades and putting out fires. Pfeffer's group also carried water from a pump for tenants hiding in a basement nearby, whose water-supply had been cut off. Eventually their commander gave them guns, and they were sent 'from one post to another, wherever the fighting was the hardest'.[51]

Such informal participation was widespread, and Jews were also accepted without difficulty into the formations of the left-wing fighting groups, the PAL, AL and SOB. Indeed, Jews comprised a substantial part of the leadership and combat forces of the AL. But Jews who attempted to join the AK formally were often rebuffed. Chaskielewicz puts the matter delicately when he writes that he had 'the impression that the Jewish question still remained significant in many insurrectionary circles', and therefore opted for informal co-operation rather than trying to join the AK.[52] Jews who did not drop their Aryan identities of course did not have such problems, unless their Jewish identity was suspected. Thus, Simcha Rotem ('Kazik') recounts that on the first day of the uprising, seeing a group of insurgents running by, he simply joined them and was accepted, no questions asked.[53]

The largest group of Jewish combatants was drawn from the several groups of Jews freed from German captivity by the AK. On the first day of the uprising, the 'Kolegium A' battalion liberated a school in Niska Street that the Germans had used as a prison for about a hundred Hungarian Jews, and on the fifth day, the 'Zośka' battalion liberated the Gęsia Street prison, where 348 Jews were held who were being used for cleaning up the ruins of the ghetto. These included eighty-nine Polish Jews as well as Jews from Greece, Hungary, Romania and other countries. Despite their emaciated condition and all the sufferings they had endured, the liberated Jews were unanimous in their desire to join the uprising and fight the Germans (in part, as Prekerowa points out, because they had nowhere else to go).[54]

Most were taken in, often by the AK units that had liberated them, but in view of the shortage of weapons, mainly by formations not directly involved in the fighting. More than a dozen were seconded to the 'Brody' quartermaster brigade; about fifty joined the 'Zośka' battalion (some of them forming a Jewish platoon), where they were employed in the repair of captured tanks and other weapons; 150 were formed into the International Jewish Auxiliary Brigade of the AL, used in the construction of barricades. Another large group made its way to the Old City, where forty-four of them joined the quartermaster's section of the 'Wigry' battalion, commanded by Feliks Cywiński, together with twenty-four of the twenty-six Jews whom he had protected over the previous eighteen months. Their direct commander was Shmuel Kenigswein. Another twenty-odd were formed into a rescue brigade, which fought fires and dug people out of the ruins. Yet another small group joined the 'Parasol' battalion, the 'Kolegium A' battalion which had liberated the Niska Street School, and the 'Gozdawy' battalion, among others.

As a result of the assignment of Jews to non-combat roles, AK counterintelligence observed: 'There are general complaints in the army that Jewish soldiers are mainly employed in the kitchens [. . .] or in other cushy jobs.'[55] But Simcha Rotem has a somewhat different recollection of the treatment of these liberated prisoners:

One day Irena [Gelblum] and I [...] saw a large group of people in prisoners' uniforms being pushed into [...] burning buildings by armed members of the AK, who ordered them to pull the food stored there out of the fire. [...] As I came closer, I learned that the prisoners were Hungarian Jews who had been brought to Warsaw as laborers by the Germans. During the fighting they were 'freed' by the AK fighters, only to be forced to perform dangerous and humiliating functions.[56]

'Antek' Zuckerman also encountered such cases, though he noted significant differences between districts: 'I wasn't in central Warsaw, where the fate of the Jews was different because, there, the AK sent the Jews to the barricades or to clear mines. In my area, as soon as I came across such a case, I immediately appealed to the AK commander.'[57] In part no doubt as a result of such mistreatment,

[u]nfortunately the majority [of the liberated prisoners] did not manage to survive. The International Jewish Brigade of the AL suffered such losses that it ceased to exist. Its last remaining members tried to make their way individually to the City Centre. Before the end of August, over a hundred Jews were evacuated to Żoliborz by AK routes. But the Germans threw explosives down the manholes. A few people died, the rest panicked and made their way back to the Old City. Probably all of them died.[58]

The attitude of the AK leadership to these prisoners was also not quite what one would have wished. General Tadeusz Pełczyński ('Grzegorz'), AK Chief of Staff, wrote to Chruściel on 4 August:

I inform you that in Wola the question of interned Jews from Yugoslavia, Greece, etc. has come to the surface. Some of these Jews have been liberated from German hands by our units. Anticipate the preparation of a temporary camp, to which all the liberated Jews and other undesirable elements could be directed. Our units should receive instructions that would exclude the possibility of excesses against the Jews.[59]

The last remark shows that the AK leadership was well aware of the problem of antisemitism in the ranks, which latter-day apologists deny.

Cichy explains that camps were in fact set up, where Germans and members of 'national minorities collaborating with the Germans' (Germans, *Volksdeutsche*, Ukrainians, etc.) were interned, but not Jews. But in addition, all foreigners, defined as 'all persons of a nationality other than Polish, even those who possessed Polish citizenship [...] before 1939', were required to register with the local post of the Security Corps, which served as the police force during the uprising. I have not come across any memoir that mentions this registration process, so that it seems to have been mainly ignored in practice, at least with respect to Jews; but Cichy's research did turn up one local registration list, in which a Polish-Jewish couple was listed among twenty-five foreigners.[60]

Finally, one must mention the participation of the ŻOB in the uprising as an organized unit. On 3 August, 'Antek' Zuckerman published an appeal

> formulated very diplomatically. That is, no emotions or ideology, but an appeal to the remnant of the Jewish Fighting Organization and young Jews, who were armed, to join the uprising for a free Poland, democracy, and so forth. [...] That proclamation was published in the press, which was no longer an underground [press]. It appeared in the press of the London people and the PPR, and in all kinds of other presses and that was significant.[61]

Subsequently, Antek's group, meeting in its headquarters at Leszno 18, decided to support the uprising as an organized and independent unit. The number of fighters involved was not large: a single platoon of twenty ghetto fighters, commanded by Zuckerman and including Tsivia Lubetkin, Simcha Rotem, Tuvia Borzykowski, Józef Sak, Stefan Grajek, the lawyer Zygmunt Taberman, and Dovid Klein and Marek Edelman of the Bund. There were also some small groups elsewhere that fought under the ŻOB banner.[62]

Antek's platoon applied to join the AK, but after much 'hemming and hawing'[63] from the high command, ended up fighting as an autonomous Jewish unit under the command of the AL. Zuckerman is full of praise for the treatment that he and his colleagues received:

> if there are days of honor in Polish or Jewish history, they were the days of this war [i.e. the uprising]. When I passed by with my comrades, they would applaud us from both sides. Maybe such a thing also happened in 1863, during that Polish uprising, too? It didn't matter if we held some position; any other group could have done that. What was important was that it expressed the participation of a nation.[64]

Indeed, Polish uprisings have historically been times of 'Polish-Jewish brotherhood', and a similar cameraderie was noted by many observers during the defence of Warsaw in 1939.

The ŻOB platoon fought with its own weapons in the Old City, on a barricade in Mostowa Street opposite a German stronghold called the Red House. The barricade was manned by AK and AL detachments as well as ŻOB, with each tour of duty followed by twenty-four hours' rest in the rear. 'Antek' explains that the barricade was less dangerous than the rear, since the Germans were reluctant to use artillery so close to their own position; at any rate, the platoon was able to hold this position without losses until the Old City fell, and then withdrew through the sewers to Żoliborz: 'When we got to Żoliborz, people were waiting for us. [...] They welcomed us as the heroes of the day. [...] The care was nice, friendly, extraordinary. We were exhausted and hungry, and people waited on us and took care of us.[65]

Again we can see that there were differences in the way the Jews were treated between the various enclaves, with the atrocities happening almost exclusively in the city centre. Zuckerman partly blames the Jewish leadership for their failure to intervene there: 'How did the Jews get murdered there?! Why wasn't there an immediate Jewish representation? With us, in the Old City, there was an address right away where people could come, an address known both by the AK and the AL.'[66] To which the short answer is that the Bermans and the rest of the political leadership were in Żoliborz, cut off from the city centre.[67] But since most of the murders were committed by a single renegade unit and the rest by unknown individuals not accessible to political influence, simple coincidence is probably a stronger explanation.

The Treatment of Jewish Civilians by the Insurgent Authorities and Population

Even though the plans to intern or register Jews were not put into practice, these proposed policies are indicative of the attitudes of at least some of the AK leadership: foreign Jews were considered an 'undesirable element', and even Polish Jews were regarded as aliens. The authorities did nonetheless treat the Jews as equals when it came to providing them with food and shelter. For example, a communal kitchen that a group of Jews set up in Mariańska Street, in order to avoid interaction with Poles, received food from the Delegatura in the same way as Polish communal kitchens.[68] Hana Gorodecka, lodged with her children in an insurgents' hospital after her shelter was destroyed by a bomb, writes that they received the same food and space as the wounded soldiers.[69] Chaim Goldstein and a friend, after being escorted to Żoliborz through the sewers by an AK patrol, were received hospitably in the insurgent headquarters and, when they had to make their way back after four days, were given supplies of food and tobacco to take with them.[70] Local welfare officials were instructed to make no distinctions in requisitioning accommodation and food. But the head of the civil administration for the city centre reported that 'the carrying out of the requisition order meets with strong opposition from the air-raid wardens and inhabitants'. The same source added that 'one should bear in mind that the [...] attitude of the Polish population towards the Jews may take broader and more antagonistic forms'.[71]

Antagonisms flared up especially over the problem of space in air-raid shelters. The residents of a three- or four-storey housing block would have to crowd into the building's basement during aerial or artillery bombardment, and space was therefore scarce. Residents of buildings that had been destroyed would then have to squeeze into their neighbours' shelters, and as the area controlled by the insurgents became more and more constricted, refugees from areas that had fallen to the Germans crowded in as well. Gorodecka describes the conditions in such a shelter:

> When I got used to the darkness and saw my surroundings, I regretted that I had not appreciated the time when we had sat quietly in confinement, not seeing the beautiful world before our eyes. There were about fifty people in the cellar; it was very tight and dirty. The stench was choking. Lice crawled over people and things. Many people were scratching themselves, because they had scabies. There was very little water in the taps, everyone pushed and shoved to catch a little. The women were angry as wasps.[72]

Such a situation was bound to lead to friction, and instances were reported of people being refused entry into cellars or forced out of them. Jews were not the only victims of such actions, but were the most likely to be singled out. Many memoirs recount stories of this kind of discrimination:

> Clara Falk, her son, and an engineer named Golde [...] were informed by their Polish neighbors that they were not welcome. After several days of persecutions and anti-Semitic insults, the engineer was forced to leave the bunker during a heavy German bombardment. He was killed by shrapnel.[73]

George Pfeffer writes:

> In a few days the Poles in the basement discovered our masquerade. Most were friendly. One of these was a Polish judge. He uncovered a plot to murder us. He told the plotters sternly that if they harmed us, after all we had suffered, he would tell the Polish police they had killed innocent people.[74]

Janina Bauman was told by another Jew in her shelter, a Mr Handelsman, that he and his companion had had to leave their previous shelter after a drunken AK man had threatened them with a pistol. But she also recounts that she was seriously ill at the time, in the late stages of tuberculosis, and that various other people in the bunker tried in their own ways to help: she recalls a Mrs Kozłowska, who kept making her barley soup; a doctor who examined her; a sculptress who produced some aspirin and her maid who tried cupping glasses; a man who tried to find some meat for her. When the uprising was over and the Poles left the bunker, Bauman received a shawl and a pair of boots from the sculptress, and a pair of trousers and an anorak from a man she did not know.[75] Chaskielewicz similarly recalls that near the end of the uprising

I observed with interest the behaviour of people from various social spheres, sometimes noting with surprise how unjustly I had judged them before. [...] I will never forget a certain tenant of our house in Krucza Street, a woman previously unknown to me, who, seeing that my suit had been torn on the barricades, [...] offered me a jacket and linen, bristling when I protested that I had no money to pay her.[76]

He adds that 'As time passed, one heard less and less about the Jews. The common danger and common struggle, and especially the common enemy, united the whole population of the city without exception.'[77] Thus the uprising reached its third and final phase. The danger to the Jews was greatest during the second phase, when the initial euphoria gave way to paranoia and a search for scapegoats as the prospect of defeat came into view. Now the magnitude of the disaster sank in, producing depression and dejection. Superstitions and suppositions about Jews yielded to experience, as the mythical Jew was displaced by the actual Jew, who had participated and suffered like everyone else.

The Aftermath of the Warsaw Uprising

As Jews found themselves once more under German control they were faced with a number of unpalatable choices. If they had fought with the AK, they could accept internment as prisoners of war, under the terms of the AK's surrender agreement (the same option was not open to those who had fought with the AL or PAL). Otherwise, they could go along to Pruszków and the other transit camps, hoping to remain unnoticed amongst the mass of Poles. They could, as many Poles did, escape from the evacuation columns and try to hide in the surrounding towns and villages; they could try to make their way across the Vistula to the Soviet-occupied right bank; or they could hide in one of the numerous bunkers that the insurgents had left behind, many of them now well concealed by heaps of rubble, and await liberation.

Few if any of the Jewish AK fighters trusted the Germans or their Polish comrades enough to accept internment as PoWs: at any rate, I have encountered no such case. Many Polish AK men, for that matter, also preferred to take off their armbands and mingle with the civilian population. In this way, Simcha Rotem's group found itself in Pruszków, from where it was deported to Suchedniów, near Kraków. The main ŻOB battle group, including 'Antek' Zuckerman, Cywia Lubetkin and Marek Edelman, was rescued from a bunker in Promyka Street in Żoliborz and, in a daring operation mounted by one Polish and two Jewish hospital workers, brought through German lines to Brwinów, to the southeast of Warsaw and ironically only three kilometres from Pruszków.[78] Rotem made his way back to Warsaw and then eventually rejoined his comrades in Brwinów.

With the fall of Praga, the Vistula became part of the Eastern Front. The Germans destroyed the bridges, and crossing the river became difficult and dangerous. Nevertheless, some people did succeed in getting across, mostly Communists or other people with AL connections. The attempt was best made at night, and at some distance from the city, where the river was less heavily guarded. Anna Lanota, whose husband was a member of the AL General Staff, made her way to Kampinos to the north of the city and then crossed by boat near Jabłonna, while the uprising was still on.[79] The ŻKN activist 'Krystyna' (Izolda Kowalska) also managed it during the uprising; by mid-September she was broadcasting to Warsaw on the Soviet-sponsored Radio Lublin. Basia Temkin-Berman credits her with influencing the Soviets to drop arms and food to the insurgents, and providing them with information to help target the drops effectively.[80] The AL staff planned to withdraw all AL units, which included individual Jews as well as the ŻOB platoon, across the river in co-ordination with the Soviets, but only a few members of the first group survived the crossing, after which the attempt was abandoned.[81] In the end, only a handful of the Jews who survived the uprising managed to make it to safety by this route.

Several hundred Jews decided to dig in again. With Soviet forces on the other side of the Vistula, no one expected that more than three months would elapse before they were freed. (It is indeed a curiosity that it took the Red Army longer to get across the Vistula than to reach Warsaw from the pre-war Polish–Soviet border, or to cover the distance from Warsaw to Berlin.) Few of those who hid were therefore prepared for such a long wait, or for the winter. Food was very scarce by the end of the uprising, and water supplies had been disrupted. Those Jews who hid in bunkers thus had to forage for food, fuel and water. While on foraging expeditions they were in danger of running across German patrols or Polish scavengers; and if the Germans suspected anything they could use dogs to sniff them out. As the bunkers were mainly in cellars concealed by rubble, a cave-in could mean being buried alive. With the return, or even impending return, of the Germans, other dangers reappeared too: the odd *szmalcownik* went back into business, extorting money from Jews setting up bunkers on the threat of exposing their locations to the Germans.[82]

What proportion of those who went into hiding perished is hard to say; probably the majority. Naturally, we have mostly accounts by survivors;[83] but they record the deaths of many others. Alicja Haskelberg gives a short, poignant, fairly characteristic account of life and death in these bunkers:

In the first days of October, everyone had to leave Warsaw, but we couldn't, because we were Jews. We were advised to hide in [...] a bunker that was created when the former garage of our building was covered in rubble [...] We hid there literally at the last moment, because the Germans, shouting and shooting, were again taking over all the houses. We managed to gather a little water in barrels and to take a little food (porridge and biscuits). Three Jews whom we didn't know hid with us, and a Jewish couple, also strangers. Jews who had come out of their hideouts during the uprising now wandered the streets like stray dogs, looking for some hideout, so as not to fall into the hands of the German beasts. We stayed in this shelter for 16 weeks, suffering terribly from hunger, and even more from thirst. The three Jews left, promising to look in on us and bring a little food. Unfortunately, our strength left us completely, and with every day we felt that we would all die. My little son, with his broken legs in plaster, began to swell up and on 30 December 1944 he died. Likewise the husband of the woman who had gone down into the bunker with us lay in agony, and my brother, who was little by little reaching the end. The body of my little son lay with us for a long time. Only later the three Jews showed up; they had been hiding nearby. They brought us a little food and took my son, to bury him temporarily in a cellar. Miraculously we were still alive on 17 January 1945. [...] Those three men came and brought us the news [of liberation]. Unfortunately, our chance acquaintance also died.[84]

Most of those who 'wandered like stray dogs' simply went to Pruszków with the rest of the city's population, hoping they would not be noticed in the general chaos. This included even people with 'bad looks', who had previously lived under the surface: for example, Janina Bauman and her family, the Lewinsons.

The first difficulty that these Jews faced was the trek to the camp. Most people made their way on foot, under the eyes of German soldiers, to one of the railway stations on the Skierniewice line, most commonly Warsaw West, Włochy or Ursus. Some people had to walk the whole 20 kilometres to Pruszków, an all-day journey under the circumstances. Along the way, there were many opportunities for hostile Poles to spot and denounce Jews, and the rumour circulated that the Germans were using Polish helpers for this purpose. However plausible these fears may have been, no concrete evidence has come to light of Jews being betrayed during this exodus.

The Pruszków camp itself was merely a transit point; the average length of stay there was only a day or two. Nevertheless, numerous dangers again lurked for the Jews. Some memoirists report having to take a communal shower at the camp, an obvious danger for circumcised men. A selection was also carried out, to separate those fit for work (who were taken to labour camps in Germany) from others (who were taken to various places in the General Government and released). Anyone identified or denounced as a Jew in the process would be shot. Daniel Falkner says that he and his father therefore stayed inside the whole time they were at Pruszków, fearing that the Poles would denounce them.[85]

Despite these obvious dangers, it does not seem that more than a handful of Jews died in the Pruszków camp, and perhaps none at all. The General Commission for the Investigation of Hitlerite War Crimes in Poland found evidence of at least 118 deaths in the camp. Sixty-three people died of disease or starvation, since epidemics of several diseases raged and in the first days of the camp prisoners were not fed. In the first two weeks of August, fifty-five young men were executed on suspicion of involvement in the underground. In addition, 'there were cases when people who tried to avoid being assigned to the group designated for deportation to the Third Reich were shot'.[86] All these groups, especially the last, may have included some Jews. But there is no evidence that any Jews died as a result of denunciation or of being recognized as Jews.

It did happen that Jews were recognized. Janina Bauman relates the following story:

> We see a German soldier approaching. He strolls along lazily, enjoying the beautiful weather and looking around. He stops in front of us, ready for a friendly chat. Suddenly his face twists into a nasty grin. '*Jude!*' he shouts, '*Sie sind Jude!*'. [...] Petrified, we pretend not to understand. But the soldier knows the Polish word for Jews. '*Żydówki!*' he roars in a fit of fury. Everyone around us holds his breath. [...] He grabs his gun and points it at us. [...] But suddenly the man changes his mind. 'Wait here', he shouts and runs off to fetch his superiors. [...] Only now do the people crouching nearby come to life again. 'Run away, ladies, run away', they beg us. 'Hide somewhere, try to save your lives.' Yes, but where can we go? The camp is surrounded by barbed wire and guards. There's no place to hide. Out of the blue, a tall man in high boots comes to our rescue [....] He scoops up the three of us with his strong arms and makes us run with him. [...] We stop at the far end of the camp away from the barracks, the crowds and the guards. There's a deserted barn here, full of rotting straw. The stranger tells us to bury ourselves in the straw and stay there till the following day. [...] Then off he goes. We shall never meet him again nor find out who he was.[87]

It is worth reflecting on this episode. The Lewinsons, besides having a conspicuously Semitic appearance, were publicly exposed as Jews in front of a crowd of strangers. All the onlookers saw the tall man take them away. We may assume that the German soldier eventually returned, when any one of the bystanders could have shown him where they had been taken. Furthermore, people may well have feared reprisals for not doing so. Yet not a single person denounced them.

Here again, then, is another situation of the kind we have seen before, and the same reasoning applies: since a single malicious person would have been enough to betray the Lewinsons, whereas their safety depended on the unanimous silence of the whole crowd, even one such occurrence would border on the miraculous if any significant proportion of the population had been sufficiently hostile. For several thousand Jews to pass through Pruszków without a single known instance of betrayal is strong evidence that there was a general attitude of solidarity at that time.

Relations on the trains from Pruszków were a reprise of those in the bunkers in Warsaw. Hanna Piżyc gives an account of her trip from the Ursus camp to the Reich, in an open goods wagon, shared by chance with representatives of the 'third Warsaw': 'Most of the society of the wagon were people with ideal faces from an album of criminals. And this predominant group gave the whole wagon its tone.' Piżyc describes the behaviour of her fellow-passengers, who seemed not the least concerned that their city had been destroyed and that they were heading into the unknown, but joked, quarrelled, traded looted goods for bread and sausage at the stations, and seemed to look on their new circumstances as merely a new chance to make money.

The train was laboriously climbing a hill, rain was pouring down mercilessly, bravely seconded by the wind, people swayed on tired legs, but such weather didn't deprive everyone of an appetite for quarrelling. And just such a worthy suddenly bestirred herself, because suddenly she didn't have enough space. With a wild screech she began to threaten her neighbour that if she didn't clear out then she would tell everyone who she was. And the poor woman ran off, alarmed, into a corner of the wagon, completely extinguished, because a new cloud had appeared on her Aryan horizon.[88]

The Lewinsons had a similar experience:

The empty, roofless cattle trucks stand waiting to be filled. People push forward. [...] The truck we have climbed into fills in no time. More and more people are forced in by the guards, until we can all hardly breathe. Children are crying, men cursing and swearing, someone becomes hysterical. 'Let's throw these three Jewesses out!' a woman suddenly exclaims. 'We'd be better off without them.'

But this proved unpopular with the crowd: 'A powerful hushing makes her hold her tongue. "One more word", a crippled man says sternly, "and you'll be thrown out yourself".'[89]

An anonymous deponent writes that he spent his time in labour camps in Germany 'living in constant fear and threatened by my Polish compatriots who were suspicious of my origin'.[90] But such antisemitism did not necessarily mean betrayal. Isaiah Trunk interviewed another survivor of these camps:

[A] woman in the bunk on top of me dropped some straw on me. I lost my temper at her, but she let fly with such curses that I got hot and cold all over: 'Stuff it, stinkin' Jewess'. Two days before, a German had threatened that if there were any Jews among us and we didn't turn them over immediately, we'd all be exterminated. I felt I was beginning to swoon. I [...] barely survived till morning. I was the first one into the latrines so I could meet the woman and beg her not to cause my death. But as soon as she saw me, she waved me away with her hand. 'Just don't you worry yourself'. But she knew I was a Jew, and all the other women had heard about it, too. The women I shared my bunk with now made life unbearable for me, but they didn't denounce me.⁹¹

Undoubtedly cases of denunciation did occur in the labour camps, but none have so far come to light. Again, these are situations where a Jew could have died through denunciation by a single malevolent person, but it required the unanimous silence of the whole barrack – in the face of death threats – to ensure the Jew's survival. That denunciations in these circumstances seem to have been rare is once more impressive evidence of the solidarity of the Warsaw deportees, even though old attitudes persisted.

If the deportees from Warsaw were united, not exactly in brotherly love, then at least in a degree of tolerance for their Jewish fellow-victims, the same cannot always be said of the inhabitants of the many cities and towns to which the refugees from Warsaw were taken. The Germans made no provision for the deportees: the passengers were simply unloaded at their destination, and the local population were expected to take them in. In general, the refugees were met hospitably, villagers sharing their homes and meagre food with them, but occasionally they were resented. The Germans tried to disperse the refugees from Warsaw throughout the parts of the General Government that they still controlled, but the places near Warsaw were also burdened with those who had escaped from the trains or columns of march to Pruszków, and such people had difficulty finding shelter. For example, J.G., interviewed by Chaskielewicz, escaped from the camp to the town of Pruszków. He felt it necessary to have his hair cut as soon as possible, since 'I had a lion's mane, and I was afraid to let anyone at all see me like that, because they would have known right away that I was from Warsaw'. He adds that 'In Pruszków I was unclean [*trefny*] as a Varsovian, not as a Jew.'⁹² Thus, these difficulties beset everyone, not just the Jews, but as usual the Jews also had special problems of their own.

On the one hand, the Jews did not especially stand out among the crowds of refugees: they were now no shabbier, no sadder-looking and no more out of place in the Polish countryside than the hundreds of thousands of other displaced city-dwellers. The German presence in the countryside and the smaller towns was not so ubiquitous and oppressive as it had been in Warsaw, and if the Jews' support networks had been disrupted, so had the networks of the *szmalcowniks* and informers. On the other hand, it was now impossible to live 'under the surface', and antisemitism in the smaller localities was cruder and perhaps more dangerous than the more sophisticated version found in the capital. The ONR had little support in the provinces, almost none in the countryside; there were thus fewer believers in the *żydokomuna*, but more who held to the old religious and folk superstitions about Jews. Such views are still in evidence in some scenes from Claude Lanzmann's documentary film *Shoah*, filmed four decades later. Even as late as 1996 – thirty-one years after the Catholic church officially renounced such views – a survey conducted by Polish sociologists showed that as many as 41 per cent of respondents still expressed some of the tenets of 'traditional antisemitism'.[93] Since such unsophisticated attitudes are found mainly in the countryside, it is likely that most rural Poles hold such views even now, and that in 1944 nearly all did.

Much depended on the parish priest. Janina Bauman, whose experiences in the countryside near Kraków were idyllic, was made to go to mass by her landlady, who, Bauman thinks, suspected that she was Jewish and did not want her to stand out. She recounts that '[t]he sermon was simple and clear. It was about the equality of all humankind in the eyes of Almighty God and the sacred duty of every Christian soul to help those who were in peril, no matter which race they belonged to or which faith they espoused.'[94] Such preaching was the exception rather than the rule, however. The period of hiding in the villages fortunately did not include Good Friday, when the service dwelt on the betrayal of Christ and (until 1959) included a prayer for the 'perfidious Jews'.

Jews once again had to conceal their identities, if they could. If not, they were exposed to negative experiences of many kinds. The same woman who described the Warsaw Uprising as a 'golden dream' gives a fairly characteristic account: 'We escaped from a transport that was taking us to a camp. And we wandered from place to place, working and lying. We changed our names several times. Everywhere, the hatred spread by the Germans persecuted and oppressed us.'[95] Stella Kutner, orphaned in the uprising, writes that she stayed in the countryside with people who knew she was Jewish. They kept her captive, forcing her to work as a domestic, allowing the children to mistreat her and locking her up at night. She managed to escape, and then wandered from town to town, eventually finding a sympathetic woman in Radom who took her in and kept her until liberation.[96] Another child who was deported to the countryside after the uprising was Marysia Szmuel, who managed to stay together with the woman who had been hiding her. Her guardian found her a place in Podgórze with a Mrs Berezyn´ska, a devout and proselytizing Catholic. Berezyn´ska told her that the Jews poison children who convert to Christianity, 'and therefore', Szmuel writes, 'I was afraid of Jews for a long time after the war'.[97] Heniek Akierman was deported from Pruszków to Gockowice with his mother, but had to be sent away when people started saying he was a Jew. He survived, but his mother was killed.[98]

Exploitation, denunciation, prejudice and the occasional murderer were not the only problems. Jews who had endured so much over the previous five years were often in poor health: for example, Bauman, as we have noted, was suffering from tuberculosis. Their resistance to disease was not enhanced by the living conditions that many had to endure in these final months. Thus, Tamara Buchman's family hid in a probably unheated attic after the uprising; she lost her mother, not to denunciation but to rheumatic fever.[99]

Despite the various dangers, the number of Warsaw Jews who lost their lives in the aftermath of the Warsaw Uprising does not seem to have been large. This can be attributed to a variety of factors. Only a few months remained until liberation; the German network of spies and informers had been disrupted; Jews were relatively inconspicuous among the flood of refugees; the shared experience of the uprising created an atmosphere of solidarity among its survivors, which to some degree extended to the Jews as well; the mood among most of the survivors was sombre and subdued. On the other hand, those who hid in bunkers could rarely gather large reserves of food and water, and could not anticipate that liberation would be delayed for so long. Many therefore died of starvation or thirst. Jews hiding in more favourable circumstances sometimes died because years of privation and stress had undermined their resistance to disease. Jews among the Warsaw refugees had a good chance of remaining unrecognized, but if their identity did become known, they could be exploited, abused or driven from pillar to post. Only on rare occasions, however, does it seem that they were denounced or murdered.

Summary and Conclusions

The number of Jews who took part in the Warsaw Uprising is hard to estimate. Perhaps a hundred or 150 fought with guns in their hands: the twenty members of Zuckerman's platoon, a second ŻOB platoon in Okęcie, Miciuta's Jewish platoon in the Wigry battalion, individual ŻOB members and a few members of ŻZW in scattered units of the AK, AL and PAL, and an unknown number fighting as Poles. Another 300–350, mostly prisoners liberated from the *Gęsiówka*, belonged to underground organizations but performed auxiliary (though still dangerous) functions. A much larger number – probably most of the able-bodied Jews in areas included in the uprising – acted as couriers, doctors, nurses, rescue workers, fire-fighters and the like. Thus, something like 400–500 people participated formally and thousands more informally. The mortality rate was high: all but a few of the Gęsia Street prisoners perished, as well as a disproportionate number of Jewish civilians. This was mainly because of the coincidence that most of the areas where Jews were hiding were encompassed by the uprising, but several dozen Jews were killed by extremists, especially in the Jew-hunt carried out by the AK unit commanded by Capt 'Hal' (Wacław Stykowski). Attempts to prosecute the offenders were derailed by antisemites within the AK and by the defeat of the uprising. Jews also died because some unit commanders used them as cannon fodder, because they were sometimes excluded from or forced out of air-raid shelters, and because they were denounced and sometimes summarily executed as a result of various absurd suspicions.

These persecutions were evidence that there existed a malignant element in Warsaw society which, though small, managed, in the anarchic atmosphere of the uprising, to do significant damage to the small and vulnerable minority of Jews. Out of 17,000 Jews then in hiding, perhaps fifty were murdered by Poles; this would correspond to an annual murder rate of about 1,700 per 100,000. By comparison, about 500 per 100,000 Polish Jews were murdered in post-war killings in 1945–46, while the 30,000 victims of the 1944–47 civil war represent about 150 per 100,000 of the general population. There was, therefore, clearly a pattern of specifically anti-Jewish violence in Poland at that time which cannot be explained by any normal political or 'criminogenic' factors. Of course, we do not need statistics to prove the point: a specifically anti-Jewish pathology was evident in each individual case, as it was also in the pogroms in Jedwabne, Radziłów and Kielce. I dwell on this matter because there are still authors who try to write antisemitism out of Polish history, finding ingenious explanations for each of these events and ignoring the overall pattern.

As we also saw in Chapter 4, the malignant element that was responsible for crimes against Jews was not confined to the *canaille*, but included brave and patriotic members of the underground, who subscribed to an ideology that numbered Jews among the nation's enemies. Others had accepted the Nazi characterization of the Jews as racially inferior and believed that, as one commander put it, 'your lives as Jews aren't worth much'. Paranoid suspicions centred on the belief that Jews could have survived only by working for the Germans. In one way or another, antisemites, as usual, found reinforcement for their views. Sensing this atmosphere, most Jews sensibly chose not to reveal themselves.

Nevertheless, most Jews report the Warsaw Uprising as a positive experience, characterized on the whole by solidarity and feelings of euphoria, with the exception of a phase dominated by paranoia, which took hold in late August and early September as the belief in victory faded. The visible participation of many Jews in the fighting, together with the feeling of shared calamity, helped to calm this mood towards the end of the uprising.

Objectively, the Warsaw Uprising and its aftermath were the final disasters to befall the Jews of Warsaw. Some 4,500 Jews died in the uprising, mostly through military action, and about 900 more in the aftermath. Though antisemitism was in evidence after the uprising, betrayal at the hands of fellow refugees from Warsaw seems to have been rare; it was somewhat more common at the hands of country- and townsfolk in other parts of the General Government, who had not had the shared experience of the uprising. Most wretched of all was the fate of the few hundred Jews who opted to hide in bunkers in the city's ruins. Having had little time to prepare, and not anticipating that liberation would be so long delayed, these Jews had to endure more than three months of thirst, hunger and freezing cold before the Red Army finally freed the 200 or so survivors.

As the final chapter will show, 17,000 Jews were still living in Warsaw when the uprising broke out, of whom about 11,500 lived to see liberation.

6 Numbers

During the [1944] uprising ... I met and spoke with a good many friends, Poles and Jews. I was quietly astonished that such a significant number of Jews had survived.

Stefan Chaskielewicz[1]

Introduction

Now that the situation of the Jews on the Aryan side has been described, we can turn, as promised at the outset, to the task of justifying the various estimates that have been put forward.

A health warning: this chapter is a 'change of gears', an exercise in statistical reasoning that some readers may find heavy going. Although the chapter is really at the core of the argument that this book makes and essential for gimlet-eyed sceptics, much of it is not altogether necessary for the reader who dislikes numbers or is prepared to take them on faith. To those who find the detailed argumentation tedious, I would suggest reading this introduction, casting an eye over the various tables and figures, and then skipping to the 'Summary and Conclusions' section, where the basic case is made.

Because the wartime and post-war situation was chaotic, few hard figures are available; there are, for example, no reliable statistics on the number of survivors from Warsaw. We therefore have to rely on inference, using whatever indirect indications we can find. I have tried whenever possible to use several independent approaches; usually, as we shall see, they corroborate each other reasonably well.

To simplify matters, I have not presented estimates in the form of ranges, as is the historian's usual practice; rather each estimate is to be understood as an approximation, typically accurate to within about 20 per cent one way or the other. Statistically minded readers might prefer to see the figures accompanied by formal error bars; I have provided enough information to allow those knowledge-able in such matters to calculate these for themselves. But I believe that the test of historical plausibility, the requirement of overall consistency, and the good agree-ment between different approaches constrain the estimates more closely, and allow us to have more confidence in them than formal statistical methods can.

Many of the estimates fit together like the pieces of a jigsaw puzzle. For example, I have asserted that there were about 28,000 Jews in hiding in Warsaw at one time or another. Could the true number have been higher? We have observed that most escapes took place after the Great Deportation, and I have estimated that nearly a quarter of the Jews who were still in the ghetto then managed to flee. This is already a rather surprising figure, and the higher we push it, the more surprising it becomes – not statistically, but historically. Could the number have been lower, on the other hand? If it was, then we shall have trouble accounting for the number of people who appear still to have been alive on the eve of the Warsaw Uprising in 1944 – 17,000, as calculated below, on the basis of fairly solid evidence. Given that we know that about 3,500 Jews 'fell in' at the Hotel Polski, for so many to have survived until the summer of 1944 the rate of attrition on the Aryan side must have been rather low: surprisingly low, many readers will feel. And the lower we push it, the more surprising it becomes. Thus, the estimate of 28,000 in hiding is trapped, as it were, between two opposite poles of historical implausibility, and – being consistent with all the evidence – is also the number that makes the best sense of the whole picture.

I have rounded most estimates to the nearest 100, 500 or 1,000, to avoid giving a spurious impression of accuracy. As a result of the rounding procedures, there are minor discrepancies: here and there: for example, a number that is given in one place as 2,700 may elsewhere be rounded down to 2,500 or up to 3,000. The implication is that all three numbers are 'within the error bars', and can be used interchangeably.

The argument will take the following course: I will estimate the number of Jews under the care of the aid organizations, on the basis of the surviving activist records that are the evidentiary backbone of this study. I will then try to ascertain what proportion of Jews in hiding were receiving aid from these organizations, and on that basis, to estimate how many Jews were in hiding during the period (late 1943 and early 1944) to which these records pertain. This in turn will lead to an estimate of the number of Jews in hiding on the eve of the 1944 Warsaw Uprising. Cases described by memoirists will then be analysed to determine when and how people died, leading among other things to an estimate of how many ultimate survivors there were. This estimate, which is much higher than those usually found in the literature, will be corroborated by a number of other approaches, while the weaknesses of the traditional estimates will be demon-strated. Having thus gained confidence not only in the final tally but also in the evidence provided by the memoirs, we will add up the number of known survivors on the eve of the Warsaw Uprising (31 July 1944) and the number estimated to have died before that date, to arrive at the total number of people in hiding all together. This number, as we have already seen, is also constrained by historical 'sanity checks' and can thus be taken as reasonably solid.

The rate of attrition among the Jews in hiding will then be calculated and tested against several independent indicators, to make sure that we are on the right track and to lay the basis for comparisons. Next, the activist records will be used to develop some demographic statistics, whose significance will be discussed. It will be shown that both attrition rates and demographic patterns corroborate assertions made in Chapter 2 about the decision to escape and its timing, and confirm once again the consistency of the evidence provided by the memoirs. Finally, broader conclusions will be drawn.

Study 1. How Many Jews Were Hiding on the Eve of the Warsaw Uprising?

The most extensive information about the Jews of the secret city comes from the surviving records of the organizations that distributed money to them, particularly the Berman archive, kept at the Ghetto Fighters' House (*Beit Lohamei Hagetaot –* BLHG), which contains the records of the Jewish National Committee (*Żydowski Komitet Narodowy –*ŻKN). These and other records were compiled into a computer database; the methodology has been described in a previous publication.[2]

The documents from the Berman archive that are of greatest interest here concern people who were receiving financial assistance from the committee (BLHG 357 and 358). At the time I examined them, these files had not been internally organized, so that I had to impose my own system. For the purposes of the analysis that follows, these files are organized into numbered 'lists', reflecting the fact that most of the records are lists of aid recipients. These lists contain, all told, about 7,500 individual entries: 6,004 were entered into the database, and there were about 1,500 more consisting of rough notes, that were judged not to contain enough reliable new information to be useful in the analysis. Each entry consists of some of the following information: name (of an individual or family group); number of people in the group; receipt number and amount received; age, or date and place of birth; other identifying information such as occupation and place of origin; name of the responsible activist; and comments of various kinds. For security reasons, the recipients' real names were used, rather than the pseudonyms by which they were known to the world at large.

Two more sources were used in constructing the database: the previously published records of the 'Felicja' cell of the Polish aid organization, Żegota (1,155 entries dated December 1943–May 1944, with partial receipts for November 1943 and June 1944)[3] and recipient lists for the Bund (2,209 entries, covering March to June 1944).[4] Each entry in these lists contains at least the name of a recipient, the number of people in the receiving group, and the amount paid out.

The database thus contains 9,368 entries. Of these, 126 were judged irrelevant to the present study (for example, because they pertained to people outside the Warsaw area), or were illegible or undecipherable. The remaining 9,242 entries were assigned 4,751 distinct identifying numbers, representing 4,592 named individuals or family groups and 159 groups of entries which contained no surname but enough other information to distinguish individual cases. All told, the database is calculated to represent 6,515 distinct individuals.

The interpretation of these documents requires some knowledge of the structure and functions of the ŻKN, and indeed of the whole organized effort to bring relief to Jews in hiding. Quite a bit has been written about the Polish Council to Aid Jews (Żegota), much less about Jewish self-help. Indeed, apart from scattered references in memoirs and books on related topics, the only published description of the ŻKN and its work is a short article by Dr Berman himself which appeared in 1953.[5] Berman was the director of CENTOS (*Centrala Opieki nad Sierotami* – Central Organization for Orphan Care) in the Warsaw Ghetto. He was a prominent Left Labour Zionist, and edited the left-wing underground newspaper *Der Ruf* ('The Call'). In the course of the Great Deportation in 1942 the ghetto's child-welfare institutions were liquidated, rendering CENTOS superfluous. After having been rescued three times from the *Umschlagplatz*, Berman escaped from the ghetto on 5 September 1942.

The ŻKN was formed within the ghetto on about 20 October, as an umbrella group uniting the Zionist parties and youth groups (excluding the Revisionists and their youth group, Betar). Shortly afterwards, the Jewish Co-ordinating Committee (*Żydowski Komitet Koordynacyjny* – ŻKK) was established, with representation from the Bund as well as the ŻKN. The impulse for the formation of the ŻKN and ŻKK was the decision by the underground political parties in the ghetto to prepare for armed resistance: the ŻKK was meant to present a united front in negotiations with the Polish underground and to provide political leadership for the Jewish Combat Organization (*Żydowska Organizacja Bojowa* – ŻOB), which had been formed in July by Zionist youth groups.

Berman was named the representative of the ŻKN, and its representative on the ŻKK, on the Aryan side. Dr Leon Feiner, long-established on the Aryan side, represented the Bund. Berman had extensive pre-war professional contacts with the Polish intelligentsia, and as director of CENTOS had also maintained sporadic contact during the ghetto period with the Polish above-ground relief organization, the RGO. Through these contacts, Berman became drawn into the Temporary Committee to Aid Jews (*Tymczasowy Komitet Pomocy Żydom* – TKPŻ), founded at about the same time as the ŻKN at the initiative of the Catholic activist Zofia Kossak-Szczucka and the Socialist activist Wanda Krahelska-Filipowicz. When this body was reorganized in December into the Council to Aid Jews (*Rada Pomocy Żydom* – RPŻ, codenamed Żegota), under the umbrella of the Polish civil underground, he became the ŻKN's representative on its governing council. After the

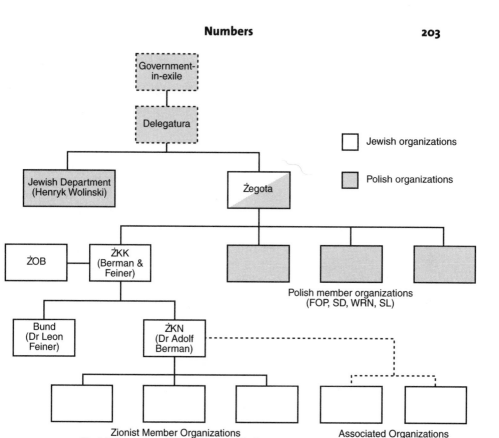

Figure 6.1   Organizational Structure of Aid Organizations

defeat of the Ghetto Uprising and the final liquidation of the ghetto, Berman became the chairman of the ŻKN. From this point on, relief work among Jewish fugitives became the committee's chief focus.

The aid organizations clustered under the financial umbrella of Żegota comprised a multi-tiered federative structure, with Żegota at the top (Figure 6.1). At the next level, on the Jewish side, was the ŻKK, and then its component organizations, the Bund and the ŻKN. Below that were ŻKN's member organizations, the Left and Right Labour Zionists, the General Zionists, the youth groups Hashomer Hatzair, Dror Hehalutz, Akiba and Gordonia, and the Joint Distribution Committee (JDC or 'the Joint'). The ŻKN also channelled funds to the religious party Agudas Yisroel and the Revisionist Zionists, and maintained fraternal contacts with the (Communist) Polish Workers' Party (PPR) and its associated organizations. In addition, ŻOB continued to exist on the Aryan side, supported by the Bund and the ŻKN through the ŻKK. A few ŻOB activists lived in hiding in Warsaw, others operated as partisans in nearby forests.

On the Polish side, Żegota was supported by its member organisations, political parties of the left and centre as well as the Catholic FOP (*Front Odrodzenia Polski*). Many of the Żegota activists were also active in Polish relief organizations – above ground, the RGO, the Catholic welfare organization Caritas, and the Polish Red Cross; underground, the Social Self-Help Organization (*Społeczna Organizacja Samopomocy* – SOS), formed in 1942 by the Democratic Party. Kossak-Szczucka declined to work with RPŻ and formed a Jewish branch within SOS instead; this served mainly as a liaison with convents and Catholic orphanages caring for Jewish children.[6] The PPR looked after its Jewish members directly, as did the two branches of the Polish Socialist Party (PPS), the right-wing Freedom-Equality-Independence (WRN) and particularly the left-wing Polish Socialists (PS; later the Workers' Party of Polish Socialists, RPPS), who maintained fraternal contacts with the Bund. The underground military arm of the Polish Scouts, *Szare Szeregi*, co-operated with Hashomer Hatzair. Individual members of these organisations provided the bulk of the manpower on which the ŻKN and the Bund relied.

On the Jewish side, each organization provided financial support as required for its own members, and also for whatever Jews came to its attention. In time, the distinction between the ŻKN and its member organizations became blurred, and the latter became in effect cells of the ŻKN. The ŻKN's work expanded rapidly in 1943 and 1944 (Figure 6.2), as it and the Jewish fugitives managed to find each other, and as the fugitives' own resources ran out. Though most of the recipient lists in the Berman archive are undated, it can be inferred that these records pertain mainly if not exclusively to the period from October 1943 onwards, and especially to the spring and summer of 1944.[7]

By this time, the number of cells had grown to fifty or a hundred, according to Berman,[8] each employing a group of activists and communicating through a single contact person with the central organization. It can be inferred that the average cell had some fifty Jews under its wing. As it finally evolved, the ŻKN had a three-tiered structure. At the top was a Central Committee, consisting of Berman and his wife Basia, the Committee's secretary, Hirsch Wasser, and representatives of member groups.[9] At the next level, Berman names twenty individuals as the 'central team'.[10] Below that were the local cells. It follows that each member of the 'central team' served as the contact for several different cells.

Information flowed upwards through the organization, and money flowed downwards. A person in need would in some way establish contact with one of the cells and thereby with one of the Committee's activists. Sometimes she or he would submit a written plea for assistance (Berman preserved some of these – List 33). This, or simply the activist's recommendation, would be transmitted to the central cell, which after vetting it would allocate appropriate additional funds to the activist. Each activist would then receive a monthly sum to distribute, normally 500 zł per recipient, at times reduced to 400 or even 300 zł as the organization's growth outstripped its resources.

As the ŻKN was financially accountable to the Financial Review Committee of Żegota, aid recipients were asked to sign receipts. These were written on small scraps of paper, which activists concealed, typically under their watchbands. A few of these receipts are preserved in the archive (List 21). Individual activists were asked to tabulate the receipts (e.g. List 1, signed by 'Helena'), and these individual lists would filter up to the leadership. Not all activists kept such lists, however, many feeling it to be too dangerous.[11] Attempts by the Central Committee to keep central records seem to have been sporadic and incomplete, probably also for security reasons. No central register was kept, but activist lists were used for a time to prepare monthly statements to the Financial Review Committee (List 5, consisting of monthly sublists 5.1 [October 1943] to 5.6 [March 1944]). In addition, several members of the Central Committee seem to have tried to collate activists' lists into an alphabetical register (Lists 4 and 6, kept by Hirsch Wasser; List 3, by Basia Berman; List 2, typed and unsigned, consisting of sublists 2.1–2.9, divided into categories of some kind). In addition to the monthly registers of List 5, there is another, similar, but much rougher monthly tabulation (List 7, with sublists 7.1 [January 1944] to 7.6 [June 1944]). In the case of List 5, the sublists were written up neatly on slips of paper and signed and dated by 'Borowski' (Berman), 'for the presidium of the ŻKN'. They are countersigned, all on 14 June 1944, by three members of the Financial Review Committee of Żegota, 'Lasocki' (Feiner), 'Łukowski' (Marek Arczyński), and 'Różycki' (Tadeusz Rek). In the case of List 7, the sublists take the form of rough notes with liberal use of abbreviations and cryptic notations.

The function of the individual lists is in some cases identified explicitly, while in other cases it has to be inferred. List 7.4 is identified as '*subwencje indywidualne*' (individual subsidies), that is to say, people under the care of the ŻKN directly rather than of one of its member organizations. List 14 is marked '*Podopieczni Ż.K.K.*', that is to say, people under the direct care of the ŻKK. In general, the lists fall into the following categories:

1. Letters requesting assistance (eighty-two letters, most dated June–July 1944)
2. Thirty individual receipts.
3. Monthly registers of receipts (Lists 5 and 7). The Bund and 'Felicja' recipient lists are similar, and were designated Lists 40 (sublists 1–4, March–June) and 50 (sublists 1–7, October–April), respectively.
4. Reports from individual activists, some dated.
5. Larger registers of recipients, each probably for a high-level cell (the ŻKN: Lists 2, 3, 4, 6; ŻKK: List 14).
6. Notes and jottings of various kinds.

Development and Finances of ŻKN

The ŻKN received money from Żegota, which in turn received it from the Polish Government-in-Exile. Starting in mid-1943, however, money raised in the US was channelled to the ŻKN through the Government-in-Exile: payments of $10,000 were received each month from June until September. (As a benchmark both of the value of the złoty at the time and of the rate of inflation, it is worth noting that Berman was able to convert this money on the black market at the rate of 66.15 zł to the dollar in June and 90.34 by September. At these rates, the standard monthly relief payment of 500 zł was worth $7.55 in June and $5.53 in September).

It offers some insight both into the structure of the ŻKN and the scale of its operations to examine the disposal of the $40,000 received between June and September 1943. The total sum obtained on the black market was 3,030,550 zł, and this was distributed as follows:

Table 6.1 ŻKN Financial Report for 1 January–31 October 1943

General Zionists	335,000
Right Labour Zionists	355,000
Hehalutz and other youth organizations	335,000
Left Labour Zionists	285,000
Camps and ghettos	585,000
Individual grants (includes small allowances for Aguda and Revisionists)	350,000
Donations to Żegota	250,000
Administrative expenses	30,550
[Unaccounted for]	505,000
Total	3,030,550

Source: YV O6/48.

The body of the report mentions subsidies to ŻOB for the purchase of weapons, upkeep of fighters in forests near Warsaw and travel expenses. These are said to amount to a 'significant portion of the ŻKN budget' and probably account for the missing sum, which seems to have been omitted through a clerical error.

On this basis, it would appear that at this point the ŻKN and its member organizations were providing financial support for some 800 people, not counting camps and ghettos. But Berman complained that towards the end of this period individual grants had to be cut to 300–400 zł monthly, at the very time that favourable black-market rates were effectively increasing the sums at the Committee's disposal. Therefore, a more realistic picture would be that the number of recipients during this four-month period grew from about 600 to 1,000 or more. This comprised about 300 activists of the member organizations (assuming that their support consumed half the amounts disbursed to the organizations), a

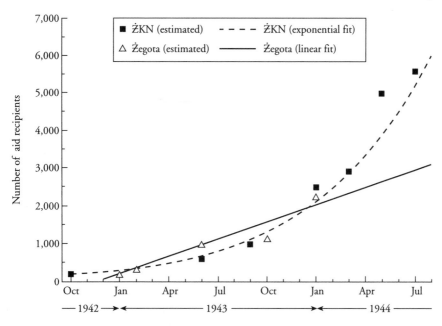

Based on activists' estimates; the true numbers may have been slightly lower.

Figure 6.2   Growth of Żegota and the ŻKN in Warsaw

number that probably declined gradually, and an ever-increasing number of individual recipients who had managed to make contact with one of the cells of the ŻKN. According to a note in the Berman archive (BLHG 357, List 7.1), the number of recipients had grown to 2,500 by January 1944. In a letter to the Plenipotentiary of the Government-in-Exile dated 20 March 1944 (BLHG 310), Berman estimated the number at just under 3,000. In a report on the Committee's activities on 24 May, his estimate has risen to 5,000 (BLHG 309), and at a meeting with the Plenipotentiary on 17 July (BLHG 313) to 5,600. (See Figure 6.2.)

The evidence from the recipient lists only generally supports Berman's claims, which have met with strong scepticism in some quarters.[12] The database contains concrete evidence of 4,271 people under the care of the ŻKN, and, as I have noted, about 1,500 entries were not tabulated. Though most of these merely duplicate existing entries, they might represent a few hundred more people. In addition, the preserved records may well be incomplete. We can probably therefore accept Berman's estimates, with a small pinch of salt; for the sake of round numbers, we shall say that the ŻKN had about 5,000 people under its care.

Berman claimed further that Żegota had an additional 4,000 people under its care in the Warsaw area and the Bund 1,500–2,000, making for a total of 11,000–12,000 in the Warsaw area alone. But this claim does not stand up. As to Żegota, Teresa Prekerowa puts forward the more modest figure of 3,000 (another

1,000 were hiding elsewhere, mainly in Kraków). Her estimate is based on the organization's financial reports, and we can probably trust Żegota activists to have been honest: they were surely people of the highest probity. The claims for the Bund do seem to be reasonable: 1,736 people are represented in the Bund lists, which do not include party activists; furthermore, the Bund lists stop in June 1944, leaving room for additional growth before the outbreak of the Warsaw Uprising on 1 August.

But we cannot simply add up the numbers, as Berman did. Comparison of the recipient lists reveals considerable overlaps between them – that is to say, there were quite a few people who drew money from two or even three sources, either at the same time or first from one and then another. There was perhaps some welfare fraud, but a more likely explanation is that the three organizations handled their budgetary problems by transferring people to each other. Reasonable assumptions yield the picture shown in Table 6.2.

Small numbers of people also received aid from other organizations such as the PPR, PPS, RGO, the Warsaw Housing Co-operative and the SOS.

Of course, not all people in hiding received money from the aid organizations, but the recipient lists can be used to estimate what proportion did. Starting with a list of 2,356 names of aid-recipients, I looked up the names of 131 people who, according to the memoirs, were in hiding at the outbreak of the Warsaw Uprising. I found fifteen exact matches, and on this basis we could conclude that the recipient list represents about 15/131 of the Jews in hiding, who therefore numbered about 20,576 (2,356 × 131/15).

But there were also some inexact matches, for example on surname only. There were fourteen such matches among the 131, of which I judged ten to be 'possible' and four to be 'remote'. If we guess that half of the possibles and one of the remotes were real matches, then we would have another six, or twenty-one out of 131. In that case, there would have been about 14,697 Jews in hiding (2,356 × 131/21).

Of course, there is also the converse possibility that some names were similar by coincidence, and we really cannot tell how many of the possible matches were real. Therefore, the true number of Jews in hiding at this time might have been

Table 6.2 Case Loads of Aid Organizations, 1943–44

Organization	People under care	Overlapping cases (percentage)	Net people under care
Żegota	3,000	21.3	2,300
Bund	2,000	28.9	1,400
ŻKN	5,000	16.1	4,200
Multiple			1,000
Total			8,900

anywhere in this approximate range. In round numbers, this method of calculation thus broadly confirms activists' estimates that there were 15,000–20,000 Jews in hiding on the eve of the Warsaw Uprising, the period to which the recipient list pertained.

There are also independent indications, to be discussed below, of how many people ultimately survived and of how many died during and after the Warsaw Uprising. Adding up these numbers should give the number of people in hiding just before it broke out. On this basis we shall come to about 17,000, which is consistent with the previous calculation and falls at about the mid-point of the range.

Since two independent methods lead to the same conclusions, we can consider it fairly solidly established that about 17,000 Jews were in hiding on the eve of the Warsaw Uprising. It follows that the aid organizations between them eventually reached about half of this remnant group.

Most observers, myself among them, would have regarded this claim with scepticism until now: memoirists, other than the organizations' own activists, rarely mention having received aid, and most survivors deny it when questioned. Gutman and Krakowski estimated that only 5 per cent of Warsaw-area memoirs mention financial aid, the extent of which they therefore believe was 'greatly exaggerated'.[13] But Teresa Prekerowa always maintained, relying as I have noted on Żegota's financial statements, that the claimed figures were realistic. She wrote to me that

> Jews receiving aid from Żegota gave receipts, some of which have been preserved. I sought out a few [of these Jews]. At first they denied it: nobody had given them anything. Only when I showed them the receipt with their signature on it did they stop objecting, they recognized their signatures. But they kept insisting that they didn't remember anything. They explained that they were very young, or in a state of shock because of the situation, that when they got money they didn't ask where it was coming from, and so on.[14]

Now we have further evidence that this is probably a correct reading.

Before leaving the question of numbers and growth, one feature of Figure 6.2 is worth discussing. The numbers of recipients for the ŻKN are fitted very closely by an exponential growth curve, whereas the corresponding data for Żegota are fitted equally closely by a straight line. In short, the ŻKN's activity grew exponentially, that is to say, according to the 'laws of natural growth', and Żegota's linearly, as if constrained. This reflects, first of all, the fact that the ŻKN catered to all comers, and that news of its activities spread by word of mouth: one person told two people, who told four people, and so on. Żegota, on the other hand, cut its cloth to fit its pocket, accepting only as many cases as its financial state allowed. The rest, I suspect, were passed on to the Jewish organizations, and this would help to account for the high degree of overlap between the three organizations' recipient lists. Second, growth of the type experienced by the ŻKN is actually characteristically not exponential but sigmoid, that is to say, it eventually levels off. Growth was ultimately limited, of course, by the fact that there were only so many Jews in hiding. The data would be fitted even better by a sigmoid or S-shaped curve with its point of inflection in April 1944, when there were claimed to be 4,000 (in reality more likely about 3,500) under care. This would suggest that the ŻKN's outreach would eventually have levelled off at about 7,000 and all the organizations between them might eventually have reached 12,500 people or so. The rest would have been people who were either so well situated that they preferred not to reveal themselves by seeking out aid, or else dead by then.

Study 2. How Many Warsaw Jews Survived the War?

We shall now try to determine how many of the 17,000 survivors at the outbreak of the Warsaw Uprising lived to see the end of the war, and in the process construct an overall picture of what fates met the Jews of the secret city.

The straightforward approach is to look up some of the names from the database in the standard post-war survivor list, which contains some 58,000 entries and was published in June 1945 by the Central Committee of Polish Jews (CKŻP). The CKŻP's leading historian, Philip Friedman, used this list as the basis for what have become the standard estimates of the numbers and types of Holocaust survivors in Poland. According to Friedman, 40,000–50,000 Jews had survived 'on the soil of Poland', some of whom had survived not in hiding but as partisans or in family camps.[15] A subsequent register published in December 1945 did contain 80,000 names, but this number includes 25,000 Jews repatriated from concentration camps in Germany (in addition to 5,446 registered in the camps in the June list), and also the first few Jews repatriated from the Soviet Union. The register of 58,000 names was therefore 'purer' for Friedman's purposes.

When the CKŻP June register was searched for a sample of 265 names drawn from the database, only eighty-two were found, about 31 per cent. On the face of it, this gives a direct indication of how many died. But when the exercise was repeated with a control sample of 112 people whose fates were known, only thirty out of eighty-six known survivors were found, about 35 per cent – only marginally more. The low number of 'hits' is probably due in part to the fact that the June register is incomplete – some survivors had not yet registered, and some never registered at all – and partly due to research artefacts. For example, the names of 11 per cent of the people known *not* to have survived turned up on the survivor list: these were mainly people with common surnames, where by coincidence, somewhere in Poland someone with the same name had survived.

We might, however, estimate the true attrition between the summer of 1944 and the end of the war at 4 per cent, the difference between the test sample and the control. But this approach is not a reliable one. The samples are small, and the process of matching names is by nature error-prone. The experience of those who were receiving institutional aid may not be typical, and the apparent conclusion – that 96 per cent of the 17,000 Jews survived – flies in the face of accepted wisdom, common sense, and other lines of evidence. At most we can conclude that the rate of attrition may have been lower than has been supposed, but we need to try a few other approaches first.

The existing literature does not provide a well-grounded estimate of how many Warsaw Jews survived, though the general impression is that there were very few. Israel Gutman estimates that one-quarter to one-third of the Jews in hiding survived; since he estimates the total number of the latter at 15,000–20,000, one could deduce that the survivors numbered 4,000–7,000.[16] In conversation, he has mentioned a figure of 5,000, but this was accompanied by a shrug. Michael Marrus, who has studied post-war population movements, gives the same figure, and the same shrug. Shmuel Krakowski supposes that 25,000 Jews escaped from the ghetto,[17] but does not venture to guess how many survived, beyond writing that 'the majority were murdered on the Aryan side or fell in the Polish uprising in 1944'.[18] Helen Fein took up the question in connection with her seminal study *Accounting for Genocide*, and after analysing the CKŻP survivor lists (more on her work below) concluded that '[p]erhaps one Jew in 100 in Warsaw' – therefore fewer than 5,000 – 'evaded capture by the Germans, usually living in continual fear and isolation'.[19]

The Evidence of the Memoirs

A close examination of the memoirs contradicts these very low estimates. Given that there were 17,000 Jews in hiding on the eve of the Warsaw Uprising, if there were only about 5,000 survivors at the end of the war it would follow that more than two-thirds – 12,000 people or so – had perished in the uprising or subsequently. But a third-person study of 234 Jews whose fates were recorded by memoirists showed that only fifteen were reported to have died during the Warsaw Uprising, and two more in its aftermath.

These figures need further analysis, however. Despite the fact that the memoirists themselves are excluded, the sample still clearly overrepresents survivors, who make up 131 of the 234. Why do memoirists report the fate of survivors more often than that of non-survivors? Often memoirists simply lost track of people, usually because they had died under unknown circumstances, whereas most adult survivors registered with the CKŻP after the war and so could generally find each other.[20] In addition, survival was perceived to be such an exceptional, almost miraculous outcome that memoirists often feel the need to record it for posterity by meticulously listing the names of all friends and family members who came out of the war alive.

A further 133 cases were left out of this study for lack of the necessary details. When they are included, we have a total of 367 people, of whom 101 died and 171 survived; the fates of ninety-five were not recorded. On the assumption that these last were people who died in unknown circumstances, causing the memoirists to lose track of them, we can conclude that 196 died and 171 survived, an overall survival rate of 47 per cent. As we shall see, this is still slightly too high, so that we are unlikely to have erred too much in assuming that all ninety-five were killed.

The chaos of the uprising and its aftermath, and the isolation of the insurrectionary enclaves, represented the circumstances under which people were most likely to lose track of friends and relatives in hiding, so that we might surmise that at least half of the ninety-five people whose fate is not reported died during this period. In that case, the number killed during and after the uprising would have been between fifty-five and 112 out of 367, or 4,000–8,000 in all. We can narrow this down further. A detailed breakdown of the time and manner of death of the 113 non-survivors for whom these details were known gives the results shown in Table 6.3. On this evidence, deaths during and after the Warsaw Uprising totalled about 5,400, and the ultimate survivors should therefore have numbered about 11,600 or, within 5 per cent error bars, 9,400–13,800. The established estimates that there were between 4,000 and 7,000 survivors on the Aryan side in Warsaw are obviously well outside these error bars, and require there to have been either substantially fewer Jews in hiding, or else a substantially higher death rate during and after the uprising than seems to be indicated by the evidence.

Helen Fein also used quantitative methods to arrive at her estimate; let us therefore evaluate her approach to see why it differs from mine. Fein examined the card-file of survivors accumulated after the war by the CKŻP, now held at the Jewish Historical Institute. This card file is a treasury of information useful to the present study. Registrants were asked to state, among other things, their pre-war, wartime and post-war names and addresses and their method of survival, as well as information that would be useful in constructing a demographic profile. Many answers are contained in this card-file. On the basis of a 3 per cent sample study, Fein found about 10,000 survivors who gave Warsaw as their pre-war place of residence, not counting repatriants from the USSR. From this number she deducted an estimate of the number of people who survived in camps rather than in hiding to arrive at her estimate of 5,000 or so Warsaw survivors 'on the soil of Poland'.[21] But things are not so simple.

Table 6.3   Time and Manner of Death of Non-Survivors among Warsaw Jewish Fugitives Mentioned in Memoirs

Time and manner of death		Number	Percentage	Projection
On Aryan side:	Not known how	30	26.5	†
	Betrayed or murdered	9	8	3,600
	Caught, not betrayed	6	5.3	2,400
	Natural causes*	2	1.8	800
(Subtotal)		*47*	*41.6*	*6,800*
Returned to ghetto		4	3.5	600
Hotel Polski		24	21.2	3,500
After leaving Warsaw area		1	0.9	150
During Warsaw Uprising		15	13.3	4,500
After Warsaw Uprising		3	2.7	900
Time and manner unknown		19	16.8	‡
Total		113	100.0	16,450

Projections are based on the estimate that 3,500 Jews died as a result of the Hotel Polski affair (see Chapter 4). Projections are rounded to the nearest 100; to the nearest 10 if under 1,000.
† In forming the projections, these cases were redistributed among the known categories of death on the Aryan side.
‡ For reasons explained in the body of the text, these people were assumed to have died during or after the Warsaw Uprising and in forming the projection were redistributed proportionally between these two cases.
* Deaths due to 'natural causes' were of course influenced by the stresses and living conditions of life in hiding.

Sources: selected memoirs from the AŻIH 301 and YV O3 collections; memoirs of Janina Bauman, Adina Blady-Szwajger, Jacob Celemenski, Stefan Chaskielewicz, Zofia Kubar, Vladka Meed, Eugenia Szajn-Lewin, 'Antek' Zuckerman; selected relations from Bartoszewski and Lewin, *Righteous among the Nations*; selected files from Yad Vashem, Department of the Righteous.

We cannot assume that people who came from Warsaw spent the war years there, nor, conversely, that people who survived in Warsaw came from there. As to those who spent the war years elsewhere, the largest group were the 30,000 or so who fled to the Soviet occupation zone in 1939–40. The great majority of these were later deported to the depths of the Soviet Union, and most of the others were then either massacred when Germany invaded the Soviet zone in 1941, or made their way back to their families in Warsaw. Jewish PoWs form another large group: those captured by the Soviets were either, again, deported to the depths of the Soviet Union, or else were among the officers massacred at Katyń. Those who were captured by the Germans were eventually killed or released, and most of the latter went back to their families. In short, most Warsaw Jews who left the city early in the war either perished, or ended in the depths of the Soviet Union and therefore were eliminated from Fein's study, or returned to Warsaw in due course. And once the ghetto was closed, few people left except to go into hiding. I would not suppose that more than 1,000–2,000 Warsaw Jews survived the war somewhere else in Poland. We would have to eliminate these from Fein's 10,000 putative Warsaw survivors, to arrive at 8,000–9,000.

Those are the subtractions; now for the additions. Warsaw was a major concentration point for Jews, not only from the surrounding area but from places as far afield as Germany and Czechoslovakia, and these refugees (as they were called in the ghetto) made up as much as a third of the ghetto's population.[22] They had worse chances of survival than Warsaw natives, and fewer prospects on the Aryan side, but some did go into hiding, especially those from nearby towns who knew the area well. Further, if the refugees were underrepresented among those who escaped deportation then *ipso facto* they were overrepresented among deportees, and thus presumably among survivors in the camps. Conversely, therefore, we should expect native Warsaw Jews to be underrepresented in the camps, and Fein's deduction for survivors in camps is thus too high. (In fact, it is much too high, as we shall see below.) Finally, a substantial number of Warsaw Jews who survived in camps were there as Aryans, usually having found their way into them via Pruszków after living in hiding until the Warsaw Uprising. Within the present terms of reference, such people should be counted as survivors 'on the Aryan side', though not necessarily 'on the soil of Poland'.

Still further additions need to be made. Not all Jews registered with the CKŻP; indeed, we have seen that investigations using the published register, which is a subset of the card catalogue, indicate that the number of non-registrants may have been quite large. Recall that the names of known survivors turned up in the register only half as often as they should have.[23] Jews registered with the CKŻP so that surviving family members could find them, but as long as relatives had some point of contact it was not necessary to register everyone, particularly children. For example, three of the six surviving members of the Brzostek family (AŻIH 301/5861) registered, but three others – Bernard, Lejbe and Perła – did not. There is a Saba Brzostek; possibly Perła registered under that name. Rywa Kaganowicz (AŻIH 301/5865) registered herself, but not her son, Grzesio. My own suspicions about the completeness of the CKŻP register were first aroused when of three close relatives of mine who survived in hiding, I found only my grandmother in the register. My mother ended the war in Sweden and registered there; my sister, four years old at the time, was being looked after by Polish relatives who did not register her (She was eventually registered by her grandmother, but not in time for her name to appear in the June lists). My sister was one of many Jewish children in the care of Polish families that were often reluctant to give them up. Not a few adults elected to conceal their Jewish identity after the war, converts and Communists in particular. Finally, there were Jews liberated in camps who never returned to Poland: for example, my mother was one of more than 4,000 Polish Jews who registered in Sweden and do not appear in the CKŻP lists.[24] Another 6,000 Jews from Warsaw alone are listed in a register compiled by the *Landsmanschaft* (regional association) of Warsaw Jews in the US occupation zone in Germany in 1948; more than 80 per cent of the names in this register do not appear in the CKŻP June list.[25] Presumably there were still more unregistered Polish Jews in the other occupation zones. Jews who found themselves abroad at the end of the war often knew that their families had perished and sought out relatives abroad, or simply were glad to have done with Poland and never wanted to see it again. Thus, of six people in the sample who memoirists say were living abroad after the war, only one appears in the June list. Of the Jews who stayed abroad, a certain proportion were again survivors 'on the Aryan side', though not 'on the soil of Poland'.

We can attempt to quantify some of these categories. As the 'refugees' constituted one-third of the ghetto population, pro rata they should have contributed a further 4,000–4,500 survivors. Since their chances of finding hiding places were not as good as those of the natives, though, perhaps a more reasonable estimate would be half that number, 2,000 or so. To this we should add the survivors among the 2,700 who came to Warsaw to hide – about 1,000, say. Thus, we can guess that there were 3,000 survivors 'on the Aryan side' in Warsaw who were not from Warsaw, as against 1,000–2,000 Warsaw Jews who survived elsewhere. After these adjustments to Fein's estimate, we would come to 11,000–12,000 surviving Warsaw Jews. We should then have to take into account all the categories of non-registrants, so that the overall total would be higher still, perhaps 13,000 or more. From this number we have to subtract those who were in the camps as Jews and not as Aryans, and also those who survived as partisans, or in 'family camps' in the forest.

To deal with these questions, and as a further check, we shall next look at two more sources, the American *National Registry of Jewish Holocaust Survivors* and the inventory of longer memoirs published by the Jewish Historical Institute, supplemented by published summaries and excerpts.[26] Unlike the memoirs considered so far, these sources pertain to the whole of Poland and will thus allow some comparisons to be made.

Analysis Using the National Registry

The National Registry is a computer database claimed to contain more than 80,000 names of Holocaust survivors living in the US and Canada. Of these, some 32,000 are listed in the published volume used for this study.[27]

The published registry lists each registrant's place of residence before the war, and all places during the war. A sample study was undertaken of people in the registry who mention locations in Poland as either their place of origin or among 'places during the Holocaust'. Cases were classified on the following assumptions:

1. Someone who lists one or more concentration camps or places in Germany among 'places during the Holocaust' is assumed to have ended the war in a camp or at labour in Germany. This will be wrong only in the few cases of people who managed to escape from the camps, or who were transferred from these camps to labour camps in Poland, and liberated there.
2. Someone who lists no concentration camp or place in Germany, but does list the name of one or more of the labour camps in Poland, probably ended the war 'on the soil of Poland' but in one of these camps. Again this will be wrong in the case of people who escaped from such camps.
3. Someone who lists no concentration camp or labour camp, and who mentions the name of a forest, or gives 'forest' or 'partisans' among the places during the Holocaust, is assumed to have ended the war in a family camp or in a partisan unit. This will be wrong in some cases of people who had mixed experiences of hiding and fighting in partisan units.
4. Someone who mentions none of the above, and whose list of places during the Holocaust either includes the word 'hiding' or mentions only places in Poland is assumed to have ended the war 'on the Aryan side' in Poland.

The following kinds of registry entry were eliminated from the sample, however:

1. People whose places during the Holocaust include 'Siberia', 'USSR', or places within the pre-war boundaries of the USSR, who are assumed to have fled to the Soviet Union in 1939–40. In principle, the registry is not supposed to include such people, but in practice there are many exceptions.
2. Entries that duplicate other entries or represent aliases or wartime names of people for whom full information is given elsewhere in the registry.
3. People who give no information about either place of origin or pre-war residence or about places during the Holocaust. People who mention only places outside Poland were retained for comparative purposes, but only a gross count of such cases was made.

People who mentioned Warsaw were further divided into the following categories:

1. People who mention Warsaw as both a pre-war place and a place during the Holocaust.
2. People who mention Warsaw as a pre-war place but not as a place during the Holocaust.
3. People who mention Warsaw as a place during the Holocaust but not as a pre-war place.

Of the entries in the registry, 4.49 per cent were sampled at random, 2,233 cases

Table 6.4 Broad Breakdown of Cases in the National Registry

Category	No. of cases in sample	Projected no. in registry	Percentage
Eliminations:			
Aliases and duplications	783	17,443	
USSR	55	1,225	
No places given	434	9,669	
Total eliminations	1,272	28,337	
Polish cases (after eliminations)	545	12,141	56.7
Non-Polish cases (after eliminations)	416	9,268	43.3
Total (after eliminations)	961	21,409	100.0
Grand total	2,233	49,746	

out of 49,746 (estimated) in total. The first and most general analysis yielded the results shown in Table 6.4.

We may note without further comment the extraordinary proportion of Polish Jews in the registry.

The Polish cases were then subjected to a more detailed analysis, with Łódź as well as Warsaw cases isolated for comparison; the results are shown in Table 6.5.

Table 6.5 Sample Counts of Polish Cases in the National Registry of Holocaust Survivors, by Inferred Wartime Experience

Location		Type of Experience Inferred				
Pre-War	During war	Camps or Germany	Aryan side	Forests/ Partisans	Other/ Unknown	Total
Warsaw	Warsaw	5	17		4	26
	Not Warsaw	1	6			7
Non-Warsaw	Warsaw	4	12		2	18
	Łódź	70	20		13	103
	Other	181	109	15	86	391
Total		261	164	15	105	545

(Most cases classified as Other/Unknown represent people who give a pre-war place of residence but no places during the war).

After consolidating and simplifying, we arrive at the following proportions:

Table 6.6 Methods of Survival, Warsaw and non-Warsaw Compared (based on the National Registry)

(Places during the War)	Camps Germany	Aryan side	Forests/ Partisans	Total
		(percentage)		
Warsaw	23	77	0	100
Non-Warsaw (all)	63	34	3.7	101
Łódź	78	22	0	100

(Totals do not always equal 100 per cent because of rounding errors)

Two oddities may be noted in Table 6.5. First, what seems an extraordinarily large proportion of survivors in Warsaw were not from Warsaw, more than 40 per cent. Can this really be so? Recalling that resettled Jews constituted one-third of the ghetto's population, they would then have constituted, *pro rata*, about 8,000 of the Jews who fled the ghetto or never entered it. As they were joined by 2,700 who came to Warsaw to hide, the total number of non-natives among the fugitive population would then have been 10,700 out of 27,000: indeed, about 40 per cent. This would suggest that, contrary to expectations, non-natives were no less likely than natives to find hiding places. If this is the case, then we should add another 2,000 to Fein's estimate.

A second oddity is that only 33/545 = 6 per cent of the sample were from Warsaw before the war, whereas Fein projected 10,000 out of some 80,000, 12.5 per cent. The National Registry, since it includes only emigrants to North America, is clearly not a representative sample: evidently it overrepresents Polish Jews but underrepresents Jews from Warsaw, perhaps because of demographic factors. Since Warsaw was the main centre of both assimilationism and Zionism, perhaps an unusually large proportion of Warsaw Jews either stayed in Poland or emigrated to Israel. The National Registry is therefore not a good basis for estimating the overall number of Warsaw survivors, but it does have other uses.

In particular, we may note the striking difference between Warsaw and non-Warsaw cases in the proportion of survivors in camps and on the Aryan side. As Table 6.6 shows, this difference is especially marked in the case of Łódź: 78 per cent of Łódź survivors survived in the camps and 22 per cent on the Aryan side, whereas in the case of Warsaw these proportions are almost exactly reversed. It would seem that Fein was broadly right in supposing that about half of the Jewish survivors in Poland had survived in camps rather than in hiding, but not in assuming that this proportion would also hold good for Warsaw.

Why is there such a sharp discrepancy between Warsaw and non-Warsaw cases? First, the non-Warsaw cases are skewed by the very large group from Łódź. The

Łódź ghetto was the last one to be liquidated, surviving until August 1944, and a large proportion of the remaining Jews were taken to labour camps – particularly the large HASAG camp near Częstochowa – rather than to Auschwitz. Even at Auschwitz, which was not a pure extermination camp like Treblinka but also a huge labour-camp complex, the last major *Aktion* (against the Hungarian Jews) had already ended, and because of the desperate military situation conditions at the camp had eased somewhat in the interests of war production. Thus, Łódź Jews had better chances of survival in the camps than any other group of Polish Jews, and this accounts for the fact that the Jews of Łódź were the largest single group of Jewish survivors in Poland. On the other hand, the Łódź ghetto had been nearly hermetically sealed, and few if any of the Łódź Jews escaped to the Aryan side. (In fact, so poor were the chances of hiding on the Aryan side in Łódź that I suspect that the few cases in the registry really represent people who fled from Łódź early in the war and hid somewhere else.)

Warsaw stands at the other extreme. The great majority of Warsaw Jews were taken to the death camp at Treblinka, with practically no survivors. Some 80,000 were taken instead to Majdanek or to labour camps in the Lublin area (mainly Trawniki and Poniatowa). Jews in these camps were, in principle, eliminated in the *Erntefestaktion* of 3 November 1943, and the few survivors of this 'Harvest Festival' then still had to endure one-and-a-half years of concentration-camp conditions and death marches before liberation. It is not surprising that there were very few left alive. In addition, many of the Warsaw Jews who did survive in camps were there as Aryans, either because they 'fell in' as Aryans, or after the deportations from Pruszków. Of the 150,000-odd people who were sent to work in Germany from Pruszków, *pro rata* some 2,000–3,000 should have been Jews, most of whom (in the camps as Aryans, at a time when their labour was desperately needed) probably lived to see the end of the war. These 2,000–3,000 would amount to about 22 per cent of the 11,600 survivors estimated above, and would thus account for essentially all the Warsaw camp survivors in the National Registry study.

Finally, the study supports the conclusion that more people came to Warsaw than left it – nearly three times as many, in fact. On this evidence, if we accept the estimate that 1,000–2,000 Warsaw natives had left the city and survived elsewhere than in the Soviet Union, then the number of survivors who came to Warsaw from elsewhere must have been about three times higher, or 3,000–6,000. This roughly supports the estimate made above.

Analysis Using the Inventory of Memoirs

A smaller-scale but more closely focused study was carried out using the published inventory of memoirs in AŻIH collection 302, supplemented by published digests and summaries. One hundred and seventy cases of known survivors were found in these sources whose place and method of survival could be ascertained. This analysis yielded the results shown in Table 6.7.

Table 6.7   Place and Method of Survival, Based on 170 Memoirs

	Place during Holocaust		
Method of Survival	**Warsaw**	**Non-Warsaw**	**Total**
Camps	16	41	57
Oskar Schindler	0	1	1
Aryan Side	64	32	96
Forests, Partisans	0	16	16
Total	80	90	170

Six of the camp survivors from Warsaw were in the camps as Jews, 7.5 per cent of the Warsaw cases. This would point to about 1,000 true camp survivors.

The general pattern broadly agrees with that observed in the National Registry study: roughly 80 per cent of Warsaw Jews survived on the Aryan side and most camp survivors were there as Aryans. Both sources agree that very few of the Jews who spent time in Warsaw during the war fought as partisans or hid in the forests. There were small partisan groups in the forests near Warsaw, associated mainly with ŻOB, but most of these partisans were killed, and the rest mostly returned to Warsaw and went into hiding. Partisan groups and family camps were to be found mainly in the east of Poland.

Recall now that Fein had estimated that 5,000 of the 10,000 Warsaw cases in the CKŻP card-file had survived in the camps. We have shown that this is too high; the true number was nearer to 1,000, if not fewer. Recall also that we had concluded that there were 13,000 Warsaw survivors including those in the camps: on this line of analysis, the total number of survivors would come to 12,000, in fairly close agreement with the estimate of 11,600 developed on the basis of the memoirs (see p. 212).

Additional Approaches

A number of less formal approaches help to reinforce these conclusions. It was noted in the introduction that 11.8 per cent of the relations in AŻIH 301 pertained to Aryan Warsaw; as there were about 80,000 survivors according to the CKŻP December register, this would point to about 9,500 survivors in Aryan Warsaw; perhaps 2,000 more when non-registrants are taken into account. The proportions between Righteous Gentiles in Warsaw and elsewhere can act as a further check. Mordechai Paldiel, Director of the Department of the Righteous, estimates that about a quarter of the Polish Righteous Gentiles are from Warsaw. They account for rather more than a quarter of the case histories in Michał Grynberg's *Księga sprawiedliwych* [Book of the Righteous], but after eliminating activists (who were both concentrated in Warsaw and especially likely to come to our attention), the Grynberg case histories roughly support Paldiel's estimate. Therefore, we might surmise that Warsaw cases also account for about one-quarter of all survivors on the Aryan side in Poland. Recall now Philip Friedman's estimate that there were 40,000–50,000 survivors 'on the soil of Poland'. To arrive at survivors 'on the Aryan side', we have to subtract those who survived in Poland in labour camps in Poland, as partisans, or in family camps; on the other hand, we have to account (as before) for non-registrants and survivors as Aryans in the camps. If we assume that the additions and subtractions will be roughly equal, then the total number of survivors on the Aryan side we will come once more to 40,000–50,000, and 10,000–12,500 of these will therefore be from Warsaw. This again agrees quite closely with the previous estimates, and also helps to confirm that these are consistent with established estimates of the number of Jewish survivors in Poland as a whole.

Conclusions

All methods of calculation thus lead to the same conclusion, that the secret city had (in round numbers) 11,500 Jewish survivors.

How Many Jews Were Hiding in Warsaw All Told?

We have established to this point that about 17,000 Jews were still in hiding on the eve of the 1944 uprising, and that about 11,500 survived. What is equally important, we have established that the projections in Table 6.3, based on memoir evidence and an independent estimate of the number of Hotel Polski cases, give a credible overall picture. Readers will recall that it was estimated that 5,400 people had died during and after the Warsaw Uprising, leaving 11,600 post-war survivors, and a number of independent lines of investigation have supported this estimate. Since according to the same projections 16,500 people died in all, we can conclude that about 11,000 died before the Warsaw Uprising, so that to account for the presence of 17,000 Jews in August 1944 we would have to suppose that about 28,000 Jews went into hiding in all, QED.

Attrition

Let us consider the fifteen months between 1 May 1943, when the secret city reached its peak size, and 1 August 1944, when it ceased to exist. Although we have shown that about 28,000 people were in hiding in total, some of them died or returned to the ghetto before May 1943. Therefore, the number of people in hiding at the peak moment, or arriving in Warsaw subsequently, was somewhat smaller – let us say 26,000. In that case, the population of the secret city declined by 9,000 during these fifteen months, an average of 600 per month or twenty per day. But much of this decline was the result of the single dramatic episode of the

Hotel Polski, which we should remove from the equation if we are to draw meaningful conclusions and comparisons. If we therefore take into account only the 22,500 people who did not volunteer for the Hotel Polski scheme, then the attrition rate works out as 1.9 per cent per month: an average of about 370 people per month or twelve per day.

Contemporary testimony points to roughly similar numbers. Ringelblum maintained that 150 Jews had been caught on the 'other side' during the 1942 *Aktion*, which lasted fifty-three days;[28] later, he estimated that 'tens' (*kilkadziesiąt*) of people were being caught each day.[29] Probably more soundly based is the testimony of Julien Hirshaut, who spent a year in the Pawiak prison after having been caught on the Aryan side in the summer of 1943. Hirshaut was kept in cell 258, where people suspected of being Jews were held while their cases were investigated. This cell had some twenty-eight inmates, he tells us, with 'a few' arriving and leaving each day, and the neighbouring cell 257, where condemned Jews were kept prior to execution, housed 'several' Jews at any one time. Hirshaut estimates that on average 500 Jews per month passed through the Pawiak, and that 8,000 Jews died there in all.[30]

These estimates do not quite add up. Five hundred Jews a month would mean seventeen a day, about eight to nine from each cell. As to cell 258, this would be rather too large a fraction of twenty-eight to be described as 'a few', and, on this scale certainly the largest number in cell 257 that could be described as 'several'. We know from the memoirs of the relatives and friends of prisoners that investigations could be quite lengthy and thorough, so that people could spend weeks or even months in the prison before their cases were disposed of. If we suppose that one week represented an average stay, then the number of people removed from the cell would have been of the order of four per day. Not all this number, furthermore, were taken to be shot: some were released, because their documents had stood the test, or a bribe had been paid, or someone had vouched for them. Those who were to be killed were normally first transferred to cell 257, so that simply adding the numbers taken from the two cells would involve double counting. All things considered, it is therefore doubtful that the number of Jews killed in the prison reached even half the total claimed by Hirshaut. In addition, several hundred of them were 'wild' Jews who had gone to the Hotel Polski, rather than people who had been caught.

Of course, not all Jews who were caught came to the Pawiak, but most did. Many people suspected as Jews were interned pending investigation in local stations of the Blue police, at Kripo headquarters at Ujazdowskie 8, or at the Daniłowiczowska Street prison, or were taken for questioning to Gestapo headquarters in Szucha Avenue. Normally, such people were eventually either released or transferred to the Pawiak. There were other possibilities, however. During the ghetto period, Jews caught on the Aryan side were held in the Gęsia Street prison or *Werterfassung* headquarters, or else they were taken to the *Umschlagplatz* directly.

As I have noted, children returned from the Aryan side were placed in a special orphanage in Dzika Street, and taken thence eventually to the *Umschlagplatz*. Other Jews were simply shot on the spot. Reliable estimates of the number of people killed in these various ways are very hard to come by.

Not all those caught on the Aryan side were true fugitives from the ghetto. Many who were captured while the ghetto was still in existence were food-smugglers, and probably a few were Christians who had been falsely accused. On the other hand, there were Jews who were killed for political or other reasons, without their identities having been discovered. Such cases are difficult to identify, let alone count. The question of attrition is therefore complex and difficult to answer on the basis of direct evidence, but certainly these partial estimates are not inconsistent with the claim (see Table 6.3 again) that some 6,000 Jews died after being caught or betrayed: half of them, let us say, at the Pawiak, and half in other ways.

A direct method of estimating attrition rates is available through the analysis of monthly receipt registers. The published register of *Żegota* receipts spans the period from December 1943 to May 1944, with fragmentary records for November 1943 and June 1944. Of the eighty-four people on this list who received money in November or December, seventy-nine also received money in May or June. On the most unfavourable assumption, that all those who dropped off the list had been captured, this represents a six-month attrition of about 6 per cent, or just over 1 per cent monthly. This group, at any rate, had a considerably better than average survival rate.

A similar study of cases drawn from the Bund lists indicates a much lower rate of survival. Of 175 people listed as receiving aid in March 1944, 114 were also listed in June, three months later. People who dropped off the list often reappeared later, and some turn up in the survivor lists or in later lists of the other organizations. It was calculated, taking these factors into account, that about thirty-seven of the 175 can be presumed to have been killed, which is equivalent to an attrition rate of about 5 per cent monthly.

April 1944 was a bad month for the Bund, however. The number of people on their lists dropped from 461 to 368 (against the overall trend: by June, they were carrying 807 people). The decline among the selected group between May and June was eight out of 116, half of whom were likely to have been temporary absences, giving an attrition rate of about 3 per cent for that month. This may have been more typical.

Different ways of calculating attrition rates thus give somewhat different results, ranging from 1 per cent to 5 per cent monthly, but it is natural that there was a great deal of variation between one organization and another, and one time period and another. The best measure of attrition is the most broadly based one: about 2 per cent per month if the Hotel Polski is omitted and 3 per cent if it is included. The other estimates are roughly similar.

Data on attrition within the ghetto are readily available, and a comparison with the attrition rates calculated above allows us to assess whether it was rational to stay in the ghetto before the liquidation actions. Thus in 1941 there were 42,239 recorded deaths in the ghetto, out of a peak population estimated at 460,000 – an attrition rate of 0.8 per cent monthly. Of the approximately 490,000 people who passed through the ghetto all told, about 350,000 were still in the ghetto on the eve of the liquidation action, twenty months after the ghetto was closed. This represents a rate of loss due to all factors, including deportation to labour camps, of 1.7 per cent monthly. Thus even with the benefit of hindsight, and with calculator in hand, there is little reason to recommend flight from the ghetto before the liquidation started. Indeed, since those who had the best chances of escaping from the ghetto also had the best means of surviving within it, it must be reiterated that remaining outside the ghetto in 1940, or escaping before 22 July 1942, was (without benefit of hindsight) not a reasonable course of action for the great majority of Jews.

Demographic characteristics

The Berman archive permits some rudimentary demographic studies of the Jews in hiding. Of those whose sex could be determined, there were 2,025 women and 1,360 men, so that women made up 60 per cent of those in hiding. Information about age was available in 225 cases; Table 6.8 shows the age and sex distribution of the Jews in hiding, on the basis of these cases. For comparison, Table 6.9 shows figures for the beginning of the occupation and 6.10, for the final period of the ghetto. Figures 6.9 and 6.10 summarize these tables graphically.

Table 6.8   Age and Sex Distribution of Jews on the 'Aryan Side' in Warsaw, 1943–44

Age group	Male Number	%	Female Number	%	Total Number	%
0–9	1,042	9.5	1,953	11.5	2,995	10.7
10–19	1,823	16.7	2,214	13.0	4,037	14.4
20–29	2,605	23.8	4,428	26.0	7,033	25.1
30–39	2,344	21.4	4,428	26.0	6,772	24.2
40–49	1,433	13.1	1,433	8.4	2,866	10.2
50–59	521	4.8	1,172	6.9	1,693	6.0
60–69	781	7.1	781	4.6	1,562	5.6
70+	391	3.6	651	3.8	1,042	3.7
Total	10,940	1,000	17,060	100.2	28,000	99.9

Male–Female ratio: 39:61
(Percentages do not necessarily add up to 100 per cent because of rounding errors.)

Table 6.9 Age and Sex Distribution of Jews in Warsaw, Census of 28 October 1939

Age groups	Men	Percentage	Women	Percentage	Total
0–15	46,172	28.1	45,439	23.2	91,611
16–59	104,273	63.5	131,784	67.4	236,057
60+	13,325	8.1	16,933	8.7	30,258
Undetermined	537	0.3	1,364	0.7	1,901
Total	164,307	100.0	195,520	100.0	359,827

Male–Female ratio: 46:54
Source: Joseph Kermish, ed., *To Live with Honor and Die with Honor: Selected Documents from the Warsaw Ghetto Underground Archives* 'O.S.' (Oneg Shabbath) (Jerusalem: Yad Vashem, 1986), 137.

Table 6.10 Comparative Age and Sex Distribution among Jews in the Ghetto before and after the Main Deportation Action and on the Aryan Side

| | In the ghetto* | | | | In hiding | |
| | Early 1942 | | End October 1942 | | 1943–44 | |
Age group	Male	Female	Male	Female	Male	Female
0–9	16.3	12.2	1.3	1.6	9.5	11.5
10–19	22.4	18.8	11.0	14.6	16.7	13.0
20–29	12.5	17.1	19.5	29.5	23.8	26.0
30–39	18.5	19.4	34.2	30.8	21.4	26.0
40–49	13.4	14.5	21.9	16.5	13.1	8.4
50–59	9.4	9.9	10.2	6.1	4.8	6.9
60–69	5.6	5.8	1.8	1.0	7.1	4.6
70+	1.8	2.4	0.2	0.1	3.6	3.8
Total	99.9	100.1	100.1	100.2	100.0	100.2

Male–Female ratio: see Table 6.11
* From (no author) 'Materialn tsu demografishe forshungen vegn der yidishe bafolkerung in Varshe beys der Hitleristisher okupatsye', *Bleter far Geshichte* 1955, 206–8.

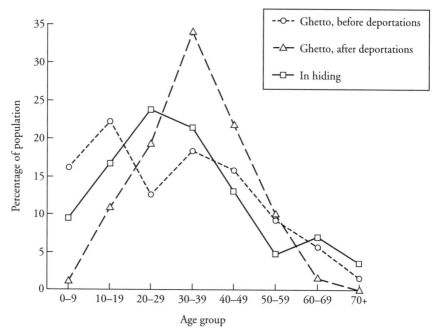

Figure 6.3   Age Distribution (Male)

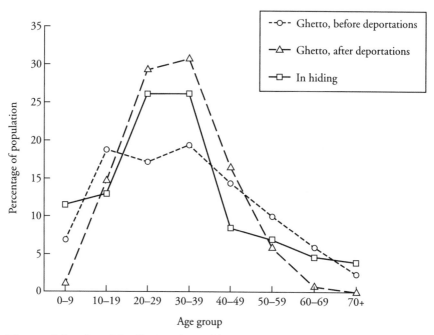

Figure 6.4   Age Distribution (Female)

It can readily be seen from these graphs that both the age distribution and the gender ratio of the Jewish population shifted quite dramatically as a result of the 1942 deportations, which struck disproportionately at the most vulnerable: the very young, the very old, and women. The age-distribution pattern can be seen more clearly if ages are grouped into broader bands. This is done in Table 6.11, where the 'expected' distribution is obtained by combining the pre- and post-deportation figures for the ghetto in the proportions suggested by analysis of the memoirs (see Chapter 2, Table 2.1).

The figures for October 1942 reflect the Darwinian effects of the first liquidation action on the ghetto community. Among the very young and the very old, losses approached 100 per cent. None of the ghetto's 890 octogenarians survived, and only 498 out of 51,458 children under ten. Out of 7,804 people over seventy, there were forty-five survivors. Women were more vulnerable than men: overall, 93 per cent of the ghetto's women were taken, compared with 87 per cent of the men. The difference between the sexes was greatest among the middle aged: 20 per cent of men aged thirty to fifty-nine, survived, but only 9 per cent of women.

As we saw in Chapter 2 (Table 2.1), some 54 per cent of escapes from the ghetto took place after the end of the first *Aktion*, and the distribution of the population in hiding – intermediate between those before and after the *Aktion*, but more closely resembling the latter – reflects (and corroborates) this fact. However, comparison of the actual distribution of Jews in hiding with the expected distribution computed according to this proportion shows clearly that the population in hiding favoured the young and the old over the middle-aged, and women over men. Escape from the ghetto, unlike the chaotic attempts to evade deportations within the ghetto, was thus not based on the principle of *sauve qui peut*; rather, families preferentially rescued women, children and the elderly when they could.

Table 6.11   Broad-Band Age and Sex Distribution (Percentages)

	Male			Female			Overall	
	0–19	20–59	60+	0–19	20–59	60+	M	F
Ghetto before deportations	38.7	54.8	7.4	31	60.9	8.2	43	57
Ghetto after deportations	12.3	87.8	2	16.2	76.8	1.1	56	44
In hiding, actual	26.2	63.1	11	24.5	67.3	8.4	42	58
In hiding, expected	22.9	74.6	4.2	22.1	70.4	3.9	51	49

Distribution by Occupational Category

Among the papers in BLHG 358 is a tabulation in Basia Berman's hand of some people according to their pre-war profession, which is reproduced in Table 6.12.

Table 6.12 Distribution of Population on the Aryan Side by Occupational Category

Occupational category	Number
Clerical workers	25
Trade and industry	45
Journalists	4
Literature, arts and science	16
Teachers	26
Doctors and related professions	14
Engineers and technicians	15
Lawyers	11
Military	2
School-age children	17
Blue-collar trades	8
Unknown or unclassified	103
Total	286

The last category no doubt includes housewives and reflects the prevalence of women within the sample. Apart from that, the overwhelming predominance of the intelligentsia and middle class is apparent. ('Trade and industry' probably includes a substantial proportion of owners and managers of enterprises; the activists' comments note a good many of these.)

The sample is no doubt biased, since the relief organizations made a special effort to reach just such people; for example, as is well known, Żegota activists managed to arrange Ringelblum's escape from the Trawniki labour camp, and the famous educator Janusz Korczak was offered a chance to escape from the ghetto (which he refused). Also ŻKN activists were themselves members of the intelligentsia; that was where their contacts were and where they began their activities. There can be little doubt, however, that the Jews in hiding were indeed largely drawn from these classes, since these were the Jews in Poland who spoke Polish well, and who had contacts with the Polish side, through whom the necessary arrangements could be made. Another indication is the overwhelming preponderance of Polish over Yiddish manuscripts among the testimonies on file both at ŻIH and Yad Vashem.

The survival of the elderly also reflects the prevalence of the intelligentsia. Here is a complete list from the database of people known to be over sixty-five:

Idalia Bejlin (70)	teacher
Felicja Bloch (70)	teacher
Ignacy Bruner (73)	lawyer
Mrs Fajgenbaum (72)	profession unknown
Leopold Hausner (68)	engineer
Janina Lipszyc (70)	lawyer's widow
Kazimierz Majzel (83)	history teacher
Marta Pfefferberg (72)	merchant's widow
Ludwika Zelcer (80)	profession unknown
Michał Piszczakowski (71)	profession unknown
Helena Sołowicz (66)	profession unknown
Leokadia Szenwic (70)	profession unknown

It will be noted that four of the five people whose profession is unknown were women, and that two of the four remaining women are identified by the professions of their deceased husbands. This reflects the traditional social structure of, especially, the older generation of Warsaw Jews, in which it was very unusual even in progressive circles for women to work outside the home. It also reinforces the supposition advanced above, that Berman's 'unknown or unclassified' cases are largely housewives.

While hardly the leading lights of Jewish Warsaw, most of these people are among its respected elders, with seven out of twelve known to be members of the intelligentsia and middle class, and the remaining five very likely to be so as well. Thus, there is a still heavier predominance of these classes among the elderly than is observed in the fugitive population as a whole. In rescuing the elderly, the ghetto community was not only respecting age but trying to rescue what was left of its intellectual leadership.

Summary and Conclusions

On the basis of activist records, it seems that the various aid organizations had between them some 8,900 people under their care in the Warsaw area in the spring and summer of 1944, and that about twice that number of Jews were in hiding during that period. They were the remnant of about 28,000 Jews who had been in hiding at one time or another. Of these 28,000, about 16,500 died and 11,500 survived, an overall survival rate of 41 per cent. Many of the casualties were the result of two episodes that were unique to Warsaw, the Hotel Polski affair and the Warsaw Uprising.[31] Between them, these episodes account for about 8,000 deaths. If we take into account only the period before the Warsaw Uprising, and remove the Hotel Polski from the equation, we arrive at an attrition rate of about 2 per cent per month. On this basis, it can be calculated that, but for the Warsaw

Uprising, about seven-eights of those in hiding on 1 August 1944 would have survived to see liberation in January. This would have yielded about 15,000 survivors out of the 24,500 who avoided the Hotel Polski. Thus, after we remove the two idiosyncratic episodes from the equation, we would be left, notionally, with an overall survival rate of about 61 per cent.

For the sake of comparison, the case of the Netherlands might be examined. There, 20,000–25,000 Jews are estimated to have gone into hiding, mainly in Amsterdam, of whom 10,000–15,000 survived the war.[32] The overall survival rate in the Netherlands was thus 40–60 per cent – broadly in the same range as in Warsaw. Deportations from the Netherlands began in July 1942; the last transport left Vught transit camp on 5 September 1944, when liberation was already under way. The threat to the Jews in hiding thus stretched out over twenty-seven months. Taking numbers in the mid-point of these ranges – supposing, that is, that 22,500 Dutch Jews went into hiding, of whom 12,500 survived these twenty-seven months – the attrition rate among Jews in hiding in the Netherlands would work out to 2.2 per cent per month, slightly higher than in Warsaw. Even in Denmark, where the Jew-hunt lasted only three weeks and was not carried out with any severity, some 120 of the country's 7,800 Jews were betrayed: also about 2.2 per cent per month.[33]

This leads us to the startling conclusion that, but for the Hotel Polski and the Warsaw Uprising, the survival rate among Jews in hiding in Warsaw would have been about the same as that in Western Europe, contrary to all expectations and contemporary perceptions.[34]

Summary and Conclusions

I have estimated that the secret city consisted of some 28,000 Jews in hiding, in addition to 70,000–90,000 Poles who helped them and a few thousand criminals and policemen who preyed on them. Criminal element and all, the secret city thus numbered at least 100,000 people, 10 per cent of the population of Aryan Warsaw. It was linked, as all cities are, by a complex network of personal relationships, of which the individuals who comprised it were only dimly aware.

I have also estimated that about 11,500 of these Jews survived. If these figures are correct, then despite the distress that the city of Warsaw suffered during the war, despite the dangers that all its citizens faced, despite the special dangers that confronted the Jews, and despite the dangers unique to Warsaw, such as the 1944 Warsaw Uprising and the Hotel Polski trap, the survival rate among the Jewish fugitives of Warsaw (about 40 per cent) was not much less than that observed in a Western European country such as the Netherlands, where it has been estimated that 40–60 per cent survived. In Warsaw, some 61 per cent of those in hiding (17,000 out of 28,000) survived until the 1944 uprising; some 69 per cent of those who avoided the Hotel Polski.

The fugitives may have amounted to only a small proportion of the nearly 490,000 Jews who passed through the Warsaw ghetto, but as we have seen, the bulk of escapes occurred only after the Great Deportation of 1942, when the ghetto population had been reduced to 55,000–60,000: no fewer than 13,000 escapes took place after that point, nearly a quarter of the remaining population. No less remarkable is that a city so overcrowded, impoverished and terrorized managed to find room for 28,000 Jewish refugees, more than most of the neutral countries of Europe took in over the entire war (spacious Sweden, the land of my fathers, absorbed about 9,000).[1]

Depending on one's point of view, therefore, the number of Jewish fugitives and ultimate survivors in Warsaw was either very small (5 per cent and 2 per cent of the Jewish population, respectively) or very large (more than anywhere else, remarkable under the circumstances). Both are legitimate points of view. Therefore, two complementary questions can be asked: why so few, and why so many?

Why so few? The most obvious reason is that escape on a large scale took place only at a late date, when the great majority of the Jews of Warsaw were already dead. How we evaluate the importance of this factor depends on our assessment of how many more fugitives the city could have accommodated, a question that can only be a matter for speculation. Certainly the wave of escapes was showing no signs of abating when the Ghetto Uprising broke out: if escape had continued at the same rate for another six months, half the remaining Jews would have got away; by August 1944 they would all have gone. But it is unlikely that this rate of escapes could have been sustained. As even the Germans were having trouble finding space for their refugees in 1944, it must be assumed that the possibility of accommodating such large numbers of additional Jews was slim. Indeed, the difficulties that the activists had in placing the surviving ghetto fighters in the summer of 1943 suggests that their possibilities were well-nigh exhausted at that point, though the same may not have been true of the wider network. With an organized effort, it would in principle have been possible to transfer Jews to other centres, or to rural estates like those of the Bersons. But this is a speculation made with the benefit of hindsight: no one at the time seems to have thought of such a scheme. On the contrary, Jews hiding elsewhere were advised to come to Warsaw, as the main centre of Polish resistance and of the aid effort. Jews did to some extent find hiding places on their own initiative in outlying towns, or left the Warsaw area altogether, but the net flow of Jews seeking hiding places was towards Warsaw, not away from it.

The lateness of escape, rather than a shortage of hiding-places, explains why 95 per cent of the ghetto population did not flee; the fact that flight was all but cut off by the third *Aktion* and the outbreak of the Ghetto Uprising accounts for the fact that 77 per cent of the remnant did not flee. Had it been otherwise, it is likely that the city's absorptive capacity would have been reached at some point, but we cannot know for certain when.

A variety of factors in turn account for the lateness of escape. When the ghetto was sealed off in 1940, no one knew what the future held, and it is not surprising that few people wanted to chance disobeying German orders. Nevertheless, more Jews might have stayed out of the ghetto but for the fact that those who did, and even those who escaped in 1940–41, were regarded virtually as traitors, and certainly as cowards. The ghetto famine of 1941–42 might have induced more people to escape, but paradoxically the success of the smuggling effort meant that escape was never perceived as the best prospect for survival. Even Poles who extended aid to their Jewish friends in the ghetto helped by bringing them food, medicine and money, and rarely by proposing escape. The introduction in October 1941 of the death penalty for leaving the ghetto acted as a further disincentive, making Poles think twice about helping Jews and Jews think twice about exposing their Polish friends. Ominous news reaching the ghetto in the first half of 1942 did induce slightly more people to escape, but the news was contradictory, unreliable and hard to interpret. By the eve of the first *Aktion*, in July 1942, only about 5,000 Jews were to be found on the Aryan side, a little more than 1 per cent of the Jewish population of Warsaw.

Once the first *Aktion* started, escape immediately became more difficult, as the established smuggling routes were sealed off. It took some time before the ghetto became persuaded that those 'deported to the east' were in fact being killed, and before new means of escape were worked out. At the same time, the ghetto remained unaware of the scope of German plans, and many people believed that the deportation was to be limited to 'unproductive elements', sparing those with essential jobs. The Germans took care to promote such illusions by announcing various classes of exemption, which were cancelled one by one.

Even for those who were convinced that the ghetto was doomed, escape was by no means an easy or obvious choice. The chaotic conditions of the *Aktion* left people with little time and energy to organize escape, and adults were reluctant to leave their families and community behind. Many of those who left the ghetto during the *Aktion* were therefore children sent out of the ghetto by their parents, who hoped to be able to follow eventually.

During the *Aktion*, and even more so after its completion, the idea of escaping from the ghetto had to compete with that of building 'bunkers' in which to last out any future deportations. It was theorized that the Germans would wait until the last possible moment before destroying their labour force, so that if you could survive underground for a few weeks or months, the war would be over. Also, such shelters seemed to offer an extra chance of survival: in the worst case, you could leave the shelter and try your luck on the Aryan side. This therefore became the most popular method of evasion. The decision to opt for bunkers within the ghetto was further influenced by stories about Jews being robbed by *szmalcowniks*, the expectation that a hostile reception awaited Jews on the 'other side', and the belief that 'good looks', money and direct contacts with Poles were prerequisites of escape. As we have seen, these negative expectations were not wrong, but exaggerated.

In the final stage of the ghetto's existence, during the Ghetto Uprising and its aftermath, escape was effected in a few cases through sewers and tunnels, but more often by jumping from deportation trains, hiding in the abandoned areas of the ghetto and then crossing to the Aryan side under cover of darkness, or fleeing from the labour camps at Trawniki and Poniatowa, where the guard was fairly lax. People who escaped during this period acted out of desperation, and rarely had well-prepared hiding-places, documents or money. Jumping from trains was physically risky and mainly for the young and agile; in addition, those who were still with their families were again unwilling to leave them behind. Many who made the attempt were gunned down by the guards who manned the trains, or injured themselves during the jump and could not proceed farther. Such people were robbed and either murdered or left to die by scavengers who patrolled the tracks. Nevertheless, a few hundred people did manage to make their way back to Warsaw and find places to hide. Of those who found themselves in the labour camps, the majority seem to have been overcome with apathy as a result of the experiences of the last few years, and did not take opportunities to escape, even though they were available. Almost all perished in the 'Harvest Festival' of 3 November 1943.

Those who did manage to make their way to the Aryan side, by one route or another, found themselves hunted by German gendarmes, Polish Blue policemen and an army of *szmalcowniks*. In addition, they had to deal with the complications of underground life in a dictatorship, which aimed to enmesh every citizen in a web of documentary controls, and were also faced with a critical shortage of housing, especially of a kind that offered the privacy that Jews living underground needed. Jews seem to have been easily detectable by the Poles, less because of their Semitic appearance, as was supposed, than by more subtle traits: a characteristic accent or manner of speech, unfamiliarity with Polish cultural and religious traditions, and various other signs – above all, a furtive manner and sad eyes – so that practically every Jew in hiding was successfully tracked down by *szmalcowniks* at least once, and often many times. In addition, Jews could be recognized by prior acquaintances, who were not necessarily friendly, or by other residents in the same building, who might denounce them or put pressure on the porter to have them removed; or rumours might reach them that the police or blackmailers were on their trail. Any of these situations, which Jews in hiding encountered on average seven or eight times in the course of their ordeal on the Aryan side would force a change in hiding place. Each such move confronted Jews with new dangers and uncertainties, and forced them to deal afresh with the problems of housing and documentation.

Money posed a major problem for Jews in hiding, for whom working meant additional public exposure as well as the need to obtain more documents. Some worked nevertheless, preferably at home or as domestics; others operated on the black market, exposing themselves to additional dangers. About a third eventually received financial support from Żegota, The ŻKN, the Bund or other welfare agencies, but the amounts were small and came late in the day. Most lived either by selling their possessions, or on the charity of their Polish hosts. Those who carried all their possessions with them were soon stripped of them by *szmalcowniks* or unscrupulous landlords, in some cases being left literally penniless and naked. Many Jews therefore left goods for safekeeping with Polish friends, most of whom discharged their obligations honestly; but some, including highly respectable members of Polish society, had no scruples about robbing them. This could leave them in a disastrous situation.

On top of these special difficulties and dangers, Jews also faced the same dangers as the Polish population. The Germans carried out frequent house searches, meant to discover hidden weapons, underground newspapers and people in hiding, including Jews. Hundreds of Jews were caught in this way. Frequent document checks were carried out on the street, as well as round-ups for forced labour, although these had become less frequent by the time of the major wave of escapes. In any case, some Jews volunteered for labour in Germany, on the theory that Germans, unlike Poles, could not tell the difference between a Pole and a Polish Jew. This strategy proved to offer reasonable prospects of survival.

Adding to the terror to which the Jews were subjected, finally, was the unrelenting barrage of antisemitic propaganda, emitting not only from street loudspeakers and the Nazi-sponsored 'reptile' press, but also from the underground organs of the Polish right, which for example told Poles to be wary about hiding Jews, since Jews who were captured were supposedly known to denounce their benefactors. Together with the widespread pre-existing antisemitism in Polish society, which found its expression in malevolent remarks and, in extreme cases, in denunciation or murder, these expressions of hostility made Jews more apprehensive and hence easier for *szmalcowniks* to recognize, dissuaded many Jews from escaping from the ghetto, and persuaded others to return to the ghetto or take advantage of the various German schemes and 'amnesties'. The most elaborate of these schemes, the Hotel Polski affair, cost the lives of some 3,500 Jews – most of them drawn to it, however, less by fear of the Poles than by weariness with the constant strain of running and hiding, and the illusory prospect of a normal life.

The harrowing underground existence of the Jews of the secret city ended with the outbreak of the Warsaw Uprising on 1 August 1944, but old dangers were now replaced by new ones. By coincidence, the majority of hiding places were located in areas controlled by the insurgents, so that Jews formed a disproportionate number of those killed by military action. Jews were also at risk in various ways from the Polish population. A renegade unit of the AK murdered at least twenty-three Jews in and near the area that they controlled, and there were many other individual murders and summary executions as well. Jews were suspected of being German agents (on the logic that 'since they survived, they must have collaborated'), and were arrested and sometimes killed out of hand on the basis of absurd 'evidence'. Jews descending into bomb shelters often encountered hostility from the Polish occupants, and in at least one case a Jew was forced to leave his shelter during a bombardment and was killed by shrapnel. In total, some 4,500 Jews died during the uprising, several dozen at the hands of Poles.

After the Warsaw Uprising, a few hundred Jews decided to hide in bunkers under the city's ruins. With the Red Army already across the Vistula, they expected to be liberated quickly, but they had to endure four months of hunger, thirst and winter weather, and were also vulnerable to German patrols and Polish scavengers.

About 200 survived to see liberation on 17 January 1945. A few Jews managed to reach the right bank of the Vistula, which was liberated by Soviet troops on 15 September 1944. But most Jewish survivors of the uprising mingled with the Poles and were evacuated with them to nearby transit camps, chiefly the one at Pruszków. Thence they were taken either to Germany for forced labour, or to various places in Poland and released. After the uprising, the Warsaw population was subdued and united in the solidarity and depression of defeat. Despite occasional eruptions of antisemitic behaviour, in general the Warsaw natives were protective towards the Jews, so that no Jews seem to have been betrayed at Pruszków, and few in the camps in Germany. The same cannot be said of the Polish countryside, where Jews report being harassed and exploited, and sometimes report also that Jewish friends or relatives were denounced or murdered by Poles. A few hundred Jews died under these circumstances.

It can readily be seen that Jews in hiding faced extraordinary difficulties and dangers, and that every Jew in hiding ran a gauntlet in which a single misstep could be fatal. It is no wonder that authors who consider only the negative aspects of this story conclude that the Jews' chances of survival on the Aryan side were 'negligible'. I have estimated (see Table 6.3, p. 213) that 16,450 Jews died on the Aryan side in the Warsaw area: 5,400 during and after the Warsaw Uprising, 3,500 as a result of the Hotel Polski trap, a few hundred of what one might call accelerated natural causes, another few hundred for various other reasons, and 6,000 as a result of being caught, betrayed or murdered. Nevertheless, I have also estimated that there were 11,500 survivors. Even the reader who is disinclined to believe such a high estimate – and who would need not only to refute my evidence and reasoning, but also to show how all my other estimates should be adjusted to maintain a consistent picture – even a reader who might prefer, for example, Israel Gutman's estimate that only one-quarter to one-third of these Jews survived, would still have to admit that this number is somewhat more than 'negligible'.

We therefore need also to ask the complementary question 'Why so many?' How was it possible for nearly a quarter of the remaining ghetto population to escape, once the necessity of escape became evident? And how was it possible for such a relatively large proportion of them to survive the seemingly insuperable challenges that faced them? The following reasons can be adduced:

1. The Jews of Warsaw had many pre-existing links with the Gentile community, despite the apparent mutual isolation of and frequent friction between the two societies. A bridging community existed, consisting mainly of converts and people in mixed marriages, who had friends and relatives on both sides of the wall. Jewish assimilants also often had Polish friends and colleagues to whom they could turn, especially those who were politically engaged in the three political parties (the SD, PPS, and PPR) that had both Jewish and non-Jewish

members. The small number of Jews – about 2,400 – who stayed out of the ghetto in 1940 frequently maintained contacts with their friends and relatives inside the ghetto, as did some Poles. From this nucleus of primary contacts, a network spread out that reached into all milieus on both sides of the wall, so that most Jews had some direct or indirect contacts on the Aryan side.

2. Various factors made the ghetto wall porous. The Warsaw ghetto was in the heart of the city, and not in the outskirts as was originally planned. This in turn was a result of the very large number of Jews in Warsaw, which made it impracticable to relocate them all, and also of their economic importance, which persuaded the authorities that isolating or hermetically sealing the ghetto would be disadvantageous. German policies that predated the creation of the ghetto had already given rise to an extensive black market in Warsaw, and this market continued to operate, on both sides of the ghetto wall and across it. The links that were formed and the methods that were worked out at that time served well later on, when the trade was in guns and people.

Physical channels of contact across the ghetto wall included telephones and the postal service, both of which continued to operate until a surprisingly late date, evidently an oversight on the part of the authorities. In addition, some Poles had passes that allowed them to enter the ghetto legally, or else they entered the ghetto with work parties, while others crossed the wall illegally. Through these channels, Jews contemplating escape from the ghetto could get in touch with friends on the 'other side', who could make the necessary arrangements.

Once on the Aryan side, Jews typically had to keep finding new quarters to avoid blackmailers and police; in the process, they were forced to rely on help from people with whom their connections were increasingly tenuous. That is to say, the group of people involved in helping Jews spread from the original bridging community to encompass a much wider circle, which, I have estimated, ultimately numbered 70,000–90,000 people.

3. In this and other ways the networks that individual Jews relied upon became interconnected to form a single 'secret city'. Many strands of evidence show that this was so. The rapidity with which news of the Hotel Polski spread, and the fact that organized aid eventually reached about a third of the fugitives (despite their reluctance to expose themselves even by asking for help), testify to the existence of an effective communications system. So does the fact that an argot developed, which included such words as *melina*, *szmalcownik* and so on (which have become a permanent addition to the Polish language). Most Jewish memoirists report encountering other Jews in hiding, previously unknown to them: each such encounter demonstrates a point of contact between individual networks. The same is true of contacts with previously unknown Poles, and conversely of the involvement of Poles in hiding Jews previously unknown to

them. The secret city also had its institutions, its meeting places, its intellectual life, even its publications and nascent culture. If we take into account Jews and their helpers, the secret city numbered about 100,000 people, or one-tenth of the population of supposedly *judenrein* Warsaw.

4. The Germans were almost certainly unaware of the size and extent of this secret city, estimating the number of Jews who had fled the ghetto at only 5,000–6,000. After they had caught 3,500 Jews through the Hotel Polski scheme, they must have thought they had nearly all of them. Subsequent Jew-hunting from the German side was fairly desultory, and took second place to action against the Polish underground.

5. Warsaw was the centre of this underground, and also accommodated a large number of people who were hiding for various reasons. This meant that there was a parallel Polish 'secret city', offering Jews further contacts and opportunities. For example, an extensive document-forging operation came into existence, which also became available to the Jews. Clerks in the municipal administration succeeded in delaying the introduction of the German identity document, the *Kennkarte*, with the fortuitous result that the period of the greatest number of escapes from the ghetto coincided with the registration of the entire population of Warsaw. Thus, thousands of Jews could obtain authentic *Kennkarten* without attracting attention. The large number of non-Jews in hiding also provided a certain amount of camouflage for the Jews, although they also drew the unwelcome attention of the police.

6. The Blue police were somewhat cautious about turning suspected Jews over to the Germans, since there were known cases of Poles who had been mistaken for Jews. Therefore, Jews who were arrested were not killed on the spot, as the German authorities had ordered, but were held for investigation. This provided opportunities for even those who had been caught to free themselves through bribes, or for Polish friends to come and vouch for them. The other main group of Jew-hunters, the *szmalcowniks*, were for the most part interested in money, not blood. Those who accosted Jews on the street were generally satisfied with relatively small sums, while those who found out their victims' hiding places would take whatever they could find. Although in the latter case Jews could be left destitute and desperate, and often died as a consequence, it was relatively uncommon for *szmalcowniks* to turn them over to the police, contrary to the general belief. Actual denunciation was done for personal or ideological reasons, was usually anonymous, brought little material benefit to the denouncer and was relatively rare.

7. Although some Poles to whom Jews had entrusted their belongings for safe-

keeping betrayed this trust, the majority did not; and although some Poles who hid Jews for money failed to honour their promises or otherwise cheated or exploited the Jews, the majority did not. Most Poles who were hiding Jews did not make money a condition of rescue, and some even refused to accept money when it was offered. Many Jews were thus able to support themselves on the Aryan side through selling their belongings, or by relying on the help of faithful friends. Work opportunities were very limited, and exposed Jews to additional dangers; nevertheless, some Jews were able to support themselves at least partially by working, most commonly as domestics or doing work that could be performed at home. Some, finally, received help from *Żegota*, the Jewish National Committee, the Bund or other aid agencies, or if politically engaged were supported by their parties.

8. German policy was in many respects self-defeating. Irrational economic policies created the underground economy that sustained the ghetto; they necessitated the use of Jewish labour outside the ghetto, which provided the most frequent means of escape; and they ensured that nearly everyone was engaged in some kind of illegal activity, creating a generally anarchic atmosphere. Indiscriminate and excessively draconian measures, instead of taming the population, forced it into bravado and lawlessness; as a result, hiding Jews became merely one of the many illegal activities for which people routinely risked their lives. The principle of collective responsibility backfired as well: denouncing Jews also meant exposing their Polish helpers to danger, a severe violation of the wartime code of solidarity. (Some Jews, on the other hand, were denounced precisely in order to strike at their helpers, as a result of private vendettas.)

9. The secret city was a self-selecting conspiracy of mainly decent and honest people, which remained secret not only from the Germans but also from the bulk of the Polish population. In this the Jews benefited from, among other things, the unspoken rules of behaviour in occupied Poland – at the minimum, to mind your own business. This is, of course, more generally a principle of big-city life, and was one of the things that attracted Jews to Warsaw as a place to hide. When Jews were exposed in front of Poles who were not involved in the conspiracy, the latter, though not especially sympathetic to the Jews and sometimes openly hostile, rarely went so far as to denounce them. This could be seen most clearly in the aftermath of the Warsaw Uprising, when few if any Jews were betrayed at Pruszków or in the German labour camps. That the same was true during the period preceding the uprising is more difficult to demonstrate, but we have noted numerous situations in which Jews were publicly exposed as Jews and yet no one in a large crowd denounced them. Keeping in mind that it required only one person to denounce a Jew but the unanimous silence of the whole crowd to allow him or her to escape, that a significant

number of Jews did survive such situations is testimony that most Poles were passively protective towards the Jews, even when their attitudes were anti-semitic, while only a small minority were actively hostile.

Some broader conclusions also can be drawn. We have seen that the three police forces, all of them much reviled, played an active part in the smuggling of food, goods, guns and people. The German police consisted mainly of an Order Police unit similar to that recently studied by Christopher Browning and Daniel Goldhagen, and their behaviour in this context casts some light on the controversy that followed the appearance of Goldhagen's book, *Hitler's Willing Executioners*. Briefly, we have seen the whole gamut of responses from these policemen, from the sadistic 'Frankenstein' who killed Jews for pleasure, to an SS man, Schmedke, who went out of his way to help the Jews of his work detail, without any financial reward. In between, there were those who were officious and carried out their duties punctiliously, and a good many who were willing to turn a blind eye in return for a bribe. There is no evidence among these men of a generalized 'elimi-nationist antisemitism'; indeed, on the testimony of the Jewish policeman Szapse Rotholc, many policemen regarded the battle with the Jews as 'only politics', whereas they hated the Poles 'from the heart'. (Chaim Kaplan attributes the same sentiment to Ludwig Fischer, the governor of the Warsaw District: 'The Poles we hate instinctively; the Jews we hate in accordance with orders'.) German colleagues tell me that this was a popular saying at the time.[2]

The Polish Blue police can also be divided into three types: those who hunted Jews with enthusiasm or co-operated with blackmailers; those who were willing to turn a blind eye in return for a bribe; and those, like Mieczysław Tarwid or Eliasz Pietruszko, who used their positions actively to help Jews. The great majority of escapes were accomplished by leaving the ghetto with a work party; this required the guards at the ghetto gate (one from each police force) to miscount the members of the party and the party's overseer to allow people to slip away once outside. This could not have been accomplished without the co-operation of a sufficient number of German and Polish policemen, who usually had to be bribed but sometimes acted voluntarily.

Neither the Polish nor the Jewish underground acquitted itself particularly well in helping Jews to escape, both becoming involved in helping Jewish fugitives only on a comparatively small scale and relatively late in the day. The Jewish underground had its sights fixed on armed resistance, and generally persuaded itself that escape was impossible, although each organization managed to smuggle some of its activists out. The organizational structure – the Jewish Co-ordinating Committee, the Jewish National Committee and the Bund – that later carried out relief work among the Jews in hiding came into existence not for that purpose but as the political arm of the Jewish Combat Organization (ŻOB), to organize arms for the ghetto and maintain contacts with the Polish underground. It did not organize escapes from the ghetto (although there is evidence that some ŻOB members operated an 'underground railroad' from the Poniatowa labour camp), and its relief operations reached a significant scale only towards the end of 1943.

The Polish underground likewise was not involved in arranging escapes from the ghetto. The Jewish Bureau under Henryk Woliński – with a Jewish wife, he was a member of the 'bridging community' described above – had only the functions of observing and reporting, and later served as liaison between Polish and Jewish leaders. Żegota, the initiative for which came again from the 'bridging community', in this case a group of Jewish converts who were members of the Democratic Party, came into existence only in October 1942 and operated at first on a very small scale. Like the Jewish organizations, whose representatives joined the Żegota council in January 1943, it reached a larger group of fugitives only in the second half of 1943. Eventually the Polish and Jewish underground, between them, provided financial assistance to about 8,900 Jews in hiding.

The roles played by the Polish culture of the time, especially its rampant antisemitism, and by the Catholic church need to be assessed. Here we might reflect on two instances, recounted by Michael Zylberberg and Stefan Chaskielewicz respectively. In each case, a woman who was risking her life to hide Jews – in Zylberberg's case, refusing to accept money for it – felt obliged to go to her parish priest and confess to this 'sin'. In each case, the priest reassured her that she was doing a fine and noble thing, and Chaskielewicz writes of his landlady that she subsequently lost her fear and stopped asking him to find another hiding place. These examples show the Catholic church at its best. But it is notable that in both cases an essentially good person had become so confused by Catholic teachings concerning Jews that she was no longer sure where her duty lay. It is no wonder, then, that people who were less good persuaded themselves that hiding Jews was disreputable, or even disgraceful. Churchmen on the whole acquitted themselves well: for example, the prelate of All Saints' Church in the ghetto, Msgr Marceli Godlewski, though notorious before the war as an antisemite, became actively involved in smuggling Jewish converts out of the ghetto. Other priests provided forged parish documents to Jews, and it appears to be true that virtually every convent in the Warsaw area was hiding a few Jewish children. The Father Boduen orphanage also distinguished itself in this regard. Nevertheless, it is also true that the traditional prayer 'for the perfidious Jews' continued to be said on Good Friday; that priests were on occasion heard to express crude antisemitic sentiments (and continue to do so even today)[3] and on occasion even denounced Jews personally. The record and influence of the Catholic church, which by its own standards should have been unambiguously on the side of the oppressed and persecuted, was in fact mixed: the church was a force for evil as well as good. This was true not only in Poland: in Slovakia, the head of state, Josef Tiso, a Catholic priest, allowed his country's whole Jewish community to be deported to their deaths, exempting only converts. In Lithuania, Bishop Vincent Brizgys of Kovno instructed his subordinates not to intervene on behalf of the Jews. The Vatican informed the Vichy régime in France that it had 'no objection in principle' to its anti-Jewish laws.

Zylberberg, on one occasion, having read the book of medieval lamentations *Gorzkie Żale* (Bitter Sorrows), marvelled that despite such influences many ordinary Poles had managed to retain a humane and compassionate attitude towards the Jews. This can be attributed, first, to the more positive aspects of Polish culture: traditions of hospitality (*'Gość w dom, Bóg w dom'* – 'When a guest is in the house, God is in the house'); Catholic teachings such as the Parable of the Good Samaritan or the Old Testament principle, 'Love thy neighbour as thyself' (not to mention 'Thou shalt not kill'); the Catholic veneration of altruism and martyrdom and related nationalist traditions of heroic self-sacrifice in adversity; a Polish literary tradition that has generally been sympathetic to the Jews (Mickiewicz, Prus, Orzeszkowa, Boy-Żeleński, Konopnicka); historic traditions of toleration and liberality stretching back to the old Commonwealth of Both Nations. Less positively, Catholics were moved by the hope of gaining converts. Second, the sheer familiarity of the Jews led to curiously inconsistent attitudes, which I have described as antisemitism 'present company excepted'. We may recall the paradox of the woman who expressed satisfaction that 'the Jewish bedbugs are burning' while serving a meal to a Jewish couple for whom she was risking her life. The strength of family ties in Poland also made a contribution: if some members of a family had made a commitment to helping Jews, other members would know that by betraying the Jews they would also be betraying their own family. Third, despite the strength of right-wing politics and antisemitic attitudes, there was also a considerable left in Poland, particularly in the capital, which rejected antisemitism in principle and had been known to defend Jews against antisemitic attacks before the war.

The question of the effects of Nazi actions and propaganda is controversial, some authors maintaining that these created sympathy for the Jews and others that the Nazi example served to embolden and radicalize Polish antisemites. The question of the difference between traditional and 'racial' antisemitism is also sometimes raised in this connection, the argument being made that the traditional antisemite wanted to eliminate the Jews by conversion, whereas the 'racial' antisemite has to resort to biological extermination to achieve the same end. It is then argued, on the one hand, that Poles were traditional antisemites and therefore not murderous, and on the other, that racial and therefore murderous ideas were rapidly gaining ground, especially on the far right, and that the Nazi example was admired in some circles.

In my view, the difference between these two varieties of antisemitism is overplayed: traditional antisemites have murdered Jews on occasion, whereas 'racial' antisemites, including the pre-war Nazis, have usually advocated expulsion or isolation rather than mass murder. 'Racial' antisemitism is in any event neither new nor clearly distinct from the religious variety, since it can be seen in an early form in the 'purity of blood' (*limpieza de sangre*) laws of sixteenth-century Spain, under which people descended from converts suffered discrimination even many generations later. Rather than the 'racial' definition extending antisemitism to converts, I suspect it was the other way around: suspicion of converts ('once a Jew, always a Jew') led to the 'racial' definition of Jews.

The distinction between Polish and Nazi antisemitism, I believe, does not lie in their respective attitudes to the 'racial' question, but in two main differences: first, the Nazis consciously and deliberately rejected all ethical restraints, whereas the Catholic church and the great majority of Poles did not; second, the Nazis had such extreme plans for Poland that no patriotic Pole could contemplate collaboration with them (nor were the Nazis interested in such help). For this reason, even radical Polish antisemites, unlike ultra-rightists elsewhere in Nazi-occupied Europe, had no reason to admire or emulate the Nazis, and they were strongly anti-German historically as well. That did not mean that they rejected Nazism root and branch: they admired the Nazis' handling of the 'Jewish question' when it coincided with their own ideas. Some of them were prepared to admit that 'objectively' the Nazis had done Poland a favour by getting rid of the Jews, or even to complain that they had not done a thorough enough job, while hastening to add that they themselves would of course never have done anything like that.

My own impression is that the Poles, regarded by the Nazis as *Untermenschen*, were driven by the need to salve their considerable and wounded pride. They did so sometimes by lording it over the still more inferior Jews, but also by a thorough contempt for the Germans. The mass killing of the Jews was viewed by most Poles as proof of the depravity of the German occupier and the moral superiority of their own culture, as well as of a frightening bestiality that might soon be visited on them, too. Nazi Jewish policy in its early, pre-genocidal stages might have won the approval of many Endeks, and the right-wing underground press continued to maintain that Jewish property should not be restored, that Jews returning after the war should not be readmitted to Poland, that Jews should be stripped of their citizenship, and so forth. But as Nazi policy became more radical and more murderous, it left a larger and larger proportion of Polish public opinion behind. As the Nazis would have put it, the Poles, like most traditionally antisemitic societies, did not have a sufficiently advanced understanding of the Jewish question. Only those who were the most radical in their political outlook, the most criminal by nature or the most corrupted by the war were prepared to follow the Nazi example and murder Jews or betray them.

Things naturally looked different from the point of view of the Jews, who were a small and vulnerable minority, and even smaller and more vulnerable when they took up life on the Aryan side. They were also, of course, especially sought out by these malicious elements, and so were acutely aware of their existence when most

Poles were not. To the Jews, a few thousand dedicated enemies were a serious threat, even though they probably constituted less than 1 per cent of the Polish population. And it cannot be said that these enemies, as Poles would like to believe, were drawn only from criminal and other marginal elements of Polish society: some were thoroughly respectable Polish patriots, who risked their lives for their country in the Warsaw Uprising or in the underground movement, and were even decorated for it by their government; while other thoroughly respectable Poles were prepared to steal property entrusted to them, on which Jews relied for their subsistence. There are concentric circles of responsibility: few Poles were directly involved in putting Jews to death, but larger numbers contributed indirectly or unintentionally to their destruction. The refusal of the National Party to participate in Żegota, its opposition to creating the organization, and the antisemitic propaganda that continued to emanate from its press even after the liquidation of the ghetto, must stand as a condemnation of the hypocrisy, bigotry and small-mindedness of this party and its various offshoots and supporters. The atmosphere created by such people drove many Jews to surrender at the Hotel Polski, to return to the ghetto, to commit suicide or to think twice about escaping to the Aryan side. Finally, ambiguous attitudes towards Jews left many Poles paralysed and indecisive in situations where their duty should have been clear, and allowed the criminals to do their work with impunity, even believing that they were acting in the national interest and with popular approval. Indeed, antisemitism was regarded as a respectable opinion by most Poles, even by those who did not share it. The commission of crimes against the Jews was not considered a reason for ostracism or condemnation, as crimes against Poles would have been: even a murderous antisemite was still considered swój ('one of us'), and hence entitled to communal solidarity and protection. Obstruction from 'ordinary antisemites' prevented criminals from being brought to justice, as we saw in the case of Stykowski's group in the Warsaw Uprising; and there was little enthusiasm for such prosecutions after the war.

The most vivid example of native antisemitism in Poland and its evil effects is the case of the massacres in Jedwabne and other towns near Białystok, to which Jan T. Gross has recently drawn attention.[4] Costing the lives of thousands of Jews, these massacres took place in July 1941 with German encouragement and possibly at their instigation, but were largely or entirely carried out by Poles. Whether it is fair to say, as Gross does, that 'one half of the town murdered the other half', or whether responsibility was limited to a smaller group, is still an unsettled question, but it is also not an especially relevant one. Enough people were involved to murder virtually all the Jews in these towns, and it would be disingenuous to suggest that they were not influenced by the pre-war antisemitic propaganda that emanated from the most respectable circles. The convicted perpetrators, after serving short sentences, returned to the community, where they lived normally, apparently without suffering social disadvantages and in some cases even becoming folk heroes. The *Endecja's* ideological heirs have responded to Gross's book with denials, evasions and counterattacks, to the disgust not only of most Jews but fortunately of many Poles as well. In post-Communist Poland, such issues no longer have a 'Polish side' and a 'Jewish side': a substantial proportion of Poles, including most intellectuals, now realize that antisemitism is a blot on Poland's reputation and are prepared to oppose it strenuously, at least in theory. But a 1992 nationwide survey carried out by Polish academics showed that antisemitic stereotypes persist. The survey found that 17 per cent of respondents were 'consistent' antisemites of the 'modern' type, 11 per cent were 'consistent' traditional antisemites, 39 per cent agreed with the statement 'I'm not an antisemite, but you have to watch out for the Jews', 52 per cent felt that 'there are some exceptions, but all Jews are alike', and fully 78.8 per cent agreed that 'the Jews always stick together' – a belief that betray's ignorance of the diversity and, indeed, often bitter divisions within the Jewish community, that justifies collective attributions and is the foundation of antisemitism of any kind.[5] There is evidently still much work to do.

Attitudes, however, are not necessarily translated into actions. Jedwabne was a specific occurrence at a specific historical moment; it was an outbreak of mob violence that, like other such outbreaks – lynchings in the US, for example – required not only a prior prejudice but also leadership, organization, a catalyst and the dynamics of a mob. The situation in Warsaw – or indeed in Jedwabne before and since – was quite different. Betrayals and individual killings did take place, but similar things happened elsewhere as well (recall, for instance, that Anne Frank was betrayed). There were people everywhere who were prepared, for whatever motives, to do the Nazis' work for them. And if there was more antisemitism in Poland than in many other countries, there was also less collaboration.

Individual incidents aside, there seems to be no firm connection between the strength of native antisemitism and overall rates of Jewish survival. In Warsaw, the great majority of Jews were taken to their deaths directly from the ghetto, allowing no realistic possibility of intervention by the Poles, whereas among those who escaped, the rate of survival seems to have been no worse, *ceteris paribus*, than it was in comparable cases in Western Europe. Native antisemitism seems to have played only a marginal role in determining the fate of the Jews of Warsaw, and one that was offset by other factors, such the positive aspects of Christian faith, anti-German solidarity, and the strength and efficiency of the Polish underground. The secret city also effectively isolated the Jews under the protection of what I have called a spontaneous, self-selecting conspiracy of honest and decent people, so that what mattered was not how many enemies the Jews had, but how many friends.

Antisemitism, I would conclude, made life dangerous for the Jews, but the danger was not necessarily realized. The Nazis generally preferred not to count on outbursts of 'emotional antisemitism', when what was needed to realize their plans was 'rational antisemitism', as Hitler himself put it. For that, they neither wanted nor received significant help from the Poles.

Collective attributions are not made only by antisemites or Poles, but are well-nigh universal in relations between ethnic groups. Stereotypes and prejudices also existed on the Jewish side, and can be added to the factors that inhibited escape. One need only consider the widespread conviction that one had to be blond and blue-eyed to look like a Pole to realize that Jews in the ghettos had developed an oversimplified view of Polish society in their years of separation from it. While it was no doubt natural for the pre-war experience of antisemitic violence and propaganda to lead to the conclusion that Polish society as a whole was so hostile to the Jews that survival outside the ghetto was impossible, and while it was a normal consequence of the nationalistic outlook that the other nation was viewed as a monolithic whole, these assumptions were usually not put to the test; and even when they were, perceptual filters often remained in place. How else can one account for the fact that Jews in secure hiding places gave them up in favour of the Hotel Polski, or even that Jews who found themselves homeless went there, preferring to trust the Germans, after all that had happened, rather than the Poles? Objectively and in hindsight, a Jew with nowhere to go had a better chance to save himself by knocking on a random door and asking for asylum than by giving himself up to a proven gang of murderers. Objectively, also, a Jew's best chance of saving himself was to flee if he could, even if he had no money, no contacts, 'bad looks' and every other disadvantage. To return once again to the point made by Hannah Arendt: half or more of those who fled may have perished, but so did 99 per cent of those who did not flee. The conclusion is that a vulnerable minority needs to have an accurate view of the society around it, and that in extreme conditions such as those of the *Shoah* both excessive optimism and excessive pessimism could kill.

To conclude, I shall return to the question of evasion as a Jewish response to the Holocaust. Evasion is Hilberg's term, and carries pejorative connotations: we evade responsibilities, evade awkward questions, evade the draft and so on. We are not pleased to be accused of evasiveness: evasion seems dishonourable, and smacks of cowardice. That is perhaps why it has remained an invisible topic in writing on the Holocaust. We might choose a different word – avoidance, perhaps – or we could simply learn to hear it differently: it is not dishonourable to evade an enemy, a boxer does well to evade a blow. In fact, we would do well to get beyond the question of honour altogether: there are more important questions concerning how the Jews reacted to their plight than whether their responses meet some arbitrary standard.

In particular, our fixation with honour has led not only to the neglect of evasion because it sounds dishonourable, but to lumping everything that we do consider honourable under the catch-all and increasingly meaningless category of resistance. Evasion is not a form of resistance: resistance, we might say, means trying to overcome hostile force, whereas evasion means getting out of its way. More succinctly, resistance is *fight* and evasion is *flight*, and these are very basic and important categories. If we conflate them, we fail to understand the choices that the Jews were forced to make.

Evasion – the attempt of the victims to save themselves – should also not be conflated with rescue, which is a response of the bystanders. The literature on rescue tends to portray the Jews themselves as passive recipients of aid, and at the same time tends to paint the rescuers as noble, heroic and rare – and therefore altogether too lofty to serve as role models for ordinary mortals. When, on the other hand, we look at it from the point of view of the Jews, we find that they did make efforts to save themselves and each other – evasion is an active and not a passive response – and also that rescue is rarely an appropriate term for what the bystanders did. Rescue, properly speaking, should mean an action initiated by the rescuer and resulting in the victim's survival (there is also attempted rescue, when the victim does not survive). But most Jews who evaded the deportations and went into hiding sought help on their own initiative, and received help from many different people. Rarely was a single act of help enough to bring about survival. Therefore, we have not rescuers but helpers, whose actions, for the most part, are altogether on a more human and comprehensible scale. Not many of us would be up to risking our lives, day in, day out, to save a stranger, or even a friend. Most of us, though, would help a little if we were asked for it, even if some risk were involved, and would otherwise at least have the decency to keep *shtum*. The Jews did not need to be loved, or rescued: they needed to be helped to save themselves.

This study has shown that evasion was possible and did take place on a large scale, even in a place where the conditions for it seemed most unpropitious. It took place thanks to the initiative, ingenuity, courage and perseverance of the Jews themselves, who saved not only themselves but also others, and lived to fight another day. It took place thanks to the network that arose spontaneously to help them, in which there were genuinely heroic people, but also others who were simply decent, or out to make a buck, or to gain converts for their faith, or had other reasons of their own.

Evaders also received help from an unexpected quarter: the perpetrators, who appear here in a new and unfamiliar light. For once, we have policemen – German, Polish and Jewish – helping to save lives as well as take them. Having the most power to harm, they also had the most power to help. The fact that some of them did help, however small the proportion, belies the protestations of the others that they had to carry out orders, or that there was nothing they could do.

The fugitives faced a nerve-racking and protracted struggle for existence, which, thanks to help from various quarters, was nevertheless successful as often as not. Evasion was therefore not only possible, but of all responses offered the best chance of survival. It has been unjustly neglected by historians.

I hope therefore that this book will help to found the study of evasion as a response to the Holocaust – a subject that might indeed be of use beyond the boundaries of Holocaust studies. Every larger human crisis confronts people with the fight-or-flight decision, and there may well be something to be learnt from the experiences of the Jewish fugitives of Warsaw that would serve in Bosnia, or

Rwanda, or wherever people think of crossing some metaphorical ghetto wall and going into hiding.

The conditions in Warsaw were inauspicious: a vicious dictatorship intent on destruction, a history of troubled ethnic relations, a nasty criminal element, no possibility of getting to a safe sanctuary abroad, economically difficult conditions all around. As a case study it represents a stiff test. In the end, however, the phenomenon of the Jews on the Aryan side in Warsaw must be assessed positively rather than negatively. To reiterate, the number of Jews who escaped from the ghetto was small in proportion to the whole ghetto population, but large – even extraordinarily large – as a proportion of those who might realistically have been expected to realize the need to escape. It was also extraordinarily large considering the traditional social isolation of the Polish Jews, a situation that had existed for centuries by mutual consent, and considering the conditions of life in occupied Warsaw, particularly the shortage of housing and the prevailing poverty and terror. It was, finally, extraordinarily large in comparison with other cities and even whole countries, which had more space, more resources, fewer barriers and more freedom. I have estimated that 7–9 per cent of the city's population was involved in helping Jews, including 6 per cent who knowingly provided hiding places; and it is possible that even more people would have risen to the occasion if they had been asked: the invisible walls that protected the secret city could at times exclude potential friends as well as enemies. The overcrowding in Aryan Warsaw, amounting to almost two people per habitable room, also meant that many people of goodwill lacked the physical circumstances to provide significant help, while others were restrained by fear. Finally, the proportion of Jews who survived, after hiding for between twenty months and four years, is surprisingly high in view of the dangers that beset them. I have pointed to the 'gauntlet effect', which multiplied even a small degree of risk through repeated exposure: that so many Jews ran the gauntlet successfully is evidence that the great majority of the population, even people who were hostile, were not prepared to go so far as to hand Jews over to be killed. The secret city protected the Jews; its criminal element hounded them; the rest of Warsaw, whatever it may have thought and felt about the Jews, provided camouflage and above all kept the secret. Thus – under the noses of one of the harshest occupation regimes in history – 28,000 Jews managed to hide, and a good number of them lived to see the end of the war.

The secret city of the Jews of Warsaw, 1940–45, was in short a remarkable achievement, made possible by the initiative, courage and perseverance of the Jews, the heroic altruism of some Poles and the common decency of many others, and of some of the Germans as well. It casts a welcome and entirely unfamiliar light on the Holocaust as a whole, and for its own sake, and as an excursion into the uncharted continent of evasion as a response to the Holocaust, is a phenomenon well worth further reflection and study.

Notes

Foreword

1. Yitzhak Arad et al., eds, *Documents on the Holocaust* (Jerusalem: Yad Vashem, 1981), 214–15.
2. Tomasz Szarota, *Warszawy Okupacyjnej dzień powszedni* (Warszawa: Czytelnik, 1988), 67–70.
3. Ibid., 515.

Acknowledgments

1. Dariusz Stola, *Nadzieja i Zagłada* (Warszawa: Oficyna Naukowa, 1995). Małgorzata Melchior, *Społeczna tożsamość jednostki* (Warszawa: Uniwersytet Warszawski, Instytut Nauk Społecznych, 1990).
2. Barbara Engelking, *Nałące popiołów; Zagłada i pamięć; 'Czas przestał dla mnie istnieć'* (Warszawa: Czytelnik, 1993). Also *Holocaust and Memory* (London: Leicester University Press, 2001); Engelking and Jacek Leociak, *Getto warszawskie: Przewodnik po nieistniejącym mieście* (Warsawa: IFiS PAN, 2001).
3. Jonathan Glover, *Humanity: A Moral History of the Twentieth Century* (London: Pimlico, 2001).

Introduction

1. Entry for 26 September 1939.
2. Entry for 29 December 1942.
3. The Mongols are said to have massacred 800,000 people in Baghdad in 1258, but like most medieval estimates of this sort, this is probably a considerable exaggeration.
4. The full name of the holiday is *Yom haZikharon l'Shoah v'l'Gvurah*, the Day of Remembrance of Destruction and Heroism. It falls on the 26th Nisan, or on the 27th if the 26th is the Sabbath. The 26th Nisan 5703 corresponded to May Day in 1943, when the Warsaw Ghetto Uprising was at its height. Thus, the date celebrates both Jewish and labour militancy, in keeping with the Socialist character of most of the ghetto fighters and of post-war Israel. Yom haShoah also comes a week before Yom haZikharon, which commemorates those who have died for Israel and which in turn is the eve of Yom haAtzmaut, Israel's Independence Day. In the middle of this period is Rosh Khodesh Iyar, the beginning of the new month, with its theme of renewal. The whole eight-day period has thus come to symbolize the

birth of the State of Israel out of the ashes of the Shoah, hence 'Destruction and Heroism', of which the Warsaw Ghetto Uprising is the leading symbol.

5. Raul Hilberg, *The Destruction of the European Jews* (London and New York: Holmes & Meier, 1985), 514.

6. Susan Zuccotti, *The Holocaust, the French, and the Jews* (Lincoln NB and London: University of Nebraska Press, 1993), 161, 199, 237. According to Zuccotti, 140,000–150,000 Jews went into hiding in France as a whole; she offers no estimate of how many of these were in Paris. There was no ghetto in Paris, however, and it was never illegal for Jews to live there openly. Only people who chose to evade orders to report to the transit camp in Drancy needed to hide. There were about 150,000 Jews living in Paris at the time of the German invasion, of whom a substantial number fled to the unoccupied south.

7. Yisrael Gutman, *The Jews of Warsaw, 1939–1943* (Bloomington IN: Indiana University Press, 1989).

8. See Chapter 3.

9. Michal Borwicz, *Arishe papirn* (Buenos Aires, 1955); *Vies interdites* (Tournai: Casterman, 1968).

10. 'Ringelblum Revisited: Polish–Jewish Relations in Occupied Warsaw, 1940–1945', in *Contested Memories: Poles and Jews during the Holocaust and its Aftermath* (Rutgers University Press, 2002).

11. Yehuda Bauer, *Rethinking the Holocaust* (New Haven: Yale University Press, 2000).

12. This section is partly adapted from my paper of the same title in *Remembering for the Future: The Holocaust in an Age of Genocide* (London: Palgrave, 2001), I: 302–18.

13. Hilberg, *Destruction*, 1030.

14. Hannah Arendt, *Eichmann in Jerusalem* (Harmondsworth: Penguin, 1977), 117.

15. Ibid., 125.

16. Reuben Ainsztein, *Jewish Resistance in Nazi-Occupied Eastern Europe* (London: Paul Elek, 1974).

17. Adapted from Yehuda Bauer, *The Jewish Emergence from Powerlessness* (Toronto: University of Toronto Press, 1979), after Bauer, *Rethinking*, 119.

18. Hilberg, *Destruction*, 1036.

19. Ibid., 514.

20. Ibid., 1036.

21. Arendt, *Eichmann*, 124

22. Ibid., 125.

23. E.g. Bob Moore, *Victims and Survivors* (London: Arnold, 1997); Jacob Presser, *Ashes in the Wind* (Detroit: Wayne State University Press, 1988). Moore, for example, cites recent estimates that 24,000–25,000 Dutch Jews went into hiding, of whom 16,000–17,000 survived, but describes these estimates as 'problematic' (p. 146). Among other things, these figures appear to include people who were exempted from deportation, of whom there were 15,632 in April 1943 (p. 103). Most but not all of these exemptions were eventually cancelled, and some holders of exemptions went into hiding in anticipation that they would lose theirs as well. Both Moore and Presser state that the majority of those in hiding were concentrated in Amsterdam, but neither ventures an estimate of how many.

24. The experience of the Jews in Soviet-occupied areas in 1939–40 has been researched by Ben-Cion Pinchuk (*Shtetl Jews under Soviet Rule*, Oxford: Basil Blackwell, 1990) and others (A. Polonsky and N. Davies, eds, *Jews in Eastern Poland and the USSR, 1939–1946*, Basingstoke: Macmillan, 1991), but this research has concentrated on ethnic relations, especially the question of Jewish–Soviet collaboration. These Jews, of course, include both fugitives from German-occupied Poland and those who would subsequently flee to the Soviet interior in June 1941, but in this literature there is very little discussion of flight itself. The problem of Jewish refugees in the Soviet Union was raised as early as 1959 by Meir Korzen ('Problems Arising out of Research into the History of Jewish Refugees in the USSR during the Second

World War', *Yad Vashem Studies 3* (1959)); Korzen proposed a questionnaire to be administered to Jews who had returned from the Soviet Union after the war, but this appears never to have been done. Mordechai Altschuler, taking up the topic of flight in 1993 ('Escape and Evacuation of the Soviet Jews at the Time of the Soviet Occupation', in L. Dobroszycki and Jeffrey S. Gwock, *The Holocaust in the Soviet Union: Studies and Sources on the Destruction of the Jews in the Nazi-Occupied Territories of the USSR 1941–1945* (London: M.E. Sharpe, 1993), 77–104), still had reason to complain that 'this subject has been given scanty attention in the vast Holocaust literature' and that 'Soviet and Western historiographies of the war refer only incidentally to escape and evacuation' (p. 77). Pinchuk deals with the question in a ten-page chapter entitled, characteristically, 'Why Did They Stay?'.

25. Abraham Shulman, *The Case of the Hotel Polski* (New York: Holocaust Library, 1982), 22.

26. Emmanuel Ringelblum, *Polish–Jewish Relations during the Second World War* (New York: Howard Festig, 1976), 101.

27. Zofia S. Kubar, *Double Identity* (New York: Hill and Wang, 1989), 5.

28. I conducted interviews with the following people: Nina Assorodobraj (Warsaw); Renia Brus (Oxford); Daniel Falkner (London); Helena Merenholc (Warsaw); Diana Sternick (Warsaw); Janina Brandwajn-Ziemian (Tel Aviv).

29. Bronia Klibanski, *Yad Vashem Central Archives, Collection of Testimonies, Memoirs and Diaries (Record Group O33)* (Jerusalem: Yad Vashem, 1990), I: vi.

30. Archiwum Akt Nowych 30/III, t.5, pp. 18–46; Teresa Prekerowa, 'Komórka "Felicji": Nieznane archiwum działaczy Rady Pomocy Żydom w Warszawie', *Rocznik Warszawski* 15 (1979).

31. *Register of Jewish Survivors, II: List of Jews in Poland (58,000 names)* (Jerusalem: Jewish Agency for Palestine/Search Bureau for Missing Relatives, 1945); *List 1: About Jews Liberated from German Concentration Camps Arrived in Sweden in 1945;* (Stockholm: WJC Relief and Rehabilitation Dept., 1946) *Liste fun di lebngeblibene Warszewer Jidn in der US Zone in Dajczland* (Centrale fun di Warszewer Landsmanszaftn in der US Zone in Dajczland, 1948); *National Registry of Jewish Holocaust Survivors* (Washington: American Gathering of Holocaust Survivors and U.S. Holocaust Museum, 1993). The National Registry is now the Benjamin and Vladka Meed Registry of Holocaust Survivors.

32. Jan Thomasz Gross, *Neighbors: The Destruction of the Jewish Community in Jedwabne, Poland* (Princeton: Princeton University Press, 2001), 139–40.

33. Antony Polonsky, ed., *My Brother's Keeper* (London: Routledge, 1990), 193.

34. Ibid., 195.

35. Sara Kraus-Kolkowicz, *Dziewczynka z ulicy Miłej* (Lublin: Agencja Wydawnictwo-Handlowe, 1995).

36. Hana Gorodecka, *Hana: pamiętnik polskiej Żydówki* (Gdansk: Wydawnictwo ATEXT, 1992).

37. YVO33–2374.

38. Marek Edelman, *Getto walczy* (Warszawa: CK Bundu, 1948), 14.

39. Joseph Kermish, ed., *To Live with Honor and Die with Honor* (Jerusalem: Yad Vashem, 1986), 682 (from AŻIH, Ring/JM/202).

40. Florian Znaniecki and William Isaac Thomas, *The Polish Peasant in Europe and America* (Urbana IL.: University of Illinois Press, 1984).

Chapter 1

1. Conversation with the author, April 1994.

2. Marian Fuks, *Żydzi w Warszawie* (Poznań: Sorus, 1992), 271.

3. *Mały Rocznik Statystyczny 1939* (Warszawa: Główny Urząd Statystyczny, 1939), pp. 22, 24. The overall annual rate of population growth dropped from 1.7 per cent in 1921–31 to 1.2

per cent in 1931–39, reflecting the effects of the Depression. The growth rate of the urban population was higher. In 1921–31 it was 2.9 per cent; the *Mały Rocznik* does not give a figure for 1931–39, but it would have been 2.0 per cent if it declined in proportion to that of the country as a whole. The overall population of Warsaw in 1931 was 1,179,500; at the latter rate of growth it would have increased to 1,381,972 by 1939. The 1931 Jewish population was 353,000; it would have increased to 413,596. If the number of assimilants increased proportionally, it would have grown from 19,300 to 22,613.

4. Of a sample of 113 Jewish testimonies pertaining to the Aryan side in Warsaw, drawn from ŻIH collection 301, 106 were in Polish. For summaries of some of these (in Polish and English), see *Relacje z czasów zagłady: Inwentarz, Archiwum ŻIH-INB, zespół 301, Tom I (1–900)* (Warszawa: ŻIH, 1998). By contrast, of a random sample of a hundred testimonies listed in this inventory, pertaining to Poland in general, fifty-nine were in Yiddish and forty-one were in Polish.

5. See, for example, Władysław Bartoszewski and Zofia Lewin, *Righteous among Nations* (London: Earls Court, 1969), 332–4 *et passim*. Father Tadensz Puder, prelate of the other Catholic church in the ghetto, was a converted Jew.

6. For Yad Vashem's policy for recognizing non-Jews as 'Righteous among the Nations', see Mordechai Paldiel, 'The Righteous among the Nations at Yad Vashem', *Journal of Holocaust Education* 7 (1998), 45–66. Among the obvious requirement are that the person helped was a Jew and that the person helping was a non-Jew, and for these purposes the criteria mentioned are applied.

7. Cited in Alina Cała, *Asymilacja Żydów w Królestwie Polskim* (Warszawa: Pi W, 1989), 89–91.

8. Ibid.

9. *Gazeta żydowska* 13 V 1941, nr 38. Cited in Ruta Sakowska, *Ludzie z dzielnicy zamkniętej* (Wydawnictwo Naukowe PWN: 1993), 28n.

10. Ringelblum, *Relations,* 94–5.

11. It should not, of course, be concluded that the *Hassid* had the same chance of survival as a fully assimilated, middle-class Jew; in fact, I have not come across a single case of a Hassidic Jew on the Aryan side in Warsaw, though Rabbi Moshe Prager apparently knows of some. The more direct one's contacts were, the better. Additionally, the thought of chancing it on the Aryan side rarely occurred to traditional Jews, especially if they were poor.

12. Interview with author.

13. Ronald Modras, *The Catholic Church and Antisemitism: Poland, 1933–1939* (Reading: Harwood, 1994), *passim.*

14. Ibid., 346–7.

15. Jolanta Żyndul, *Zajścia antyżydowskie w Polsce w latch 1935–1937* (Warszawa: Fundaja im. K. Kelles-Krausa, 1994), 52–5.

16. The Warsaw Positivist movement at the end of the nineteenth century understood this point: its doyen, Aleksander Swiętochowski (1849–1938), published a celebrated article entitled 'Jewish Gold' which argued that Jewish capital and skills were a valuable economic asset for Poland. Later in his life, however, Świętochowski became a supporter of Dmowski.

17. *Unconquered Poland* (New York: Polish Labour Group, 2nd edn, Sept. 1943, 1st edn, April 1943). Wiktor Ehrenpreis describes the genesis and activity of the Polish Labour Group in 'Socialiści Polscy w Nowym Jorku', in Edward Hałoń, ed., *Polska Partia Socjalistyczna w latach wojny i okupacji 1939–1945* (Warszawa: Polska Fundacja Upowszechnania Nauki, 1994), I: 301–8. According to Ehrenpreis, a number of Jews were active in this group, notably the sociologist Aleksander Hertz, and the group's programme of action was formulated by a colleague from the Bund, Szlama Mendelson.

18. Olena Zaremba-Blatonowa *et al*, eds, *'My tu żyjemy jak w obozie warowym': Listy PPS-WRN Warszawa-Londyn 1940–1945* (London: Puls, 1992).
19. Ibid., 161–2.
20. Helen Fein, *Accounting for Genocide* (London: Collier Macmillan, 1979).
21. AŻIH 301/4235; AŻIH 301/4659; AŻIH 301/5815; Michał Grynberg, ed., *Księga sprawiedliwych* (Warszawa: Wydawnicto Naukowe PWN, 1993), 77, 326, 327; AŻIH 301/5008; Bartoszewski and Lewin, *Righteous*, 182–5, and Grynberg, *Księga*, 91, 410, 643.
22. Grynberg, *Księga*, 90; also AŻIH 301/5711, YV-RG0221 1966, and Bartoszewski and Lewin, *Righteous*, 181–5 (from the recollections of Henryk Joffe). Bocheński's name is spelt 'Buchański' by Joffe and 'Bachański' elsewhere.
23. Bartoszewski and Lewin, *Righteous*, 4–5 (extract from the memoirs of Adolf Berman), 492–3 (extract from the memoirs of Rachel Auerbach), 496–7 (extract from the memoirs of Basia Temkin-Berman), 500–3 (extract from the memoirs of Janina Buchholtz-Bukowska). Temkin-Berman was introduced to Buchholtz-Bukolska on the Aryan side, in October 1942, by a mutual acquaintance, Dr Jadwiga Zawirska. Adolf Berman, Buchholtz-Bukolska and Zawirska were all psychologists. Berman and his wife also mention another psychologist in their circle who was involved in Żegota, Professor Maria Grzegorzewska (pp. 5, 494–5). The 'Polish engineer' mentioned by Auerbach (p. 493) is undoubtedly Cywiński.
24. Shmuel Krakowski, *The War of the Doomed* (New York: Holmes & Meier, 1984), 278.
25. AŻIH 301/5175 (deposition of Stefan Koper), and Bartoszewski and Lewin, *Righteous*, 450–2 (memoirs of Marek Stok). The Kopers were a working-class family: Stefan Koper had been an army clerk before the war, and the nephew had been a porter.
26. Supporting letter to Chmielewski's deposition, AŻIH 301/5815.
27. Janina Bauman, *Winter in the Morning* (New York: Free Press, 1986), 104–5 *et passim*: Bauman refers to him as Karol; he was her mother's cousin.
28. Rotholc (AŻIH 301/4659) says he was taken prisoner by the Soviets in 1939 and held in the PoW camp at Kozielsk, and then was sent to a German camp in Lower Silesia by way of a prisoner exchange. He spent six months there, until all Jews were released from German PoW camps, whereupon he returned to Warsaw. He does not explain why Germany and the Soviet Union would have exchanged Polish prisoners.
29. AŻIH 301/5815, 4
30. Ibid., 6. 'Beat the Jew!' (*Bij Żyda!*) was a common incitement, particularly among right-wing student gangs that attacked Jews in the street before the war. The Camp of Great Poland: see 'OWP' in the Glossary. The National Radical Camp: see 'ONR' in the Glossary.
31. Mosdorf was the pre-war editor of *Prosto z mostu*, the main organ of the ONR. As a prisoner in Auschwitz, he became involved in the camp underground and devoted particular attention to helping Jewish prisoners. He perished in the camp. See Philip Friedman, 'Za naszą i waszą wolność', in Bartoszewski and Lewin, eds, *Ten jest z ojczyzny mojej* (Kraków: Znak, 1969), 90–91, and relation of Mieczysław Maślanko, in ibid., 668–70.
32. Ringelblum, *Kronika getta warszawskiego*, ed. Artur Eisenbach (Warszawa: Czytelnik, 1988), 204.
33. AŻIH 301/4659.
34. AŻIH 301/5815, 12.
35. Ibid., 13.
36. Ibid., 18–19.
37. Computer printout of the Yad Vashem database on Righteous Gentiles (Polish cases only) in author's possession, as of April 1994; kindly provided by Dr Mordechai Paldiel.
38. Bauman, *Winter*, 52.
39. Ibid., 121.

40. Bauman uses various pseudonyms in her memoir. For Stefania Bergman: Aunt Maryla; for Bielińska: Zielińska; for Stanisław: Edward; for Kulesza: Koterba; for Dr Płocker: Uncle Leo; for Simonis: Serbin; for Szawernowski: Sokolnicki; for Tom's partner Wanda: Krystyna; for Zina Ziegler: Zena Richter. She could not remember the real names of the Majewski family or of the prostitute Lily.

41. Ibid., 141.

42. Ibid., 145.

43. Ibid., 33.

44. Nechama Tec, *When Light Pierced the Darkness* (Oxford: OUP, 1986), 150–83; Michael Marrus, *The Holocaust in History* (Toronto: Lester & Orpen Dennys, 1982), 106.

Chapter 2

1. Yisrael Gutman, *Jews of Warsaw*, 211.

2. Jürgen Stroop, *The Stroop Report: The Jewish Quarter of Warsaw Is No More!*, ed. Sybil Milton (London: Secker & Warburg, 1980, n.p.), report for 24 May 1943. Stroop reports that 6,929 Jews 'were destroyed via transport to T.II' and that 'about 7,000 were destroyed directly', 'making the total number of Jews destroyed 13,929'. Obviously the accuracy of this last number, and hence of the overall total, is spurious.

3. Tatiana Berenstein and Adam Rutkowski, 'Liczba ludności żydowskiej i obszar przez nią zamieszkany w Warszawie w latach okupacji hitlerowskiej', *Biuletyn ŻIH* 6(1958), 83.

4. Adolf Berman, 'Ha-Yehudim b'tsad ha-Ari', in *Entsiklopedia shel galuot*, vol. 7.8 'Varshe' (Jerusalem: Encyclopedia of the Jewish Diaspora Co. Ltd, 1953), 685.

5. Deposition of 'Citizen Frajnd', AŻIH 301/4651.

6. Michael (Michał) Borwicz, 'Factors Influencing the Relations between the General Polish Underground and the Jewish Underground', 346.

7. Report of Waldemar Schön 20 January 1941, cited in Bartoszewski and Lewin, *Righteous*, 627–32.

8. AŻIH 301/4651.

9. See, for example, Noemi Szac-Wainkranc, *Przeminęło z ogniem* (Warszawa: CŻKH, 1947), 18.

10. For example, A.P. married a Catholic in May 1940; both she and her mother (her only close living relative) had to be provided with Aryan papers (personal relation to author). Henryka Wanda also married a Catholic in the hope of staying out of the ghetto; according to the testimony of her husband, Antoni Kolbarczyk, she later entered the ghetto as a result of harassment and threats from their neighbours (AŻIH 301/5187).

11. In many cases, assimilants not only had a weak attachment to the Jewish community, but also exhibited an active antipathy towards traditional Jewish society. For example, Władysław Smólski mentions a woman named Jola whom he persuaded to leave the ghetto just before it was closed. Smólski tells us that she was so thoroughly assimilated that she disliked the Jewish milieu and everything connected with it (Smólski, *Zaklęte lata*, 52–3). Such disdain for the 'uncivilized' Eastern Jews was common among assimilated Jews, not only in Poland but also – or, rather, especially – in Western Europe. It should not be confused with antisemitism.

12. Several memoirists or persons mentioned by memoirists who stayed out of the ghetto were married to non-Jews before the war, or had established close relationships with non-Jews before the ghetto was closed; e.g. Janina Mądra (AŻIH 301/5824), Janina Bauman's uncle and great-uncle (Janina Bauman, *Winter*, 35–6), Ada Blitzer's husband (AŻIH 301/5120).

13. A.P.'s husband was a member of the Polish underground, and a first cousin of the chief prosecutor of the underground courts, Kazimierz Moczarski (personal relation to author);

an anonymous deponent relates that she stayed out of the ghetto because she was having trouble finding lodgings under her real identity and knew a few prominent figures on whom she could count for references (AŻIH 301/5680). The best-known case of a Jewish convert who stayed out of the ghetto is that of the economist Ludwik Landau, who maintained a chronicle of the occupation with the help and encouragement of the Polish underground. Later published in three volumes, this is one of the fundamental sources for the period. (Ludwik Landau, *Kronika lat wojny i okupacji* (Warszawa: PWN, 1963), xiii–xxiii.)

14. A.P.'s mother, Ada Blitzer's son, Bauman's uncle Władek and his son and the daughter of Władysława Kubena (AŻIH 301/5178).

15. Henryka Wanda (see note 10 above).

16. Ada Rolnicka's son (AŻIH 301/5717).

17. Ludwik Landau, arrested on 29 February 1944; Ada Blitzer's husband, arrested in December 1942 and sent to Auschwitz; Janina Bauman's great-uncle Ludwik, place and manner of death unknown.

18. Report of Waldemar Schön, 20 January 1941, in J. Noakes and G. Pridham, eds, *Nazism: A History in Documents and Eyewitness Accounts 1919–1945* (New York: Schocken, 1988), vol. 2, 1064–5.

19. Ibid., 1066.

20. AŻIH, Ring II 274–7, cited in Y. Arad *et al.*, eds, *Documents*, 228.

21. AŻIH 301/5003.

22. Jack Eisner, *The Survivor* (New York: Morrow, 1980).

23. Relation of Szapse Rotholc, AŻIH 301/4235.

24. Personal relation to the author.

25. AŻIH 301/5717.

26. Relation of Stanisław Lenartowicz, AŻIH 301/5298.

27. AŻIH 301/4629.

28. AŻIH 301/4235.

29. Ibid.

30. Ibid.

31. *Raporty Ludwiga Fischera*, 530.

32. Chaim Lazar mentions the following tunnels constructed by ŻZW: the well-known tunnel under Muranowska Street, connecting ŻZW headquarters at number 6 to number 7 on the Aryan side; a second tunnel, partly excavated and partly using sewers, from the ŻZW bunker at Karmelicka 5 to the Carmelite Hospital opposite; a third, leading from the Church of the Holiest Virgin Mary in Leszno Street; and 'other tunnels' besides. All but the first two had been 'rendered unusable' for unspecified reasons by the time arms smuggling on a larger scale began. Lazar maintains that the Karmelicka Street tunnel was used among other things 'for evacuating people from the ghetto during the period between the major *Aktion* and the outbreak of the [ghetto] uprising' (Chaim Lazar, 'The Jewish Military Organization in the Warsaw Ghetto', in David Wdowiński, *And We Are Not Saved* (New York: Philosophical Library, 1985), 184).

33. Reproduced in Bartoszewski and Lewin, *Ten jest*, 892.

34. Ibid.

35. AŻIH 301/5003.

36. AŻIH 301/5011.

37. Brunon Sikorski, 'Handel Warszawy okupacyjnej', in *Studia Warszawskie*, vol. 7., i, 73; Ruta Sakowska, *Ludzie* (Warszawa: Instytut Historyczay PAN, 1971), 63. There are small discrepancies between the two, and Sakowska does not give the average. On the basis of the breakdown figures given by both authors, the average given by Sikorski seems too low.

38. Houses set aside for refugees and the destitute. Kermish notes the mortality rate in one of these houses, a foundlings' home at Dzielna 39, where 331 out of 600 children died in May and June 1941 (Kermish, *To Live*, 396n). Detailed reports on the food, sanitary conditions and mortality rates in the various 'points' can also be found in Kermish, *To Live*, 324–31. Constituting less than 1 per cent of the ghetto's population (2,977 out of some 400,000 in January 1942), the 'points' accounted for 19 per cent of its mortality. At Stawki 9, 25 per cent of the inhabitants died in January 1942, and overall more than 18 per cent of the refugees died in the same month.

39. Memoirs of A.P., 37–38, MS in author's possession.

40. P.D. in conversation with Stefan Chaskielewicz, in Chaskielewicz, *Ukrywałem się w Warszawie* (Kraków: ZNAK, 1988), 150–1.

41. AŻIH 301/3006.

42. Józef (Joseph) Ziemian, *Papierosiarze z placu Trzech Krzyży* (Warszawa: Niezależna Oficyna Wydawnicza, 1989).

43. Kaplan, Chaim, *Scroll of Agony* (Bloomington IN: Indiana University Press, 1999), 20. Entry for 1 September 1939. The reference is to Hitler's speech in the Reichstag of 30 January 1939, on the sixth anniversary of his accession to power (see note 45).

44. Ibid., 296

45. Ibid., 297. The reference is to Hitler's speech to the Reichstag on 30 January 1942, the ninth anniversary of his accession to power. In this speech he referred to the 'prophecy' that he had made in his speech of 30 January 1939: 'if the international Jewish financiers ... should succeed once more in plunging the nations into a world war, then the result will not be the ... victory of Jewry, but the annihilation of the Jewish race in Europe' (Arad, *Documents*, 134–5).

46. ARI/JM/202 (Kermish, *To Live*, 682).

47. Kaplan, *Scroll*, 274–5.

48. Ibid., 22–3.

49. Abraham Lewin, *A Cup of Tears* (London: Fontana/Collins, 1990), 61–2.

50. ARI/PH/10-4-3 (Kermish, *To Live*, 116–20).

51. Kaplan, *Scroll*, 305–6 (entry for 23 March). On 1 March the population of the Łódź ghetto stood at 142,079 and on 1 April at 115,102: rather more than 'a meager remnant' (Source: Lucjan Dobroszycki, ed., *The Chronicle of the Łódź Ghetto 1941–1944, passim*).

52. Kaplan, *Scroll*, 309 (6 April 1942) and 321 (30 April 1942).

53. On the other hand, Emmanuel Ringelblum wrote on 10 June that 'Unproductive elements – children under ten and old people – are loaded into sealed wagons ... and carried in an unknown direction. Usually in the direction of Bełżec, where all trace of the resettled Jews is lost. The fact that no-one has managed to save themselves from the death camp in Bełżec, that there is so far not a single Polish or Jewish witness to the extermination being carried out in Bełżec, is the best evidence of how diligently they take care that this sort of information should not spread among the Germans. If the German people knew about this [it would] certainly not [be possible] to carry out such mass murder' (*Kronika*, 392).

54. Dobroszycki, *Chronicle*, 234.

55. Kaplan, *Scroll*, 297. Entry for 22 February 1942.

56. Ringelblum, *Polish–Jewish Relations during the Second World War* (New York, Howard Festig, 1976), ed. J. Kermish and Shmuel Krakowski, 95.

57. Arad, *Documents*, 281–2.

58. Ibid., 275.

59. Kaplan, *Scroll*, 379.

60. Ibid., 381.

61. Jacob Celemeński, *Elegy to my People* (unpublished translation of *Mitn farshnitenem folk*; copy of ts. in author's possession). According to Marek Edelman (*Getto Walczy*, 32), in *Oyf der Wach*.

62. Gutman, *Jews of Warsaw*, 222, 219.
63. Kaplan, *Scroll*, 397.
64. A. Lewin, *Cup of Tears*, 148.
65. Ibid., 153.
66. Ibid., 157.
67. Gutman, *Jews of Warsaw*, 219–27.
68. Adam Starkopf, *There is Always Time to Die* (New York: Holocaust Library, 1981), 110–11.
69. YVo33-239.
70. Kaplan, *Scroll*, 387.
71. Ibid., 19–21.
72. London: Valentine, Mitchell, 1970.
73. Jerzy Himmelblau (AŻIH 301/3073).
74. Helena Szereszewska, *Krzyż i mezuza* (Warszawa: Czytelnik, 1993), 195–7.
75. AŻIH 301/5960.
76. Ringelblum, *Relations*, 89–91.
77. A. Lewin, *Cup of Tears*, 179.
78. Gutman, *Jews of Warsaw*, 269.
79. A. Lewin, *Cup of Tears*, 186–7. The word *szaber*, now a standard Polish word meaning loot (also *szabrowanie*, looting, and *szabrować*, to loot), comes from pre-war thieves' slang, which often appropriated Yiddish words – in this case *shaber* (שאבער), crowbar, and *shabreven* (שאברעווען), to break with a crowbar. The ultimate root may be the German *Schaber*, scraper, or the Hebrew שבר, to break.
80. Trade during the 'shops' period is described by Ringelblum, *Kronika*, 420.
81. Ringelblum, *Relations*, 99.
82. Ibid., 27.
83. Gutman gives the following figures: October, 360; November, 121; December, 65; January (including resistance to the second *Aktion*), 1,171 – compared with an average of 75 per month in the three months preceding the first *Aktion*, when the ghetto was of course much larger (Gutman, *Jews of Warsaw*, 277).
84. Ringelblum, *Kronika*, 438.
85. Cf. Gutman, *Jews of Warsaw*, 353.
86. Simcha Rotem, *Memoirs of a Warsaw Ghetto Fighter* (New Haven and London: Yale University Press, 1994), 26.
87. 'Z pamiętnika Stefana Ernesta', in Michał Grynberg, ed., *Pamiętniki z getta warszawskiego* (Warszawa: Wydawnictwo Naukowe PWN, 1993), 98. This passage is cited from Emma Harris's translation in Barbara Engelking, *Holocaust and Memory* (London: Leicester University Press, 2001).
88. AŻIH 302/195, cited in Grynberg, *Pamiętniki*, 197.
89. Ringelblum, *Kronika*, 441.
90. Adina Blady-Szwajger, *I Remember Nothing More* (New York: Pantheon, 1991), 157.
91. Ringelblum, *Kronika*, 440.
92. Szac-Wainkranc, *Przeminęło*, 58.
93. Ringelblum, *Kronika*, 422.
94. Lewin, *Cup of Tears*, 188.
95. Ringelblum, *Kronika*, 438.
96. Ibid., 410 (15 October 1942).
97. Ibid., 419.
98. Ibid., 424.
99. Ibid., 97.

100. Ringelblum himself recognized quite candidly the provisional nature of his work, which he characterized as a 'contribution for a future historian of the Polish Jews during the Second World War.' (*Stosunki polsko-żydowskie w czasie drugiej wojny światowej* (Warszawa: Czytelnik, 1988), 28).
101. Eugenia Szajn-Lewin, *W getcie warszawskim: lipiec 1942 – kwiecień 1943* (Poznań: Wydawnictwo a5, 1989), 50.
102. Blady-Szwajger, *Nothing More*, 73.
103. Szac-Wainkranc, *Przeminelo*, 70.
104. Ibid., 71.
105. Szajn-Lewin, *W getcie*, 50–1.
106. AŻIH 301/5882.
107. Anna Lanota, in conversation with Stefan Chaskielewicz, in Chaskielewicz, *Ukrywałem*, 135.
108. Ringelblum, *Kronika*, 434–6.
109. Emmanuel Ringelblum, letter to Adolf Berman, 25 November 1943 (BLHG 358). The proposal of smuggling Jewish intellectuals to Hungary had been put by Ignacy Szwarcbart, the Zionist representative on the Polish National Council in London; the affair is also mentioned by Itzhak Zuckerman *(A Surplus of Memory* (Oxford: University of California Press, 1993), 439).
110. Chaskielewicz, *Ukrywałem*, 26.
111. Anna Winawer, in conversation with Stefan Chaskielewicz, ibid., 155–6.
112. AŻIH 301/5543.
113. AŻIH 301/5544.
114. Szajn–Lewin, *W getcie*, 55.
115. Blady-Szwajger, *Nothing More*, 74.
116. AŻIH 301/5085, 5.
117. Szajn-Lewin, *W getcie*, 57–8.
118. AŻIH 301/5603.
119. AŻIH 301/5049.
120. E.g., Janina Baran writes that her journey to Poniatowa (near Lublin) took twenty-eight hours. (AŻIH 301/5085, 5).
121. YVO33-1418, 21.
122. Deposition of Eliasz Pietruszko, AŻIH 301/5222.
123. AŻIH 301/5692.
124. AŻIH 301/5583a.
125. Ringelblum, *Kronika*, 406.
126. YVO33-1418, 49.
127. AŻIH 301/5085, 6.
128. Zuckerman, *Memory*, 514.
129. Ibid., 513.
130. Ibid., 418.
131. Ibid., 419.

Chapter 3

1. Vladka Meed, *On Both Sides of the Wall*, (New York: Holocaust Library, 1979), 79.
2. Kaplan, *Scroll*, 356 (entry for 19 June 1942).
3. Interviewed by Engelking, *Na łące*, 205.
4. AŻIH 301/4651.
5. Ibid.

6. Szarota, *Okupowanej*, 34.
7. AŻIH 301/4651.
8. Sara Bergazyn (AŻIH 301/5681), for example, mentions a clerk at the Warsaw records office named Antoni Hochaubel who made forged documents for her, evidently without payment since she says she had left the ghetto with 14 zł in her pocket.
9. Ringelblum, *Relations*, 104.
10. Szajn-Lewin, *W getcie*, 51.
11. Cf. Bartoszewski and Lewin, *Righteous*, 250–3, 254n.
12. AŻIH 301/4651.
13. Szarota, *Okupowanej*, 36–37.
14. Quoted in ibid., 35–6.
15. Quoted in ibid., 38.
16. Marek Arczyński and Wiesław Balcerak, *Kryptonim 'Żegota'* (Warszawa: Czytelnik, 1979), 75–7. Arczyński claims, apparently on the basis of these figures (cf. ibid, 82), that 50,000 Jews were hidden in Warsaw; this is clearly a considerable exaggeration. A single Jew required a suite of half a dozen documents, and might need to change identity several times. A count of 50,000 documents would thus correspond well enough to the 4,000 Jews under Żegota's care throughout Poland, with perhaps some documents that were manufactured on behalf of the Bund and ŻKN as well. (Jews under care of the PPR received documents from its own legalization cell or *paszportówka*: testimony of Renia Brus, in conversation with the author.)
17. Not only second-generation converts were uncircumcised, but also sometimes secular Jews. For example, Alina Margolis-Edelman writes that her parents, both doctors, were atheists and determinedly rejected all religious practices. Thus, her brother Olek was not circumcised, and survived an encounter with *szmalcowniks* for this reason (Alina Margolis-Edelman, *Ala z elementarza*, 46). Jewish boys born during the war were usually not circumcised, even if their parents were religious, since *halakhah* allows for exemptions to save life; but some parents felt that circumcision was a declaration of loyalty that was more important then than ever.
18. The microbiologist Adam Drozdowicz (*né* Gutgisser) (YVO3–3647) writes that he had held discussions with other medical people over how such an operation could be carried out, but that it was decided that it would be impossible to do anything that would pass muster. 'An operation was devised and tried out on corpses, but the results were easy to detect. . . . Also the rumour came to us that the Germans knew about our discussions and were thinking along the same lines.' However, a group of Polish doctors drawn from the Council of Democratic and Socialist Physicians, particularly the eminent surgeon Professor Andrzej Trojanowski, did develop and perform the operation, as well as plastic surgery to alter the shape of the nose. Trojanowski and several other physicians from his circle have been recognized as Righteous Gentiles. (Bartoszewski and Lewin, *Righteous*, 47, 60, 112, 113.)

Attempts to reverse circumcision have a long history, dating back to the Hellenistic period; the first surgical procedures were described by the First-Century Roman physician Celsus. During the Holocaust, such operations were performed by a Dr H. Feriz in the Netherlands as well as in Poland (see Dirk Schultheiss et al., 'Uncircumcision: A Historical Review of Preputial Restoration', *Plastic and Reconstructive Surgery*, 101, (1998), pp. 1990–8). The authors describe the methods used by Polish doctors as follows: 'The first and crudest method was to pull forward the penile skin over the glans, scarify the new prepuce edges, and avoid recession by suturing them together, thus producing a phimosis. This implied a high failure rate because the sutures were often extruded and the skin was retracted to the former position. The second method was quite similar to the second procedure of Celsus, resulting in a single-layered new prepuce. The main disadvantage of this way of foreskin restoration was the high infection rate. Finally, the last and most sophisticated method was performed by using a skin graft from the area over the iliac crest serving as the new prepuce.' The second method of Celsus was as follows: 'A coronary incision was made, and the penile skin was mobilized along the whole length of the penis to the root [....] The skin was thus stretched over the glans and recession was now prevented by means of a bandage fixed securely over the penile shaft from the pubis to the glans [....]; adhesion was counteracted by the application of additional saturated dressings and plasters.' (Ibid.)

19. AŻIH 301/5768.
20. Szereszewska, *Krzyż*, 25.
21. Philip Friedman, 'The Karaites under Nazi Rule', in Ada June Friedman, ed., *Roads to Extinction: Essays on the Holocaust* (Philadelphia: The Jewish Publication Society of America, 1980), 153–75.
22. Julien Hirshaut, *Jewish Martyrs of Pawiak* (New York: Holocaust Library, 1982), 20–2.
23. Margolis-Edelman, *Elementarza*, 109–10.
24. Miriam Peleg-Mariańska and Mordechai Peleg, *Witnesses: Life in Occupied Kraków* (London: Routledge, 1991).
25. Ringelblum, *Relations*, 103.
26. YVO33–1510.
27. Hitler, recorded in Rosenberg's diary, 27 September 1939. Reproduced in Noakes and Pridham, eds, *Nazism*, 2:927.
28. Ludwik Landau, *Kronika*, 392 (entry for 6 May 1943).
29. Ringelblum, *Relations*, 103.
30. Michael Zylberberg, *A Warsaw Diary, 1939–1945* (London: Valentine, Mitchell, 1969), 152–3.
31. This was a common wartime joke. Another version was 'he looked like three Jews' (*wyglądal jak trzech Żydów*), or 'he looked like a Czech' (Czech sounds like *trzech*, three). Possibly by extension, Jews were called 'people from Częstochowa'; more likely, though, this is a pun on *często chowa* ('often hides').
32. Personal relation to author.
33. Chaskielewicz, *Ukrywałem*, 35.
34. Ibid., 88.
35. Ringelblum, *Relations*, 104; Samuel Willenberg, *Surviving Treblinka* (Oxford: Basil Blackwell, 1989), 157.
36. Chaskielewicz, *Ukrywałem*, 39, 35.
37. Szereszewska, *Krzyz*, 300.
38. AŻIH 301/4242.
39. Alicja Kaczyńska, *Obok piekła* (Gdansk: Marpress, 1993), 48.
40. Ibid.
41. In addition, such services were sometimes antisemitic in content. Luba Bat reports that the porter in her building would in his prayers regularly thank Jesus for sending Hitler to rid Poland of the Jewish plague (HU 84(3)).
42. M.M. Mariańscy, *Wśród przyjaciół i wrogów* (Krakow: Wydawnictwo Literackie, 1988), 29.
43. Kaczyńska, *Obok piekła*, 62.
44. Zylberberg, *Warsaw Diary*, 125, 121, 148, 120.
45. Adina Blady-Szwajger, *I Remember Nothing More: The Warsaw Children's Hospital and the Jewish Resistance* (New York: Pantheon, 1991), 87 and *passim*; Meed, *Both Sides*, 216 and *passim*.
46. AŻIH 301/5853.
47. Anna Lanota, in conversation with Stefan Chaskielewicz, Chaskielewicz, *Ukrywałem*, 138.
48. Jonas Turkow, *Noch der bafrayung* (Buenos Aires: Tsentral Farband fun Poilishe Yidn in Argentine, 1959), 254.
49. Albert Nirenstein, *A Tower from the Enemy: Contributions to a history of Jewish resistance in Poland* (New York: Orion Press, 1959) 257.

50. Mathematically, if the probability that any one person is a 'hooligan' is one in fifty or .02, then the probability that a given person is not a hooligan is conversely .98, and the probability that there are no hooligans in a crowd of 50 people is $.98^{50} = .36$ approximately, or one in 2.7. These would be the odds of surviving one such encounter. If the crowd numbered 100 people, then the odds of surviving would drop to about one in 7.5.

51. AŻIH 301/4632.

52. For a summary of the extraordinary variety of social psychological approaches to the problem of crowd violence and non-intervention, see Don Foster, 'Crowds and Collective Violence', in Don Foster and Joha Louw-Potgieter, eds, *Social Psychology in South Africa* (Johannesburg: Lexicon, 1991), 441–83.

53. Calculated on the basis of figures given in Szarota, *Okupowanej*, 69, 277. Szarota's pre-war figures, however, are inconsistent with those that he cites for the wartime period. Szarota estimates the population of Warsaw on 1 September 1939 at 1.25 million (p. 69) and says that 78,000 rooms were destroyed in the subsequent bombardment, amounting to 10.3 per cent of the city's housing stock. This would imply that there were about 760,000 rooms before the war, giving a density of 1.64 people per room. The property 'census' carried out by the occupation authorities on 28 November 1939, on the other hand, indicated that there were 582,940 rooms in the city at that time (Szarota, table, p. 279. Note that Szarota's total is calculated incorrectly.) This would then imply a pre-war housing stock of about 661,000 rooms, yielding a density of 1.89 people per room, and destruction of 11.8 per cent of the housing stock in the bombing. According to official census figures, in 1931 the city's population was 1,179,500 and the average population density 2.1 people per room, implying 561,667 rooms at that time (*Mały Rocznik 1939*, 12, 61).

54. *Biuletyn statystyczny judenratu w Warszawie*, 11(18 Dec 1940), reproduced in T. Berenstein and A. Rutkowski, 'Liczba ludności żydowskiej i obszar przez nią zamieszkiwany w Warszawie w latach okupacji hitlerowskiej', *BŻIH* 26(1958), 105–10.

55. Noakes and Pridham, eds, *Nazism*, 2:1063–7.

56. Hilberg, *Destruction*, 152.

57. Gutman, *Jews of Warsaw*, 60, 432n.32.

58. See, for example, Szarota, *Okupowanej*, 60 and Antony Polonsky, introduction to A. Lewin, *Cup of Tears*, 2. Szarota does give the correct figure elsewhere (p. 283), apparently without noticing the inconsistency.

59. That the commonly repeated statistics are exaggerated does not mean that it is impossible to find individual cases where the number of people per room was as great as the claimed average or even greater. For example, Jakub Herzog wrote that he 'moved into a single room ... in which over a dozen [*kilkanaście*] people were living' (AŻIH 301/5974). Szarota, on the other hand, notes that there were single-room flats on the Aryan side in which 'as many as twelve' people lived (Szarota, *Okupowanej*, 279).

60. *Mały Rocznik 1939*, 12, gives the area of Warsaw as 141 square kilometres = 14,100 hectares; the area of the ghetto when it was closed was 403 hectares. The densities are derived from the population figures given above. Various authors give various and sometimes absurd figures: for example, Szarota (*Okupowanej*, 283) gives the density of the Aryan district as 38,000 per square kilometre = 380 per hectare. The population density of Warsaw in 1931 was eighty-three people per ha.

61. The most densely populated district of Hong Kong had 2,521 people per hectare in 1976. Population statistics for Hong Kong and the City of London are taken from *The Guinness Book of Records 1991*.

62. Engelking, *Zagłada i pamięć* (Warszawa: Wyd. IFiS PAN, 1994), 85–91; *Holocaust and Memory* (London: Leicester University Press, 2001), 91–115.

63. Szarota, *Okupowanej*, 279.

64. Ibid., 85.

65. Ibid., 77.

66. Ibid., 80.

67. Ibid., 81.

68. Ibid., 81.

69. Ibid., 87.

70. Ibid., 85.

71. Ibid., 279.

72. Ibid., 280.

73. Some authors give the address as Grójecka 84.

74. BLHG 308.

75. Orna Jagur, *Bunkier 'Krysia'*, 14.

76. BLHG 308.

77. AŻIH 301/5544. Letter to Adolf Berman, 6 January 1944.

78. Bauman, *Winter*, 121ff.

79. Tuvia Borzykowski, *Between Tumbling Walls* (Tel Aviv: Ghetto Fighters' House, 1972), 107–17.

80. Michał Grynberg, *Księga*, 90; also AŻIH 301/5711 and YV–RG0221 1966.

81. For example, George Pfeffer (YVO33–1418, 66–7) was hidden for a time, along with another Jew, by a German woman and her Jewish husband. Pfeffer also encountered (p. 78) a man who had previously stayed in a *melina* run by a Jewish woman living on Aryan papers. Joseph Steiner, eight years old at the time, and his older sister were under the care of the sister's fiancé's brother, a Jew, who arranged *melinas* for them (in Jane Marks, *The Hidden Children* (London: Piatkus, 1994), 127–38). Many other examples could be cited.

82. For example, Michael Zylberberg lived in the block at Sapieżyńska 7, where the porter was said to have turned three Jews over to the Germans. Nevertheless, he encountered other Jews living in the building, some of whom even socialized with the porter. During the 1944 Warsaw Uprising, he writes, 'the mystery ... was cleared up. [...] It turned out that some of the tenants were part of a huge conspiracy. The block housed an illegal printing press for an underground news sheet; ammunition was stored here; many Poles who were politically suspect lived here; and so Jews could be the more easily hidden. The story about the three Jews discovered by the porter was deliberately allowed to circulate; it was a fabrication which helped to avert suspicion' (*Warsaw Diary*, 110–11). The porter Stefan Giemza (AŻIH 301/4242, 2) reports that in his block 'There was a drunken woman in the courtyard who shouted that there were Jews living there, but she was hiding two Jews herself. Maybe for money.' Similar stories are not uncommon.

83. Ringelblum, *Relations*, 116.

84. YVO3–824.

85. YVO3–824, 2.

86. Teresa Prekerowa, in conversation with author.

87. Ewa Kurek-Lesik, *Gdy klasztor znaczył życie* (Krakow: Znak, 1992), 121–2.

88. Szajn-Lewin, *W getcie*, 13.

89. Ibid., 14.

90. Kurek-Lesik, *Gdy klasztor*, 137–8.

91. Józef (Joseph) Ziemian, *Papierosiarze z placu Trech Krzyży* (Warszawa: Niezależna Oficyna Wydawnicza, 1989) 4. See also (English edition) *The Cigarette-Sellers of Three Crosses Square* (Minneapolis: Lerner, 1971).

92. Jack Klajman, *Out of the Ghetto* (London: Valentine Mitchell, 2000).

93. Foreword to Ziemian, *Papierosiarze*.

94. Ringelblum, *Relations*, 133.
95. Blady-Szwajger, *Nothing More*, 81–2.
96. Tec, *Light*, 218–19n.
97. Szarota, *Okupowanej*, 30.
98. Bartoszewski and Lewin, *Righteous*, 891–2.
99. Kazimierz Brandys, *Miasto Niepokonane* (Warszawa: Państwowy Instytut Wydawniczy, 1960), 151.
100. Mordechai Paldiel, 'The Righteous among the Nations at Yad Vashem', *Journal of Holocaust Education* 7 (1998), 45–66.
101. Ringelblum, *Relations*, 247.
102. Bernard Mandelkern, *Escape from the Nazis* (Toronto: James Lorimer, 1987), 90ff.
103. Professor Andrzej Trojanowski (YV–RG 66–0109) or Dr Stanisław Trojanowski (YV–RG 90–4485), both physicians and members of the Co-ordinating Committee of Democratic and Socialist Doctors. *Vide* Bartoszewski and Lewin, *Righteous*, 112–16; Grynberg, *Księga*, 580; Kubar, *Double Identity*, 106. Uklejska is described on 43–4, Dobrowolski on 44, Szczypińska on 12, 82.
104. The number of Righteous Among the Nations from Poland had reached 5,632 at the time of writing, of whom Mordechai Paldiel has estimated in conversation that about a quarter are from Warsaw. Even if only 10 per cent of helpers were to deserve the title, it would follow that only a fraction of them have received it. In fact some benchmark cases suggest that the number of 'Righteous Gentiles' who have been recognized across Europe represents a similarly small fraction of the deserving cases. See my article, 'The Rescue of Jews by Non-Jews in Nazi-Occupied Poland', *Journal of Holocaust Education* 7 (1998) 19–44. Of the cases in my files that seem to merit the title, about 20 per cent have received it – and these are cases for which full documentation is already on file.
105. Szarota, *Okupowanej*, 141 and 139, the former after a Delegatura report (CA KC PZPR 202/I–30, 32).
106. *Raporty Ludwika Fischera*, 529.
107. Szarota, *Okupowanej*, 139.
108. Ibid.
109. *Ludwika Fischera*, 366.
110. *Nowy Kurier Warszawski*, 8 March 1940, quoted in Szarota, *Okupowanej*, 282.
111. Ringelblum, *Relations*, 140.
112. Ibid., 133.
113. Berman archive, LHG 358 (numbered 1203).
114. Ibid., unnumbered.
115. Szarota, *Okupowanej*, 139–42.
116. Meed, *Both Sides* (1972 edition), 252.
117. Bartoszewski and Lewin, *Righteous*, 183.

Chapter 4

1. Nathan Eck, 'The Rescue of Jews with Aid of Passports and Citizenship Papers of Latin American States', *YVS* I (1957), 142. Eck states that the shipments comprised 2,500–3,000 holders of Latin American documents and 250 people on the 'Palestine list', i.e. with immigration certificates to Palestine.
2. Ibid., 141.
3. J. Bauman, *Winter*, 121.
4. Celemenski, *Elegy* (copy of typescript in author's possession), 206–8. Accounts of Henryk

Zamoszowski, reproduced in Shulman, *Hotel Polski*, 80–2, and Józef Gitler-Barski, ibid., 156–61. Gitler-Barski gives an account of the affair in his memoirs, based largely on a diary that he kept at Bergen-Belsen: Józef Barski, *Przeżycia i wspomnienia z lat okupacji* (Wrocław, 1986), *passim*. Zuckerman, *Surplus*, 438–9; Wdowinski, *Not Saved*, 209–10.

5. Blady-Szwajger, *Nothing More*, 133.
6. AŻH 301/5034, 67.
7. AŻH 301/5034, 13.
8. Maria Kann, 'Na oczach świata' (wartime pamphlet), cited in Szarota, *Okupowanej*, 187.
9. Jan Ciechanowski, in R.F. Leslie, ed., *The History of Poland since 1863* (Cambridge: CUP, 1980), 217.
10. Szarota, *Okupowanej*, 541–4.
11. Jan Tomasz Gross, *Polish Society under German Occupation* (Princeton: Princeton University Press, 1979), 164–5.
12. Jan Tomasz Gross, *Revolution from Abroad* (Princeton: Princeton University Press, 1988), 116 *et passim*.
13. Kubar, *Double Identity*, 73–4.
14. AŻIH 301/5830.
15. Berman archive, BLHG 315.
16. Letter of denunciation signed 'Dr Rosenmann' and [illegible], Berman archive, LHG 315.
17. Ringelblum, *Relations*, 133–4.
18. See Bożena Szajnok, *Pogrom Żydów w kielcach* (Warszawa: Bellona, 1992). There is a theory, popular in Poland, that the pogrom was a provocation instigated by the authorities to distract attention from the obviously falsified referendum ratifying Communist rule that was then in progress. Whatever the merits of this theory, this is not the incitement referred to here, but rather the fact that individual militiamen seemed ready to believe in the story that the Jews had kidnapped a Polish child and helped disseminate it.
19. Adam Hempel, *Pogrobowcy klęski* (Warsawa: PWN, 1990), 233 *et passim*.
20. Zuckerman, *Surplus*, 370.
21. Marek Getter, 'Policja "granatowa" w Warszawie 1939–1944', in *Studia Warszawskie*, 7: *Warszawa lat wojny i okupacji*, t. II (Warszawa, 1972), 215–37.
22. Hempel, *Pogrobawcy*, 92.
23. Ibid., 125.
24. *Ludwiga Fischera*, 218.
25. Hempel, *Pogrobowcy*, 172–3.
26. Ibid., 177. Hempel refers to surviving police records from the right-bank suburb of Praga; the records for left-bank Warsaw were destroyed in the 1944 uprising. It is therefore not clear how representative these records are. It should be noted that Hempel is generally quite apologetic.
27. Cited in ibid., 175–6.
28. AŻIH 301/5539.
29. See the discussion of Leon Wanat's testimony in Chapter VI.
30. YVO3–824.
31. E.g. AŻIH 301/3073, 5543, 5222, 5717; Mandelkern, *Escape*, 91 *et passim*.
32. YVO3–824.
33. Meed, *Both Sides*, 91.
34. Ringelblum, *Relations*, 124.
35. YVO6/48.
36. AŻIH 301/5830.
37. Bauman, *Winter*, 122–9.
38. E.g. Meed, *Both Sides*, 93.

39. Meed, *Both Sides, passim.*
40. Zylberberg, *Warsaw Diary*, 115.
41. Meed, *Both Sides*, 182.
42. E.g. YVO33–1418; AŻIH 301/5537; Szac-Wajnkranc, *Przeminęło*, 19–20, 78; Chaskielewicz *Ukrywałem*, 56.
43. Ibid., 40, 49.
44. Mandelkern, *Escape*, 25, 104.
45. Ringelblum, *Stosunki polsko-żydowskie* (Warszawa: Czytelnik, 1988), 134.
46. HU 84(3). (Original in English.)
47. HU 222(10). (Original in English.)
48. Mandelkern, *Escape*, 110.
49. Engelking, *Holocaust*, 56.
50. Ringelblum, *Stosunki*, 135.
51. Landau, *Kronika*, 357.
52. Meed, *Both Sides*, 141, 143, 147.
53. Chaskielewicz, *Ukrywałem*, 42.
54. Zuckerman, *Surplus*, 374.
55. Blady-Szwajger, *Nothing More*, 130–1.
56. HU 3(84), 13.
57. Mandelkern, *Escape*, 114–16.
58. Nechama Tec, *Dry Tears* (New York: OUP, 1984), 122.
59. Mandelkern, *Escape*, 120.
60. Paweł Szapiro, ed., *Wojna Żydowsko-niemiecka* (London: Aneks, 1992).
61. *Walka*, an organ of the National Party, 28 July 1943; reprinted in two other papers, one of them a press digest published by the *delegatura*. In Szapiro, *Wojna*, 299–300.
62. *Walka*, 5 May 1943, in ibid., 128.
63. *Prawda Młodych*, April–May 1943, in ibid., 218.
64. Arad, *Documents*, 322–3.
65. Szapiro, *Wojna*, 436.
66. Tec, *Light*, chapter heading.
67. *Prawda Młodych*, in Szapiro, *Wojna*, 218–9.
68. Teresa Prekerowa, 'The "Just" and the "Passive"', in Polonsky, ed., *My Brother's Keeper*, 75.
69. AŻIH 301/5882.
70. Peleg-Mariańska and Peleg, *Witnesses*, 38–9.
71. Borwicz, *Vies interdites*, 240.

Chapter 5

1. Polonsky, *My Brother's Keeper*, 213–15.
2. *Biuletyn Głownej Komisji Badania Zbrodni Niemieckich w Polsce*, 1 (1946), 264–5.
3. For example, Ludwig Fischer estimated civilian losses at 'at least 180,000 and probably over 200,000' (*Raporty Ludwiga Fischera*, 837).
4. The General Commission for the Investigation of Hitlerite War Crimes in Poland gives the following figures for Pruszków alone: 650,000 people passed through the camp, 550,000 from Warsaw and 100,000 from nearby towns. Of this number, 400,000 were deported to other parts of the General Government or to concentration camps, 150,000 to the Reich for forced labour, and 100,000 were freed. (*Obozy hitlerowskie na ziemiach polskich*, 406–7.)
5. *Raporty Ludwiga Fischera*, 831 (editor's note).
6. See, for example, the deposition of Jakoba Blidsztein (Danuta Dąbrowska) (AŻIH 301/5719), who lived in the co-operative (WSM – *Warszawska Spółdzielnia Mieszkaniowa*) before the war.

She was allocated a room there, together with her mother and aunt, by Witold Rogala, a member of the WSM governing council. WSM also helped this family escape from the ghetto at an early stage. Her mother and aunt were later hidden by WSM resident Julia Imach. Later, all three received Aryan documents at no cost, arranged by friends at WSM, mainly the pae-diatrician Dr Alexander Landy, whose sister also later provided Blidsztein with a *melina*. She and other members of the Landy family, among them the well-known Żegota activists Dr Irena Kanabus (Dr Landy's niece) and her husband, Dr Felix Kanabus, were very actively involved in rescuing Jews. Blidsztein writes that WSM was 'swarming' (*roiło się*) with Jews in hiding, and adds the names of several other activists involved in this effort.

7. 'Antek' Zuckerman writes of Żoliborz: 'How many Jews were there? We know of thou-sands. Zolibórz [*sic*] was a neighborhood of laborers and working intelligentsia, where the PPS, the Communists and the Democrats were very influential. Naturally it was more com-fortable for a Jew to hide there than in other parts of the city' (Zuckerman, *Surplus*, 546). On the other hand, Żoliborz elected an ONR city councillor in 1938.

8. Zuckerman, *Surplus*, 521.

9. Chaskielewicz, *Ukrywałem*, 71.

10. YVO33-1418, 87.

11. Marian Berland, *Dni długie jak wieki* (Warszawa: Niezleżna Oficyna Wydawnicza, 1992), 454.

12. Borzykowski, *Tsvishn*, 243.

13. AŻIH 301/5525.

14. Chaskielewicz, *Ukrywałem*, 71–2.

15. Zuckerman, *Surplus*, 561.

16. Cywia Lubetkin, *Zagłada i powstanie* (Warszawa: Książka i Wiedza, 1999), 150.

17. Cited in Michał Cichy, 'Polacy – Żydzi: Czarne Karty Powstania', *Gazeta Wyborcza* (29–30 January 1994) 13–16.

18. Relation of Efraim Krasucki, AŻIH 301/1539.

19. Prekerowa, 'Żydzi w Powstaniu Warszawskim', in *Powstanie Warszawskie* (Warszawa: Instytut Historyczny PAN (1995)89.

20. Meed, *Both Sides*, 254.

21. Prof. Zbigniew Ryszard Grabowski, 'Strzelał do mnie sierżant AK', in *Gazeta Wyborcza*, 12–13 February 1994, 10.

22. Ibid.

23. Ibid., 10–11.

24. Ibid., 11. In *Ukrywałem*, Chaskielewicz expresses a slightly different opinion: 'the war years taught me that a significant number of Poles, degraded by the Germans, on their part displayed contempt for the Jews, thinking themselves better.' Probably both factors were operative.

25. Prekerowa, 'Żydzi', 91.

26. Berman Archive, LHG 315. Bracketed details from Cichy, 'Polacy', 15, after Turkow and Bursztyn.

27. Among the other sources are the memoirs of Jonas Turkow, *In kamf far leben* (Buenos Aires: Tsentral. Farband fun Poilishe Yidn, 1949), the relation of Henryk Bursztyn (AŻIH 301/1106), and the prosecutorial records uncovered by Cichy (AAN 203/X–32, AWIH III/43/72), cited in Cichy, 'Polacy'. Turkow's account is secondhand and erroneous in some details, for example, Ostoja's name is given as 'Okrzeja'. Bursztyn was an eyewit-ness to events in the bunker: hidden in its deeper recesses, he escaped detection. Three other residents of the bunker were not present at the time, and observed the events over the courtyard wall. These were Avram Bursztyn, Henryk Herszbajn and Josek Tenenbaum. Samuel Willenberg (*Treblinka*) gives another secondhand account, based on conversations with them. He also claims to have seen the piled-up bodies in the cellar.

It should be noted that the men from Prosta 4 were shot on the grounds of Twarda 30, with the result that some authors have assumed that these were two separate massacres and have counted the victims twice. Cichy maintains that both Shmuel Krakowski and Martin Gilbert have exaggerated the number of victims for this reason (Cichy, 'Polacy', 16).

28. Willenberg, *Treblinka*, 186.
29. AAN 203/X-32 k. 64–5, cited in Cichy, 'Polacy', 15.
30. E.g. Turkow, Willenberg and Henryk Bursztyn. Bolesław Chrobry (the Valiant, r. 992–1025) was the first crowned king of Poland. In the pre-war period, extreme nationalists wore a miniature of Chrobry's sword as a lapel pin, symbolic of smiting the nation's enemies. The accusations against the Chrobry II battalion seem unsubstantiated by the evidence, and are perhaps the result of this pre-war association of Chrobry's name with right-wing causes.
31. Wacław Zagorski, *Wicher wolności: Dziennik powstańca*, cited in Cichy, 'Polacy', 15–16.
32. Cited in ibid., 16.
33. AWIH III/43/72 t. 4, k. 23, cited in Leszek Żebrowski, *Paszkwil wyborczej* (Warszawa: Burchard Edition, 1995, 48–9. Żebrowski's book is largely a scurrilous, *ad hominem* attack on Cichy and the *Gazeta Wyborcza*, with an apologetic and poorly argued defence of the AK and NSZ, but it does have the virtue of quoting certain documents at greater length than Cichy does.
34. E.g. Bursztyn, AŻIH 301/1106.
35. Cited in Cichy, 'Polacy', 16.
36. YV O33–1157, cited in Cichy, 'Polacy', 16.
37. Ibid., 16.
38. AŻIH 301/470, cited in ibid., 15.
39. Rotem, *Memoirs*, 114.
40. Berman Archive, LHG 315.
41. Meed, *Both Sides*, 257.
42. Cited in Prekerowa, 'Żydzi', 91.
43. Zuckerman, *Surplus*, 529.
44. Willenberg, Treblinka, 182–3; Prekerowa, 'Żydzi', 86; Cichy, 'Polacy', 14. In the slang of the day, German agents who were supposed to frequent the rooftops, acting as lookouts or snipers, were called 'pigeon-fanciers' (*gołębiarze*).
45. Charles Goldstein, *The Bunker* (Philadelphia: Jewish Publication Society of America, 1970), 105–7.
46. Prekerowa, 'Żydzi', 90.
47. AŻIH 301/470, cited in Cichy, 'Polacy', 15.
48. Zuckerman, *Surplus*, 530.
49. Goldstein, *Bunker*, 101.
50. Cited in Prekerowa, 'Żydzi', 90.
51. YVO33-1418.
52. Chaskielewicz, *Ukrywałem*, 71.
53. Rotem, *Memoirs*, 118.
54. Prekerowa, 'Żydzi', 86.
55. *Archiwum Wojskowego Instytutu Historycznego* (AWIH III/43/72 t.III k.128), cited in Cichy, 'Polacy', 14; according to Cichy, probably from AK counterintelligence.
56. Rotem, *Memoirs*, 123–4.
57. Zuckerman, *Surplus*, 540.
58. Prekerowa, 'Żydzi', 87.
59. AWIH III/40/12, k. 25. Cited in Cichy, 'Polacy', 13.
60. Ibid.
61. Zuckerman, *Surplus*, 533 .

62. 'Antek' visited a group of Hashomer Hatzair fighters in Okęcie, a district that was quickly mastered by the Germans. He believes they all perished (ibid., 530). Individual ŻOB members participated in AK and PAL units. There were various organized ŻOB groups fighting as partisans near Warsaw, and another in the Ursus tractor factory, but these areas were not encompassed by the uprising.

63. Ibid., 534.

64. Ibid., 530.

65. Ibid., 544.

66. Ibid., 531.

67. B. Temkin-Bermanowa, 'Akcja pomocy Żydom w okresie okupacji hitlerowskiej,' *BŻIH*, 22(1957), 71.

68. Prekerowa, 'Żydzi', 86.

69. Gorodecka, *Hana*, 74.

70. C. Goldstein, *Bunker*, 124.

71. AAN 202/XX-24 k. 152, cited in Cichy, 'Polacy', 13–14.

72. Gorodecka, *Hana*, 73.

73. Meed, *Both Sides*, 256–7.

74. YVO33-1418, 88.

75. Bauman, *Winter*, 159–62.

76. Chaskielewicz, *Ukrywałem*, 72–3.

77. Ibid., 73

78. An account of this dramatic operation from the Polish side can be found in Stanisław Śwital, 'Siedmioro z ulicy Promyka', *ŻIH* 65–6(1968), 207–10, and from the Jewish side in Zuckerman, *Surplus*, 553–5, and Borzykowski, *Tsvishn*, 199–215, Alina Margolis-Edelman, *Elementarza,* 129–34; and Lubetkin, *Zagłada*, 151–2.

79. Chaskielewicz, *Ukrywałem*, 141.

80. Temkin-Bermanowa, 'Akcja', 82.

81. Zuckerman, *Surplus*, 548.

82. Chaskielewicz, *Ukrywałem*, 79.

83. The best known of these was the bunker (New York, 1961) that served the Bundist leader, Bernard Goldstein ('Comrade Bernard'), and also David Guzik of the Joint and several other prominent Jews. It is described in Goldstein's memoir, *Five Years in the Warsaw Ghetto*, and also by another of its inmates, one of the few surviving ŻZW fighters, Joseph Greenblatt (YVO33-1313). Charles Goldstein, *Bunker*, describes a somewhat different kind of bunker, connected to the sewers and prepared well in advance. Chaskielewicz hid in a bunker with a group of chance-met Jews (Chaskielewicz, *Ukrywałem,*, 79–93), as did Dawid Fogelman ('Pamiętnik pisany w bunkrze', *BŻIH* 52(1964), 107–41).

84. AŻIH 301/5745.

85. Interview with author.

86. GK, *Obozy hitlerowskie*, 406–7.

87. Bauman, *Winter*, 166.

88. AŻIH 301/5523.

89. Bauman, *Winter*, 168.

90. YVO33-1510 (anon.).

91. Isaiah Trunk, *Jewish Responses to Nazi Persecution*, (New York: Stein and Day, 1979), 138. (Testimony no. 16)

92. Chaskielewicz, *Ukrywałem*, 129, 131. The Polish word *trefny* in this sense comes from the Hebrew טרף.

93. Bauman, *Winter*, 180.

94. Ireneusz Krzemiński, *Czy Polacy są asntysemitami?* Warszawa: Oficyna Naukowa, 1996), 33.

The scale of 'traditional antisemitism' consisted of two questions, one asking whether the Jews were responsible for the death of Christ, the other, whether they had brought their own suffering down upon themselves. Regrettably, we are not told the raw results: the analyst, Helena Datner-Śpiewak, tells us only that 41 per cent of respondents expressed agreement with at least one of these propositions and that 11 per cent agreed with both (p. 61). An additional 37 per cent gave at least one 'undecided' answer, a response that Datner-Śpiewak interprets as '*de facto* pro-Jewish' (p. 33).

Both doctrines were repudiated by the Catholic church in the encyclical *Nostrae Aetate*, published in 1965.

95. AŻIH 301/5524. Memoirs 5524 and 5525 are by the same person, identified by the archivist as 'C., name illegible'. 5525 expands on the period of the Warsaw Uprising.
96. AŻIH 301/5526.
97. YVO33-644.
98. AŻIH 301/5511.
99. AŻIH 301/5509.

Chapter 6

1. Chaskielewicz, *Ukrywałem*, 72.
2. Gunnar S. Paulsson, 'The Demography of Jews Hiding in Warsaw, 1943–1945', *Polin* 13 (2000), 78–103. Where there are discrepancies between that article and this book, the book should be taken as authoritative.
3. Teresa Prekerowa, 'Komórka'.
4. AAN 30/III t. 5, 18–46.
5. Adolf Berman, 'Hayehudim', 685–731. Additional sources: 'Rozwój działalności Ż.K.N. po stronie aryjskiej', YVO33-238; Zuckerman, *Surplus*; Simcha Rotem, *Wspomnienia bojowca ŻOB* (Warszawa: Wydawnictwo Naukowe PWN, 1993); Gutman, *Jews of Warsaw*.
6. Berman claimed (ibid.), and later authors have repeated, e.g. Joseph Kermish, 'The Activities of the Council for Aid to Jews ("Żegota") in occupied Poland', in Yisrael Gutman and Efraim Zuroff, eds, *Rescue Attempts during the Holocaust: Proceedings of the Second Yad Vashem International Conference* (Jerusalem: Yad Vashem, 1977) pp. 367–96, here p. 382), that FOP withdrew from Żegota because an increased atmosphere of antisemitism made involvement with Jewish affairs unpopular. There is nothing to support this assertion, however. Kossak-Szczucka personally withdrew when Żegota was formed because she objected to its 'political' character: she wanted the aid effort to be a pure act of Christian charity not involving the Jews, who, she felt, had their own organizations. She therefore transferred her activity to SOS. FOP continued to be represented on the board of Żegota by Witold Bieńkowski and Władysław Bartoszewski. Berman further takes credit for creating the children's branch of Żegota, but, as is clear from the surviving protocols of Żegota, the initiative for this came from SOS.
7. Paulsson, 'Demography', 87–8.
8. In his report to the *Delegatura* on 20 March, 1944 (BLHG 313), Berman claimed that the organization had fifty cells, while in his report 'Rozwój działalnosści Ż.K.N. po stronie aryjskiej' (YVO33-238) on 24 May he claims a hundred cells.
9. Daniel Kaftor (David Guzik) for the 'Joint'; Szymon Gottesmann for the General Zionists (in Kraków); Avram Warman for Hashomer Hatzair (in Lwów); and a number of others who were unable to participate actively in the ŻKN's work activities because they were forced to hide 'under the surface', but who took part in it internally. These included Tsivia Lubetkin, Józef Zak, Stefan Grajek, Lejzer Lewin, Pola Elster, Dr Emmanuel Ringelblum and Hersch Berlinski (Berman, Hayehudim, 711).

10. Basia or Batya Berman, Symcha Rathajzer (Simcha Rotem — 'Kazik'), Bela Elster, Klima Fuswerk, Anna Gotesman, Irena Gelblum, Helena Merenholc, Dr Lota Wegmajster, Jakub Roth, Joseph Zysman, Dr Nina Asserodobraj, Anatol Matywiecki, Halina Gertner, Pola Bugajska, Riva Moszkowicz, Zofia Kimelman, Joanna Tykocińska, Jakub Wiernik, Emilka Kossower and the mother of Mark Folman (YV-E/238).

11. Author's interview with Helena Merenholc, 8 June 1995.

12. For example, Yisrael Gutman and Shmuel Krakowski describe this and related estimates as 'greatly exaggerated' (*Unequal Victims: Poles and Jews during World War II* (New York: Holocaust library, 1986), 266). Gutman (in conversation with the author) has theorized that Berman exaggerated the Committee's activities in reports to London so as to justify requests for increased funds. After the war, he thinks, Berman was too embarrassed to admit his deceit, so that these exaggerated estimates 'just stuck'.

13. Gutman and Krakowski, *Unequal Victims*, 266.

14. Private letter to the author, undated, 1994.

15. Philip Friedman, 'The Extermination of the Polish Jews', in Ada June Friedman, ed., *Roads to Extinction*, 235–6.

16. Gutman, *Jews of Warsaw*, 265.

17. Shmuel Krakowski, 'Avidot Yehudei Polin b'Shoah', *Studies of the Holocaust Period*, vol. II (Tel Aviv: Hakibutz Hame Uchad Publishing House, 1981), 234.

18. Ibid., 235.

19. Fein, *Accounting*, 261

20. CKŻP (*Centralny Komitet Żydów w Polsce*) was formed in Lublin in July 1944 and set up branches in the major Polish cities as they were liberated. It carried out relief work and, through its subsidiary organization CKŻH (*Centralny Komitet Żydowski Historyczny* – Central Jewish Historical Committee), began gathering historical materials and preparing documentation for the prosecution of war criminals. Among other things, CKŻP provided a registration service to aid Jews in locating surviving relatives. The CKŻP register was published in May 1945, when it contained some 58,000 names, and again in December, when the number had grown to about 80,000.

21. Fein, *Accounting*.

22. The pre-war Jewish population of Warsaw was about 360,000; this was diminished by deaths in the 1939 campaign and flight to the Soviet zone, so that there were probably not more than 330,000 native Warsaw Jews in the ghetto when it was closed. 490,000 Jews passed through the Warsaw ghetto in all (see Berenstein and Rutkowski, 'Liczba ludności, 73–105. Thus there were 160,000 non-natives, 33 per cent of the total. The first wave of non-natives consisted of people who fled to Warsaw from the Incorporated Territories, especially Łódź, in 1939–40. Subsequently Jews from outlying communities were forced to enter the ghetto, and once 'deportation to the East' got under way, also German and Czech Jews.

23. Lest readers suspect that the methodology was at fault, it should be explained. The published register has some idiosyncrasies, for example, the last part of the sections for the letters P and S are missing; names falling into these ranges were eliminated from the study. All the many possible spelling variations were taken into account; for example Ajzenman, Eisenmann, Ejsenman; Neu, Ney and Noj; Cymerman and Zimmerman, and so forth. Names in the register are not always in strict alphabetical order, and a conscientious search was carried out whenever a surname did not appear in the expected place. Where a person was known by several names (real and Aryan names, for example, or maiden and married names), all were searched for. Cases where a person might have given a different first name on different occasions – for example, Bogusław for Boruch or Janek for Jankiel – were noted; if all such possible matches were treated as real, then the number of matches in the control study would increase to about 55 per cent, still well below expectations (and in view

of the large number of false positives, certainly too high). There remain the possibilities that memorists sometimes give names incorrectly or are mistaken in stating that someone has survived, but I doubt that such problems could account for all of the remaining difference.

24. List 1: About Jews Liberated from German Concentration Camps Arrived in Sweden in 1945 (Stockholm: WJC Relief and Rehabilitation Dept., 1946).

25. Liste fun di lebngeblibene Warszewer Jidn in der US Zone in Dajczland ([no city of publication], Centrale fun di Warszewere Landsmanszaftn in der US Zone in Dajczland, 1948).

26. National Registry of Jewish Holocaust Survivors (Washington: American Gathering of Holocaust Survivors and U.S. Holocaust Museum, 1993); Apolonia Umińska et al., eds, Inwentarz zbioru "Pamiétniki Żydów"; Michał Grynberg, Pamiętniki.

27. There are more than 50,000 entries in the 1993 edition of the National Registry, but many are aliases or duplicates.

28. Ringelblum, Kronika, 419.

29. Ringelblum, Stosunki, 81.

30. Hirshaut, Jewish Martyrs, 36–40.

31. The statement that the Hotel Polski affair was unique to Warsaw requires some clarification. The affair was part of a two-pronged German programme, originating in the Foreign office, called the Heimschaffungsaktion (Repatration Action) and the Austauschaktion (Exchange Action). The purpose of the first was to 'repatriate' Jews to neutral countries that would accept them (Spain, for example, took in a number of Sephardic Greek Jews because of their 'historic' connection with Spain), and the second aimed to exchange Jewish citizens of states with which Germany was at war for interned German civilians. The two 'actions' were pursued across Europe between 1942 and 1944, but never in quite the same way as in Warsaw. Elsewhere there were still people living openly as Jews, either in transit camps, or enjoying exemptions through mixed marriages or for other reasons, and it was these people who were targeted. They were mainly well-to-do people from whom – or on whose behalf – the Nazis hoped to extort ransom payments and whom they had therefore some interest in preserving. Those who volunteered for these schemes – including the Hotel Polski Jews – were interned either in the 'Exchange Camp' (Austauschlager) at Bergen-Belsen (AL Bergen-Belsen), or in one of the 'Civil Internment Camps' (Zivilinternierungslager) at Biberach, Libenau, Tittmoning-Laufen, Vittel or Wurzach. The Zivilinternierungslager were under the jurisdiction of the Wehrmacht rather than the SS, and were regularly inspected by the International Red Cross: the conditions in these camps were therefore quite good. AL Bergen-Belsen was under SS control, but it was kept separate from the notorious concentration camp of the same name (KL Bergen-Belsen). Conditions in the AL were also quite good, or at any rate not life-threatening, until the last few weeks of the war. The great majority of the internees in all these camps survived, except for those whose documents the issuing states refused to honour and who were therefore sent to Auschwitz for extermination. This inlcuded nearly all the Hotel Polski Jews, whose documents were bogus: only the 200-odd Jews on the 'Palestine List' were spared. Most Western Jews, on the other hand, had obtained quite legal documents, in their own names, which were honoured. Some Western Jews did perish, however. The second-largest group of victims were from the Netherlands: about 2,000 Dutch Jews were killed, of the 8,000–10,000 who were interned at Bergen-Belsen. But only a small fraction had been in hiding. (See Alexandra-Eileen Wenck, Zwischen Menschenhandel und 'Endlösung': Das Konzentrationslager Bergen-Belsen (Paderborn: Verlag Ferdinand Schöningh, 2000).

32. Various estimates are cited by Presser, Ashes, 383. The one used here is the most favourable to the Dutch, for which Presser cites 'K.P.L. Berkley op. cit. 94', but the full citation for Berkley is never given. Bob Moore in Victims cites an estimate of 16,000–17,000 survivors out of 24,000–25,000 (64–71 per cent), but describes it as 'problematical' (See Introduction, note 24).

33. Leni Yahil, *The Rescue of Danish Jewry* (Philadelphia: 1969), 269. See also Gunnar S. Paulsson, 'The Bridge over the Øresund: The Histiography on the Expulsion of the Jews from Nazi-Occupied Denmark', *Journal of Contemporary History* 30 (1995), 431–64.
34. Thus, Emmanuel Ringelblum writes: 'In Western Europe, especially in Holland, the Aryan population has hidden Jews on a mass scale', and later that 'Poland has not taken an equal place alongside the Western European countries in rescuing Jews,' (Ringelblum, *Relations*, 246–7).

Summary and Conclusions

1. Complete figures are surprisingly hard to find. In 1943, 7,230 Jews arrived from Denmark, joining about 800 Norwegian Jews who had fled a year earlier and perhaps 1,000 from Poland and the Baltic States who had come in 1939–40. Another 1,000 Jews arrived from Finland in the final year of the war, but they cannot really be classified as refugees from Nazism; another 10,000–11,000 came after March 1945, when the war was effectively over. (Sources: Paul Levine, *From Indifference to Activism*, 243; Marrus, *The Unwanted*, 271–2; Sune Persson, 'Folke Bernadotte and the White Buses', in David Cesarani and Paul Levine, eds, *Bystanders to the Holocaust: A re-evaluation* (London: Frank Cass, 2002), 243–4.
2. Diary of Chaim Kaplan, entry for 4 October 1940 (p. 204).
3. Thus, Father Henryk Jankowski of Gdańsk, Lech Wałęsa's parish priest, was barred from preaching for a year because of his antisemitic sermons; Father Edward Orłowski, the parish priest in Jedwabne, after saying that there was no problem of antisemitism in the town, told reporter Anna Bikont an idiotic story about a Jewish industrialist, supposedly known to Orłowski, who sold his factory to the Nazis at a good profit and emigrated to New York while his people were being killed. Thrust into prominence by the Jedwabne 'affair', Orłowski has said more such things. Jankowski and Orłowski became prominent by chance, and are presumably fairly typical of the parish clergy. Even senior members of the Polish church hierarchy have recently made offensive remarks: for example, Bishop Stefanek of Łomża, in whose parish Jedwabne lies, denounced publicity on the 1941 massacre in Jedwabne as a 'provocation', motivated by a desire to extort money from Poles. The Primate of Poland, Cardinal Glemp, initially declared that the massacre was a 'local tragedy' of no interest to the church, and later retorted that 'history and recollections also note Jews destroying their own'. He added that 'Poles also suffered injuries, for example they were killed by the Nazis for helping Jews or suffered as a result of the evil dealt out by Jews, for example when Communism was being introduced into Poland. I expect that the Jewish side will carry out an accounting of its conscience and will come around to apologizing to Poles for these crimes.' A similar response was offered by Bishop (later Cardinal) Wyszyński in 1946, when a Jewish group asked him to condemn the Kielce pogrom.

    The Polish Catholic church is of course not monolithic; a group of liberal clerics, particularly those connected with the liberal Catholic journals *Więź* and *Tygodnik Powszechny*, have worked diligently to change attitudes. Archbishops Henryk Muszyński and Józef Życiński, bishops Stanisław Gądecki, Marian Gołębiewski, and Tadeusz Pieronek, and Fathers Michał Czajkowski and Stanisław Musiał particularly deserve recognition. The highest-ranking Polish Catholic of them all, Pope John Paul II, has never expressed antisemitic ideas and, despite a few controversial actions, has generally been a positive force in Catholic–Jewish relations.
4. Jan T. Gross, *Neighbors*.
5. Ireneusz Krzemiński, ed., *Czy Polacy są antysemitami?* (Warszawa: Oficyna Naukowa, 1996), 33, 271.

Bibliography

This bibliography does not pretend to completeness, but lists all the sources I have cited and others that I have found useful in my research.

A. Manuscript Sources

Archiwum Akt Nowych, Warsaw
    AAN 30/III t. 5   List of persons receiving monetary assistance from the Bund.

Beit Lohamei ha-Getaot, Israel: the Berman archive
    BLHG301   Letters to Dr Berman from 'Antek' Zuckerman
        308   Letters to Dr and Mrs Berman from Emmanuel Ringelblum, his wife Józia and Marek Passenstein
        309   Copies of reports from 'Wacław' (Henryk Wolinski) to the Delegatura. Rough notes and typed reports.
        310   Letters from ŻKN and Bund to the Delegate. Żegota reports.
        313   Minutes of meetings of the Presidium of Żegota with the Delegate, Jan Jankowski. Pamphlets and leaflets.
        315   Files on blackmailers: accusatory letters, lists of accused persons, notices of sentences carried out against blackmailers clipped from the underground press.
        324   Two ghetto memoirs by Ber Warm.
        328   Two memoirs from the ghetto and Pawiak prison by Dr Leon Polisiuk.
        331   Relations by members of the Polish underground: Capt. Grom-Potyka of the Socialist underground organization PAL about action at the ghetto walls during the uprising; testimony concerning the rescue of Jews by Father Kazimierz Ptaszek.
        357   Records of persons receiving money from ŻKN: lists of names with amounts received and other information; receipts; partial accounts; copies of letters asking for help; lists of names classified by profession.
        358   Continuation of BLHG 357.
        592   Two draft chapters of a book by Berman about the Aryan side (Yiddish, 10pp).

Hebrew University, Institute of Contemporary Jewry, Jerusalem
   Oral History division
   HU 84(3), 222(10)

Manuscripts in author's possession
   Memoirs of Jacob Celemenski, *Elegy to my People* (English translation of *Mitn farshnitenem folk*), courtesy of Prof. Kenneth Waltzer.
   Memoirs of Maria Ejzen, courtesy of Yvonne Bogorya.
   Memoirs of Daniel Falkner, courtesy of Mr Falkner.
   Memoirs of Florian Mayevski, courtesy of Alex Keller.
   Memoirs of A. P.
   Memoirs of Ruth Skorecka, courtesy of Prof. Lawrence Powell.

Underground Poland Study Trust, London
   B.I   Testimonies about Polish–Jewish affairs.
   B.II   Reports. Jewish affairs.
   MSW   t. 2a, postal bundle 16/43, sent to Poland September 1943
          6   Despatches concerning the Warsaw Ghetto Uprising
          16, 17, 27 Letters of Ignacy Szwarcbart to ŻKN.
          31   Materials for ŻKN.
          41a, 41c   Letters from Szwarcbart to ŻKN covering transmission of $20,000 from American Jewish Committee and other funds, with instructions for disbursement.
          t. 2b, postal bundle 17/43, sent to Poland 6 October 1943
          21   Letter from 'Luc' to Bund.
          30   Szwarcbart to ŻKN. Coded names of Jews to whom money is to be paid; proposal to send nineteen Jewish activists (including Berman and Ringelblum) to Hungary.
          t. 3–4,   postal bundle 20/44 sent 18 February 1944.
          3   Letters of Ignacy Szwarcbart and 'Arieh' to ŻKN.
          87, 100   Letters of Emmanuel Scherer to Leon Feiner.
          91, 92   Letters of 'Anzelm' to ŻKN.
          t. 5–6,   postal bundle 21/44 sent April 1944.
          11, 16   Letter from Emmanuel Scherer to Leon Feiner.
          t. 46   (Transmission from Poland)
          9   Bund report for October 1942–November 1943, acknowledging receipt of $58,000 from Delegatura.
                    ŻKN report for 1 November 1943 to 20 May 1944, acknowledging receipt of $100,000 from JDC, $20,000 from WJC and other funds.
          t. 50–II (Transmission to Poland, July–August 1944).
          187   From ORKAN to Delegatura, authorizing disbursement of $50,000 each to Bund and ŻKN from JDC, $50,000 to RPŻ from Government-in-Exile, $50,000 from Jewish Agency to ŻKN.
   M.V   Maps of Warsaw.

Yad Vashem, Jerusalem
   Archives:
   YV–M13   Żegota (Warsaw).
   YV–O3   Testimonies.
   YV–O17   YIVO testimonies, files O17/17, 19, 38, 44.

YV–O33   Memoirs and Diaries. Files YV–O33/50, 224, 238, 239, 258, 259, 285, 729, 769, 949, 959, 990, 1012, 1034, 1072, 1138, 1182, 1280, 1466, 1491, 1510, 1521, 1524, 1533, 1551, 1566, 1572, JM/2856.

YV–O51   Nazi documents.
(8) Files of Ludwig, Leist, October 1940–March 1941; Correspondence of Heinz Auerswald, 1941–42

YV–O62   Memoirs collected by Michał Borwicz; Files O62/379, 367, 452, 469, 545, 547.

Department of the Righteous:
YV–RG 16   Wojcik, Władysław.
YV–RG 170   Żabiński, Jan and wife Antonina.
YV–RG 208   Jarmiołkowski, Jan.
YV–RG 511   Woliński, Henryk.
YV–RG 922   Kosek, Edmund, and family.
YV–RG 1136   Zelwerowicz, Aleksander, and wife Helena.
YV–RG 1222   Walter, Mada and sons Edmond and Ryszard.
YV–RG 1265   Abramowicz, Józef.
YV–RG 1608   Wróblewski, Henryk.
YV–RG 2377   Dunin-Wąsowicz, Krzysztof, Prof., and mother Janina.
YV–RG 2619   Piętak, Zygmunt.
YV–RG 2756   Krasna, Maria, and son Jan Krasny.
YV–RG 2773   Kwiatkowska-Biernacka, Wanda, and family.
YV–RG 3217   Komorowska, Maria, and sister Sofia Śląska.
YV–RG 3429   Chądzyński, Edward, and sister Janina Zaremba.
YV–RG 3624   Pietrów, Stefania, and brother Aleksander.
YV–RG 3888   Kartaszwew, Jakub, and wife Anna.
YV–RG 4027   Tęgi, Stanisław, and wife Irena-Kazimiera.
YV–RG 4689   Antoni Stefan Koper.
YV–RG 5246   Stefania Matraszek.
YV–RG 5388   Woźniak, Stanisław.
YV–RG 5502   Renata and Izabella Kossobudzka.
YV–RG 5799   Klewicka, Stanisława, and son Leszek Klewicki.

Żydowski Instytut Historyczny, Warsaw
AŻIH 301, Relations.
AŻIH 302, Memoirs.

B. Published Sources

Abbreviations:
BŻIH   Biuletyn Żydowskiego Instytutu Historycznego w Polsce.
CKŻH   Centralny Komitet Żydowski Historyczny.
GK   Główna Komisja Badania Zbrodni [(Niemeckich) (Hitlerowskich) w Polsce] [Przeciwko Narodowi Polskiemu]
IFiS   Instytut Filozofii i Socjologji.
IH   Instytut Historyczny
PAN   Polska Akademia Naukowa.
PIW   Państwowy Instytut Wydawniczy.

PWN   Polskie Wydawnictwo Naukowe.
YVS   Yad Vashem Studies.

1. Primary Sources

Adler, Stanislaw, *In the Warsaw Ghetto 1940–1943: An Account of a Witness* (Jerusalem: Yad Vashem, 1982).

Arad, Yitzhak *et al.*, eds, *Documents on the Holocaust* (Jerusalem: Yad Vashem, 1981).

Ajzensztajn, Betti, and Michał Borwicz, eds, *Ruch podziemny w gettach i obozach: materiały i dokumenty* (Warszawa: CKŻH, 1946).

Archiwum Ringelbluma: Konspiracyjne Archiwum Getta Warsawskiego, vol 1: *Listy o zagładzie* ed. by Ruta Sakowska (Warszawa: Wydawnictwo Naukowe PWN, 1997).

Arczyński, T., T. Rek, W. Bieńkowski, S. Sendlak, E. Wąsowicz, J. Żabiński, A. Staśkowa, Z. Myczko, 'Rada Pomocy Żydom w Polsce (Żegota): Wspomnienia centralnych i terenowych działaczy RPŻ', *BŻIH* 65–66 (1968), 173–205.

Barski, Józef, *Przeżycia i wspomnienia z lat okupacji* (Wrocław, 1986).

Bauman, Janina, *Winter in the Morning* (New York: Free Press, 1986).

Berland, Marian, *Dni długie jak wieki* (Warszawa: Niezależna Oficyna Wydawnicza, 1992).

Berman, Adolf, *Bim'kom Asher Ya'ad li ha-Goral: Am Yehudi Varsha, 1939–1942* (Beit Lohamei Hagetaot, 1977).

Bermanowa, Basia, ' "Pierwsza Irena", wspomnienia o Irenie Sawickiej', *Przełom* 15.10(1947), 10.

Bermanowie, Adolf and Barbara, 'Zagłada getta w Warszawie (szkic kronikarski)', *BŻIH* 1963, 138–58.

Birenbaum, Halina, *Hope Is the Last to Die: A Personal Documentation of Nazi Terror* (New York: Twayne Publishers, 1971).

Birenbaum, Halina, *Nadzieja umiera ostatnia* (Warszawa, 1967).

Birnbaum, Irena, *non omnis moriar: pamiętnik z getta warszawskiego* (Warszawa: Czytelnik, 1982).

Blady-Szwajger, Adina, *I Remember Nothing More: the Warsaw Children's Hospital and the Jewish Resistance* (New York: Pantheon, 1991).

Borkowicz, Maryla, Krzysztof Dunin-Wąsowicz and Teresa Kowalska, eds, *Raporty Ludwika Fischera Gubernatora dystryktu warszawskiego, 1939–1944* (Warszawa: Książka i Wiedza, 1987).

Borzykowski, Tuvia, *Tsvishn falndike vent* (Beit Lohamei ha-Getaot, 1976).

Brandys, Kazimierz, *Miasto niepokonane* (Warszawa: Państwowy Instytut Wydawniczy, 1960).

Chaskielewicz, Stefan, *Ukrywałem sih w Warszawie: Styczeń 1943 styczeń 1945* (Kraków: ZNAK, 1988).

Cukierman, Icchak (Antek), 'Dzielna 34', *BŻIH* 161(1992), 67–78.

Czapska, Maria, *Gwiazda Dawida: Dzieje jednej rodziny* (London: Oficyna Poetów i Malarzy, 1975).

Czerniaków, Adam, *Adama Czerniakowa dziennik getta warszawskiego 6.IX.1939–23.VII.1942* (Warszawa: PWN, 1983).

David, Janina, *A Square of Sky and A Touch of Earth: A Wartime Childhood in Poland* (Harmondsworth: Penguin, 1966).

Dawidowicz, Lucy, ed., *A Holocaust Reader* (New York: Behrman House, 1976).

Donat, Alexander, *The Holocaust Kingdom: A Memoir* (New York: Holt, Rinehart & Winston, 1965).

Dunin-Wąsowicz, Janina, 'Wspomnienia o akcji pomocy łydom podczas okupacji hitlerowskiej w Polsce', *BŻIH* 45–46 (1963).

—, *Wspomnienia* (Warszawa: Lampa i Iskra Boża, 1995).

Dzieci żydowskie oskarżają (Warszawa: Fundacja 'Szalom', 1993).

Edelman, Marek, *Getto walczy* (Warszawa: CK Bundu, 1948, 2nd edn).

—, *The Ghetto Fights: Warsaw 1941–43* (London: Bookmarks, 1970).

Eisner, Jack, *The Survivor* (New York: Morrow, 1980).

Fater, Czesława, *Aniołowie bez skrzydeł* (Warszawa: PIW, 1995).

Fisher, Josey G., *The Persistence of Youth: Oral Testimonies of the Holocaust* (Westport: Greenwood, 1991).

Fogelman, Dawid, 'Pamie,tnik pisany w bunkrze', *BZ IH* 52 (1964).

Fortunoff Video Archive for Holocaust Testimonies, *Guide to the Yale University Library Holocaust Video Testimonies*, vol. 1 (New York: Yale University Press, 1990)

Games, Sonia, *Escape into Darkness* (New York: Xlibris, 2002).

Gładysz, Antoni, *Piekło na ziemi: Wspomnienia z lat 1939–1945* (Doylstown, PA, 1972)

Goetzel-Leviathan, Sophie, *The War from Within* (Berkeley: Judah L. Magnes Museum, 1987).

Goldstein, Bernard, *The Stars Bear Witness* (London: Victor Gollancz, 1950).

Goldstein, Charles [Chaim], *The Bunker* (Philadelphia: Jewish Publication Society of America, 1970).

—[Goldsztejn, C.], 'Ze wspomnień Żyda uczęstnika powstania warszawskiego, *BŻIH* 37 (1961), 89–97.

Gorodecka, Hana, *Hana: Pamiętnik polskiej Żydówki* (Gdańsk: Wydawnictwo ATEXT, 1992).

Grabowski, Zbigniew Ryszard, 'Strzelał do mnie sierżant AK', *Gazeta Wyborcza* (12–13 February 1994), 10–11.

Gross, Nathan, 'Days and Nights in the "Aryan" Quarter: The Daily Worries of a Jew Carrying Aryan Papers, *Yad Vashem Bulletin* 4–5 (1959), 12–13.

—, 'Unlucky Clara', *Yad Vashem Bulletin* 15 (August 1964), 55–60.

Grynberg, Michał, *Pamiętniki z getta warszawskiego: Fragmenty i regesty* (Warszawa: Wydawnictwo Naukowe PWN, 1993).

Gurdus, Luba Krugman, *The Death Train: A Personal Account of a Holocaust Survivor* (New York: Holocaust Library, 1978).

Guz, Leon, *Targowa 64: Dziennik 27.I.1943–11.IX.1944* (Warszawa: Czytelnik, 1990).

Hirshaut, Julien, *Jewish Martyrs of Pawiak* (New York: Holocaust Library, 1982).

Hirszfeld, Ludwik, *Historia jednego życia* (Warszawa: Czytelnik, 1946).

Horn, Maria Halina, *A Tragic Victory* (Toronto: ECW Press, 1988).

Huberband, Shimon, *Kiddush Hashem: Jewish Religious Life in Poland during the Holocaust* (New York: Yeshiva University Press, 1987).

Jabrzemski, Jerzy, ed., *Szare szeregi: harcerze 1939–1945*, 3 vols. (Warszawa: PWN, 1988).

Jaworski, Michał, 'Plac Muranowski 7 (Fragment wspomnień)', *BŻIH* 90 (1974), 69–89.

Kaczyńska, Alicja, *Obok piekła* (Gdańsk: Marpress, 1993).

Kaplan, Chaim, *Scroll of Agony: The Warsaw Diary of Chaim A. Kaplan* (Bloomington, IN.: Indiana University Press, 1999).

Karpiński, Emil, 'Wspomnienia z okresu okupacji', *BŻIH* 149(1989), 65–90.

Kermish, Joseph, ed., *To Live with Honor and Die with Honor: Selected Documents from the Warsaw Ghetto Underground Archives 'O.S.' ['Oneg Shabbath']* (Jerusalem: Yad Vashem, 1986).

Klajman, Jack, *Out of the Ghetto* (London: Vallentine Mitchell, 2000).

Krall, Hanna, *Shielding the Flame: An Intimate Conversation with Dr. Marek Edelman, the Last Surviving Leader of the Warsaw Ghetto Uprising* (New York: Henry Holt & Co., 1986).

Krawczyńska, Jadwiga, *Zapiski dziennikarki warszawskiej, 1939–1947* (Warszawa: PIW, 1971).

Kubar, Zofia, *Double Identity* (New York: Hill & Wang, 1989).

Landau, Ludwik, *Kronika lat wojny i okupacji* 3 vols. ed. by Zbigniew Landau and Jerzy Tomaszewski, (Warszawa: PWN, 1962).

Lazar, Chaim, *Muranowska 7: The Warsaw Ghetto Uprising* (Tel Aviv: Masada-PEC, 1966).

Lewin, Abraham, *A Cup of Tears* (London: Fontana/Collins, 1990).

Lewin, Rhoda G., ed., *Witnesses to the Holocaust: An Oral History* (Boston: Twayne Publishers, 1990).

Lichtensztejn, J., 'Un es iz geven', *Bleter far Geshichte* II/1–4 (1949).

List 1: About Jews Liberated from German Concentration Camps Arrived in Sweden in 1945 (Stockholm: WJC Relief and Rehabilitation Dept, 1946)

Lubetkin, Cywia, *Zagłada i powstanie* (Warszawa: Książka i Wiedza, 1999).

Makower, Henryk, *Pamiętnik z getta warszawskiego. Październik 1940–styczeń 1943* (Wrocław: Zakład Narodowy im. Ossolińskich, 1987).

Mandelkern, Benjamin, *Escape from the Nazis* (Toronto: James Lorimer, 1988).

Mariańscy, M.M., *Wśród przyjaciół i wrogów: Poza gettem w okupowanym Krakowie* (Kraków: Wydawnictwo Literackie, 1988).

Meed, Vladka, *On Both Sides of the Wall: Memoirs from the Warsaw Ghetto* (New York: Holocaust Library, 1979).

Meroz, Anna, *W murach i poza murami getta: Zapiski lekarki warszawskiej z lat 1939–1945* (Warszawa: Czytelnik, 1988).

Moczarski, Kazimierz, *Rozmowy z katem* (Warszawa: Wydawnictwo Naukowe PWN, 1992).

Modrzewska, K., 'Pamiętnik z okresu okupacji hitlerowskiej', *BŻIH* 31–32 (1959).

'My tu żyjemy jak w obozie warownym': Listy PPS-WRN Warszawa-Londyn 1940–1945 ed. by Olena Zaremba-Blatonowa, Lidia Ciołkoszowa, and Wanda Czapska-Jordan (London: Puls, 1992).

National Registry of Jewish Holocaust Survivors (Washington: American Gathering of Holocaust Survivors and U.S. Holocaust Museum, 1993).

Noakes, J., and G. Pridham, eds, *Nazism: A History in Documents and Eyewitness Accounts, 1919–1945*, vol. 2 (New York: Schocken, 1988).

Nowakowska, Krystyna [Felicja Zygler], *Moja Walka o Życie* (Warszawa: Książka, 1948).

Peleg-Mariańska and Mordechai Peleg, *Witnesses: Life in Occupied Kraków* (London: Routledge, 1991).

Perechodnik, Calel, *Am I a Murderer? Testament of a Jewish Policeman* (Oxford: Westview, 1996).

——, *Czy ja jestem mordercą?* (Warszawa: KARTA, 1995).

Persson, Sune, 'Folke Bernadotte and the White Buses', in David Cesarani and Paul Levine, eds, *Bystanders to the Holocaust: A re-evaluation* (London: Frank Cass, 2002), 237–68.

Polish Help for the Jews (1939–1945): Documents (London: Underground Poland Study Trust, 1988).

Prekerowa, Teresa, 'Komórka "Felicji": Nieznane archiwum działaczra Rady Pomocy Żydom w Warszawie', *Rocznik Warszawski* 15 (1979).

Register of Jewish Survivors, II: List of Jews in Poland (58,000 Names) (Jerusalem: Jewish Agency for Palestine/Search Bureau for Missing Relatives, 1945).

Ringelblum, Emmanuel, *Notes from the Warsaw Ghetto* (New York: Schocken, 1981).

——, *Polish–Jewish Relations during the Second World War*, ed. by Joseph Kermish and Shmuel Krakowski (New York: Howard Fertig, 1976).

——, *Stosunki polsko-żydowskie w czasie drugiej wojny światowej*, ed. by Artur Eisenbach (Warszawa: Czytelnik, 1988).

——, *Kronika getta warszawskiego, wrzesień 1939–styczeń 1943*, ed. by Artur Eisenbach (Warszawa: Czytelnik, 1988).

Rosenberg, Carl, *As God Is my Witness* (New York: Holocaust Library, 1990).

Rosenberg, Maxine B., *Hiding to Survive: Stories of Jewish Children Rescued from the Holocaust* (New York: Clarion, 1994).

Rotem, Simcha, *Memoirs of a Ghetto Fighter: The Past within Me* (London: Yale University Press, 1994).

—, *Wspomnienia bojowca ŻOB* (Warszawa: Wydawnictwo Naukowe PWN, 1993).

Rudnicki, Klemens, *Na polskim szlaku: Wspomnienia z lat 1939–1947* (Londyn: Polska Fundacja Kulturalna, 1983).

Rzepecki, Jan, *Wspomnienia i przyczynki historyczne* (Warszawa: Czytelnik, 1983).

Sakowska, Ruta, *Archiwum Ringelbluma* (Warszawa: PWN, 1997).

—, 'Relacje Daniela Fligelmana – członka "Oneg Szabat"', *BŻIH* 137–8 (1986) 167–94.

—, 'Archiwum Ringelbluma – ogniwem konspiracji warszawskiego getta. Cz. III', *BŻIH* 155–6 (1990) 153–60.

Sendlerowa, Irena, 'Ci, którzy pomagali Żydom (Wspomnienia z czasów okupacji hitlerowskiej)', *BŻIH* 45–6 (1963) 234–47.

Smakowski, Jakub (ps. 'Czarny Julek'), 'Fragment pamiętnika ("Życie i zmagania")', *BŻIH* 2(1975), 81–91.

Starkopf, Adam, *There Is Always Time to Die* (New York: Holocaust Library, 1981).

Stroop, Jürgen, *The Stroop Report: The Jewish Quarter of Warsaw Is No More*, ed. Sybil Milton (London: Secker and Warburg, 1980).

Śwital, S., 'Siedmioro z ulicy Promyka (w Warszawie)', *BŻIH* 65–6 (1968).

Szac-Wajnkranc, Noemi, *Przeminęło z ogniem* (Warszawa: CŻKH, 1947).

Szajn-Lewin, Eugenia, *W getcie warszawskim: Lipiec 1942–kwiecień 1943* (Poznań: Wydawnictwo a5, 1989).

Szapiro, Paweł, ed., *Wojna żydowsko-niemecka: Polska prasa konspiracyjna 1943–1944 o powstaniu w getcie Warszawy* (London: Aneks, 1992).

Szereszewska, Helena, *Krzyż i mezuza* (Warszawa: Czytelnik, 1993).

Szmidt, Leokadia, *Cudem przeżyliśmy czas zagłady* (Kraków, 1983).

Szpilman, Władysław, *Śmierć Miasta* (Warszawa: Spółdzielnia Wydawnicza, 1946).

Szwajger, Adina Blady, *I Remember Nothing More: The Warsaw Children's Hospital and the Jewish Resistance* (New York: Pantheon, 1990).

Szwarcbard, M., 'Notitsn fun geto Varshe', *Bleter far Geshichte* VIII/3–4 (1955).

Szymańska, Zofia, 'Ratunek w klasztorze (wspomnienie)' *BŻIH* 4 (1973).

—, *Byłam tylko lekarzem* (Warszawa: Pax, 1979).

Tec, Nechama, *Dry Tears: The Story of a Lost Childhood* (New York: OUP, 1984).

Trunk, Isaiah, *Jewish Responses to Nazi Persecution* (New York: Stein and Day, 1979).

Turkow, Jonas, *Azoy iz es geven: Churbn Varshe* (Buenos Aires: Tsentral-Farband fun Poilishe Yidn, 1948)

—, *In kamf farn leben* (Buenos Aires: Tsentral-Farband fun Poilishe Yidn, 1949).

Tusk-Schweinwechslerowa, Franciszka, 'Cena jednego życia', *BŻIH* 33 (1960), 58–104.

Tyszkowa, Maria, 'Eksterminacja Żydów w latach 1941–1943: Dokumenty Biura Informacji i Propagandy i Informacji KG AK w zbiorach Biblioteki Uniwersytetu Warszawskiego', *BŻIH* 162–3 (1992), 35–62.

Unconquered Poland (New York: Polish Labour Group, July 1943, revised edn).

Wanat, Leon, *Za murami Pawiaka* (Warszawa: Książka i Wiedza, 1958).

Wdowiński, David, *And We Are Not Saved* (New York: Philosophical Library, 1985).

Willenberg, Samuel, *Surviving Treblinka* (Oxford: Basil Blackwell, 1989).

Wojciechowski, Kazimierz, 'Wspomnienia okupacyjne oświatowca', *BŻIH* 3–4 (1988), 211–16.

Wyleżeńska, A., 'Z notatek pamiętnikarskich (1942–1943)' *BŻIH* 45–6 (1963).

Zelichower, N., 'Siedem obozów hitlerowskich', *BŻIH* 68 (1968).

Ziemian, Joseph, *The Cigarette-Sellers of Three Crosses Square* (Minneapolis: Lerner Publications Group, 1975).

—[Ziemian Józef], *Papierosiarze z placu Trzech Krzyży* (Warszawa: Niezależna Oficyna Wydawnicza, 1989).

Zuckerman, Yitzhak, *A Surplus of Memory: Chronicle of the Warsaw Ghetto Uprising* (Oxford: University of California Press, 1993).

Zylberberg, Michael, *A Warsaw Diary, 1939–1945* (London: Valentine, Mitchell, 1969).

Zylbersztejn, S., 'Pamiętnik więźnia dziesięciu obozów koncentracyjnych', *BŻIH* 68 (1968).

Żywulska, Krystyna, *Pusta woda* (Warszawa: Iskry, 1965).

2. Secondary Sources

Abramsky, Chimen, Maciej Jachimczyk and Antony Polonsky, eds, *The Jews in Poland* (Oxford: Blackwell, 1986).

Ainsztein, Reuben, 'The Jews of Poland Need Not Have Died', *Midstream* 2–4, 101–3 Autumn 1958.

—, *Jewish Resistance in Nazi-Occupied Eastern Europe, with a Historical Survey of the Jew as Fighter and Soldier in the Diaspora* (London: Paul Elek, 1974).

Arczyński, Marek, and, Wiesław Balcerak, *Kryptonim 'Żegota': z dziejów pomocy Żydom w Polsce 1939–1945* (Warszawa: Czytelnik, 1979).

Arendt, Hannah, *Eichmann in Jerusalem: A Report on the Banality of Evil* (Harmondsworth: Penguin, 1977).

Balcerak, Wiesław, '*Stronnictwo Demokratyczne* w akcji pomocy Żydom', *BŻIH* 2 (1987) 117–24.

Ball-Kaduri, K.Y., 'Evidence of Witnesses: Its Value and Limitations', *YVS* 3 (1959), 79–90.

Bar-On, Zvi, and Dov Levin, 'Problems Relating to a Questionnaire on the Holocaust', *YVS* 3 (1959), 91–117.

Bartoszewski, Władysław, *Warszawski pierścień śmierci* (Warszawa: Interpress, 1970).

—, *The Warsaw Death Ring, 1939–1944,* (Warszawa: Interpress, 1968).

—, *The Blood Shed Unites Us* (Warszawa: Interpress, 1970).

—, *The Warsaw Ghetto: A Christian's Testimony* (Boston: Beacon Press, 1987).

— and Zofia Lewin, *Righteous among Nations: How the Poles Helped the Jews, 1939–1945* (London: Earlscourt, 1969).

— and Zofia Lewin, *Ten jest z ojczyzny mojej* (Kraków: Znak, 1969).

— and Marek Edelman, *Żydzi warszawy, 1939–1943* (Lublin: Towarzystwo Naukowe Katolickiego Uniwersytetu Lubelskiego, 1993).

Bartoszewski, Władysław T., and Antony Polonsky, eds, *The Jews in Warsaw* (Oxford: Basil Blackwell, 1991).

Bauer, Yehuda, *The Jewish Emergence from Powerlessness* (Toronto: Toronto University Press, 1979).

— *Rethinking the Holocaust* (New Haven: Yale University Press, 2000).

— ed., *Guide to Unpublished Materials of the Holocaust Period*, 5 vols, (Jerusalem: Alpha Press, 1975).

Bauman, Zygmunt, *Modernity and the Holocaust* (Cambridge: Polity, 1989).

Berenstein, Tatiana, 'Documents in the Archives of Poland', *YVS* 3 (1959), 67–76.

— and Adam Rutkowski, *Assistance to the Jews in Poland 1939–1945* (Warszawa: Polonia, 1963).

—, 'O ratownictwie Żydów przez Polaków w okresie okupacji hitlerowskiej', *BŻIH* 35 (1960), 3–46

—, 'Liczba ludności żydowskiej i obszar przez nią zamieszkiwany w Warszawie w latach okupacji hitlerowskiej', *BŻIH* 26 (1958), 73–105.

Bergman, Stefan, 'Przyczynki do historii Bundu', *BŻIH* 162–3 (1992), 107–32.

Berman, Adolf, 'Ha-yehudim b'Tsad ha-Ari', in *Entsiklopedia shel galuot*, vol. 7.8 'Varshe' (Jerusalem: Encyclopaedia of the Jewish Diaspora Co. Ltd, 1953), 685–732.

—, 'Ruch oporu w getcie warszawskim', *BŻIH* 29 (1959).

Biuletyn Glownej Komiski Badania Zbrodni Niemieckick w Polsce, 1 (1946).

Block, Gay, and Malka Drucker, *Portraits of Moral Courage in the Holocaust* (New York: Holmes & Meier, 1992).

Borwicz, Michał, *Arishe papirn*, 3 vols (Buenos Aires: Tsentral-Farband fun Poilishe Yidn, 1955).

— [Borwicz, Michel] *Vies interdites* (Tournai: Casterman, 1968).

— [Borwicz, Michael] 'Factors Influencing the Relations between the General Polish Underground and the Jewish Underground' in *Jewish Resistance during the Holocaust* (Jerusalem: Yad Vashem, 1971)

Brustin-Berenstein, Tatiana, 'O hitlerowskich metodach eksploatacji gospodarczej getta warszawskiego', *BŻIH* 4 (1953), 42.

Burstin, B.S., *After the Holocaust: the Migration of Polish Jews and Christians to Pittsburgh* (Pittsburgh: University of Pittsburgh Press, 1989).

Cała, Alina, *Asymilacja Żydów w Królestwie Polskim (1864–1897): Postawy, Konflikty, Stereotypy* (Warszawa: PIW, 1989).

Cargas, Harry James, *Voices from the Holocaust* (Lexington KY: University of Kentucky Press, 1993).

Chądzyński, Edward, 'Pomoc Żydom udzielana przez konspiracyjne biuro fałszywych dokumentów w okresie okupacji hitlerowskiej (1939–1945)', *BŻIH* 75 (1970), 129–32.

Chlebowski, Cezary, *Reportaż z tamtych dni* (Warszawa: Krajowa Agencja Wydawnicza, 1986).

Chrzanowski, Bogdan, 'Eksterminacja ludności żydowskiej w świetle polskich wydawnictw konspiracyjnych', *BŻIH* 133–4 (1985), 85–104.

Cichy, Michał, review of Calel Perechodnik, *Czy ja jestem mordercą?* , in *Gazeta Wyborcza, Gazeta o Książkach*, n. 11/93.

—, 'Polacy – Żydzi: Czarne Karty Powstania', *Gazeta Wyborcza* (29–30 January 1994), 13–16. Foreword by Adam Michnik, 12.

Czarnomski, Tadeusz, 'Pomoc ludności żydom udzielona przez pracowników Wydziału Ewidencji Ludności zarządu M. St. Warszawy w okresie okupacji hitlerowskiej (1939–1945)', *BŻIH* 75 (1970), 119–28.

Datner, Szymon, 'Zbrodnie niemieckie na Żydach zbiegłych z gett', *BŻIH* 75 (1970), 7–29.

—, *Las sprawiedliwych: Karta z dziejów ratownictwa Żydów w okupowanej Polsce* (Warszawa: Książka i Wiedza, 1968).

Dawidowicz, Lucy, *The Holocaust and the Historians* (Cambridge, MA: Harvard University Press, 1981).

Dobroszycki, Lucjan, ed., *The Chronicle of the Lodz Ghetto 1941–1944* (London: Yale University Press, 1984).

— and Jeffrey S. Gurock, eds, *The Holocaust in the Soviet Union: Studies and Sources on the Destruction of the Jews in the Nazi-Occupied Territories of the USSR, 1941–1945* (London: M.E. Sharp, 1993).

—, *Reptile Journalism: The Official Polish-Language Press under the Nazis, 1939–1945* (London: Yale University Press, 1994).

Dunin-Wąsowicz, Krzysztof, 'Życie, walka i zagłada ludności żydowskiej w czasie II wojny światowej w Polsce w świetle polskich wspomnień i relacji', in *Powstanie w getcie warszawskim*, 62–74.

Eck, Nathan, 'The Rescue of Jews with Aid of Passports and Citizenship Papers of Latin American States', *YVS* 1, (1957), 125–52.

Ehrenpreis, Wiktor, 'Socialiści Polscy w Nowym Jorku', in Edward Haloń, ed., *Polska Partia Socjalistyczna w latach wojny i okupacji 1939–1945* (Warszawa: Polska Fundacja Upowszechniania Nauki, 1994), I: 301–8.

Elster, Roma, *28, rue Nowolipki (Varsovie 1939–1945)* (Aix-en-Provence: Alinea, 1983), Fictionalized memoir.

Engel, David, 'The Polish Government-in-Exile and the Deportations of Polish Jews from France', *YVS* 15 (1983).

—, *In the Shadow of Auschwitz: The Polish Government-in-Exile and the Jews, 1939–1942* (Chapel Hill: NC: University of North Carolina Press, 1987).

—, *Facing a Holocaust: The Polish Government-in-Exile and the Jews 1943–1945* (Chapel Hill NC: University of North Carolina Press, 1993).

Engelking, Barbara, *Na łące popiołów.*

—, *Zagłada i pamięć: Doświadczenie Holocaustu i jego konsekwencje opisane n podstawie relacji autobiograficznych* (Warszawa: IFiS PAN, 1994).

—, *'Czas przestał dla mnie istnieć . . .'* (Warszawa: IFiS PAN, 1996).

—, *Holocaust and Memory* (London: Leicester University Press, 2001).

—, and Jacek Leociak, *Getto warszawskie: Przewodnik po nieistniejącym mieście* (Warsawa: IFiS PAN, 2001).

Fąfara, Eugeniusz, *Gehenna ludności żydowskiej* (Warszawa: Ludowa Spółdzielnia Wydawnicza, 1983).

Fein, Helen, *Accounting for Genocide: National Responses and Jewish Victimization during the Holocaust* (London: Collier Macmillan, 1979).

Fijałkowski, Zenon, *Kościół katolicki na ziemiach polskich w latach okupacji hitlerowskiej* (Warszawa: Książka i Wiedza, 1983).

Fischer, Ludwig, *Raporty Ludwiga Fischera, gubernatora dystryktu warszawskiego 1939–1944*, ed. Krzysztof Dunin-Wąsowicz, Marek Getter, Józef Kazimierski et al (Warszawa: Książka i Wiedza, 1987).

Foster, Don and Joha Louw-Potgieter, eds, *Social Psychology in South Africa* (Johannesburg: Lexicon, 1991)

Fracek, Teresa, *Zgromadzenie sióstr franciszkanek rodziny Marii w latach 1939–1945* (Warszawa: Akademia Teologii Katolickiej, 1981).

Friedman, Ada June, ed., *Roads to Extinction: Essays on the Holocaust* (Philadelphia: The Jewish Publications Society of America, 1980).

Friedman, Philip, 'Righteous Gentiles in the Nazi Era', in Ada June Friedman ed., *Roads to Extinction*, 409–21.

—, 'Problems of Research on the European Jewish Catastrophe', *YVS* 3 (1959), 25–39.

Friszke, Andrzej, 'Słowa przed zbrodnią', *Gazeta Wyborcza* (19–20 February 1994), 11.

Fuks, Marian, 'Pomoc Polaków bojownikom getta warszawskiego', *BŻIH*, 149 (1989), 43–52.

—, 'Żydowska inteligencja w Polsce 1918–1939', *BŻIH* 3–4 (1988), 127–34.

—, *Zydzi w Warszawie: Zycie codzienne, wydarzenia, ludzie* (Poznań: Sorus, 1992).

Garliński, Józef, *Poland in the Second World War* (Basingstoke: Macmillan, 1985).

Getter, Marek, 'Policja "granatowa" w Warszawie, 1939–1944', *Studia Warszawskie*, 8:215–37.

Gilbert, Martin, *The Holocaust: A Jewish Tragedy* (London: Fontana, 1987).

Glover, Jonathan, *Humanity: A Moral History of the Twentieth Century* (London: Pimlico, 2001).

Grinberg, Daniel, ed., *The Holocaust Fifty Years After. Fiftieth Anniversary of the Warsaw Ghetto Uprising: Papers from the Conference Organized by the Jewish Historical Institute of Warsaw March 29–31, 1993* (Warszawa: Wydawnictwo DiG, 1993).

Gross, Jan Tomasz, *Polish Society under German Occupation: The Generalgouvernement: 1939–1944* (Princeton: Princeton University Press, 1979).

—, *Revolution from Abroad: The Soviet Conquest of Poland's Western Ukraine and Western Belorussia* (Princeton: Princeton University Press, 1988).

—, *Ten jest z ojczyzny mojej–ale go nie lubę* (London: Aneks, 1986).

—, *Neighbors: The Destruction of the Jewish Community in Jedwabne, Poland* (Princeton: Princeton University Press, 2001).

Gross, Leonard, *The Last Jews in Berlin* (London: Sidgwick & Jackson, 1982).

Gross, Nathan, 'Aryan Papers in Poland', in *Extermination and Resistance, Historical Sources and Material* 1 (1958), 79–86.

—, 'Research into the Question of Aryan Papers', *Yediot Yad Vashem* 10–11 (1956), 34.

Grynberg, Henryk, *Żydowska wojna* (Warszawa: Czytelnik, 1989).

Grynberg, Michał, 'Pomoc udzielana Żydom w czasie okupacji hitlerowskiej w Polsce (uwagi i refleksje)', *BŻIH* 2 (1987), 125–33.

—, 'Bunkry i schrony w warszawskim getcie', *BŻIH* 149 (1989), 53–64.

—, ed., *Księga sprawiedliwych* (Warszawa: Wydawnictwo Naukowe PWN, 1993).

Guide to the Moreshet Archives in Giv'at Haviva (Jerusalem: Yad Vashem), vol. 1, ed. Shmuel Krakowski (1979); vol. 2, ed. Iris Berlatzky (1985).

Gutman, Yisrael, *The Jews of Warsaw 1939–1943* (Bloomington IN: Indiana University Press, 1989).

—, *Fighters among the Ruins: The Story of Jewish Heroism during World War II* (Washington: B'nai B'rith, 1988).

— and Efraim Zuroff, eds, *Rescue Attempts during the Holocaust: Proceedings of the Second International Yad Vashem International Conference, Jerusalem, April 8–11, 1974* (Jerusalem: Yad Vashem, 1977).

— and Gideon Greif, eds, *The Historiography of the Holocaust Period: Proceedings of the Fifth Yad Vashem International Conference* (Jerusalem: Yad Vashem, 1988).

— and Krakowski, Shmuel, *Unequal Victims: Poles and Jews during World War II* (New York: Holocaust Library, 1986).

Hałoń, Edward, ed., *Polska Partia Socjalistyczna w latach wojny i okupacji 1939–1945* (Warszawa: Polska Fundacja Upowszechniania Nauki, 1994), vol. 1.

Hanson, Joanna K.M., *The Civilian Population in the Warsaw Uprising of 1944* (Cambridge: CUP, 1982).

Hempel, Adam, *Pogrobowcy klęski: Rzecz o policji 'granatowej' w Generalnym Gubernatorstwie 1939–1945* (Warszawa: PWN, 1990).

Hertz, Aleksander, *The Jews in Polish Culture* (Evanston, IL: Northwestern University Press, 1988).

Hilberg, Raul, *The Destruction of the European Jews* (London and New York: Holmes & Meier, 1985).

—, and Josef Kermisz, eds, *The Warsaw Diary of Adam Czerniaków: Prelude to Doom* (New York: Stein and Day, 1979).

Hołuj, Tadeusz, 'Jan Mosdorf's Truce', in Adolf Rudnicki, ed., *Lest We Forget* (Warszawa: Polonia Foreign Languages Publishing House, 1955), 118–24.

Horn, Maurycy, 'Działalność naukowa i wydawnicza Centralnej Żydowskiej Komisji Historycznej przy CKŻWP i Żydowskiego Instytutu Historycznego w Polsce w latach 1945–1950', *BŻIH* 133–4 (1985).

Huberband, Shimon, *Kiddush Hashem: Jewish Religious Life in Poland during the Holocaust* (New York: Yeshiva University Press, 1987).

Iranek-Osmecki, Kazimierz, *He Who Saves One Life* (New York: Crown Publishers, 1971).

Irwin-Zarecka, Iwona, *Neutralizing Memory: The Jew in Contemporary Poland* (London: Transaction Publishers, 1989).

—, 'Problematizing the "Jewish Problem"', *Polin* 4 (1989) 281–95.

Jagur, Orna, *Bunkier 'Krysia'* (Lodz: Oficyna Bibliofilow, 1997).

Kermish, Joseph, 'On the Underground Press in the Warsaw Ghetto', *YVS* 1 (1957), 85–123.

Klibanski, Bronia, *Yad Vashem Central Archives, Collection of Testimonies, Memoirs and Diaries (Record Group O33)* (Jerusalem: Yad Vashem, 1990).

Korbonski, Stefan, *The Polish Underground State: A Guide to the Underground 1939–1945* (New York: Hippocrene, 1981).

Korzec, Paweł, 'The Government Delegacy in Nazi-Occupied Poland and Funds for the Rescue of Jews – Selected Documents', in Emmanuel Melzer, and David Engel, eds, *Gal-Ed: On the History of the Jews in Poland* (Tel Aviv: Diaspora Research Institute), vol. 13 (1993), 129–60.

Korzen, Meir, 'Problems Arising out of Research into the History of Jewish Refugees in the USSR during the Second World War', *Yad Vashem Studies* 3 (1959), 119–40.

Krajewska, Barbara, 'Ludność Warszawska w latach 1939–1945', *Studia Warszawskie*, vol. 7, 185–207.

Krakowski, Shmuel, 'Avidot Yehudei Polin be-Shoah – ha-Aravah Statistit', in *Studies of the Holocaust Period* vol 2 (Tel Aviv: Hakibbutz Hame Uchad Publishing House, 1981), 231–7.

—, 'The Holocaust in the Polish Underground Press', *YVS*, 16 (1984), 241–70.

—, *The War of the Doomed: Jewish Armed Resistance in Poland, 1942–1944* (New York: Holmes & Meier, 1984).

—, 'The Holocaust of Polish Jewry in Polish Historiography and Polish Émigré Circles', in Gutman and Greif, *The Historiography of the Holocaust Period*, 117–32.

—, 'Relations between Jews and Poles during the Holocaust – New and Old Approaches in Polish Historiography', *YVS* 19 (1988), 317–40.

—, 'The Polish Underground and the Extermination of the Jews', *Polin* 10 (1996), 138–47.

Krall, Hanna, *Dowody na istnienie* (Poznań: Wydawnictwo a5, 1996).

Kraus-Kolkowicz, Sara, *Dziewczyna z ulicy Miłej, albo świadectwo czasu Holokaustu* (Lublin: Agencja Wydawniczo-Handlowa AD, 1995). Fabricated antisemitic memoir.

Kroll, Bogdan, 'Organizacja polskiej samopomocy społecznej w Warszawie październik 1939–lipiec 1944', *Studia Warszawskie*, vol. 7, no. 1 (Warszawa: Instytut Historyczny PAN, 1971), 87–138.

Krzemiński, Ireneusz, ed., *Czy Polacy sa antysemitami?* (Warszawa: Oficyna Naukowa, 1996).

Kurek-Lesik, Ewa, *Gdy klasztor znaczył życie: udział żeńskich zgromadzeń zakonnych w akcji ratowania dzieci żydowskich w Polsce w latach 1939–1945* (Kraków: Znak, 1992).

Landau-Czajka, Anna, 'The Ubiquitous Enemy: The Jew in the Political Thought of Radical Right-Wing Nationalists in Poland, 1926–1939, *Polin* 4 (1989), 169–203.

Langer, Lawrence L., *Holocaust Testimonies: The Ruins of Memory* (London: Yale University Press, 1991).

—, *Versions of Survival: The Holocaust and the Human Spirit* (Albany: SUNY Press, 1982).

Lazar, Chaim, 'The Jewish Military Organization in the Warsaw Ghetto', in David Wdowinski, *And We Are Not Saved* (New York: Philosophical Library, 1985), 125–207.

Legec, W. i S., 'Żołnierze ŻOB i ich przyjaciele', *BŻIH* 5 (1953).

Lenski, Dr Mordechai, 'Problems of Disease in the Warsaw Ghetto', *YVS* 3 (1959), 283–93.

Leslie, R.F., ed., *The History of Poland since 1863* (Cambridge: CUP, 1980).

Levine, Paul A., *From Indifference to Activism: Swedish Diplomacy and the Holocaust, 1938–1944* (Uppsala: Acta Universitatis Uppsaliensis, 1996).

Lukas, Richard C., ed., *Out of the Inferno* (Lexington, KY: University of Kentucky Press, 1989).

—, *The Forgotten Holocaust: The Poles under German Occupation 1939–1944* (Lexington KY: University of Kentucky Press, 1986).

—, *Did the Children Cry? Hitler's War against the Jewish and Polish Children, 1939–1945* (New York: Hippocrene, 1994).

Maciejewska, Irena, *Męczenstwo i zagłada Żydow w zapisach literatury polskiej* (Warszawa: Krajowa Agencja Wydawnicza, 1988).

McWhirter, Norris and Ross, eds, *The Guinness Book of Records 1991* (London: Guinness Superlatives, 1991).

Madajczyk, Czesław, *Generalna Gubernia w planach hitlerowskich: studia* (Warszawa: PWN, 1961).

—, *Polityka III rzeszy w okupowanej Polsce* (Warszawa: PWN, 1970).

Maly Rocznik Statystyczny 1939 (Warszawa: Głowny Urząd Statystyczny, 1939).

Marcus, Joseph, *Social and Political History of the Jews in Poland 1919–1939* (New York: Mouton, 1983).

Margolis-Edelman, Alina, *Ala z elemetarza* (London: Aneks, 1994).

Mark, Ber [Bernard], *Uprising in the Warsaw Ghetto* (New York: Schocken, 1975).

——, *Powstanie w ghetcie warszawskim na tle ruchu oporu w Polsce: Geneza i przebieg* (Warszawa: ŻIH, 1953).

——, 'Problems Related to the Study of Jewish Resistance Movement in the Second World War', *YVS* 3 (1959) 41–65.

Marks, Jane, *The Hidden Children* (London: Piatkus, 1994).

Marrus, Michael R., *The Holocaust in History* (Toronto: Lester & Orpen Dennys, 1987).

——, *The Unwanted: European Refugees in the Twentieth Century* (Oxford: OUP, 1985).

'Materialn tsu demografishe forshung vegn der yidisher bafolkerung in Varshe beis der hitleristishe okupatsye', *Bleter far Geshichte* (1955), 185–208.

Melchior, Małgorzata, *Społeczna tożsamość jednostki* (Warszawa: Uniwersytet Warszawski – Instytut Nauk Społecznych, 1990).

Mendelsohn, Ezra, *The Jews of East-Central Europe Between the World Wars* (Bloomington, IN: Indiana University Press, 1987).

Modras, Ronald, *The Catholic Church and Antisemitism: Poland, 1933–1939* (Reading: Harwood, 1994).

Moore, Bob, *Victims and Survivors: The Nazi Persecution of the Jews in the Netherlands 1940–1945* (London: Arnold, 1997).

Netzer, Shlomo, 'The Holocaust of Polish Jewry in Jewish Historiography', in Gutman and Greif, *The Historiography of the Holocaust Period*, 133–48.

Nirenstein, Albert, *A Tower from the Enemy: Contributions to a History of Jewish Resistance in Poland* (New York: Orion Press, 1959).

Obozy hitlerowskie na ziemiach polskich 1939–1945: Informator encyklopedycny (Warszawa: PWN, 1979).

Oliner, Samuel P. and Pearl M., *The Altruistic Personality: Rescuers of Jews in Nazi Europe* (New York: Free Press, 1988).

Paldiel, Mordechai, 'The Righteous among the Nations at Yad Vashem', *Journal of Holocaust Education* 7 (1998), 45–66.

Pankowicz, Andrzej, *Polski czerwony krzyż w Generalnej Gubernii, 1939–1945* (Kraków: Uniwersytet Jagielloński, 1985).

Passenstein, Marek, 'Szmugiel w getcie warszawskim', *BŻIH* 26 (1958), 42–72.

Patterns of Jewish Leadership: Proceedings of the Third Yad Vashem Conference (Jerusalem: Yad Vashem, 1977).

Paulsson, G.S., 'The Bridge over the Øresund: The Historiography on the Expulsion of the Jews from Nazi-Ooccupied Denmark', *Journal of Contemporary History* 30 (1995), 431–64.

——, 'The Demography of Jews Hiding in Warsaw, 1943–1945', *Polin* 13 (2000), 78–103.

——, 'Evading the Holocaust: The Unexplored Continent of Holocaust Historiography', in *Remembering for the Future: the Holocaust in an Age of Genocide* (London: Palgrave, 2001), I: 302–18.

——, 'Ringelblum Revisited: Polish–Jewish relations in occupied Warsaw, 1940–1945', in *Contested Memories: Poles and Jews during the Holocaust and its Aftermath* (New Brunswick, NJ: Rutgers University Press, 2002).

Perle, J., 'Khurbn Varshe', *Bleter far Geshichte* 5:3 (1952).

Pilichowski, Czesław, *No Time Limit for these Crimes* (Warsaw: Interpress, 1980).

——, *et al.*, eds, *Obozy hitlerowskie na ziemiach polskich 1939–1945: Informator encyklopedyczny* (Warsaw: PWN, 1979).

Pinchuk, Ben-Cion, *Shtetl Jews under Soviet Rule: Eastern Poland on the Eve of the Holocaust* (Oxford: Basil Blackwell, 1990).

Podolska, Aldona, *Służba porządkowa w getcie warszawskim w latach 1940–1943* (Warszawa: Wydawnictwo Fundacji 'Historia pro Futuro', 1996).

Polish Help for the Jews (1939–1945): Documents (London: Underground Poland Study Trust, 1988).

Polonsky, Antony, 'Polish–Jewish Relations and the Holocaust', *Polin* 4 (1989), 226–42.

—, *My Brother's Keeper: Recent Polish Debates on the Holocaust* (London: Routledge, 1990).

—, and Norman Davies, eds, *Jews in Eastern Poland and the USSR 1939–46* (Basingstoke: Macmillan, 1991).

Powstanie w getcie warszawskim: sesje w 45-ą rocznicé (14–15 kwietnia 1988r) (Warszawa: GK, 1989).

Prekerowa, Teresa, *Konspiracyjna rada pomocy Zydom w Warszawie 1942–1945* (Warszawa: PIW, 1982).

—, *Zarys dziejów Żydów w Polsce w latach 1939–1945* (Warszawa: Wydawnictwo Uniwersytetu Warszawskiego, 1992).

—, 'Nic nie zniszczy legendy Powstania', *Gazeta Wyborcza* , 12–13 February 1994, 10.

—, 'Żydzi w Powstaniu Warszawskim', in *Powstanie warszawskie z perspektywy półwiecza* (Warszawa: Instytut Historyczny PAN, 1995), 84–94.

—, 'The Jewish Underground and the Polish Underground', *Polin* 9 (1996), 148–57.

Presser, Dr Jacob, *Ashes in the Wind: The Destruction of Dutch Jewry* (Detroit: Wayne State University Press, 1988).

Pyszka, Wladyslaw, ed., *The Warsaw Ghetto* (Warsaw: Interpress, 1988).

Relacje z czasów zagłady: Inwentarz, Archiwum ŻIH–INB, zespót 301 Tom I (1–900) (Warszawa: ŻIH, 1998).

Rescue Attempts During the Holocaust: Proceedings of the Second Yad Vashem Conference, ed. Yisrael Gutman (Jerusalem: Yad Vashem, 1974).

Ringelblum, Emmanuel, *Polish–Jewish Relations during the Second World War*, ed. Joseph Kermish and Shmuel Krakowski (New York: Howard Fertig, 1976).

—, *Stosunki polsko-żydowskie w czasie drugiej wojny światowej* ed. Artur Eisenbach (Warszawa: Czytelnik, 1988).

Roth, John K., and Michael Berenbaum, *Holocaust: Religious and Philosophical Implications* (New York: Paragon House, 1989).

— and Elizabeth Maxwell, eds, *Remembering for the Future: The Holocaust in an Age of Genocide* (London: Palgrave, 2001), 3 volumes.

Rudnicki, Adolf, ed., *Lest We Forget* (Warszawa: Polonia Foreign Languages Publishing House, 1955).

Rudnicki, Henryk, *Martyrologia i zagłada Żydów warszawskich* (Łódź: 1946).

Sakowska, Ruta, *Ludzie z dzielnicy zamkniętej: Z dziejów Żydów w Warszawie w latach okupacji hitlerowskiej październik 1939–marzec 1943* (Wydawnictwo Naukowe PWN, 1993, 2nd edn).

—, 'Biuro Informacji i Propagandy KG Armii Krajowej a Archiwum Ringelbluma', *BŻIH* 162–3 (1992), 19–34.

Schultheiss, Dirk, M.D., Michael C. Truss, M.D., Christian G. Stief, M.D. and Udo Jonas, M.D., 'Uncircumcision: A Historical Review of Preputial Restoration', *Plastic and Reconstructive Surgery*, 101 (1998), 1990–8.

Shapiro, Robert M., *The Polish 'Kehile' elections of 1936: A Revolution Re-Examined* (New York: Yeshiva University, 1988).

Shulman, Abraham, *The Case of Hotel Polski: An Acount of the Most Enigmatic Episode of World War II* (New York: Holocaust Library, 1982).

Siemaszko, Zbigniew S., *Narodowe Siły Zbrojne* (Londyn: Odnowa, 1982).

Sikorski, Brunon, 'Handel Warszawy okupacyjnej', *Studia Warszawskie*, vol. 7, no. 1 (Warszawa: Instytut Historyczny PAN, 1971), 17–85.

Silver, Eric, *The Book of the Just: The Unsung Heroes Who Rescued Jews from the Holocaust* (New York: Grove, 1992).

Skalniak, Franciszek, *Stopa życiowa społeczeństwa polskiego w okresie okupacji na terenie Generalnej Gubernii* (Warszawa: GK, 1979).

Smólski, Władysław, *Zaklęte lata* (Warszawa: Pax, 1964).

Stola, Dariusz, 'Pół wieku później: rząd polski i Żydzi w latach II wojny światowej', *BŻIH* 1–2 (1993), 151–60.

—, *Nadzieja i Zagłada: Ignacy Schwarzbart – żydowski przedstawiciel w Radzie Narodowej RP (1940–1945)* (Warszawa: Oficyna Naukowa, 1995).

Stopniak, Franciszek, ed., *Materiały i studia*, 6 vols (Warszawa, 1973. Series: *Kościół katolicki na ziemiach polskich w czasie drugiej wojny światowej*).

Suchcitz, Andrzej, *Informator Studium Polski Podziemnej 1947–1997* (London: Underground Poland Study Trust, 1997).

Szapiro, Paweł, 'Prasa konspiracyjna jako źródło do dziejów stosunków polsko-żydowskich w latach II Wojny Światowej – uwagi, pytania, propozycje badawcze', *BŻIH* 3–4 (1988) 197–210.

Szarota, Tomasz, *Okupowanej Warszawy dzień powszedni* (Warszawa: Czytelnik, 1988).

Szaynok, Bożena, *Pogrom żydów w kielcach 4 lipca 1946* (Warszawa: Bellona, 1992).

—, 'The Pogrom of the Jews in Kielce, July 4, 1946', *YVS* (1992), 199–236.

Tec, Nechama, *When Light Pierced the Darkness: Christian Rescue of Jews in Nazi-Occupied Poland* (Oxford: OUP, 1986).

—, 'Of Help, Understanding and Hope: Righteous Rescuers and Polish Jews', *Polin* 4 (1989), 296–310.

Temkin-Bermanowa, B., 'Akcja pomocy Żydom w okresie okupacji hitlerowskiej', *BŻIH* 22 (1957), 61–84.

Tomaszewski, Irene, and Tecia Werbowski, *Zegota: The Rescue of Jews in Wartime Poland* (Montreal: Price-Patterson, 1994).

Tomaszewski, Jerzy, ed., *Najnowsze dzieje Żydów w Polsce* (Warszawa: Wydawnictwo Naukowe PWN, 1993).

Turkow, Jonas, *Noch der bafrayung* (Buenos Aires: Tsentral Farband fun Polishe Yidn in Argentine, 1959).

Umińska, Apolonia *et al.*, eds, *Inwentarz zbioru "Pamiętniki Żydów" 1939–1945* (Warszawa: Archiwum ŻIH, 1994).

Wroński, Stanisław, and Zwolakowa, Maria, *Polacy i Żydzi, 1939–1945* (Warszawa: Ksiażka i Wiedza, 1971).

Wyleżeńska, A., 'Z notatek pamiętnikarskich (1942–1943)', *BŻIH* 45–46 (1963).

Wynot, Edward D., Jr, *Warsaw between the World Wars: Profile of the Capital City in a Developing Land, 1918–1939* (New York: Columbia University Press, 1983).

Yahil, Leni, *The Rescue of Danish Jewry* (Philadelphia: Jewish Publication Society of America, 1969).

Zajączkowski, Wacław, *Martyrs of Charity* (Washington: St Maximilan Kolbe Foundation, 1988).

Zalewska, Gabriela, *Ludność żydowska w Warszawie w okresie międzywojennym* (Warszawa: Wydawnictwo, Naukowe PWN, 1996).

Zaremba-Blatonowa, Olena, *et al.*, eds, 'My tu żyjemy jak w obozie warowym', *Listy PPS-WRN Warszawa-Londyn 1940–1945* (Londyn: Puls, 1992).

Żebrowski, Leszek, *Paszkwil Wyborczej* (Warszawa: Burchard Edition, 1995).

Znaniecki, Florian, and William Isaac Thomas, *The Polish Peasant in Europe and America* (Urbana, IL: University of Illinois Press, 1984).

Żyndul, Jolanta, *Zajścia antyżydowskie w Polsce w latch 1935–1937* (Warszawa: Fundacja im. K. Kelles-Krauza, 1994).

Zucotti, Susan, *The Holocaust, the French and the Jews* (Lincoln, NB and London: University of Nebraska Press, 1993).

Index